Comparative Health Policy

Comparative Health Policy

Fourth Edition

Robert H. Blank

and

Viola Burau

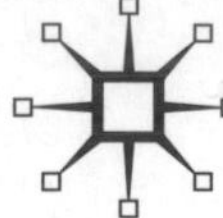

First edition 2004
Second edition 2007
Third edition 2010
Fourth edition 2014

Published by
PALGRAVE MACMILLAN

Palgrave Macmillan in the UK is an imprint of Macmillan Publishers Limited, registered in England, company number 785998, of Houndmills, Basingstoke, Hampshire RG21 6XS.

Palgrave Macmillan in the US is a division of St Martin's Press LLC, 175 Fifth Avenue, New York, NY 10010.

Palgrave Macmillan is the global academic imprint of the above companies and has companies and representatives throughout the world.

Palgrave® and Macmillan® are registered trademarks in the United States, the United Kingdom, Europe and other countries

ISBN 978–1–137–02357–5 hardback
ISBN 978–1–137–02356–8 paperback

This book is printed on paper suitable for recycling and made from fully managed and sustained forest sources. Logging, pulping and manufacturing processes are expected to conform to the environmental regulations of the country of origin.

A catalogue record for this book is available from the British Library.

A catalog record for this book is available from the Library of Congress.

Contents

List of Illustrative Material

Boxes

Figures

Tables

Preface to the Fourth Edition

We wrote the first edition of this book to fill a glaring gap in comparative health policy. Although there had been numerous books about the health policies of specific countries and a handful of books that compared a few nations, our own research in a variety of countries convinced us that a more inclusive comparative coverage would be helpful in elucidating the issues and problems surrounding health care. Therefore, we pooled our shared knowledge of a diverse set of health care systems and wrote an introduction to the health policy of nine countries. Based on numerous reviews in journals and on input from those who used the first three editions, we have extensively updated the text, statistical tables, and references to reflect the many changes that have taken place in the last several years. We have restructured some of the chapters to better cover the comparative content and expand coverage of the international context of health policy and of global health issues.

As in the earlier editions, in order to establish the extent to which the problems facing health care systems have common roots or spring from specific national circumstances, our assessment of health policy focuses on key themes, issues and tensions that run through the book. Thus, chapters are organized around these themes rather than looking country by country. How do the main types of health systems in the developed world address health care problems, and do diverse systems make a difference in policy outcomes? Is health policy in all developed countries converging due to globalization and other factors as some observers argue? This book, therefore, analyses what lessons can be learned about public/private mixes, policy and funding frameworks, professional organizations, and acute and preventive services across disparate health systems. In order to accomplish this, the systems of Australia, Germany, Japan, New Zealand, the Netherlands, Sweden, Singapore, Taiwan, the UK and the USA are covered.

Throughout the book, we put health care in a broader social context and reveal its interdependence with factors often excluded from analysis. Health care, we argue, cannot be separated from other issues that impinge on health such as economic inequalities, the environment and social services. Thus, we include analyses of home care for the elderly and an array of public health and general public policy issues that cumulatively impact on health outcomes more than medical services. We also explore whether the medical model and the heavy emphasis on medicine is the most effective way to address the health of populations.

Chapter 1 introduces health policy and the impact of global trends of population ageing, technology diffusion and heightened public expectations on the health systems of developed nations. It also discusses the importance of comparative health care analysis and presents the typologies conventionally used to classify health systems. Chapter 2 looks at the institutional, historical/cultural, and economic context of health care and proposes an integrated model of health that accounts for the variation across our countries. It also discusses differences over the definition of health, the role of alternative forms of medicine and the relationship between health status and the socio-economic milieu.

Chapter 3 shifts attention to the provision, funding and governance of health care and to the nature and scope of health reforms across the countries examined here. Our countries show considerable diversity, both among different health systems and across the sub-systems of each health system, and only a few countries neatly fit existing typologies. Chapter 4 continues and expands this discussion by examining priority-setting in health care. It illustrates the problematic allocation and rationing issues facing all health systems and discusses how these countries have responded to these challenges. It also introduces health technology assessment and the evolving integration of information technologies into health care. Chapter 5 examines the organization and power of doctors in these health systems with special emphasis on how this role has changed in light of recent health care reforms. Although the face of medical practice has altered, doctors in particular have retained considerable power and remain key players in health policy.

Chapter 6 moves the discussion to home care to elucidate the interdependence of health with other care services as countries face the dual challenges of ageing populations and social transformation in an era of cost containment. Despite diverse approaches, common trends are apparent, most notably the enhanced support for informal carers. Chapter 7 shifts focus from individual, patient-centred acute care to public health with its emphasis on the health of populations and examines the trends toward the globalization of public health. It also shows that health outcomes for populations are more closely tied to health promotion and disease prevention efforts, income distribution, housing, social conditions and the environment than to medical interventions. The concluding chapter returns to the broader themes introduced in Chapter 1 and begins by assessing the appropriateness of existing typologies of health systems. The discussion demonstrates the sustained importance of country-specific differences as well as the complexity of health systems. The chapter then moves on to discuss the possibilities and limitations of policy learning across countries that is inherent in comparative research.

We are particularly grateful to our respective universities for the different ways in which they have supported our collaboration. Moreover, at the University of Aarhus, Robert Blank received two research fellowships from the university's Research Foundation that provided valuable opportunities for working together. We would particularly like to thank Jens Blom-Hansen and Birgit Kanstrup for their help in the application process for the fellowships.

In terms of the revisions for this edition we have benefited from constructive comments from colleagues whose valuable feedback has helped us sharpen our analysis. Some of the specific changes here are responses to suggestions raised in journal reviews which were mainly highly supportive of the earlier editions. Moreover, teaching in comparative health policy has offered a welcome test ground for new ideas and we are grateful to our students for their patience and input. At the University of Aarhus, Troels Bøggild provided invaluable research assistance with updating the statistical material, while Helle M. H. Bundgaard, Anne-Grethe Gammelgaard and Lone Winther edited the bibliography with great care. We would also like to thank Steven Kennedy for his strong support and encouragement on this project over the years and for the excellent production team at Palgrave Macmillan, and outside reviewers for their valuable suggestions. In particular, we greatly appreciate the thorough review of the manuscript by Anneliese Dodds of Aston University.

University of Canterbury ROBERT H. BLANK
University of Aarhus VIOLA BURAU

List of Abbreviations

ACA	Affordable Care Act (USA)
ACC	Accident Compensation Commission (New Zealand)
AHB	Area Health Boards (New Zealand)
AIDS	Acquired Immunodeficiency Syndrome
AMA	American Medical Association
APCCP	Australian Primary Care Collaborative Program
BMA	British Medical Association
BMI	Body Mass Index
BNHI	Bureau of National Health Insurance (Taiwan)
CDC	Centers for Disease Control and Prevention (USA)
CHE	Crown Health Enterprise (New Zealand)
CPF	Central Provident Fund (Singapore)
DHBs	District Health Boards (New Zealand)
DHHS	Department of Health and Human Services (USA)
DRGs	diagnosis-related groups
ECDC	European Centre for Disease Prevention and Control
EPR	Epidemic and Pandemic Alert and Responses
EU	European Union
FCTC	Framework Convention on Tobacco Control (WHO)
FFO	Fee-for-outcomes (Taiwan)
GATS	General Agreement on Trade in Services
GDP	gross domestic product
GMC	General Medical Council
GP	general practitioner
HACC	Home and Community Care Program (Australia)
HCFA	Health Care Financing Administration (USA)
HCQI	Health Care Quality Indicator Project
HFA	Health Funding Authority (New Zealand)
HHA	Home Health Agencies (USA)
HIV	Human Immunodeficiency Virus
HTA	health technology assessment
HMO	Health Maintenance Organization
IOM	Institute of Medicine (USA)
IPA	Independent Practice Association (New Zealand)
IPCC	Intergovernmental Panel on Climate Change
JMA	Japanese Medical Association
MBS	Medicare Benefits Schedule (Australia)
MHCs	Municipal Health Centres (Japan)

MOH	Ministry of Health
MRI	magnetic resonance imaging
MSA	Medical Savings Account (Singapore)
MSAC	Medical Services Advisory Committee (Australia)
NGO	Non-Governmental Organizations
NHI	National Health Insurance (Taiwan)
NHMRC	National Health and Medical Research Council (Australia)
NHRS	National Rural Health Association (USA)
NHS	National Health Service
NICE	National Institute for Clinical Excellence (UK)
NIH	National Institutes of Health (USA)
NZMA	New Zealand Medical Association
OECD	Organisation for Economic Co-operation and Development
PACE	Program for All Inclusive Care for the Elderly (USA)
PHO	Primary_Health_Organizations (New Zealand)
PHS	Public Health Service (USA)
PPO	Preferred Provider Organization
PHI	private health insurance
RHA	Regional Health Authorities (New Zealand)
QALY	quality adjusted life years
QWB	Quality of Well Being
SARS	Severe Acute Respiratory Syndrome
SES	socio-economic status
SCHIP	State Children's Health Insurance Program (USA)
TCM	traditional Chinese medicine
UNAIDS	Joint UN Programme on HIV/AIDS
USAID	US Agency for International Development
UVB	ultraviolet B radiation
UVR	solar ultraviolet radiation
WHO	World Health Organization
WTO	World Trade Organization

Chapter 1

Comparative Health Policy: An Introduction

Health care has always been a controversial policy area, but over the last decades it has become a major issue in all developed nations. Ageing populations, the proliferation of new medical technologies, and heightened public expectations and demands, among other factors, have elevated health care to the top of the political agenda. Intensifying pressures on political leaders to meet rising public demands for expanded service conflict directly with the need to constrain health care costs and to manage scarce societal resources. Thus, despite major differences among countries as to how health care is funded, provided and governed, no government has been able to escape the controversy and problems accompanying health care in the 21st century, although some seem to be coping significantly better than others. Why is that so?

Given the universality of the problems raised by health care, one must question whether what governments do about it – the policies they adopt – makes a difference. And if policies do matter, what approaches and strategies offer the most hope of resolving or managing the dilemmas of health care? Does simply spending more money improve the health of a population? If not, what does? This book addresses these questions by examining health care policy across a collection of countries that have taken divergent approaches and instituted a variety of mechanisms for covering the health needs of their populations. It also analyses trends within and across these countries in order to determine whether or not there is a convergence in health policy among developed nations, as argued by some observers.

Health care as public policy

The term 'policy' has a wide range of meanings in current English usage. Politicians and parties present their intended actions as policies to be pursued and they defend past actions as policies to be extended. Political commentators often talk about a government's housing policy, crime policy or drug policy in general terms, while others debate a specific government action. Policy, then, can be used to refer to general statements of intention, past or present actions in particular areas, or a set of standing rules to guide actions. Although all organizations have policies, at least in the latter sense, the focus of this book is on the policies of government. 'Public policy' is defined here as a decision taken by the government or on behalf of it. Although usually viewed as an action, a decision not to act can also be a policy. All health policies then involve a fundamental choice by a government as to whether to take a specific action or to do nothing (see Howlett and Ramesh, 2009).

Only the government has the legitimate authority to make decisions that are binding and carried out in the name of the people as a whole. Other organizations, such as medical associations and nursing societies, often make decisions that affect many individuals as well as the health care system as a whole. While their decisions might indeed have a bearing on what the government ultimately does, they are not binding by force of law. Although we discuss actions by private and voluntary organizations that impact on health care where appropriate, the focus of attention is on governmental action or non-action.

It is useful here to distinguish between health policy, health care policy and health care politics. Health policy constitutes those courses of action proposed or taken by governments that affect the health of their populations. As we will see in Chapter 7, health policy overlaps with economic, social welfare, employment and housing policy, among other areas. Health policy, then, is a broad term encompassing any action that has health implications. On the other hand, 'health care' policy is a more narrow term that refers to those courses of action taken by governments that deal with the financing, provision or governance of health services. Although we use the term health policy throughout the book, given its prominence in Western countries, most attention is placed on health care policy. Only in Chapters 6 and 7 does this emphasis widen to health policy in the broader sense. Finally, 'health care politics' comprises the interactions of political actors and institutions in the health care arena in each country. It will become apparent in Chapter 2 that politics is a crucial dimension of all attempts to frame health policy; but politics is very country specific and it is impossible to cover systematically all the intricacies of health care politics of each country. Therefore, while we do not purport to analyse country-specific health politics, readings that offer such detailed analyses are detailed in the Guide to Further Reading.

It is also important to note that while health policy conceptually can be distinguished from other areas of public policy, in reality it is highly interrelated with an expansive range of social and economic policies. In fact, there are health dimensions in virtually all policy areas including national defence and security, law enforcement and labour policy. In Chapter 7 it will be argued that the health of a population can be as dependent on these policies as it is on prescribed health care policy.

Public policy can be categorized as one of three basic types: regulatory, distributive and redistributive (see Lowi, 1972). Regulatory policies impose constraints or restrictions on the actions of groups or individuals: they provide rules of conduct with sanctions backed up by the authority of government. Distributive policies are based on the notion of public goods, e.g. goods and services that benefit all individuals but which are unlikely to be produced by voluntary acts of individuals, in part because they lack the resources. Public goods are defined by each society differently depending upon how broadly government responsibility is interpreted. Often, however, distributive policies provide advantages or benefits to particular segments of society. Considerable governmental activity revolves around the provision of public services and it is often accomplished without undue controversy until scarcity forces tradeoffs to be made as to what groups get what goods. Redistributive policies, in contrast, are controversial in principle because they represent deliberate efforts by governments to alter the distribution of income, wealth or property among groups in society. The reallocation of resources through progressive taxes and other mechanisms occurs to some extent in all democracies, but it is the foundation of more egalitarian states. It should be noted that all of these policies create winners and losers although the mechanisms by which gains and losses might occur are often subtle (Hill, 2009).

Health care encompasses all three types of policy. The regulation of the health care sector through fee scales, licensing requirements, approval of drugs for use and other constraints on medical practice is extensive. Health care is one of the most regulated sectors in all developed countries in spite of their divergent types of health systems. The distributive policies of health care are most obvious in countries that have national health services, but occur to some extent in all countries through medical education programmes, the funding of health care research, the provision of public health services and health promotion activities. Finally, redistributive health care policies are based on the concepts of need and entitlement and encompass a range of efforts by government to shift resources from healthy to non-healthy citizens. They are usually based on a society's conception of equality. Mechanisms for such policies include the use of general revenues to provide services to those who lack resources, means-tested social insurance schemes for the poor and programmes that redistribute societal resources from general revenues to the elderly or indigent.

Health policy is an amalgamation of these various types of policy as governments attempt to influence the provision of health care to their citizens. Of all areas of public policy, health care is one of the most controversial because it always entails conflicts, especially in the regulatory and redistributive modes. This is not surprising given the high emotional and economic stakes involved in any policy involving life, death and huge amounts of resources.

In addition to the potential life/death stakes inherent in any policies regarding health care, health policy is distinctive because the health care profession has by virtue of its specialized knowledge a privileged status of experts in shaping and constraining it. Because of the centrality of health professionals to the delivery of health care, a policy can only be successful if it has at least the tacit support of the medical community. Furthermore, since medical professionals largely define health need and the means necessary to meet it, any attempts by a government that are perceived as imposing constraints on the profession risk condemnation from these key stakeholders. The complexity of providing health care and the inherent uncertainty surrounding medicine further reinforces the power of the health care providers to influence the delivery of medical services and thus shape health care policy.

Complicating the policy context, in part driven by the shift towards sophisticated curative care over the second half of the 20th century, is the fact that the bulk of health care spending has become concentrated on a relatively small number of patients. A minority of each population generates the most cost; approximately 10 per cent in each age group incurs 60 to 70 per cent of total health care costs each year for that group. People with these enormous medical costs are often chronically ill, disabled and/or poor (American College of Physicians, 2008). Table 1.1 demonstrates the extent of this concentration in the USA, but similar patterns have been documented in systems as diverse as Canada, France and New Zealand. In any given year, the top 1 per cent of users account for over 25

Table 1.1 ***Distribution of health expenditures for the USA by magnitude of expenditures for selected years 1963–2009***

Percentage of population ranked by expenditures	*1963*	*1970*	*1980*	*1996*	*2002*	*2009*
Top 1%	17%	26%	29%	27%	22%	21%
Top 2%	–	35%	39%	38%	–	–
Top 5%	43%	50%	55%	55%	49%	51%
Top 10%	59%	66%	70%	69%	64%	66%
Top 20%	–	–	–	–	80%	81%
Top 30%	–	88%	90%	90%	–	91%
Bottom 50%	5%	4%	4%	3%	3%	3%

Sources: Berk and Monheit (2001); Stanton and Rutherford (2005); NCHCSN (2012).

per cent of all health care expenditures; the top 5 per cent use over 50 per cent; and the top 10 per cent use about 70 per cent. In contrast, only 3 per cent of payments go to those patients in the healthiest half of the population. Those in the bottom 50 per cent incurred an average annual expenditure of $122 in medical costs compared with an average expenditure of $56,459 for those in the top 1 per cent! Likewise, only 5 per cent of beneficiaries of the US Medicare system for the elderly account for nearly half of total Medicare spending (Goetzel *et al.*, 2007). Thus, the majority of citizens are accountable collectively for a very small proportion of health care spending.

It is possible, of course, that these figures reflect the fact that while a few people become seriously ill each year and use significant resources, they are replaced by others in following years. Evidence, however, demonstrates that a small number of repeat patients consume substantial resources over a longer term (see Box 1.1). According to Berk and Monheit, there has been a 'remarkable stability in this concentration pattern over the last three decades' (2001: 12). A systematic analysis of high users by Monheit (2003) found that a majority of high users exhibit persistently high expenditures from one year to the next. Critically, the heaviest users of health care come predominantly from two groups: the elderly and those persons who engage in high risk behaviour, thus causing or contributing to their own ill health. Chronic diseases, especially prevalent in the elderly population, generate a large proportion of health care spending (Goetzel *et al.*, 2007). This concentration of the cost for health care is important because it necessitates the redistribution of significant resources from young to old and from those persons who live healthy lives to those who do not. This pattern raises questions of equity and fairness especially in times of scarce resources (see Chapter 4).

Many of the most challenging dilemmas in democracies surface as governments struggle to find the proper mixture of these policy types in the light of conflicting interests. Because of the heavy emphasis on rights to health care in many countries, the distinction between negative and positive rights is important (see Heywood, 2002). Negative rights are those rights that impose obligations on governments and other citizens to refrain from interfering with the rights bearer. They relate to the freedom

Box 1.1 Overuse of resources

Just nine individuals in Austin, Texas, accounted for nearly 2,700 emergency room visits between 2003 and 2008. The cost to taxpayers through Medicare and Medicaid exceeded $3 million. Eight of the nine patients had drug abuse problems, seven were diagnosed with mental health issues and three were homeless. They had a variety of health problems, with many simply complaining of chest pain (Associated Press, 2009).

to be left alone to use one's resources as one sees fit. Under negative rights, each person has a sphere of autonomy that others cannot violate; but no one is further obliged to take positive action to provide that person with the resources necessary to exercise that right. The only claim on others is a freedom from intrusion. Health care as a negative right would allow patients with adequate personal resources to maximize their use of health care. Thus, negative rights are always in conflict with redistributive social welfare policies that deprive individuals of the free use of their resources.

In contrast, positive rights impose obligations on others such as taxpayers to provide those goods and services necessary for each individual to exercise her or his rights. Although the level of positive rights is generally ill defined, this additional dimension requires the presence of institutions that guarantee a certain level of material well being, through governmental redistribution of resources where necessary. Positive rights imply a freedom from deprivation, the entitlement to at least a decent level of human existence. The welfare state is based to a large extent on this more expansive notion of rights. One question within health policy is whether all citizens have a positive right to health care and, if so, what it should entail. How far does a right to the freedom from ill health go in requiring societal provision of health care resources to all citizens? What limits can justifiably be set on these entitlements to health care? For instance, could treatment be denied to an individual who causes his own ill health and who refuses to change his self-destructive behaviour despite repeated warnings?

Comparative health policy

Over the last several decades, comparative policy analysis has become a growth industry (for an overview of the literature see Marmor *et al.*, 2009a). Advances in information technology have expanded the availability and dissemination of data across many countries, while at the same time many policy fields increasingly have become internationally oriented. A greater interest in information about policies in other countries has also been fostered by the perception of shared policy challenges arising from economic and welfare state crises. Deleon and Resnick-Terry (1999) refer to this development as the 'comparative renaissance'. The comparative perspective is now widely used in both the academic field of public policy analysis and in more applied policy studies (see, e.g., Castles, 1999). Parallel to discussions about the insights generated by comparative analyses is a debate about the methodologies of cross-country comparison (for comparative politics, see, e.g., Peters, 1998; for comparative social policy, see, e.g., Clasen, 1999; Hantrais and Mangen, 1996).

This book places health policy in a comparative context in order to demonstrate the similarities and differences in approach among various countries as they attempt to resolve difficult health care problems. Although it can be risky to transfer policies that work in one country to another, comparative public policy is useful in expanding policy options and demonstrating the experiences of a wide range of applications. Øvretveit argues that comparative health research has a role in building relations among different communities 'by creating knowledge that helps people understand their differences and similarities' and that 'health managers can improve their services by sensitively adapting ideas that have worked elsewhere' (1998: 15). Marmor *et al.* (2009b) distinguish among three rationales for cross-national comparative health policy research that include: 'learning about national health arrangements and how they operate, learning why they take the forms they do, and learning policy lessons from those analyses' (2009b: 10). Comparative public policy is, therefore, a source of generalizations about public policy that, in turn, are valuable for understanding policy in any particular country.

In addition, comparative policy analysis can demonstrate that factors viewed as paramount in one country, such as the attitudes of its medical profession or the distinctiveness of its political customs, might actually produce divergent outcomes in other countries. According to Immergut, the 'comparative perspective shows that some factors are neither as unique nor as critical as they appear, whereas others stand out as truly significant' (1992: 9). Ham (1997a) adds that an examination of international experience can illuminate both the difficulties faced by, and the wide range of strategies available to, policy makers. It can also elucidate the institutional context and the importance of the process by which decisions are made (Klein and Williams, 2000). Comparative studies, then, give us cross-cultural insights as to what works or does not work under an array of institutional and cultural contexts. Given the complexity of health care and the plethora of potential health care systems, only comparative studies can generate the evidence necessary to consider the full range of policy options.

Against a background of common policy problems, many comparative studies have highlighted the importance of policy convergence for understanding how health care policies are shaped (cf. Harrison *et al.*, 2002; Wessen, 1999). Convergence implies that countries increasingly rely on a similar design of policies in order to pursue their goals (Schmid and Goetz, 2009). Health policy convergence suggests that there are global trends in the formation of health policies, and that the objectives and activities of national health systems are becoming more alike. Moreover, observations of policy convergence have turned attention to international interdependence (Holzinger and Knill, 2005), the result of diffusion, which is defined as 'a pattern of successive or sequential adoption of a practice, policy, or program either across countries or sub-national jurisdictions such as states and municipalities' (Freeman, 2006: 367). Cross-national influence and the diffusion of policies are predominant topics in deliberations about health reform (Gilardi *et al.*, 2009; Okma *et al.*, 2010; Nolte *et al.*, 2008). Dobbin and colleagues (2007), for instance, offer four theories of distinct mechanisms explaining the diffusion of policies across countries: competition; coercion; emulation; and learning.

The convergence thesis, then, suggests that health policy across disparate country environments has a tendency to become similar over time. Moreover, since all countries face demographic changes and the proliferation of expensive technologies (discussed later), the pressures towards convergence are extenuated. Based on an examination of trends across industrialized democracies, Chernichovsky (1995) contends that despite the diversity of health care systems, health system reforms have led to the emergence of a 'universal outline or paradigm' for health care financing, organization and management that cuts across ideological (private versus public) lines and across conceptual (market versus centrally planned) frameworks. Other authors point to medical knowledge and technology as drivers of health policy convergence. Field (1999), for example, suggests that the means of medical production are becoming universal and that the social organization of medical work is becoming strikingly similar across systems, leading to health systems sharing more common elements.

Convergence is further bolstered by globalization (Taylor, 2009) and by the development of an international health forum through the Internet where people anywhere can obtain information as well as by the private sector that has a huge economic stake in health care (see Box 1.2). In addition, explicit efforts by international organizations such as the Organisation for Economic Co-operation and Development (OECD), the World Health Organization (WHO) and the European Union (EU) help prepare the foundations for what Harrison *et al.* (2002) in their study of evidence-based medicine refer to as 'ideational convergence'. Some argue that the World Trade Organization's General Agreement on Trade in Services (GATS) could lead to homogeny of health services such as health insurance, hospital services, telemedicine and the acquisition of medical treatment abroad. These common driving forces, then, suggest a convergence in relation to the framing of policy problems and the intellectual underpinnings of policy solutions.

There is, however, growing disparagement of initiatives such as GATS by those who contend they impose conformity at the expense of national and culturally specific health policy. Critics argue that GATS requires the privatization of health services, prevents governments from regulating health sectors and hinders a government's ability to determine the shape of its domestic health system in a democratic way. Although Belsky *et al.*

Box 1.2 Market-driven convergence

Cortez (2008a) notes that while attention has focused on 'policy' convergence in the public sphere, it is driven primarily by the private sector that pushes for convergence because it benefits from it. He contends that various methods, practices and standards in the health care industry are becoming more alike across countries through 'market-driven convergence'. For example, there are internationally recognized uses of many drugs, hospital quality standards are spreading and the expectations for doing business in health care are becoming more universal. Moreover, this trend is heavily promoted by the USA, and convergence is towards America's unique brand of health care. Although market-driven convergence presents concrete benefits including increased efficiency in health care markets, gains from trade, higher quality goods and services and enhanced patient choice, these benefits may disproportionately accrue to the private sector at the expense of already overburdened public health systems. Thus, 'policymakers should be wary of the risks of conforming to international, market-driven standards, particularly if it encourages their health care sectors to further privatize and commercialize' (Cortez, 2008a: 648).

(2004: 138) conclude there is 'little clear evidence of such adverse consequences', it is too early to tell what if any impact GATS and similar EU initiatives will have. While GATS at present does not appear to be significantly affecting health care services, Sexton (2001) contends that if current proposals are implemented, GATS could be used to overturn almost any legislation governing health services. Although the controversy surrounding GATS and its imposition on national autonomy and democratic legitimacy are bound to escalate, it is most likely that such concerns will be concentrated in low- and middle-income countries which are most vulnerable to outside pressures to adopt models that are unresponsive to the health needs of their populations.

Convergence theory, however, remains intuitively attractive because similar problems potentially make for similar solutions, and under these circumstances it becomes more likely that health policies will converge. This presumption is supported by the fact that ultimately there are a limited number of policy instruments available to address a certain policy problem, thus suggesting that function rather than politics informed by historical legacy or culture predominantly shapes health policies. As stated by Gibson and Means (2000), policy levers are limited and there are relatively few 'good ideas' around to solve a specific problem. Ideas travel around the world and influence national policy makers, although they are perceived in the context of national and system-specific experiences. Using diagnosis-related groups (DRGs) for inpatient services as an example, Schmid *et al.* (2010) show how cross-national influences as well as system-specific problems contribute to the implementation of innovative policy instruments. Although they are far from a uniform instrument and their use and implementation varies from country to country, the authors consider the spread of DRGs as an example of a convergent trend.

Policy convergence is also encouraged by the fact that all health systems must fulfil similar types of functions, for example raising public funds to pay for medical care and organizing the delivery of these services. In contrast, Schmid and colleagues (2010) and similarly Rothgang *et al.* (2010) suggest that it is the specific, type-related deficiencies of individual health systems that lead to convergence. These deficiencies cannot be resolved by routine mechanisms and, thus, non-system specific elements become integrated in individual health systems. As a result, individual health systems increasingly have a hybrid character and, overall, health systems are becoming more similar.

In contrast, critics of convergence theories argue that its proponents oversimplify the process of development and underestimate significant divergence across countries (Howlett and Ramesh, 2009). Moreover, most studies that have found evidence of convergence have failed to demonstrate that it is applicable across all domains, thus allowing for significant divergence in other areas (Blank and Burau, 2006). In their study of leadership and governance arrangements in seven developed health systems, Smith and associates (2012) came to similar conclusions. They analysed three fundamental functions (priority setting, performance monitoring and accountability arrangements), and found that approaches to leadership and governance vary substantially and have been developed piecemeal and somewhat arbitrarily. Although there appears to be practical consensus on the broad goals of the health system, there is considerable variation in approaches to setting priorities. Therefore, while one can selectively find evidence of convergence, it is by no means certain, inclusive or consistent and has not necessarily translated into similar health policies or policy directions across countries.

In their 36-year perspective of convergence patterns across 22 OECD countries, Leiter and Theurl (2009) found that convergence had taken place but the impacts are not equally pronounced for each dependent variable across health care systems and time periods. Moreover, the rate of convergence has actually decreased over time. Using a similar cohort of 19 OECD countries for the period 1972–2006, Panopoulou and Pantelidis (2011) found a convergence in per capita health care expenditures for 17 countries, but when they tested for convergence of outcome using six different health measures, they actually found a divergence of the full panel of OECD countries for all but infant mortality, thus concluding that convergence in per capita health expenditures does not lead to convergence in health outcomes. Herwartz and Theilen (2010) found that international convergence of health care expenditure across countries depends on characteristics of the age structure of the population. Likewise, Vrangbaek *et al.* (2012) found evidence of convergence among four Northern European countries in the overall policy rhetoric about the objectives associated with patient choice, embracing concepts of empowerment and market competition, but less in the design of specific policies. Similarly, in their study of six countries, Okma and associates conclude:

> The seemingly common experience in reform goals and means can easily lead to generalized conclusions of [global] convergence. However, the health politics of the six countries in this study have not converged into one common direction. Each country has implemented change within the restraints of existing national institutions and political boundaries. While the goals and range of options considered were strikingly similar, the six countries diverged widely in the actual reform models and process of implementation. Ideas, interests and political institutions played important roles...In several cases, the introduction of market competition went hand-in-hand with increased government control, leading to increased 'hybridization' of health care systems. (2010: 78)

In agreement, Grignon (2012) contends that while there is considerable dispute about whether health care systems converge (see also Paris *et al.*, 2010; Tuohy, 2012a; Narayan, 2007; Aslan, 2009), there is near universal agreement that, when there is convergence, it is invariably slow. National institutions or characteristics of health care systems die hard. Health care systems are renowned for being resistant to 'real reform', namely, reforms altering the basic rules through which individuals contribute to the financing of health care or through which care is delivered to patients. Grignon (2012) suggests that resistance to change does not mean inactivity, but despite over 1,300 reforms over eight years in 20 countries main institutions have survived essentially intact. According to Okma *et al.* (2010), major change is rare and requires the confluence of political willingness to change, popular acceptance of the need to reform and the availability of reform options that fit the national context.

According to Attia and Bérenger (2009), convergence in health care in the EU is evident at two levels: the generalization of medical coverage and the transformation of insurance schemes into universal national regimes. Moreover, the reforms surrounding disease protection, adopted in the 1990s, have coalesced around two axes: the stake in competition among the suppliers (providers) of care and the stake in competition among health insurers (purchasers). In the first instance, the reform of the UK NHS established a quasi-market for care where hospitals and health centres compete to offer their services. The mechanisms of quasi-markets served as reference to Spain where, since 1995, competition exists between the public and private establishments, a trend followed by Finland, Sweden and Denmark. The most significant example of the second is that of the German reform of 1992 under which the consumer can choose either public or private medical coverage thereby encouraging health insurance schemes to better manage their budget, offer competitive insurance services and, in the process, make the purchasers more responsible.

Overall, then, the literature on the convergence in health care systems reveals little consensus. Regardless of where they put emphasis, comparative studies of health policy largely agree on the coexistence of policy divergence and convergence (see Field, 1999; Lian, 2003; Hwang, 2008; Rico *et al.*, 2003). While some authors identify a trend towards convergence (Hitiris and Nixon, 2001; Glennerster and Lieberman, 2011; Thomas, 2011), others find no signs for convergence at all (Globerman and Vining, 1998), while still others see a mixed picture (Wendt *et al.* 2005; Blank and Burau, 2006), finding convergence for some indicators and divergence for others.

It should also be noted that health policy is not static and that movement in one direction is often followed by a move in the opposite direction as political fortunes change or the public responds negatively to a change. For instance, New Zealand was widely cited as an example of NHS convergence towards market systems in the early 1990s when it initiated strong market reforms, but most of these reforms were repealed by later governments. Finally, convergence theories beg the question of convergence to what: privatized health care, national health services, social insurance, national insurance or some new hybrids? According to Tuohy: 'mature health care states are hybridizing, resembling less closely the ideal types approximated by their founding models and increasingly incorporating elements of other models to produce distinctive national hybrids' (2012a: 612).

Classifications of health care systems

At its base, health policy is, of course, a political matter. The most obvious dimension of the political context comprises the formal institutions that have been created for making public policy decisions. The institutional setting in which policy making takes place is termed the policy arena, which includes not only formal political institutions such as legislatures, executives and courts but also regulatory agencies, semi-public bodies and specialized committees and commissions. These institutions define the distribution of power and the relationships among the political players by setting the rules of the game regarding access and interaction within arenas. As such they give distinct advantages or disadvantages to particular groups in society. Equally important to understanding public policy, then, are the informal practices and structures that have evolved within a specific formal institutional framework. These traditions and rules of the game define a special political logic in each country. They are also critical to an environment in which interest groups, political parties, bureaucrats and individual politicians vie for influence over policy.

Together these formal and informal political institutions shape how politics is conducted and create a strategic context for political conflict within the arena. 'Political factors help to determine whether a problem is defined as a public policy that requires action, they shape the way in which the problem is defined, and they intervene in the resolution of that problem' (Immergut, 1992: 10). Although institutional variables are not the only ones to matter, variation in institutional conditions across countries yields distinctive opportunities for the actors involved in policy making in each country (Timmermans, 2001; Okma *et al.*, 2010). The health system represents a set of sector-specific institutions. However, while health politics is big business for states, it often remains characterized by strong private-interest government by medical professionals.

Although no two political systems are identical, many share characteristics that allow us to develop *typologies* or ideal models. The use of typologies is central to the comparative shift in policy analysis and they have been used to conceptualize the (institutional) context in which policies are embedded. Prominent examples include: Castles' (1999) notion of 'families of nations', which describes different clusters of cultural, historical and geographical features of nations; Esping-Andersen's (1990) welfare state regimes, which identify distinct welfare state logics; and Lijphart's (1999) and Blondel's (1990) typologies of democratic and state regimes. Cross-country comparison generates an abundance of information, and ordering this information through typologies simplifies this data in order to facilitate our understanding and analysis of policy emergence, policy making and policy cycles.

Despite widespread variation among health care systems, at root they represent variants or combinations of a limited number of types. As with political systems, the comparative analysis of health policy often uses typologies of health systems to help capture the institutional context of health care and contribute to explaining health policies across different countries. 'Typologies have the advantage of allowing the inclusion of a large number of countries in the analysis. Typologies can also provide a basis for bridging the macro-micro link in comparative studies in such instances as when analyzing the outcomes of certain health policy constellations' (Marmor and Wendt, 2012: 8). While typologies can be

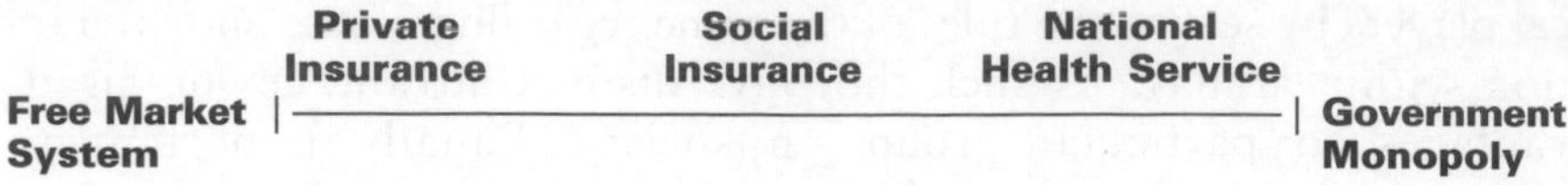

Figure 1.1 *Types of health care system by provision and funding*

Source: OECD (1987: 24).

valuable in simplifying a multifaceted set of cross-cutting dimensions, one must be cautious when interpreting them because they do represent ideal types of specific macro-institutional characteristics. As will be demonstrated in this book, the real world of health care systems is considerably more complicated.

Because of their importance in the literature, several typologies that have been used to classify health care systems are summarized here. An early typology developed in a series of OECD studies has been particularly influential (see Figure 1.1). This typology defines the health system as an ideal typical set of macro-institutional characteristics based on variations in the funding of health care and corresponding differences in the organization of health care provision. This reflects the fact that the public funding of health care (or lack of it) is often seen as the defining characteristic of the degree of public involvement in health care (Freeman, 1998).

As illustrated in Figure 1.1, the *private insurance* (or consumer sovereignty) *model* has the least state involvement in the direct funding or provision of health care services. This type is characterized by the purchase of private health insurance financed by employers and/or individual contributions that are risk oriented. This system is also largely based on private ownership of health care providers and the components of production, although it might include a publicly funded safety net for the most vulnerable groups such as the poor, the elderly or the young. The principal presumption of this approach is that the funding and provision of health care is best left to market forces.

The second basic type of health system when it comes to state involvement is the *social insurance* (or Bismarck) *model.* Although there is significant variation as to organization, this type is based on a concept of social solidarity and characterized by a universal coverage health insurance generally within a framework of social security. As a rule, this compulsory health insurance is funded by a combination of employer and individual contributions through non-profit insurance funds or societies, often regulated and subsidized by the state. The provision of services tends to be private, often on a fee-for-service basis, although some public ownership of the factors of production and delivery is commonplace. A variation of this type is represented by the Taiwan (see Box 1.3) and South Korean National Health Insurance systems. By

Box 1.3 A new health care system

Taiwan is the most recent advanced economy to adopt a universal health insurance programme. The introduction of National Health Insurance (NHI) in 1995 created a single-payer national insurance programme financed through a system jointly financed by payroll taxes, governmental subsidies and individual premiums. In the past decade, it has increased the proportion of the population with insurance coverage from 57 per cent to 98 per cent. Moreover, it has improved the delivery and availability of health care services for its citizens while managing to contain overall cost increases. The NHI is administered by the Bureau of National Health Insurance (BNHI) under the jurisdiction of the Department of Health which by law is mandated to fund and operate the NHI on a self-sustaining basis. To do this, it has been given substantial power over fees, drug prices and other 'terms of engagement' with providers (Cheng, 2003).

distinguishing between finance and provision (highly centralized/largely private in the NHIs), Lee *et al.* (2008) argue for inclusion of a fourth type, 'national health insurance'. Similarly, Kam (2012) suggests that East Asian countries do not fit the three existing categories and that there is a case for an East Asia welfare regime type or a hybrid of the liberal and conservative models. Although we see merit in this line of reasoning, in this book we will continue to treat these systems as a subset of social insurance.

The third type is the *national health service* (or Beveridge) *model*. This model is characterized by universal coverage funded out of general taxation. Although this model is most identified with the UK, New Zealand actually established the first NHS in its 1938 Social Security Act which promised all citizens open-ended access to all the health care services they needed free at the point of use. The provision of health care services under this model is fully administered by the state, which either owns or controls the factors of production and delivery.

The first of the OECD studies, then, identified three types of health system on the basis of a simple dichotomy between patient sovereignty (and the predominance of incentives) and social equity (and the predominance of government control). The NHS model is characterized by universal coverage, funding out of general taxation and public ownership. In contrast, in the social insurance model, compulsory, universal coverage is a component of a system of social security. Health care is financed by employer and employee contributions, through non-profit insurance funds, and the provision of health care is in public or private ownership. Finally, in the private insurance model, health care is funded by individual and/or employer contributions and health delivery is predominantly in private ownership.

This initial OECD typology was a descriptive categorization of how health care is organized in different countries, reflecting its origins in applied policy analysis. As Freeman (2000) observes, the typology emerged from a search, dominated by economists, for better solutions to common problems. This corresponds to a focus on the internal workings of health care rather than on its political and social embeddedness. However, this situation has changed with the wide use of the basic typology in the comparative analysis of health policy (see for example Freeman, 2000; Ham, 1997a; Raffel, 1997; Burau and Blank, 2006). Together with the increasing interest in neo-institutionalism, the typology has been a facilitator for critical analyses of the health system as the institutional framework in which health policies are embedded and how the institutions of health care (among others) shape health policies (and politics). Scott (2001), for example, uses the typology as part of her framework to analyse public and private roles and interfaces in health care across different countries. In contrast, Ham (1997a) in his cross-country comparative analysis focuses more explicitly on health reform.

These analyses also have in common their consideration of other aspects of the institutional context of health care in addition to the typology of health systems. Freeman (2000), for example, explicitly includes in his analysis the mechanisms by which health care is coordinated (health care governance). This inclusion clearly demonstrates that applying the typology of health systems to a wider range of cases has also led to its adaptation. As Collier and Levitsky (1997; also Collier and Mahon, 1993) note, such a process is typified by a tension between increasing analytical differentiation needed to capture the diverse forms of the phenomenon at hand and avoidance of the pitfalls of conceptual stretching and applying the concept to cases that do not fit. The literature on comparative health policy has addressed this tension by adding, more or less explicitly, new attributes to the definition of the health system.

Moran's work (1999, 2000) is particularly relevant here because he attempts both to better account for the institutional embeddedness of health care and to revise the typology of health systems. He starts with the observation that health policy is about more than health care and that modern health care systems are about more than delivering a personal service: 'Health care facilities in modern industrial societies are great concentrations of economic resources – and because of this they are also the subject of political struggle' (Moran, 1999: 1). This entails shifting the focus of the analysis from the organization to the governance of health care. Moran argues that with its emphasis on the access to health care the OECD typology only captures one aspect of the governance of consumption and also misses out on other important dimensions of governing health care. To that end, he introduces the concept of the health care state (see below) that consists of the institutions related to governing the consumption, provision and production of health care.

An even more intricate extension of this typology was advanced by Wendt *et al.* (2009) who distinguish health care arrangements by the roles state, non-governmental (societal) and private actors have in the financing, provision and regulation of health care. The result is a classificatory scheme of 27 types of healthcare politics. Three ideal types are based on uniform features across all dimensions of health care: state health care systems, in which financing, service provision and regulation are carried out by state actors and institutions; societal health care systems, in which societal actors take on the responsibility of health care financing, provision and regulation; and private health care systems, in which all three dimensions fall under the auspices of market actors. Interestingly, there is a predominance of mixed types where consistent features are seen along two of the three health care dimensions, thus approximating an ideal type. Moreover, in six 'pure mixed types', there is no uniformity with regard to financing, service provision and regulation, and, therefore, no resemblance to any ideal type. According to Wendt and colleagues, this expanded typology offers a wide variety of combinations that 'provide a rich basis against which real cases can be evaluated and also point to the differences in real world representation that exist' (2009: 82). Although this classification scheme is thought-provoking, problems with such a detailed categorization include the likelihood that many of the modalities, i.e., private regulation in conjunction with state-based financing and provision, do not exist in practice and that it defeats the primary goal of typologies to simplify reality and, thus, facilitate cross-national analysis.

An overlapping scheme used to categorize health care systems is based on the dimensions of the method and source of financing. At one extreme are those systems fully dependent on private sources of funding, and at the other are those fully funded by public sources. Based on this criterion there are four main types of funding:

- direct tax/general revenues
- social or state insurance
- private insurance
- direct payment by users.

Within each type, however, there are many potential variants. For instance the direct tax might be levied by the central government, by subunits such as states or provinces, or by a combination of governments. Similarly, the social insurance system might be based on a single national scheme or on multiple insurance schemes more or less rigidly regulated or controlled by the government. Furthermore, there is a wide array of possible combinations both of basic types and their variants that are used often within a single health care system, such as in the USA where only the elderly have social insurance. According to Appleby, 'all health-care systems are pluralistic with respect to financing (and organisation) with tendencies to one method rather than another' (1992: 10).

In addition to the wide variety of combinations of these funding methods in each country, different countries apply them in different ways. Some, such as the USA (and, until recently, Australia), use general taxation for particular groups such as the poor and elderly, but depend on private insurance or direct payments for the remainder of the population. Other countries distinguish between specific forms of health care. For instance, New Zealand funds hospital care through general taxation but until recently relied heavily on direct user payment for most primary care, except for specified categories of patients such as children whose care was subsidized. When examining health care policy, then, it is critical to examine not only how health care is financed based on these types, but also under what circumstances it is targeted from particular sources.

A similar classification of health systems, based on a distinction among institutions related to the governance of consumption, provision and production is offered by Moran (1999, 2000) who constructs four different types of health care states, three of which are especially relevant here. In entrenched *command and control* health care states, the governance of consumption consists of extensive public access based on citizenship and extensive control of resource allocation through administrative mechanisms. In contrast, in the *corporatist* health care state, funding through social insurance contributions makes for de facto public access to health care and gives public law bodies (such as statutory, non-profit insurance funds) an important role. This limits the public control over health care costs. The role of providers is even greater in the *supply* health care state, where funding through private insurance limits public access to health care as well as the public control of costs.

Yet another way of categorizing countries is to rank them on a single variable considered appropriate for the comparisons being made. For instance, one simple measure of state involvement that is often used to compare countries is the extent to which health care is publicly funded. Table 1.2 shows a country ranking on that criterion, ranging from over 80 per cent in the UK, New Zealand, Sweden and Japan to just over 30 per cent in Singapore (see also Box 1.4). It should be noted that this ranking, as with many typologies, can tell us nothing about whether one system is better or worse than another; it simply illustrates how the countries array themselves on this dimension. Another use of this data is to trace changes, both for particular countries and collective patterns, and to compare the comparative rankings over time.

Table 1.2 ***Public funding as percentage of health expenditures, 1970–2010, ranked by 2010***

	1970	*1980*	*1990*	*2000*	*2005*[a]	*2010*[b]	*% change*
United Kingdom	87.0	89.4	83.6	80.9	86.9	83.2	–3.8
New Zealand	80.3	88.0	82.4	78.0	78.3	83.2	+2.9
Sweden	86.0	92.5	89.9	84.9	81.7	81.0	–5.0
Japan	69.8	71.3	77.6	81.3	82.7	80.5	+10.7
Netherlands	n/a	69.4	67.1	63.1	62.5	79.2	+9.8
Germany	72.8	78.7	76.2	79.7	77.0	76.8	+4.0
Australia	n/a	62.6	66.2	67.0	67.0	68.5	+5.9
Taiwan	n/a	n/a	44.4	63.8	65.4	66.4	+21.0
United States	36.3	41.2	39.4	43.7	45.1	48.2	+11.9
Singapore	70.1	68.0	n/a	26.0	38.5	36.3	–33.7

[a] The figures for The Netherlands are 2002 and for New Zealand and Singapore are 2003.
[b] The figures for Japan, the Netherlands and Australia are from 2009.

Sources: Data from OECD (2012b).

Box 1.4 The Singapore system: low in public funding, high on individual responsibility

Of all the systems here, Singapore is most unusual in its low level of public funding. The main reason for this is that in 1984 it instituted a compulsory savings scheme that shifted primary health financing responsibility from the state to individuals (Asher *et al.*, 2008). Funds are deposited in a savings account in each contributor's name that can then be drawn on to pay for health insurance or hospital expenses incurred by that person or his immediate family. The scheme is compulsory in the form of a tax on income, but because each account is private, it is deemed privately financed. This health care system is based on a unique interpretation of individual responsibility and is designed to provide incentives to reduce consumption and offer protection against 'free-rider' abuses while guaranteeing affordable basic health care through government subsidies. Individuals can also choose the level of subsidy they wish to receive in public hospitals: if they opt for a fancy ward the subsidy is low or non-existent whereas if they go for a less fancy ward the subsidy is higher. The key principle is that patients are expected to pay part of the cost of medical services that they use, and pay more when they demand a higher level of service (Singapore Ministry of Health, 2008).

Box 1.5 Transformation and the typology

According to Wendt *et al.* (2009) three forms of transformation are possible. The most radical occurs when a system moves from one type to another, for example, when a state-based type develops into a private type. Such a 'system change' is expected to arise only in exceptional instances in which drastic turns in policy goals are met by high levels of public support. A more common form of transformation unfolds along only one of the system's dimensions and does not culminate in a larger system change. An example of an 'internal system change' of this kind would be if the provision of health care shifts from state-based to private actors, but financing and regulation remain in state hands. Therefore, while the system witnesses a significant alteration, it remains predominantly state-based. A third, milder form of transformation is that of an 'internal change of levels' in which a shift within one or more dimensions takes place without leading to an alteration of the system's main features. Although the latter does not embody the same degree of transformation as more drastic forms, it does indicate a significant development within health care systems. By virtue of its modest nature, an internal change is the most likely transformation, in particular over short periods of time which are the typical horizons of researchers and politicians. Moreover, such a change might be the antecedent to a more graduated form of transformation, especially if state, societal or private features are at risk of losing their dominant position within a given dimension.

It must be stressed that while typologies are helpful for teaching and organizing purposes by allowing us to simplify a complex reality and focus on the most important aspects, they remain problematic and offer only an estimate of the real world of health care. Even in those cases where the health system of a country is dominated by one of the types, traces of numerous variants are identifiable. Most countries reflect mixes of characteristics in finance, provision and governance across the various types and there is often variation across time and space within a single country. The specific configuration of any health care system depends on a multitude of factors including the political system, the cultural framework, the demographic context, the distinctive historical background, specific events and social structures inherent to that country (see Chapter 2). Societal goals and priorities develop over time and shape all social institutions and values, which themselves are fluid and changeable (see Box 1.5). As aptly stated by Freeman and Frisina in their analysis, although classification is the 'very stuff of the comparative analysis of health policy,' a debate continues over 'which characteristics should be taken to be definitive or constitutive of the health system; about whether or not these fall into typical clusters; about whether or not these types should be empirically or normatively defined; about which countries are instances of which types and about which countries best represent each particular type' (2012: 174).

Countries selected for study

In order to provide a constructive cross-country analysis of health policy, we have selected ten countries for primary coverage in this book. The countries were selected to give the reader systematic exposure to the full range of health systems (see Figure 1.2). Although all three have moved away from the pure model in varying degrees, Britain,* Sweden and New Zealand are examples of a national health service. Likewise, Germany, Japan, the Netherlands and Taiwan are variations of the social insurance type, while Singapore, with its compulsory Medisave system, is a variant on that theme, but with a heavy private component. Finally, the private insurance type is most clearly represented by the USA and (until recently) by Australia, although many systems contain some elements of the private marketplace. Additionally, these countries represent a wide spectrum of political, cultural and economic environments for illustrating the vagaries of health care.

Our country selection includes some, such as Germany, Sweden, the UK and the USA, that are frequently included in comparative policy studies, and others, such as Australia, the Netherlands and New Zealand that are less often included. Also covered in the analysis here are Japan, Singapore and Taiwan that offer valuable insights into health care policy regularly overlooked in the largely US/European-based literature. Individually, each of the countries has a unique contribution to make to the study of health policy. In combination, they serve as a good sample upon which to analyse the dynamics of health care policy in the 21st century.

Obviously, even the relatively large number of countries covered here does not exhaust the vast array of variation in health care systems found across the world. All of these countries are developed nations with Western-type medical systems. Even Japan, Singapore and Taiwan have

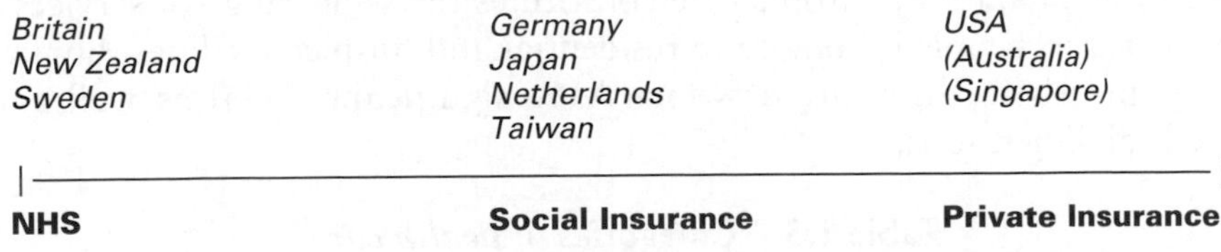

Figure 1.2 *Types of health care systems*

* In the following, when we refer to Britain or the UK we often specifically focus on the organization and policies of health care as they exist in England. Following political devolution in the late 1990s the health systems in the four countries of the UK have developed in different ways (for an overview, see Baggott, 2004).

highly sophisticated medical systems and affluent populations with high levels of expectations and demands. Missing from this analysis are cases from Africa, the Middle East, the Balkans, Eastern Europe and the former Soviet Union, which collectively represent over 4 billion people. Although inclusion of a selection of these countries would be illuminating, it would also be unwieldy and complicate the level of analysis. One of the drawbacks in trying to cover even ten countries is that it is not possible to provide a thorough analysis of any one of their health care systems. As regards specific countries, then, the objective of this book is to be an introduction, not a comprehensive analysis, and to provide a context within which to study individual countries. To this end, readers with an interest in a particular country or countries should make use of the Guide to Further Reading at the end of this book which should provide a valuable basis for building on the foundational knowledge offered in this book. In addition, the Guide to Websites provides links to the most recent information and data on these countries.

Types of health care

Another distinction that is crucial in understanding health policy relates to the types of health care. Table 1.3 describes three categories that largely define the range of activities normally incorporated under health care. Although the terms used to define these categories vary, *primary care*, *curative medicine* and *chronic care* are used here. Primary care normally encompasses visits to general practitioners (GPs), ambulatory care and health education efforts, and includes a strong health promotion/disease prevention element discussed in Chapter 7. In contrast, curative medicine, which represents the core of modern health care discussed in Chapters 3 to 5, centres on acute care in hospitals and relies on specialists and technologies to restore health to those acutely ill. Finally, as illustrated in Chapter 6, chronic care constitutes the wide range of services provided to people in long-term residential and hospice facilities, home care and so forth, many of which have significant social as well as medical dimensions.

Table 1.3 *Categories of health care*

Primary care	*Curative medicine*	*Chronic care*
General practitioners	Acute/hospital care	Long-term facilities
Well-patient physicals	Outpatient clinics	Nursing home
Ambulatory care	Technology based	Hospice
Health promotion	Specialists	Respite care
Education/prevention	Intensive care	Home care

Although the health policy of any country will comprise a mixture of these types, there is considerable variation in the weight given to each dimension depending on the assumptions and goals of the policies pursued. As illustrated by the scope of coverage in this book, health care today is dominated by curative medicine. When one thinks about health care, hospitals with highly trained specialists in the latest technologies first come to mind. As noted below in the discussion of the expansion of biomedical technology, health care is often equated with medicine despite evidence that such an unbalanced approach has limits. Even the term 'curative' is misleading because in most cases the patient is not cured, but is rather rescued or maintained, often in a state of health that is lower than it was before the person became ill. Instead of curing the person, these interventions often end up supporting or preserving a particular level of personal health by creating a continued dependence on further medical treatment or medications.

Prior to World War II, health care was normally limited to performing public health and primary care functions, in part because its curative capacities were so limited and frequently ineffective. Hospitals were primarily designed to protect the public health, often by quarantining patients rather than treating them, and largely served only persons who could not afford a private physician. Those with private resources would avoid hospitals like the plague because often plagues were found there. Families were the primary long-term care givers and most people died at home rather than in the intensive care wards of high-tech hospitals.

During the 1950s and 1960s, the emphasis on health care shifted perceptibly towards curative medicine even in health care systems in countries such as the UK, Japan and New Zealand that had strong roots in primary care and prevention. Although other countries have not bought into curative medicine to the same degree as the USA, as will be evident in the chapters that follow, there are strong pressures for aggressive medical interventions in acute care settings even in countries like Taiwan and Japan. The increased demands of the public for higher levels of technological medicine have produced indelible alterations in the health care community, most clearly manifested in the growth of medical specialities at the expense of primary care physicians and, especially, public health workers. As a result, the modern medical profession has developed primarily around the search for finding cures to disease rather than promoting health, preventing disease and protecting the public health. The growth of high-tech medical centres, the expectation of ever more sophisticated diagnostic capacity and the expansion of dramatic life-saving procedures has changed the nature of medical care. However, as evidenced in Box 1.6, shifts in disease patterns call for a corresponding shift in the balance from acute care to chronic (and

Box 1.6 Changes in patient needs: from inpatient to outpatient

The medical needs of US Medicare beneficiaries, and where they undergo treatment, have changed dramatically over the past two decades. Twenty years ago, most spending growth was linked to intensive inpatient (hospital) services, but now much of the growth is attributable to chronic conditions such as diabetes, arthritis, hypertension and kidney disease. These conditions are primarily treated not in hospitals but in outpatient settings or by patients in their home with prescription drugs. Thorpe and associates argue that health reform must address these changed health needs through evidence-based community prevention, care coordination and support for patient self-management. In 2005, among community-dwelling beneficiaries, 96.4 per cent had at least one outpatient health service (such as a doctor visit), 93.4 per cent received prescription medicines and 74.7 per cent had at least one outpatient hospital visit. Moreover, over half of Medicare beneficiaries are treated for five or more chronic conditions each year, while the typical beneficiary sees two primary care physicians and five specialists working in four different practices per year (Thorpe *et al.*, 2010).

preventive/primary) care and is certain to create heightened tensions in health care delivery in the coming decades.

Growing problems in health policy

Despite variation in health care across countries, there are several factors endemic to all developed nations that make health policy ever more problematic. In the wake of falling national incomes and increasingly scarce resources for social spending, all countries, no matter how much they vary politically or socially, face growing struggles in the financing and delivery of health care. Table 1.4 clearly demonstrates that while countries differ considerably as to the percentage of their gross domestic product (GDP) they devote to health care, in virtually all cases it has increased appreciably over the last three decades. This means that health care costs are increasing at rates exceeding that of economic growth, a pattern that is not sustainable in the long run. At present, this situation is further exacerbated by the financial crisis, which Mladovsky and colleagues (2012) characterize as an 'external shock' to health systems. In general, health systems need stable resources and arbitrary cuts can undermine health systems, especially when ageing populations require increased resources.

The increase in health care costs alone is not the problem. As Duff (2001) points out, an expansion of spending on other goods is welcomed as contributing to economic well-being; why, then, should increased

Table 1.4 *Health expenditure as a percentage of GDP, 1970–2010*

	1970	*1980*	*1990*	*2000*	*2005*	*2010*[a]	*% change*
Australia	n/a	6.3	6.9	8.3	8.8	9.1	2.8
Germany	6.0	8.4	8.3	10.3	10.7	11.6	5.6
Japan	4.6	6.5	6.0	7.7	8.2	9.5	4.9
Netherlands	n/a	7.4	8.0	8.0	9.2	12.0	4.6
New Zealand	5.2	5.9	6.9	7.7	8.9	10.1	4.9
Singapore	n/a	n/a	2.8	n/a	3.8	4.0	1.2
Sweden	6.8	8.9	8.2	8.2	9.2	9.6	2.8
Taiwan	3.6	4.8	5.5	5.9	6.3	6.4	2.8
United Kingdom	4.5	5.6	6.0	7.2	8.2	9.6	5.1
United States	7.0	8.7	11.9	13.2	15.2	17.6	10.6

[a] The figures for Australia and Japan are from 2009 and Taiwan is from 2008.

Sources: Data from OECD (2008, 2012b); Bureau of National Health Insurance (2008, 2012).

consumption on health care be a problem? Furthermore, every country spends 100 per cent of its GDP on something, so if countries spend considerably more on health care that is their choice. However, the main reason we should care about growing health care expenditure is that the extra spending might not be providing as much value as if those funds were used for education, housing, environmental protection or other private or public consumption or investment (Fuchs, 2005: 77). In economic terms, the 'opportunity costs' might be too high when excessive money goes to health care and is thus diverted from more effective areas of spending. Another reason for concern over heightened spending on medical care centres on the critical role of the state in funding it since governmental spending does not respond to normal market forces. A final cause for apprehension is the combination of ageing populations, rapid advances in medical technology and expanded public expectations and demands that exacerbates the situation. Recent reform efforts in virtually all countries are largely a reaction to these major forces, and, although there is variation by degree across countries, these trends signify ominous signs for the funding and provision of health care in the coming decades.

Ageing populations

As indicated in Table 1.5, demographic projections show that most

Table 1.5 ***Percentage of population aged 65 and over***

	1960	*1980*	*1990*	*2000*	*2020*	*2030*	*2040*	*2050*
Australia	8.5	9.6	11.1	12.4	18.3	22.2	24.5	25.7
Germany	11.5	15.6	14.9	16.4	22.7	27.8	31.1	31.5
Japan	5.7	9.1	12.1	17.4	29.2	31.8	36.5	39.6
Netherlands	9.0	11.5	12.8	13.6	19.8	23.4	25.0	23.5
New Zealand	8.7	9.7	11.2	11.8	16.7	21.1	23.8	24.6
Singapore	n/a	4.9	6.0	7.0	18.5	21.0	26.0	27.3
Sweden	11.8	16.3	17.8	17.3	21.1	22.8	24.0	23.7
Taiwan	n/a	5.8	6.2	8.6	13.6	24.0	31.8	33.0
United Kingdom	11.7	15.0	15.7	15.8	19.0	21.9	23.7	24.1
United States	9.2	11.3	12.5	12.4	16.3	19.7	20.4	20.7

Sources: Data from OECD (2009a) for all but Singapore (Ministry of Health, 2008) and Taiwan (Bureau of National Health Insurance, 2008).

countries will experience considerable ageing of their populations over the next 30 years. Although the ageing process is taking place earlier and more rapidly in some countries, all will experience it. The primary cause of the ageing of Western societies is the precipitous decline in fertility rates since the 1970s that has increased the proportion of elderly. This trend is exaggerated because the sharp upturn in birth rates after World War II produced a bloated age cohort in the baby boom generation, the first wave of which has now reached retirement age. Even if life expectancy is unaltered, this wave of ageing baby boomers, along with declining fertility rates, guarantees an increasing proportion of the elderly.

The second factor contributing to the ageing of populations is increased life expectancy. In the years between 1950 and 1980, life expectancy at birth increased by 8.5 years for females and 6.0 years for males. These significant gains reflect improved social factors, health habits and the new capacities of medicine to reduce infant mortality and extend the life span. It is important to note that in the past gains in life expectancy have been under estimated, meaning that there could be even more significant increases in average life span in the coming decades. Moreover, substantial differences in average life expectancy in OECD countries at present strongly suggest that further gains could be made in a number of countries. Ironically, these health-improving steps, together with continued low fertility rates, could exacerbate population ageing and complicate funding problems (Box 1.7).

These ageing trends are accompanied by two critical changes in the population structure. First, within the overall trends towards older populations is the ageing of these elderly populations themselves. At present the most rapidly growing segment of those 65 and over is the cohort aged 80 and over. As illustrated in Table 1.6, this proportion is expected to climb to over 30 per cent of the elderly in most countries, and over 40 per cent in Japan, by 2050. These increases are particularly significant for health policy because those over 80 are by far the heaviest users of health care. The second trend within a trend relates to the sex composition of the elderly population. As a result of their longer life expectancy, women outnumber men significantly in the elderly age cohorts. Furthermore, the sex imbalance increases with age, meaning that as the very elderly cohort expands, the proportion of elderly women will grow. Even though this imbalance is projected to narrow over time, especially at the younger end of the elderly age group, women will continue to constitute a substantial majority of the elderly, particularly among the most elderly. As with the other trends, this has considerable impact on the nature of the health care needs of the population.

Box 1.7 A warning: 'profound consequences' as the EU grows older

EU-wide, the share of the elderly in the total population is expected to rise from 21 per cent now to around 34 per cent by 2050. Those 80+ are predicted to rise from 4 per cent of today's population to 10 per cent. By 2050, 37 million people are expected to be octogenarians plus. Eurostat says these big rises in the elderly will have 'profound consequences' for social protection systems – particularly pensions, which are funded mostly by workers and employers. Health spending is also likely to 'increase significantly' (Eurostat News Release, 29 July 1999).

Table 1.6 *Share of very old persons (80+) among the elderly, 1960–2040*

	1960	*2000*	*2040*
Australia	14.3	23.6	31.8
Germany	18.4	22.3	29.9
Japan	12.6	22.0	41.1
Netherlands	15.2	23.5	30.0
New Zealand	17.1	23.8	30.5
Sweden	15.9	29.0	31.5
United Kingdom	16.4	25.4	29.1
United States	15.2	26.4	33.3

Source: Data from OECD (2005b).

What does it matter for health care if the population gets older? It matters because at present a disproportionate share of health resources go to the elderly, particularly those over age 80. As illustrated in Table 1.7, in most countries the over-65 cohort accounts for at least double the expenditures relative to its proportion of the population, and in some cases (Australia and USA) almost quadruple. In the extreme case of the USA, with its intense spending near the end of life, the 12.4 per cent of the population now aged 65 and older consumes nearly half of total health care resources. Moreover, while the average per capita expenditure is approximately four times higher for the elderly than the non-elderly, importantly, the rate of increase in spending for the elderly is nearly three times as much. Ironically, because of medical improvements and technologies that prolong life, chronic disease that requires frequent medical interventions has become a mounting drain on scarce medical resources. People who in earlier times would have died of one illness are often kept alive only to suffer long-term decline in quality of life and require even more health care as they acquire new diseases. Furthermore, because of the concurrence of multiple and frequently chronic conditions, the cost of prolonging the life of elderly patients is considerably higher than that of younger ones.

The elderly use more acute care, are hospitalized about twice as often, have longer stays in hospital and are much more likely to be readmitted to hospital (see Chapter 4 for details). The cost of ICU care in the USA for a patient over age 65, for instance, is three to five times per day the cost for the average acute-care admission. Moreover, it is estimated by the Clinical Advisory Board (2001) that current baby boomers could outlive today's elders by seven to 15 years, thus requiring a doubling of ICU care by 2020. In the USA, the prevalence of cases of Alzheimer's disease is expected to more than double in the next 20 years (Thacker *et al.*, 2006). How can health systems continue this spending pattern as the proportion of the elderly swells? Although improvements in health conditions might serve to delay the highest expenditure that occurs at the end of life for many people, cumulatively ageing populations will demand ever-greater health care spending.

As the projections in Table 1.7 illustrate, the estimated increases in health spending on the elderly are staggering in some countries, especially Sweden and the USA. Although it varies by country, the trend towards a heightened concentration of health care spending on the elderly is universal, with most countries registering over 50 per cent by 2040. The ageing population not only increases health care spending and shifts it towards the elderly, but it also has considerable potential impact on the type of health care provided. Obviously, the growing number of old people will generate a higher demand for geriatric care and thus a proportionate increase in geriatric facilities and personnel and long-term care (see Chapter 6).

Table 1.7 ***Percentage of health expenditures and persons aged 65 or more, 2003 and estimated 2020 and 2040***

	2003		*Projections*	
	% 65+	*% Total expenditure*	*2020*	*2040*
Australia	12.8	40.2	46.4	56.0
Germany	18.6	34.1	40.0	49.4
Japan	19.0	42.4	52.5	55.9
Netherlands	13.8	41.2	49.6	60.1
New Zealand	11.9	42.1	47.2	52.3
Sweden	17.2	54.2	59.6	63.3
Taiwan	9.9	25.8	36.9	44.0
United Kingdom	16.0	43.0	45.6	54.1
United States	12.4	48.8	56.9	62.9

Sources: Data from OECD (2006); Taiwan (Bureau of National Health Insurance, 2012).

Several additional aspects of the ageing of populations are critical to an understanding of the full range of implications for health policy. Although attention here has focused on the increased expenditures generated by the growing proportion of the elderly, there is also the issue that as populations age the size of the productive sector decreases, thus raising concern over the capacity of society to support the new demands. The ability of any country to finance increased costs associated with the ageing population depends upon the relative size of the productive population (usually measured by dependency ratios of some type), as well as unemployment rates and productivity. As the workforce and the tax base is reduced through ageing and continued low levels of fertility, the pressures on the remaining working age population intensifies.

Finally, just at the time where there is an increased need for long-term care giving, social changes have undermined traditional, largely informal care mechanisms for the elderly. The decline in the extended family, increased mobility and the trends towards more working women and fewer children have in many countries reduced the willingness and ability of families to care for the elderly. Although women continue to provide significant levels of long-term care for family members, coverage is saturated and as a proportion will decrease (see Chapter 6 for details). As a result, the demands for formal long-term care services will intensify and such services will depend increasingly on public funds.

Medical technology and health policy

Another force impacting on all health systems is the rapid expansion of medical technology. Simply put, there are a lot more technologies available today for intervention – and many of these new techniques are very costly on a per-case basis. Vast improvements in surgical procedures, tissue matching and immuno-suppressant drugs are making repair and replacement of organs routine. Likewise, innovations in diagnostic machinery continue to push the boundaries. Computerized axial tomography (CT) scans and magnetic resonance imaging (MRI) have been followed by positron emission tomography (PET) and other specialized diagnostic machines. Moreover, human genetic technology, stem cell research, neuroscience and pharmacology promise a dramatically expanding array of costly diagnostic and therapeutic applications that will increase both the range of intervention options and the pressures on health care systems to deliver. These innovations can enhance care but they tend to cost appreciably more than former forms of treatment.

This proliferation of new medical technologies and pharmaceuticals over the past several decades has been one of the most important drivers of health care spending growth, if not the most important (Bodenheimer, 2005). According to one study, new medical technologies account for up to one-third of the rise in annual health care costs (Zwillich, 2001). Diffusion of new technology into practice is associated with greater per capita utilization and higher spending. Medical technology affects outlays by adding to the arsenal of feasible treatments and by reducing the invasiveness of existing interventions, thus increasing the number of patients who might enjoy net gains from diagnosis and treatment. Although not every technological advance leads to increased expenditure, the net effect has tended to inflate costs due to extensions in the range and intensity of care. Thus, even relatively inexpensive advances, such as antibiotics, which appear to reduce health care costs by treating common diseases at a lower cost than conventional treatments, add significantly to medical spending.

Virtually all scholars agree that the biomedical revolution persistently drives up health care spending (Aaron, 2003). Baker *et al.* (2003) found that increases in the supply of technology tend to be related to both higher utilization and spending on the service in question. Thorpe *et al.* (2004b) found that a small number of medical conditions were associated with much of the increase in health care spending between 1987 and 2000, with the top 15 conditions accounting for approximately half of the overall growth in spending (see also Skinner *et al.*, 2006). Moreover, the problem of priority setting is destined to become more acute in the coming decade because we are seeing the rapid proliferation of costly 'last chance' therapies: technologies that represent the last chance for

Box 1.8 The cost of technology

After helping to develop some of the hottest new drugs, cancer specialist Leonard Saltz has come down with a bad case of sticker shock. The price tag for treating patients has increased 500-fold in the last decade. Ten years ago, doctors could extend the life of a patient who had failed to respond to chemotherapy by an average of 11.5 months using a combination of drugs that cost $500 in today's dollars. Now, new drugs are able to extend survival on average to 22.5 months, but at a cost of $250,000, not including pharmacy markups, salaries for doctors and nurses and the cost of infusing the drugs into patients in the hospital. That kind of cost is unsustainable. 'Sooner or later the bubble is going to pop,' according to Saltz. The question is simple: how many exorbitant cancer drugs can society really afford to stack on top of one another? 'Absent a thoughtful national discussion, the answer is none,' says Michael A. Friedman, chief executive of City of Hope, a cancer centre in Los Angeles. 'We will quickly run out of resources, leading to de facto rationing.' The rising costs, he says, are 'utterly insupportable' (Herper, 2004).

prolonging life for individuals. These are very expensive and typically yield what might be judged as marginal benefits relative to their costs (see Box 1.8).

The impact of technological advances is heightened by the increase in the very elderly since advances in technology enable the prolongation of life for persons with illnesses that until recently would have been untreatable – but at high cost. Moreover, while curative treatment may be beneficial to individual patients, the marginal gain in terms of length of survival and quality of life is difficult to judge (Lewis and Leeder, 2009). This uncertainty is complicated by the fact that most medical procedures have not been subject to controlled assessment to determine their effectiveness in particular cases and how they compare in outcome to less expensive alternative approaches. Furthermore, as noted by Campillo-Artero (2011), often health technologies do not reach their potential because they fail to change the behaviour of the health professionals that will use them or to surmount frequent environmental constraints.

Despite the fact that medical technology is global and contributes to cost escalation in all health systems, there is evidence that policies adopted by countries can have a significant impact on the use of new technologies (see Chapter 4). Although all countries feel the impact of new technologies, many try to limit the diffusion of expensive new drugs and equipment by instituting controls and requiring physicians and hospitals to work within fixed budgets (Fuchs, 2005: 76). McClellan and Kessler, for example, found 'enormous differences in how quickly and widely treatments diffused into medical practice' (1999: 253), especially those high-technology treatments with high fixed costs or high variable costs per use. They also found more modest differences in the times it takes new drugs, procedures or devices to become available. So while the approach of the USA in particular reflects the view that new technologies should be made available quickly, other countries have been more cautious. The result is that medical spending growth across nations has diverged as some countries implement cost-containment policies designed to curb the diffusion of medical technology and others fail to do so.

Rising public expectations and demands

The primary forces behind technological medicine come from the providers of the health care community who instil a demand in the public. Health professionals are trained to do what is best for their patients and in some countries this has produced a do-everything approach. Health care is big business with huge financial stakes. The health care industry itself is a powerful shaper of perceived needs and it benefits significantly from an ever-expanding notion of health care. Not surprisingly, any attempt to place limits on access to the newest technologies risks condemnation from practitioners, their patients and the public. As noted by Altman *et al.*, any limits on health spending will be strongly resisted by groups that are negatively affected. The pressure to use medical technologies past the point where they have no marginal value is very strong and as a result the long-term spending growth trend is inevitable (Altman *et al.*, 2003). Such cases of denial of access result in dramatic news stories and tough questioning of those officials who venture to deny such care (see Box 1.9).

These public expectations and perceptions of medicine have produced an over-utilization of and reliance on technology (Ubel, 2001). Patients demand access to the newest technologies because they are convinced of their value. Popular health-oriented magazines and television shows extol the virtues of medical innovations. Physicians are trained in the technological imperative, which holds that a technology should be used despite its cost if it offers any possibility of benefit. Furthermore, third-party payment provides no disincentive against the over-utilization of medical technology. Any limits on the allocation of medical technologies, then, must come from outside the health care community itself. The only agent with the power to enforce such limits on an inclusive scale is the government, but it can do so only within the context of escalating public expectations. Also, since it is natural for politicians to want to please their constituents and be re-elected, they are beholden to those interests with political power and to the claims of their constituents. As a result, they tend to over-promise and avoid proposing limits whenever possible.

Box 1.9 Media campaigns for treatment denied

In the UK, furious multiple sclerosis sufferers go to the media when the National Institute for Clinical Excellence, the government's cost-effectiveness agency, threatens to ban a new drug on the grounds that at £10,000 per year per patient it is too expensive for its relative benefits. One mother of two children with the disease is quoted as saying: 'My children are dependent on me – how can you put a price on that?' Should the government step in and fund the drug for these young children and, if so, where will the money to do so come from? Meanwhile, in New Zealand a 76-year-old man is denied kidney dialysis by the public hospital. The man and his family take his case to the media, accusing the health authorities of denying his rights to life-saving treatment. The media portray him as a victimized war veteran and include emotional interviews with family members. Unrelenting media pressure forces political officials to overrule the hospital authorities and give him dialysis despite the hospital's argument that he was an extremely poor medical risk for reasons they could not disclose due to patient confidentiality. He received dialysis but died within five months due to heart failure. Were the politicians right in bowing to public pressure?

The expectations and demands of the public for health care, then, are theoretically insatiable and they are fuelled by a medical industry that has much to gain by the continual expansion of the scope of medicine. Health care costs have increased partly because citizens expect and often demand higher and higher levels of medical intervention, levels undreamt of several decades ago. Moreover, patients have become less deferential and more informed as to their options through the Internet and the social media (Scott *et al.*, 2005). This exaggerated view of health care often is nurtured by those who place heavy emphasis on the rights of individuals to health care with few limits. It also reflects the fact that every person is a potential patient or a family member of one who at any time might need health care. Furthermore, since World War II there has been a shift towards the notion of positive rights to health care that places a moral duty on society to provide the resources necessary to exercise those rights. The long-term effect, within the context of ever more sophisticated technological options, is that setting limits has become progressively more difficult politically as the population takes health care entitlements for granted.

Moreover, the proposition that one should limit the medical expenditure on a particular patient in order to benefit the community contradicts the traditional patient-oriented mores of medicine as practised in many countries. Thus, there are strong pressures for intensive intervention on an individual basis even in the last days of life, often in spite of the enormous cost for very little return in terms of prolonging the patient's life. In countries with more communal or collectively-rounded cultures, this maximalist approach to health care is less rigid and the public more accepting of limits, but even in Taiwan the NHI reimbursement scheme has 'reinforced the perception of the goals of medicine by the public, relying more and more on making office visits and taking medicines to get well and feel better, rather than working on a change to healthier life styles' (Wen *et al.*, 2008: 266).

Public expectations may be elevated unrealistically because of a tendency to oversell medical innovation and overestimate the capacities of new medical technologies for resolving health problems. At the centre are the mass media, which are predisposed to idealistically optimistic and oversimplified coverage of medical technology. Frequently, the initial response of the media, often encouraged by medical spokesmen, is to report innovations as medical 'breakthroughs'. Because most health care is routine and not newsworthy, the media naturally focus attention on techniques that can be easily dramatized. By and large, media coverage solidifies public trust in the technological fix and 'stimulates their appetite for new, expensive, high technology procedures' (Kassler, 1994: 126). Moreover, media coverage, along with a freedom of information climate that has emerged in many countries, has forced the rationing process out into the open. Users of health care are less willing to accept a gate-keeper role for their general practitioners, especially when they read in the papers of inconsistencies and problems in the health care system. As a result, many politicians find it difficult not to join in the call for expanded access to new technologies, while the media seems to relish uncovering and sensationalizing cases where treatment is denied.

Arguments in favour of containing the costs of health care, while widely accepted at the societal level, are often rejected at the individual level. Thus, while a large proportion of the population in theory supports the need for cost containment, when one's own health or that of a loved one is at stake, constraints on the availability of health care resources are viewed as unfair: 'I know the government needs to control health care costs but not when my child needs an expensive new drug.' It is little wonder that elected officials are not willing to make decisions that jeopardize these emotionally held values. Again, it is important to note that although there are global forces working to increase public demands and expectations, these are stronger in some countries than in others.

It has been observed that no matter to what extent health care facilities are expanded, there will remain a steady pool of unmet demands. Despite the policy statements of medical advocates, there is little evidence that additional facilities and money alone will resolve the health care crisis (see Chapter 4). Although wealthier countries devote substantially higher proportions of their resources to health services than poorer countries, the demand for services does not abate; instead, the public comes to expect a level of medical care that could not be imagined by citizens of less affluent countries. Moreover, as these expectations are met, demand for expanded health services actually heightens, despite the fact that, internationally, there is virtually no relationship between health status and health spending beyond about US$1000 or so per annum per capita. The upward trajectory in health status flattens out beyond this threshold and the marginal health benefits from additional health care spending become vanishingly small. Indeed, according to Lewis and Leeder (2009), wealthy countries are all on the 'flat of the curve'.

Conclusions

Health systems of all countries face major problems regarding the issues raised here. As a result, apprehension about health care expenditure growth and its long-term sustainability has risen to the top of the policy agenda in all developed countries. As continued growth in spending places pressure on government budgets, health services provision and patients' personal finances, policy makers have begun to launch forecasting projects to support policy planning. In their comparative analysis of 25 models that were developed for OECD countries by governments, research agencies and international organizations, Astolfi *et al.* (2012) found that while virtually all models accounted for demographic shifts in the population, the least understood influences on health expenditure growth are technological innovation and health-seeking behaviour.

Whether health care represents a crisis in a particular country depends on one's perspective, but certainly there is much variation in severity across nations on more objective measures as well. To what extent are these differences the product of health policies of the countries and to what extent are the problems beyond the direct control of policy makers? Put another way, what steps can governments take, if any, to maximize the chances of framing sustainable health care systems that can weather the ageing population, the proliferation of technologies, heightened public expectations and other forces driving up the costs?

What should be already evident from the discussion so far is that there are significant differences as to how well countries are doing in constraining costs, providing universal and quality care and protecting the public health. It has yet to be demonstrated convincingly whether universal, global forces are moving the health policies of industrialized countries towards convergence. Even if that is the case, it is imperative to examine closely the variations and similarities of the health care systems of countries and to appreciate the implications for the provision of health care to populations. Chapter 2 begins this task by describing the political, cultural and historical context of the health systems of these countries in order to get a better understanding of how and why each country's health system has evolved the way it has. It presents three different sets of explanations for the divergent approaches to health care found in our countries. As such, the chapter provides a framework for studying the intricacies of the systems and the substantive issues introduced in the chapters that follow.

Chapter 2

The Context of Health Care

The health policy of any country at a particular point in time is the product of a multitude of factors, the most important of which are displayed in Figure 2.1. These factors include the intrinsic social, cultural and political fabric of a country, including its social values and structures, political institutions and traditions, the legal system and the characteristics of its health care community. For instance, policy-making authority might be highly centralized or widely dispersed across multiple levels. Moreover, in some countries unions and/or corporate structures are strong factors in determining social policy and might, in effect, have a veto power over proposed policy changes made by the government. Likewise, the influence of the medical industry and medical associations varies widely, as does the power of insurance providers in shaping health policy.

The practice of medicine can also be strongly affected by the legal system and its role in compensation claims and the definition of legal rights to health care services. Moreover, in some countries the courts can challenge and even negate government policies, while in others the government is supreme and its decisions are the law. Social values, too, are important forces, with some traditions emphasizing individual rights and entitlements and others putting heavy emphasis on collective or community good. The boundaries as to what is a 'public' good and what should remain in the private sphere also impact on health policy. Countries with stronger socialist roots are likely to define public goods and services much more broadly and include universal coverage. Furthermore, in some societies like Taiwan and Japan, the extended family still plays an important role in health care while in others even the nuclear family has diminished importance in the delivery of health care.

In addition to the values and institutions of a country, health policy is also shaped by the composition of its population and by demographic patterns. Heterogeneous, multicultural populations require more complex health systems than more homogeneous ones. Likewise, older populations have different needs from younger ones. Populations can also be more or less stratified by class, economic status or other social groupings. As noted in Chapter 1, health policy and the way in which medical resources are distributed also reflect the current state of medical technology and the public expectations and demands that accompany it.

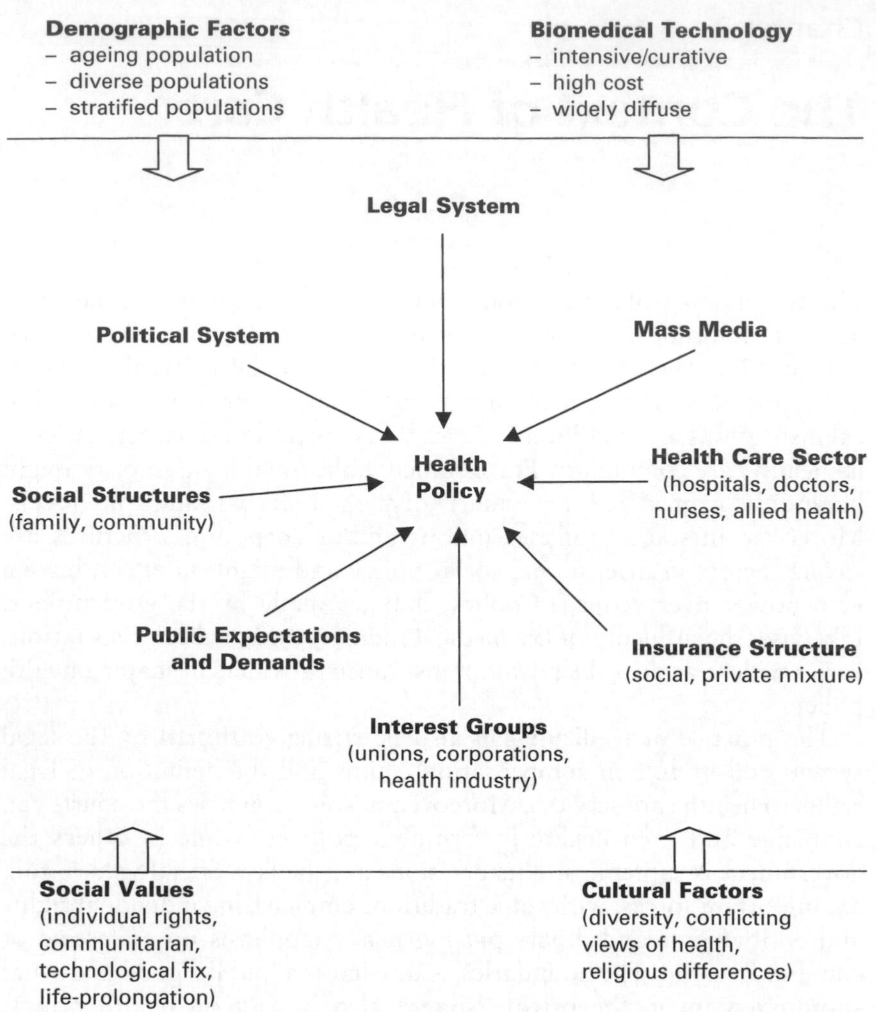

Figure 2.1 *Health policy context of developed nations*

For example, a survey of attitudes about length and quality of life among adults conducted by the UK International Longevity Centre found significant differences between the French, the Americans and the British. While 64 per cent of Americans and 55 per cent of the British wanted to live as long as possible even if that entailed pain, nearly two-thirds of the French opted to live a shorter than average life if it meant dying without being in pain or dependency on others (Carvel, 2002a).

The mass media and its coverage of medical stories clearly influence how the public perceives medicine and health care policy. Countries with 'tabloid' traditions are likely to emphasize the more sensational aspects of medicine and those with more investigative traditions are likely to look for faults in the health care system. In general, however, the mass media in these countries has tended to dramatize medicine, heighten expectations and place more demands on health managers and politicians.

Public support for policy, of course, is an important factor in democratic societies and is critical in explaining how governments with similar problems cope differently. Interestingly, levels of public support for health services across countries seem to have little correlation with levels of health spending or any objective level of services provided. Table 2.1, for instance, compares for each country the public satisfaction with their health care system with the percentage of GDP spent on health care, and it finds little relationship between higher spending and satisfaction. Spending more does not necessarily increase satisfaction levels.

Numerous statistical analyses have been offered to explain differences in aggregate health expenditure among nations and investigate the impact of institutions and other possible explanatory variables on this. Studies across developed and developing countries commonly find that the per capita income of a country is the single most important factor explaining health expenditure variation (Gerdtham *et al.*, 1998). Total health spending rises from around 2 to 3 per cent of GDP in the poorest

Table 2.1 ***Public satisfaction and percentage of GDP spent on health care***

	Satisfaction level [a]		*% GDP*	
	1991	*1996*	*1990*	1996
Australia	34	n/a	7.5	7.8
Germany	41	58	8.5	9.4
Japan	49	n/a	6.1	6.9
Netherlands	47	70	8.5	8.0
Singapore	n/a	80[b]	2.8	3.3
Sweden	32	58	8.3	8.2
Taiwan	39	80	5.1	5.7
United Kingdom	27	57	6.0	7.0
United States	10	40	11.9	12.8

[a] 1991 measured by statement, 'On the whole, the health care system works pretty well, and only minor changes are necessary to make it work better' (Blendon *et al.*, 1990). 1996 is percentage saying they were 'fairly or very satisfied' with their health system (Blendon *et al.*, 2001).
[b] Singapore figure 2006 (Lim and Joshi, 2008).

Sources: Data from OECD (2008); Blendon *et al.* (1990); Blendon *et al.* (2001), Bureau of National Health Insurance (2008).

countries to 8 to 10 per cent in the wealthiest, with the USA substantially higher (Musgrave *et al.*, 2002). Since all of our countries are quite similar in wealth, however, we suggest that differences in spending reflect a combination of economic, cultural and historical factors. Wealth still might be the most important single factor but it is only one of many that must be considered. Moreover, these statistical modelling studies cannot explain variation in how aggregate expenditure is distributed nor how the funding and provision of health services are organized.

Although health care on one level might reflect universal challenges for all countries, the political, historical and cultural context of health and health care varies from country to country as well as within countries. A main argument in this book is that variation in health policy from one country to the next can be explained only by understanding the unique combination of these variables and their interaction in each nation. This chapter examines three underlying and complementary explanations for country diversity: the institutionalist, the cultural and the functionalist (or structuralist) explanations. First, institutionalist contextual factors, specifically the political structures and institutions of these countries and their legal systems, are surveyed. Second, attention is directed towards the historical and cultural context of health care. After discussing the defining cultural characteristics of each country, different approaches to defining health and the role of traditional medicine are examined. Third, functionalist explanations are presented. These include population size and diversity, the wealth of a country and social/economic determinants of health.

Institutionalist explanations: contrasting political systems

Although the political systems of no two countries are identical and each nation has a unique history and combination of formal and informal structures (see Boxes 2.1 to 2.10), the characteristics of political systems can be categorized along several overlapping dimensions (Lijphart, 1999). The major distinguishing factor is the extent to which political power is concentrated or dispersed. As a rule, *unitary* systems concentrate political authority in a central government while *federal* systems constitutionally divide powers between the central government and states, provinces or other sub-national governments. Although the central government in a unitary system might choose to delegate specific administrative functions and responsibilities to lower units, final authority rests at the national level. In contrast, states in a federal system have constitutionally based powers that most often include health policy. Unitary governments include Japan, New Zealand, Sweden and the UK

Box 2.1 Australia

Australia is an independent nation within the British Commonwealth. The national government was created with a Constitution in 1900 patterned partly on the US Constitution, although with no bill of rights. It is a strong federal system with national powers specified in the Constitution and residual powers remaining with the six states and two self-governing territories. The national Parliament is bicameral, consisting of a 76-member Senate and a 150-member House of Representatives. Under the Westminster parliamentary system, the leader of the political party or coalition that wins a majority of the seats in the House becomes prime minister. The prime minister and the cabinet wield actual power and are responsible to the Parliament. General elections are held at least once every three years; the last general election was in September 2013. Over 670 local councils assist in the delivery of services such as road maintenance, sewage treatment, and the provision of recreational facilities (*World Fact Book*, 2012).

as well as Singapore and Taiwan, while Germany, the Netherlands, Australia and the USA are examples of the federal model.

Another institutional configuration that relates directly to the continuum of centralization is the distribution of power within each level of government. For instance, many democracies, such as New Zealand,

Box 2.2 Germany

Germany is a constitutional and federal republic that bears marks of the turbulent political history of the country. National unification occurred relatively late in the second half of the 19th century through the unification of small states; the Weimar Republic highlighted the potential instability of extreme proportionality, while the dictatorship of the Third Reich unequivocally demonstrated the dangers of a strong executive. The constitution dates back to 1949 and through the influential role of the constitutional court as an arbiter, the Basic Law puts important checks and balances on contemporary policy making. The legislature is bicameral. The Federal Chamber is the upper house and represents the 16 states (which have extensive powers), whereas the 598 members of the lower house are elected directly through an electoral system that combines elements of proportional representation and the first past the post and also includes a threshold. This typically leads to a coalition government with the chancellor as head of government. In contrast, the president as the head of state mainly has a ceremonial function (Dalton, 2008; Hague and Harrop, 2004; Sodaro, 2004). After being divided since World War II, in 1990 the process of reunification (Deutsche Wiedervereinigung) of the German Democratic Republic (East Germany) joined the Federal Republic of Germany (West Germany) and Berlin was reunited into a single city.

Box 2.3 Japan

Japan is a constitutional monarchy with a parliamentary government. Sovereignty, historically embodied in the emperor, is now vested in the Japanese people. Japan is a democracy with power resting in the National Diet of Japan (Kokkai), comprising a bicameral legislature composed of a lower house (House of Representatives) and an upper house (House of Councillors). Executive power rests in the cabinet composed of a prime minister and ministers of state, all of whom must be civilians. The prime minister must be a member of the Diet and has the power to appoint and remove ministers, a majority of whom must be Diet members. Japan is a unitary system: its 47 prefectures are not sovereign entities and depend on the central government for subsidies. Governors of prefectures, mayors of municipalities and prefectural and municipal assembly members are popularly elected to four-year terms. The Japanese constitution includes a bill of rights similar to that of the USA. The five major political parties represented in the National Diet are the Liberal Democratic Party, the Democratic Party of Japan, the New Clean Government Party (Komeito), the Japan Communist Party and the Social Democratic Party (*World Fact Book*, 2012).

Taiwan and the UK, concentrate power in parliament where the distinction between executive and legislative power is obscured or virtually non-existent. Moreover, although many parliamentary systems have upper and lower houses (e.g., the House of Lords and House of Commons in the UK), in effect most power rests in the lower houses.

Box 2.4 Netherlands

The modern political system in the Netherlands, as it emerged in the early 1800s, is characteriszd by three key tenets: a unitary state, a monarchy and bicameralism. The constitution defines the central institutions of governing and the relations among the national, the provincial and the local levels of government. The parliament consists of two chambers, the first elected indirectly from members of the provincial councils and the second elected directly through national elections. The 150 seats are allocated through a list system of proportional representation without a threshold. This typically leads to majority coalitions that are led by the prime minister. The second chamber is the main political forum, while the first chamber's role is restricted to overseeing and revising legislation. Overall, the political system works on the basis of a form of 'consociational democracy', which is characterized by grand coalitions and a high degree of autonomy to different segments of society. This reflects a society that has traditionally been dominated by Protestants and Catholics as distinct social groups and where the need to bridge the resulting cleavages has been paramount (Andeweg and Irwin, 2005).

Box 2.5 New Zealand

New Zealand is a fully independent member of the Commonwealth and has a parliamentary system of government closely patterned on that of the UK. It has no formal, written constitution. Executive authority is vested in a cabinet led by the prime minister, who is the leader of the political party or coalition holding the majority of seats in parliament. The unicameral parliament (House of Representatives) has 120 seats, seven of which currently are reserved for Maori elected on a separate Maori roll, although Maori also may run for, and have been elected to, non-reserved seats. Subnational government in New Zealand has only the powers conferred upon it by parliament. There are 12 regional councils and 74 'territorial authorities' that are directly elected, raise local taxes at rates they themselves set, and are headed by popularly elected mayors. Major parties are Labour and National and other parties include ACT, United Future, Maori Party, Progressive Party and Green Party (*World Fact Book*, 2012).

In stark contrast is the USA, with its deliberate constitutional separation of powers among a separately elected president, two houses of Congress, and a relatively active judicial system. Despite a great deal of variation in dispersion of policy-making authority in parliamentary systems, when compared to the USA they all have considerably more concentrated bases of power. Figure 2.2 presents a rough distribution of our countries in terms of centralization of institutional power along these dimensions. This distribution corresponds closely to the findings of Lijphart (1999: 189) who classifies Australia, Germany and the USA as 'federal and decentralized'; the Netherlands as 'semi-federal'; Japan and Sweden as 'unitary and decentralized'; and New Zealand and the UK as

Box 2.6 Singapore

According to the Constitution of 1959, as amended in 1965 and 1991, Singapore is a republic with a parliamentary system of government. Political authority rests with the prime minister and the cabinet. The prime minister is the leader of the political party or coalition having the majority of seats in parliament. The president, who is chief of state, is elected and exercises expanded powers over legislative appointments, government budgetary affairs and internal security matters. The unicameral parliament consists of 84 members elected on the basis of universal adult suffrage, and up to nine nominated members appointed by the president from among nominations by a special select committee. In the May 2006 general election, the governing People's Action Party won 82 of the 84 seats. The maximum term of parliament is five years. Other parties include the Workers' Party, Singapore People's Party, Singapore Democratic Party and Singapore Democratic Alliance (*World Fact Book*, 2012).

Box 2.7 Sweden

Sweden is a constitutional monarchy where political power rests with the parliament and the king as the formal head of state has only a ceremonial function. The historical roots of the parliament go back as far as the mid-16th century, when the king involved two representative assemblies in the governing of the realm. The four-part constitution sets out the basic principles of the political system, and revisions in the early 1970s led to the introduction of a unicameral parliament that consists of 349 members and works through a number of committees. The parliament has sole legislative power; it appoints the prime minister, who in turn forms a government, and the government is ultimately answerable to parliament. The parliament is elected every four years based on a system of proportional representation. In addition, there are democratically elected bodies at regional level (the county councils) and at local level (the municipal councils). Both types of bodies have tax raising powers and play a key role in the delivery of welfare services (Government Offices of Sweden, 2007; Riksdagen, 2009; Swedish Institute, 2007).

'unitary and centralized'. Singapore, a city-state of 4 million people in which all political power rests in the central government, is by far the most centralized of the countries discussed here.

The implications of these formal government types for health policy are significant. Where power is centralized, the government has the

Box 2.8 Taiwan

Until 1986, Taiwan's political system was controlled by one party, the Kuomintang (KMT), the chairman of which was also Taiwan's top leader. In 1987, President Chiang Ching-kuo ended the nearly four decades of martial law under which dissent had been suppressed. Since then, Taiwan has taken dramatic steps to improve respect for human rights and create a democratic political system. In 1989 the Legislative Yuan (LY) passed the Civic Organizations Law which allowed the formation of new political parties. In 1992, the Democratic Progressive Party (DPP) won 51 seats in the 161-seat LY and in 2000 DPP candidate Chen Shui-bian became the first opposition party candidate to win the presidency. Chen was re-elected by 50.1 per cent to a second term in 2004. The membership of the DPP is comprised largely of native Taiwanese, and it maintains that Taiwan is an entity separate from mainland China, in contrast to the KMT position that Taiwan and the mainland, though currently divided, are both part of 'one China'. In sharp contrast to the tenets of both KMT and People's Republic of China policy, a number of prominent DPP politicians openly advocate independence for Taiwan. Taiwan's second democratic transition of ruling party followed the 2008 presidential election, which went decisively (58%) to the KMT candidate (*World Fact Book*, 2012).

Box 2.9 United Kingdom

The United Kingdom has long been portrayed as a centralized, unitary state with a political system based on parliamentary sovereignty within the context of an unwritten constitution. Indeed, the United Kingdom has had the status of an archetypical example, reflecting the long history of the political system and the roots of the parliament going back to the 13th century. However, since the late 1990s the picture has been changing. The country continues to be ruled from London, although there are elected bodies in Scotland and Wales whose jurisdictions include health policy. Legislation from the EU increasingly restricts the room for manoeuvre of parliament and also strengthens the protection of individual rights. Nevertheless, there is a lot of continuity. The parliament includes the House of Lords, where appointed and indirectly elected members act in a revising and restraining capacity, and the House of Commons, which is the dominant chamber. The 659 members are elected on the basis of a first past the post system that leads to adversarial politics and a majoritarian government. The prime minister is head of government and the strength of the governing party typically gives the government considerable control over parliament (Hague and Harrop, 2004; Rose, 2008; Sodaro, 2004).

formal capacity to make more rapid and comprehensive policy changes. In the mid-1990s, Taiwan opted for a nationwide public health insurance scheme and was able to implement it in a very short time span: NHI was submitted as a bill to Parliament in 1993, passed as law in 1994, and implemented in early 1995. With similar speed, Singapore put a complicated

Box 2.10 United States

After independence from Britain, the framers of the Constitution, fearing centralized power, deliberately created a highly fragmented and decentralized political system. Moreover, because it was the 13 separate states that called the convention to create the Constitution, they were bound to create a strong federal system that protected their interests. The result is a separation of powers where among other things, the health and well-being of the citizens is a state, not national, responsibility. Also, unlike parliamentary systems, within the national government (and all state governments), there is a further division of power between the executive and legislative branches, and a separate, independent judiciary with powers of judicial review. In addition, Congress, and all but one state legislature, are bicameral institutions. The result is a system with many inbuilt veto points, resulting in slow, deliberative and reactive policy making. The winner take all system has favoured the two major parties, the Republicans and Democrats, and produced a highly pluralistic interest group-dominated political process.

Singapore	New Zealand	Taiwan	UK	Sweden	Japan	Netherlands	Germany	Australia / USA

Concentrated **Fragmented**

Figure 2.2 *Institutional power in political systems*

mix of private (but mandatory) savings schemes and public safety net funding in place (Okma *et al.*, 2010). Likewise, successive New Zealand governments have introduced almost unimpeded a range of major restructuring initiatives of the health system since the 1990s.

In contrast, the more fragmented the political authority, the higher the probability of deadlock and inaction or at best more incremental change. The USA is the prime example of a system in which making even minor changes in health policy represents a long-term struggle. Even in a relatively narrow area such as payment of prescription charges for the elderly on Medicare where almost everyone agreed something must be done, little was accomplished after over two years of political wrangling (Abrams, 2002). Australia and the USA are both federal systems, but their approaches to health care now are quite divergent. Although not as static as the USA, reform in Australia over the years has been very measured compared to that of neighbouring New Zealand.

In Germany as well health policy making tends to be highly incremental, to the extent that health policy is often locked into 'reform blockades'. Because decision-making powers are dispersed among a multitude of mainly non-state actors (insurance funds and provider organizations) across federal, state and local levels, the federal government has little direct influence on health care. This is particularly pertinent in the case of medical reform (Bandelow, 2007; Burau, 2001). Through their joint self-administration with insurance funds, doctors are at the heart of health governance, and it is difficult to address the relationship between economic and medical rationality.

Moreover, in fragmented political systems where competing political parties are able to control particular institutions, there is more likely to be a divided government where one party controls one or several branches or levels and the other party controls the rest. Although this might contribute to a more deliberative policy-making process, it can also easily degenerate into stagnation and gridlock as has been common in US health policy. Conversely, it might be expected that a highly centralized system such as the UK or New Zealand presents a policy arena characterized by more frequent and wide ranging punctuated changes such as major restructuring, often to the detriment of programme stability. For instance, instability and insecurity were major charges made by opponents of the near-continuous reforms of

Strong	Medium	Weak	None
Germany *USA*	*Australia*	*Japan* *Sweden*	*Netherlands* *New Zealand* *Singapore* *Taiwan* *UK*

Figure 2.3 *The strength of judicial review*

Source: Adapted from Lijphart (1999: 226).

the New Zealand health system in the 1990s (Martin and Salmond, 2001).

Another dimension that Lijphart (1999) sees as important in distinguishing among democracies is the strength of judicial review (the extent to which a high court can overrule elected representative bodies). Figure 2.3 demonstrates a broad range across our countries regarding the power of the courts to influence health policy. In recent decades, the German and American courts in particular have become highly activist, invalidating many laws on constitutional grounds, thus earning them the label of being an 'imperial judiciary' (Franck, 1996).

In contrast, the Netherlands, New Zealand, Singapore, Taiwan and the UK do not have systems of judicial review of policy or administrative decisions. In these countries, the will of parliament is supreme and cannot be challenged or overridden by a high court. The remaining countries have provisions for judicial review, but for a variety of reasons the courts have exercised their power with restraint and moderation. The European Court of Human Rights eventually is likely to influence health policy in member countries but its powers are still unfolding.

Legal systems

Figure 2.1 also suggests that the legal framework can have significant influence on health care. It can do this in many ways, ranging from regulating the medical professions to influencing the distribution of health care resources, to constructing liability systems that impact on both. While some countries have opted for no-fault accident compensation systems and for sanctions by medical bodies, others turn to the courts to various degrees to determine liability and the allocation of medical resources and to punish wrongdoers in the medical professions.

Not surprisingly given its emphasis on negative rights, the USA has the most extensive civil liability system with health care being no exception. Many states are considered to be in crisis with medical malpractice insurance affordability or even availability, and doctors in some states have had work stoppages or slowdowns out of protest. Insurance rates for the riskiest medical specialities have skyrocketed with annual insurance coverage for obstetricians averaging over $210,000 and for general surgery $175,000 in Florida for example (Reiss, 2003). The medical profession's response is that medical liability awards for the pain and suffering, and punishment awards, which can reach tens of millions of dollars, must be capped (a usual figure given is $250,000). However, trial lawyers, consumer groups and the Obama Administration argue that any attempt to limit awards runs counter to the rights of individuals to redress wrongs against them in a court of law and that the real problem is the failure of the medical profession to discipline negligent doctors. Most observers agree, however, that the current system is inequitable and unsustainable because most patients who go to court lose and get absolutely nothing, while in some cases persons who have suffered little or no harm receive huge monetary settlements.

There is no doubt that the US liability system contributes to inflated health care costs, although the two sides offer widely divergent estimates. The system adds to the costs in two ways. The direct cost increases come from the cost of malpractice insurance itself, most of which is passed on to patients and third-party payers. The indirect impact is even more profound, because virtually every medical decision is made within a legal context and under threat of potential litigation. This environment leads to what is termed *defensive medicine* under which doctors order all available diagnostic tests and therapeutic measures, even those that are of marginal or no benefit to a patient, in order to avert a lawsuit (e.g., the doctor did not do everything possible) or, if sued, to provide documentation that all that was possible was done for the patient. Although there are no reliable cost estimates for defensive medicine, it represents a sizeable portion of overall health spending in the USA and helps explain why US costs are so out of line with other countries (see Chapter 3).

Box 2.11 Asking for problems?

In Taiwan, citizens on average visit a doctor almost 14 times per year (over 25 for those over age 65) even though they have one of the lowest physician/population rates in the world. Doctors in Taiwan see on average 128 patients per week. As a result, doctor visits are very short, averaging three to five minutes each. Because of this haste, medical errors are bound to occur at a high frequency, although statistics are limited since no one wants to publicize such self-incriminating data. In one report, however, computer error alone on prescriptions in one medical centre was 0.34 per cent (Chen *et al.*, 2008). If extrapolated to the entire country, there would be 96 million prescription errors a year. If Taiwan operated under a US-like liability system, the courts would be submerged in malpractice suits.

Other countries have tended to depend on alternative systems to deal with medical misadventure and compensation. New Zealand, for instance, created an accident compensation system specifically to avoid the problem of costly litigation. When an individual suffers medical or other harm under this system he or she is compensated by the Accident Compensation Commission (ACC) according to a standardized formula. In return, legal remedies are severely limited, although in recent years the incidence of legal action has increased. Moreover, over the past several decades as more people have pursued medical misadventure claims, the ACC cost for health care has multiplied, as has compensation.

Although accident compensation systems are more successful in ensuring that all victims are compensated, often the compensation is small in comparison to the possible awards granted in a liability-based system. It makes sense that countries with national health services would want to avoid an unpredictable but costly liability system and opt for a predictable, less costly system even if critics argue it violates the rights of individuals to go to court. That these health systems tend to be in countries with traditions of solidarity and community rather than individual rights gives them legitimacy they would not enjoy in the USA.

In the absence of civil liability, accident compensation systems normally are linked with stricter professional self-regulating systems for medical negligence. Medical societies are given responsibility to sanction and, where appropriate, prevent such members from practising. European countries in general have traditionally put emphasis on preventing medical malpractice and disciplining problem doctors through professional self-regulation. In Germany, for example, professional chambers at state level are responsible for licensing doctors, controlling medical ethics, organizing disciplinary processes and offering specialist training. The chambers are public bodies regulated by law (Moran, 1999).

However, the case of Britain shows the limitations of this approach. In recent years, there have been a number of high-profile cases of medical malpractice (Kodate, 2012; Burau and Fenton, 2009; Fenton and Salter, 2009). One involved a pathologist who had removed organs from the bodies of dead children during post-mortem examinations without the prior consent of parents. In another case, a GP was convicted of murdering 15 of his elderly patients though a subsequent inquiry suggested that the actual number of victims exceeded 200. Both cases strongly throw into doubt the ability of the General Medical Council (GMC), the doctors' professional body, to protect patients from medical malpractice. Mounting pressure from the government and the public, as well as from within the medical profession, led to substantial reforms of the Council, including reduction in size, increased lay membership, tightened fitness-to-practice procedures and the introduction of revalidation.

At the same time, liability claims in the UK have risen sharply. According to the National Audit Office, NHS hospitals in England face massive liabilities totalling £3.9 billion. The rate of new claims rose by 72 per cent between 1990 and 1998, and, as of March 2000, around 23,000 claims of clinical negligence were outstanding (Woodman, 2001). The average value of settlement in 2000 was £87,000, excluding brain damage and cerebral palsy where courts have at times awarded more than £1 million. The Audit Office report found that the existing system for handling litigation is 'fraught with delays', and that lawyers often benefit far more than do patients (Woodman, 2001). Despite divergent legal systems, then, the problems facing the UK are reminiscent of the malpractice debacle in the USA.

Cultural explanations: cultural/historical factors shaping health care

It is argued here that each country brings to health a distinctive combination of historical and cultural factors that are crucial in explaining its proclivities and characteristics. Political culture is the complex of beliefs, values and attitudes held by the public concerning the proper role of government. To focus on those elements of culture which influence health policy, one must look at beliefs concerning definitions of health, the role of the government in the health arena, and the extent to which health care represents an individual right or a privilege granted by society. For instance, to what extent is health care a public as opposed to a private good and, if a public good, on what grounds should health services be distributed to individuals? In order to provide a basis for more in-depth comparison throughout later chapters, we will look briefly at one of the key defining cultural characteristics that shape health care across countries and then provide an overview of the most defining aspects in each country.

A crucial dimension of political culture focuses on how the individual in the society relates to the whole. What is the perceived role of the state as opposed to the citizen? Table 2.2 illustrates a rough distribution of these countries showing whether they are classified primarily as a communitarian, egalitarian or individualistic culture. Countries with communitarian traditions, based either in the family or other groupings, have designed various mechanisms to ensure the interests of the various communities. Germany, for instance, has a strong tradition of self-administration, the Netherlands guarantees empowerment of the various 'pillars' (social groups) to reach consensus, and Japan and Taiwan place strong emphasis on the family and on tradition itself (see details below).

Table 2.2 ***Distribution by type of health political culture***

Communitarian	*Egalitarian*	*Individualistic*
Germany	Sweden	USA
Netherlands	New Zealand	Australia
Japan	UK	Singapore
Taiwan		

In contrast, egalitarian cultures such as those of New Zealand and Sweden, although having divergent political systems, place emphasis on the entitlement to health care and on a societal commitment to provide health care on those grounds. Countries such as the USA and Australia due to their rugged individualism have a tendency to elevate individual rights above the welfare of the community. For such countries, it is difficult to limit these negative rights to health care even for the common good. While rights and entitlements are often used synonymously, entitlements suggest a concern for equality that can be found only in the notion of positive rights, while the individualistic version of negative, self-centred rights lacks the social dimension found in egalitarian and communitarian societies.

Although they are placed in Table 2.2 as to their predominant orientation, some countries have tended to combine aspects of these types into unique hybrids. For instance, Singapore has merged communitarian and common good features with a very strong view of individual responsibility for health and health care. Similarly, the UK culture combines a pragmatic approach to collective action with a very generous entitlement philosophy reminiscent of egalitarian cultures such as New Zealand and Sweden. In Japan, Taiwan and, to a lesser extent Singapore, meanwhile, Western medicine has introduced a form of individualism foreign to communitarian culture and created friction between generations as well as among social classes, as illustrated by the discussion of traditional medicine later in this chapter.

Germany

Germany has a strong tradition of voluntarism, self-help and family support, embedded in Christian social teachings and the idea of 'subsidiarity'. The 1873 social health insurance act, the first of its kind, built on these traditions and incorporated them in a statutory system of social solidarity. The organization of health care in Germany is marked by profound continuity and is shaped by a number of principles, among them social solidarity, freedom of choice for patients and nearly full coverage of services (Bäringhausen and Sauerborn, 2003).

In the social insurance context, access to health care is an entitlement that individuals 'earn' by virtue of paying insurance contributions. This, together with a strong legalistic approach typical of Germany, turns access to health care into the right of individuals to a defined range of services. Patients literally have 'ownership' of health services. This helps to explain why the freedom of patients to choose their doctors remains a fundamental principle of health care provision. Not surprisingly, Germany is one of the few countries that does not operate a British-style GP gate-keeping system on a compulsory basis. The individualized right to health care also goes hand in hand with the expectation that the social health insurance system provides full coverage. In conjunction with the structural features of the health system this makes cost containment and restrictions of services covered by social insurance very difficult.

The Netherlands

Another example of a communitarian country is the Netherlands, which resembles Germany in that private initiative has been a guiding principle in the organization of society. Dutch society has traditionally been organized in separate segments or pillars that represent different religious and political orientations. According to the Roman Catholic notion of subsidiarity and its Protestant counterpart of sovereignty, the different segments in society should be empowered to provide for their members (Björkman and Okma, 1997). However, the process of 'pillarization' of Dutch society began to weaken in the 1960s and state intervention in health care increased (Maarse, 1997).

This marked the modernization of the Dutch health system and a 'universalist turn'. The introduction of insurance for exceptional medical risks in 1967 is indicative here. This insurance is compulsory for all employers irrespective of income and, together with relatively generous entitlements, such insurance has helped to establish a culture of care which gives preference to formal care. However, elements of universalism do coexist with the legacy of pillarization. The provision of health care continues to be predominantly in the hands of private non-profit organizations and health policy making still requires the consensus of a large number of interest groups, to the extent that health reform becomes almost impossible.

Japan

Although for many Westerners Japan is an enigma, its health care context borrows much from Germany and is similar to the Netherlands, because at its base Japan has a communitarian, extended-family-based culture with veneration for the elderly. For health care, this has meant that universal coverage for health care is widely accepted socially as a given, although long-term care has until recently largely rested with the family, particularly women. However, during the last half-century traditional Japanese values have come into conflict with the infusion of Western, largely American, individualistic culture, thus causing significant distress, particularly among the older Japanese population.

Japanese views of medicine are an amalgamation of Buddhist, Confucian and Shinto influence, combined more recently with Hippocratic and Christian influences (Macer, 1999). During the 5th and 6th centuries, for instance, the medical profession was restricted to the privileged classes. During centralization of government in the 7th and 8th centuries, a bureau of medicine was established creating an official physician class. After the Heian period in the 9th to 14th centuries, the government-sponsored health service was replaced by professional physicians. In the 16th century, a code of practice similar to the Hippocratic code, the 'Seventeen Rules of Enjuin', was drawn up which emphasized a priestly role for the physician. Although modern Western medicine took hold in the 19th century and the rapid progress of medical technology challenged the way medicine is practised, there remains a very strong paternalistic attitude on the part of doctors and a lasting reliance on traditional practice.

Taiwan

Like Japan, in Taiwan the family traditionally has been a major social force and continues to be an important factor in health care. However, over recent generations patients have developed a physician usage culture that includes consulting physicians even for minor ailments, visiting different physicians to find one that will do what the patient wants, and finding and using the most popular doctors even if they do not specialize in what the patient really needs. As a result, the Taiwanese readily embraced the Western medical model and its accompanying dependence on medical technologies. Medical care has become synonymous with health care and health care has become the preferred linkage to health itself. Moreover, Taiwanese consume a large quantity of health/nutritional supplements, most notably Chinese herbal remedies, in addition to Western medicines, in a culture looking for short cuts to health improvement. Until 2009, when it was invited to participate in the World Health Assembly, Taiwan's situation was complicated by its political isolation because professionals had received no formal technical assistance or participated in collaborative projects with international organizations such as the WHO or World Bank for over 40 years (Yang, 2010). In public health areas, especially, activities such as information sharing and regional collaboration suffered.

Sweden

Perhaps the clearest example of an egalitarian type of culture is Sweden, which is notable for the very early provision of medical care by the state dating back to the 17th century (Glenngård *et al.*, 2005). Towns and cities employed doctors to provide public health care and municipalities also operated hospitals. In rural areas the central state paid physicians to provide basic care. State involvement in health care was consolidated in the middle of the 19th century with the creation of county councils, which had primary responsibility for health care. However, a considerable expansion of health services only occurred in the post-war period, paving the way for the universal health care system as we know it today.

The historical legacy of public involvement in health care is combined with the principle of equality, which is deeply embedded in Swedish society. People have a right to health care regardless of income and where they live (Håkansson and Nordling, 1997). The right to health care is part of people's citizenship and not an individually earned entitlement, as in the case of Germany and the Netherlands. Public funding and provision of health care are key features of the health system in Sweden, as is a strong emphasis on public health and concern for equity.

New Zealand

Although its national health system compares most closely with that of the UK and its political culture retains many features of its Commonwealth heritage, like Sweden, New Zealand has a strong tradition of egalitarianism. This was clearly reflected in the Social Security Act of 1938 that promised an open-ended provision to all citizens based on need. It is also demonstrated by the strong belief in the public consultation process and the view that office holders are holders of the public trust, not above it. New Zealand's egalitarian foundation is also illustrated by the 'tall poppy' belief which holds that people who get too successful, wealthy or powerful must be cut back to size. New Zealand politicians embraced the new-right, market-centred philosophy in the 1980s and 1990s, but the public rejected attempts to restructure the health system in ways that were seen as destroying its egalitarian foundations. The result has been a series of rather bold attempts by governments of both parties to make major changes in the health care structure, only to pull back from more extreme and unpopular tactics once the public felt threatened and demanded a return to a more egalitarian system.

Britain

In comparison to Sweden, Britain not only has had a much shorter history of public involvement in health care, but the approach to collective action has typically also been pragmatic rather than principled (Johnson and Cullen, 2000). This also helps to explain why after World War II a universal health service was introduced in what was traditionally a liberal state regime. However, the NHS did not resolve the tension between laissez-faire liberalism and collectivism and instead a generous entitlement philosophy has coexisted with rationed service provision (Moran, 1999; for more detailed historical accounts see Klein, 2001, and Webster, 1998).

The NHS enjoys high public support. The generosity of the NHS entitlement philosophy contrasts with both the failure of the earlier National Insurance arrangements and the austerity of post-war Britain, and it is deeply entrenched in the public's mind. Not surprisingly, reforms have focused on the organization of health services, and even the extensive changes under the Conservatives in the late 1980s were prefaced with the assurance 'the NHS is safe in our hands'. Universalism, together with a centralist political system, also generates expectations that health services are the same (or at least comparable) across the country. Concerns about inequities in access are prominent and are reflected in debates about the 'postcode lottery', whereby services vary significantly from one locale to the next.

United States

The USA is the prototype of an individualistic society. Although individual rights have some emphasis in all the nations examined here, in the USA rights have been elevated to a status of supremacy over collective interests. Moreover, by rights Americans mean negative rights, and, as a result, they are hesitant to sacrifice perceived individual needs for the common good. Thus, there is no guaranteed universal coverage but also no limits on what health care individuals can buy if they can afford it. This cultural tenet goes a long way to explain why the USA expends so much more of its GDP on health care than other countries, without providing universal access. Cost containment measures such as Health Maintenance Organizations (HMOs) that attempted to set limits on individual care have been widely attacked as counter to patient rights and led to calls for a 'Patients' Bill of Rights'.

In the USA, when individual rights and the common good conflict, individual claims take precedence. 'Our premium on individual rights and our emphasis on the differences between us is a far cry from the social beliefs that back the health systems of Europe, Canada, and Japan, in which more homogeneous societies band together for the common good' (Kassler, 1994: 130). Moreover, in contrast to the UK and New Zealand, in the USA there is a strong aversion by the medical community to serve as gate-keepers and professional codes of ethics refuse to

Box 2.12 Health care in the USA

American patients also expect a higher standard of care. In contrast to Japan and Taiwan, where physicians spend little time with patients, such conduct is unacceptable in the USA. Moreover, one is struck by the comparatively Spartan conditions in hospitals in other nations. In the USA, amenities commonly include satellite television, DVD libraries, bedside phones, wide menu choices and tastefully decorated rooms. These extras have little appreciable impact on health but add substantially to the costs. This value setting has contributed to the inability to control health care spending. In 2010, over $2.6 trillion was spent on health care, an average of over $8,000 per person, representing nearly 18 per cent of GDP. The Commonwealth Fund (2009) projects that without major change spending will double by 2020 and account for over 20 per cent of GDP. Many observers warn that this trend requires drastic policy changes to put the brakes on spending growth, but given the egocentric US culture this is highly unlikely (Anderson *et al.*, 2006; Borgor *et al.*, 2006).

acknowledge the existence of scarcity of resources. The idea that limits on medical expenditures for an individual patient could be set in order to benefit the wider community contradicts the traditional patient-oriented customs of medicine (see Box 2.12). Although Americans complain about high costs and high taxes, when their health or life is at stake they expect no expense to be spared and believe that medicine should not have a price tag (Ubel, 2001).

Reinforcing the predominance of negative rights, US culture is also predisposed towards progress through technological means. The result is an unrealistic dependence on technology to fix health problems at the expense of non-technological solutions. High-quality medicine is equated with high-technology medicine and the best health care is that which uses the most sophisticated new techniques. This demand for medical technology is reinforced by the dominance of medical specialists who quickly extend the indications for use of new innovations, thus leading to a very aggressive form of medicine, under which, for example, the USA carries out four operations for every one performed in Japan.

Australia

Although Australia shares the far South Pacific and a similar British heritage with New Zealand, the two cultures have diverged since independence in the 19th century, with the latter opting for a more egalitarian and collectivist political culture and Australia adopting a much more individualistic, US-type approach to defining the scope of public goods and the role of government in promoting equality. Australia's unique welfare state places it in a hybrid category value-wise, though the fragmented Australian health care system with its strong private component is closer to the USA than it is to its neighbour New Zealand (Rix *et al.*, 2005). The decentralized Australian health delivery system reflects a rugged individualism needed to survive in a hostile environment (even though Australia now has one of the highest proportions of urban population) as much as it does the fragmented federal system that defines Australian politics.

Thus, while there has been an inevitable British influence in Australia since the beginning of the first prisoner settlements and this continues to be reflected in some aspects of its health care system, the 'tendency to look to North America as a source of technology, of funding and organizational initiatives and the inspiration for new policies has continued to the present time' (Palmer and Short, 2000: 6). Australian culture, then, represents a unique combination of its European heritage with a heavy dose of individualism.

Singapore

Of all the countries, Singapore is the most difficult to classify as to cultural orientation, in part because, unlike other Asian countries, its history is short and it is thus a unique mixture of several blends of culture, East and West. Singapore has risen in the last 40 years from a Third World territory with appalling health and human conditions to a highly modern society that ranks high on health and economic measures (Ham, 2001). Its political leaders are proud of their success and angered by criticism by some Western nations that they have accomplished this by violating individual freedom. In fact, health officials argue that their health funding system based on personal savings accounts maximizes freedom of choice by focusing on the individual's responsibility for his or her own health care. Individual responsibility, not rights, is at the centre of the Singapore value system and is clearly exhibited in the health system. Thus, Singapore represents a hybrid form of individualism often at odds with that of the USA and Australia.

Singapore's approach to health policy is a distinctive combination of free-market principles and careful government control (Lim, 2004). Its philosophy is to build a healthy population through innovative preventive programmes and promotion of healthy lifestyles that individuals have a civic duty to embrace (Box 2.13). As a result, the system deemphasizes high-cost curative technologies, thereby explaining the low rates of intensive medical procedures performed in Singapore relative to other countries and the low proportion of its GDP that it spends on health care. According to Yeo Cheow Tong, the then Minister of Health: 'Our medical system is based on individual responsibility ... no Singaporean has enjoyed or expects to enjoy health services for free.

Box 2.13 Only in Singapore

A key principle of Singapore's national health scheme is that no medical service is provided free of charge, regardless of the level of subsidy, even within the public health care system. This mechanism is intended to reduce the over-utilization of healthcare services, a phenomenon often seen in fully subsidized universal health insurance systems. Patients are accustomed to cost sharing rather than depending on state largesse. The cost-sharing formula has countered the 'moral hazard' generally associated with fee-for-service, third-party reimbursement. Singapore has deliberately avoided the more costly 'leveling down' option of universal access regardless of ability to pay, in which the 'undeserving rich' enjoy the same benefits as the poor. At the highest level of subsidy, although each out-of-pocket expense is typically small, costs can accumulate and become substantial for patients and families. At the lowest level, the subsidy is in effect non-existent, and patients are treated like private patients, even within the public system (Okma *et al.*, 2010).

When hospitalized he pays part of the bill … His Medisave is his own money. This gives him the incentive to be healthy, minimise[s] the need for medical treatment, and save[s] on medical expenses.' According to Lim, Singaporeans readily accept this social contract based on individual responsibility and co-payments because of their willingness to place the common good above self-interest, the absence of any tradition of state largesse, their 'spirit of self-help' and their pragmatic nature that understands that 'trade-offs are an inevitable fact of life' (2004: 89).

As noted in Chapter 1, the convergence theory suggests that any subsequent differences in health policy will tend to fade over time as health systems of all shapes face the same problems. While this theory might or might not be borne out in the substantive discussions that follow, the presumption here is that the underlying values and beliefs of a population will be reflected in how they view health, health care and the proper distribution of health care resources. In that regard, we see how it will play out in the analysis of health care systems in the coming chapters.

Different approaches to defining health

A critical question for health policy is what is meant by the term 'health'. There are several competing models, each of which has important implications for how we organize health care. The prevailing Western medical model is primarily founded on defining health as the *absence of disease or illness*. People are healthy under this definition if they are not suffering from an illness or disease. The goal of curative medicine is to diagnose an illness and restore the health of the patient, who by definition is unhealthy. Inherent in medicine is the continual expansion of categories of disease to account for a broadening range of conditions deemed unhealthy. Moreover, such labelling of a condition as a disease tends to ingrain in medicine the notion that disease is the enemy.

A competing definition of health is the *coping* model where health is essentially an ability to adapt to the problems life gives us. Under this definition, individuals can be healthy even if they are diseased or ill so long as they have the personal strength and resilience to cope with life. The tension with the Western medical model is manifested in a concern that the latter interferes with individuals' ability to cope with their internal states and environment. Under this definition people without identifiable disease or illness are still unhealthy if they are unable to cope.

The third definition of health promulgated by the World Health Organization (WHO) is 'a state of complete physical, mental and social well-being and not merely the absence of disease or infirmity' (1946). This ambitious ideal has been widely criticized because, if taken literally, it means that individuals are unhealthy if they are unhappy with their lot in life or even if they just feel unfulfilled. Moreover, in conflict with the coping theory, individuals with any defined disease, illness or disability cannot be healthy. Although this definition is so broad as to make it almost meaningless, this is unfortunate because it does incorporate the need to expand the definition of health beyond the situation where a person has a medically defined illness or disease. To the extent that it does broaden ill health beyond the notion of biological dysfunction, the WHO definition is useful despite its operational problems.

One problem with all of these definitions is their failure to bring in the social and cultural dimensions of health and ill health explicitly. Health has both a personal and a public dimension. Although pain, suffering, disappointment and regret are individual under the WHO definition, their effect on the lives of others might be severe. Moreover, because health and illness are social constructs and culturally defined, health and disease have to be considered within each cultural context. For Callahan (1990: 103), illness itself is as much social as individual in its characteristics because tolerability will depend on the kind of care and support provided by others and by the social meaning of the disease. Good health, therefore, requires social networks and systems that are obfuscated by all of these definitions of health.

Even within particular social systems health can be a very relative term. Seedhouse (1991: 40), for instance, sees disease and health akin to the analogy of weeds and flowers. As with plants, what we perceive as undesirable in one case might be desirable in another. Pneumonia in an otherwise active 20-year-old is undesirable and it is appropriate to say she is suffering from a disease. In contrast, pneumonia in a 90-year-old victim of a severe stroke might be welcomed as offering an easier death.

Although in clinical terms pneumonia in both cases is termed a disease, the ambiguity of the disease label requires clarification of the specific context. Increasingly, it is evident that health must encompass, not only the physical and mental aspects of personal well-being, but also the social facets.

Putting health into this broader context also raises the question of why we value health in its narrow sense as freedom from disease. Although health should be highly valued since it is central to the completion of one's plan of life, health is better viewed as a means to broader goals and purposes in life. Good health is not a substitute for a good life, and good health does not guarantee a good life. Good health in itself cannot guarantee achievement of our goals, give us a reason to live, or maximize our potential to the highest order. Good health in the physical sense but without the other dimensions of health, then, is unlikely to ensure contentment. One area in which these ideas take form is in what is often termed 'alternative' or 'holistic' medicine.

Culture and traditional medicine

Although the Western medical model enjoys dominance in all of the countries examined here, traditional values continue to shape how it is practised. Therefore, although most attention in this book centres on the analysis of the similarities and differences of these countries within that broader framework, it is imperative to examine features that might be unique to, or more dominant in, particular countries. One area that offers useful insights is the extent to which various forms of traditional medicine continue to be practised alongside modern Western medicine.

Until 1875, when Western medicine became the official form of medicine in Japan, kampo and acupuncture were dominant. Kampo means 'Han Method' in Japanese because it was the Chinese who introduced the use of herbal products for medical therapy during the 7th to 9th centuries at the time of the Han Dynasty. The Japanese health care system remains an amalgamation of modern Western medicine and traditional Eastern practices, and kampo is still an important feature of medical practice. The great majority of Japanese physicians (72 per cent of all Western-style doctors in a 2000 survey) use at least some kampo formulae in their practice. Moreover, almost all pharmacies have staff trained in traditional methods of prescription and most health insurance companies recognize and support its use (Kenner, 2001). From 1974 to 1989 there was a 15-fold increase in kampo medicinal preparations in comparison with only 2.6-fold increase in the sales of mainstream pharmaceutical products in Japan (WHO, 1996). Acupuncture and other holistic practices are also integrated into the Japanese health system, in part a reflection of its Shinto/Buddhist roots.

Despite initial opposition from the medical establishment, the Taiwan NHI included coverage for traditional Chinese medicine (TCM) on an equal basis with Western medicine in its comprehensive benefits package that includes inpatient care, outpatient services, dental care, prescription drugs and home nursing care. Moreover, since the NHI is founded on a highly competitive public and private provider marketplace that offers virtually unlimited choice to the health care consumer with no formal referral requirement, people are free to choose any NHI-contracted hospital or clinic, including Chinese medicine, to receive inpatient or ambulatory care. As a result, a majority of Taiwanese patients still use TCM, in most cases in conjunction with Western medicine.

Similarly, while Singapore's health care services are based on Western medicine, it has been common practice among the various ethnic groups to contact traditional practitioners for general ailments. Although Western medicine is the principal form of health care, a variety of traditional practices continue to serve complementary roles (for implications of this clash of 'ethos', see Quah, 2003). Given the large proportion of Chinese in Singapore, TCM is an important part of Singapore's heritage and enjoys considerable popularity. Although its practice is confined to outpatient care, two acupuncture clinics are affiliated with public hospitals. The Ministry of Health estimates that about 12 per cent of daily outpatient services are delivered by TCM practitioners, the majority trained locally by specialist TCM schools (Singapore Ministry of Health, 1995). In a report, the Ministry concluded that there should be no forced integration of TCM and Western medicine and that only those persons properly trained to practice TCM should be allowed to do so. Therefore, some government regulation of TCM was necessary to safeguard patients' interests, which meant legitimizing it as a facet of health care.

Perhaps because of their location in the South Pacific and ties to Asia, the health care systems of both Australia and New Zealand have strong links to holistic medical practices. In Australia, for instance, where TCM has been practised since the 19th century, it has been estimated that over 48 per cent of the population use at least one form of alternative medicine (Maclennan *et al.*, 1996). Between 1992 and 1996, imports of Chinese herbal medicines increased four-fold in Australia, accounting for approximately $1 billion of business (Bensoussan and Myers, 1996). In 1995, the Australian State of Victoria, in response to the 'rapid expansion of the practice of and demand for TCM', created a Ministerial Committee on Traditional Medicine (Victorian Department of Human Services, 1996). In 1998, the Committee issued an extensive report on the risks and benefits of TCM and a wide range of other traditional approaches used in Australia, and a consideration of the need for regulation. A major recommendation of the Committee to the Australian Health Minister's Advisory Council was that occupational registration of the profession of TCM 'proceed as a matter of urgency' (Victorian Ministerial Advisory Committee, 1998: 1).

As in Australia, oriental medicine is well established in New Zealand with schools of acupuncture, TCM and holistic healing. Many general practitioners are trained in acupuncture, and the use of herbal products, including New Zealand native plants, is common. Although Chinese and other Asian traditional approaches are available, the most unique influence on New Zealand health policy comes via Maori and Pacific Island cultures. Considerable effort over the past decades has been directed at accounting for cultural differences in the perception of health and health care between the European and Maori populations and to integrate this into the health delivery system.

In contrast with these systems, the dominance of the American Medical Association (AMA) and other mainstream medical organizations has marginalized the scope of alternative medicine in the USA. Although recently some insurance carriers and HMOs have begun to partially reimburse selected non-traditional treatments, this practice remains the exception. Moreover, unlike even Australia and New Zealand, few medical practitioners in the USA have training in acupuncture or other alternative regimes. The predominance of the medical model even as portrayed in the media has resulted in a very narrow notion of health care among most Americans.

Although conventional medicine remains at the centre of the health service in Britain, there are moves to integrate complementary and alternative medicine into the NHS (Saks, 2002). In 2000 a report by the House of Lords called for patients to have access to unconventional medicine and to be given more and better information about alternative therapies (Mills, 2001). Here, tighter regulation was identified as a key issue and the report argued that only those therapies that were properly regulated should be accessible through the NHS. In response to this report, there have been moves to strengthen the regulation of alternative practitioners and to standardize the myriad of training schemes in unconventional therapies that currently exist. The Department of Health is also providing funding to develop the research capacity in alternative medicine as part of the drive towards evidence-based health care practice.

Functionalist explanations: population, wealth and economics

The third explanation for country-by-country variation is termed functionalist or structuralist because it centres on quantitative characteristics such as demographics and wealth. Problems facing a small highly concentrated population like Singapore are on a different scale than those facing a large, diverse population like the USA, or even those of the similar sized population of New Zealand that is sprawled across two large islands. Moreover, we would expect that wealthier nations have an easier time meeting the health needs of their populations simply because they have more resources at their disposal (Musgrave *et al.*, 2002). This section examines these functionalist contextual factors for our countries.

Population size and diversity

Not surprisingly, health policy can be significantly influenced by the demographic characteristics of a country. Moreover, because these characteristics change over time, such as the ageing or the diversification of the population through immigration, the health system must adapt to those changes. To some extent, the reform efforts of countries over the last several decades represent attempts to deal with changing needs brought about in part by demographic trends, especially population ageing. One might expect, therefore, that some of the differences in health policy among these countries described in the following chapters can be traced to disparities in the size of the respective populations, their age and ethnic diversity, and their degree of social stratification in terms of the distribution of wealth.

Table 2.3 summarizes key demographic variables across our countries. Most obvious is the vast variation in the size of population. It is not surprising that the USA struggles to devise a workable health system for over 310 million people. The State of California alone is larger than half the countries examined here. Certainly, it can be argued that countries

Table 2.3 ***Population characteristics, 2012 (est.)***

	Population	*% growth rate*	*Net migration*	*% over 65*	*% under 15*
Australia	22,015,576	1.126	5.93	14.4	18.2
Germany	81,305,856	–0.201	0.71	20.7	13.2
Japan	127,368,088	–0.077	n/a	23.9	13.5
Netherlands	16,730,632	0.452	2.02	16.6	17.2
New Zealand	4,327,944	0.863	2.26	13.6	20.2
Singapore	5,353,494	1.993	15.62	7.8	14.0
Sweden	9,103,788	0.168	1.65	20.2	15.4
Taiwan	23,234,936	0.171	0.03	11.3	14.7
United Kingdom	63,047,162	0.553	2.59	16.9	17.3
United States	313,847,465	0.899	3.62	13.5	20.0

Source: Data from the *World Fact Book* (2012).

with smaller populations ought to be better able to design a workable health policy. Since the whole populations of New Zealand and Singapore are less than at least five metropolitan areas in the USA, perhaps it would be more appropriate to compare their systems with a smaller state like Colorado which has approximately the same population as New Zealand. Large population size might also be mirrored in efforts in the UK to decentralize decision making within the National Health Service (NHS) to health authorities, or (more recently) Primary Care Trusts.

However, population size is but one important variable for health policy. Population growth rates are also crucial because they point to future health needs and relate to the dynamic composition of the population. A high growth rate requires planning for expanded services and, depending on where the growth is coming from (e.g. births, immigration), a change in types of services needed. In contrast, a low or negative growth rate might indicate difficulties in funding services even at the existing level. Singapore, New Zealand, Australia and the USA display the highest percentages of growth, indicating a need for increased services just to take care of the added numbers. In contrast, most of the European countries demonstrate smaller rates of growth, and in Germany and Japan negative growth rates, indicating shrinking populations (Box 2.14). Combined with the ageing of their populations, these low growth rates signal difficulties in maintaining existing spending patterns without increasing the tax load on the dwindling proportion that is employed.

One way of counteracting low growth rates is to increase immigration rates, which several countries, such as Germany and the Netherlands, appear to be doing. Net migration per 1,000 population ranges from zero in Taiwan to over 15 in Singapore and 6 in Australia. Again, it is important to know more details about the immigrants before estimating their

Box 2.14 Policies for older people in Sweden

Together with low rates of net migration and low growth rates of the population, Sweden has one of the highest percentages of old people. Together, these factors make Sweden something of a test bed for coping with the challenges of ageing. In the area of care of older people Sweden has responded with a combination of decentralization, service integration and de-institutionalization and targeting. In 1992 municipalities became responsible for providing health and social care to older people living in institutions; and in half of the county councils this has been extended to home-based services. In addition, the number of long-term beds has been reduced significantly, while home-based services are increasingly targeted at highly dependent older people.

Box 2.15 Migrants and the National Health Service in Britain

Migrants impact on the NHS in two ways. In an already tightly cash-limited health service any increase in the number of patients can put additional strain on existing services as recent debates about Polish migrants show (Moszczynski, 2008). This particularly applies to GPs as the first point of contact for patients. In some cases, like asylum seekers, the NHS also struggles to cope with the scale and nature of health problems of asylum seekers. In part, this reflects special needs arising from asylum seekers coming from countries with a high prevalence of infectious diseases, or having been tortured (Dunne, 2002). However, health problems are often exacerbated by the poor living conditions of asylum seekers once they arrive in the country (Casciani, 2002). Their vulnerable and very marginal position is also a major barrier to accessing health services.

impact on health policy. Are they skilled or unskilled, destitute or wealthy? Are they members of compatible cultures and religions or those likely to cause friction with the existing community? Although diverse cultures and ethnic groupings can strengthen countries in the long run and even aid in the delivery of medical care, they can also place severe strain on the health and social service systems upon arrival (see Box 2.15). Often, they bring with them disease patterns that require shifts in resources. As a result, more homogeneous countries are likely to have an easier time meeting the health needs of their population than highly ethnically diverse populations.

As was noted earlier, diverse cultures can have vastly different views of health, health care and health service delivery. These differences can be heightened when the values of a group are in conflict with those of the medical profession (e.g. female genital mutilation). With the clear exception of Japan, the countries examined here all reflect relatively high degrees of ethnic or religious diversity (Table 2.4), or, in many cases, both. While religious diversity in some cases might be a significant factor beyond simply reflecting other cleavages in society, ethnic differences can be more divisive, particularly where newer immigrants are predominantly from minority groupings such as is the case with many Southeast Asian brides of young Taiwanese men. Ethnic groups not only challenge the health system because they have differing prevalence of particular diseases and conditions, but also because they bring with them divergent views about the medical community, health and political authorities. The predicament is exacerbated, of course, when there are language difficulties.

Although most countries have a single dominant majority, except for Japan they have substantial ethnic/racial minorities that complicate the delivery of health care services. The difficulty can be aggravated where

Table 2.4 ***Ethnic and religious composition***

	Ethnic composition	*Religious composition*
Australia	Caucasian 92%, Asian 7%, aboriginal and other 1%.	Catholic 25.8%, Anglican 18.7%, other Christian 19.3%, Buddhist 2.1%, Muslim 1.7%, other or unspecified 13.7%, none 18.9%.
Germany	German 91.5%, Turkish 2.4%, other 6.1% (made up largely of Greek, Italian, Polish, Russian, Serbo-Croatian, Spanish).	Protestant 34%, Roman Catholic 34%, Muslim 3.7%, unaffiliated or other 28.3%.
Japan	Japanese 98.5%, Koreans 0.5%, Chinese 0.4%, other 0.6%.	Observe both Shinto and Buddhist 83.9%, other 16.1% (including Christian 2%).
Netherlands	Dutch 80.7%, EU 5%, Indonesian 2.4%, Turkish 2.2%, Surinamese 2%, Moroccan 2%, Netherlands Antilles & Aruba 0.8%, other 4.8%.	Roman Catholic 30%, Dutch Reformed 11%, Calvinist 6%, other Protestant 3%, Muslim 5.8%, other 2.2%, none 42%.
New Zealand	European 56.8%, Maori 7.4%, Asian 8%, Pacific islander 4.6%, other 13.5%, mixed 9.7%.	Anglican 13.8%, Roman Catholic 12.6%, Presbyterian 10%, other Christian 16.4%, Hindu 1.6%, Buddhist 1.3%, other 2.2% unspecified 9.9%, none 32.2%.

→

health services have not embraced diversity. An exception is the Chinese majority in Singapore, which seems to have been largely successful in integrating the Malay and Indian minorities into the health system. In contrast, blacks in the USA continue to be significantly less well served by the health care system than whites as measured either by access or health outcomes (Cooper *et al.*, 2012) (see Table 2.5). Similarly, the Maori minority in New Zealand has traditionally had a difficult time assimilating into the health care system. Recently, increasing numbers of asylum seekers migrating to the UK and other European countries have complicated health delivery and brought with them unique new health problems with which the health care systems must deal.

	Ethnic composition	*Religious composition*
Singapore	Chinese 76.8%, Malay 13.9%, Indian 7.9%, other 1.4%.	Buddhist 42.5%, Muslim 14.9%, Taoist 8.5%, Hindu 4%, Catholic 4.8%, other Christian 9.8%, other 0.7%, none 14.8%.
Sweden	Indigenous population: Swedes with Finnish and Sami minorities; foreign-born or first-generation immigrants.	Lutheran 87%, other (includes Roman Catholic, Orthodox, Baptist, Muslim, Jewish, and Buddhist) 13%.
Taiwan	Taiwanese (including Hakka) 84%, mainland Chinese 14%, indigenous 2%	Buddhist and Taoist 93%, Christian 4.5%, other 2.5%
United Kingdom	Caucasian (of which English 83.6%, Scottish 8.6%, Welsh 4.9%, Northern Irish 2.9%) 92.1%, black 2%, Indian 1.8%, Pakistani 1.3%, mixed 1.2%, other 1.6% (2001 census).	Christian (Anglican, Roman Catholic, Presbyterian, Methodist) 71.6%, Muslim 2.7%, Hindu 1%, other 1.6%, unspecified or none 23.1%.
United States	Caucasian 79.96%, black 12.85%, Asian 4.43%, Amerindian and Alaska native 0.97%, two or more races 1.61%.	Protestant 51.3%, Roman Catholic 23.9%, Mormon 1.7%, other Christian 1.6%, Jewish 1.7%, Buddhist 0.7%, Muslim 0.6%, other or unaffiliated 14.6%, none 4%.

Source: Data from the *World Fact Book* (2012).

The comparative wealth of countries

As discussed earlier, the most obvious determinant of health care funding and provision across countries is wealth. Rich countries on average can put considerably more resources into health care simply because they have more discretionary funds. Not surprisingly, pressures to enact the NHI came as Taiwan became more affluent. Unfortunately, very poor countries cannot compete with wealthier countries in health care spending and cannot afford the kind of medicine wealthy countries take for granted.

Table 2.5 *Health indicators by race, USA, 2011*

	White	*Black*
Low birth weight/1,000 births	7.2	13.6
Neonatal deaths/1,000 births	3.7	8.7
Infant deaths/1,000 births	5.1	11.4
Life expectancy (at birth)		
Male	76.4	71.6
Female	81.1	77.8

Source: Data from National Center for Health Care Statistics (2012).

The most used comparative measure of wealth is the GDP per capita. In 2011, the average GDP per capita of all countries worldwide was $13,802, with a low of $328 in the Congo and a high of $88,559 in Qatar. The average of the G7 industrialized countries was $39,700. Thirty-five countries had per capita GDP below $2,000 and an additional 24 between $2,000 and $4,000. From the data presented in Table 2.6, it is clear that all of our countries are relatively wealthy; in fact, they are clustered at over $30,000, with Singapore the highest at $60,500 and New Zealand the lowest near $28,000. The variance in wealth among these nations might help to explain minor economic limits on those nations near the bottom as compared to those at the top. However, the relatively minor differences in wealth among these countries means that differences in health provision and spending found among them here are not likely to be explained by this factor alone.

Table 2.6 *GDP per capita in US dollars, 2011*

Country	*GDP/capita*
Singapore	60,500
United States	49,000
Netherlands	42,700
Sweden	40,900
Australia	40,800
Germany	38,400
Taiwan	38,200
United Kingdom	36,600
Japan	35,200
New Zealand	28,000

Source: Data from the *World Fact Book* (2012).

Social and economic determinants of health

Wealth itself, however, does not guarantee the best health, nor does it ensure health that is equitably distributed. In addition to the overall wealth of a country, there is evidence that the degree of inequality or disparity in social and economic conditions at the national level is a key determinant of population health. As noted by Taylor, 'economic growth and consequent wealth, on their own and without attention to distributive policies, do not assure countries of greater health... Social inequalities play through social determinants into inequities in health' (2009: 45). Despite overall wealth ranking, countries with greater inequality tend to have poorer health outcomes overall as well as a more unequal distribution of health. Social determinants are, thus, used as shorthand for the broad and complex array of social, political, economic, environmental and cultural factors that strongly impact on health status and equity. Health systems that do not consciously address these factors exacerbate health inequities (Rasanathan *et al.*, 2011).

Concern about health inequities in the health status of different groups of people is not new, but the last two decades have seen an upsurge in the measurement and documentation of health inequities according to a range of factors including gender, ethnicity, socio-economic status and education. This new understanding has shown that, even as average health status often improves, health inequities often continue to widen, thus putting health inequities at the forefront of the health policy agenda. Success in reducing health inequities necessitates ensuring that the broad focus of primary health care and the social determinants of health are kept foremost in policy (Rasanathan *et al.*, 2011).

Navarro investigated the association between political economy type and socio-economic conditions in various countries and found that, compared to social democratic or Christian democratic political economies, liberal political economies had higher income inequality and unemployment, lower wage and salary levels and a higher proportion of people living in poverty (1999). Moreover, Navarro and Shi (2001) found that countries with liberal political economies had the largest income and wage differentials, the least redistributive impact of the state, and the lowest rate of improvement in infant mortality between 1960 and 1996. In their study of infant mortality rates in OECD countries, Navarro and associates at the International Network on Social Inequalities and Health found that political variables play an important role in defining how public and social policies determine the levels of inequalities. They found that political parties more committed to re-distributional policies, such as social democratic parties, are generally the most successful in reducing inequalities and improving infant mortality (2003).

While our country data largely support this thesis, there are exceptions. For example, Japan ranks near or at the top for most population health indicators, even though it is a liberal political economy. As Boxall and Short (2006) point out, however, many features of Japan's political economy closely resemble those of social and Christian democratic political economies, and it has a relatively equitable income distribution and high pension commitments and practices 'stakeholder' rather than 'shareholder' capitalism. They also found that Australia runs counter to the hypothesis of the relationship between political economy, inequality and population health, but they suggest that its unique welfare state model may partly account for its exceptionalism in terms of population health outcomes.

Although there is variation in health status across nations, often the variation among groups within a particular nation is even higher. For instance, in their study of 16 high-income countries, Nolte and McKee (2011) found that preventable mortality continues to fall in all countries although the USA is lagging increasingly behind the others. In the USA, however, there is considerable variation across states, suggesting that observed differences cannot be attributed solely to differences in the health system (Kulkarni *et al.*, 2011). Key factors are social and economic, which in turn might be reflected in differences in health by race, religion, class or ethnic background. Lower social class, as measured by income, education or other socio-economic status (SES) indicators, is related to higher death rates overall and higher rates of most diseases that constitute the common causes of death (Fuchs, 2004; Fukuda *et al.*, 2004). Moreover, social class differences in mortality and morbidity continue to widen (Rainham, 2007). Inequalities in mortality from selected causes suggest that some variations may be attributable to socio-economic differences in smoking, excessive alcohol consumption and access to health care (Mackenbach *et al.*, 2008). The Australian Government Department of Health and Ageing's National Primary Health Care Strategy has, therefore, identified the importance of improving access to a range of primary health care services to help overcome some of the adverse effects of income inequality on health (Harris *et al.*, 2011).

If a primary goal of health policy is to improve the health status of the population, it is essential to understand the economic and social determinants of health at the individual level as well. For instance, according to an Australian study, the prevalence of chronic disease varies across the socio-economic gradient for many specific diseases and important disease risk factors. As a result, any policy interventions to address the impact of chronic disease at a population level must take into account these socio-economic inequalities (Glover *et al.*, 2004). A workable model of health, then, requires a shift away from the dominance of the medical care system towards this more inclusive model of health (see Chapter 7). Social problems are resolved primarily through non-medical means, signifying a need to shift emphasis away from the current practice of defining and treating them as medical problems.

The over-reliance on curative-oriented medical intervention presents at least two problems for improving health and health equity. First, as noted in Chapter 1, there is convincing evidence that health expenditure does not correlate with population health or longer life expectancy, particularly when health care investments are aimed almost exclusively toward medical care. Therefore, 'responding to the (increasingly chronic) burden of illness with (increasingly expensive) technical fixatives is hardly a rational (or cost-effective) approach if the developmental goal that unites rich and poor countries is the social production of good health' (Taylor, 2009: 35).

A second problem is that health care systems, as currently commonly constituted, display a propensity to maintain and heighten health inequity (Taylor, 2009; Mooney, 2009). Health disparities or inequities are systematic, but potentially remediable, differences in one or more aspects of health across population groups defined socially, economically, demographically, or geographically (Starfield *et al.*, 2012). Although the magnitude of inequity varies across health systems, in all countries individuals in various social strata differ as to their burden of morbidity and the health care they receive. Importantly, despite public health system coverage being in place, many studies suggest that significant inequalities in health and health care remain pervasive over time (Hernández-Quevedo *et al.*, 2008). Without adequate attention to the underlying social conditions that cause ill health in the first place, health systems tend to aggrandize wider social inequalities, so that those who need health care most are those who are least able to access it, use it and benefit from it. Unfortunately, as noted by Lantz *et al.* (2007), health policy usually focuses on expanding access to personal medical services to the exclusion of expanding access to other services that affect an individual's health.

In 2008, the WHO Commission on Social Determinants of Health published its report stating that 'inequities are killing people on a "grand scale"' (WHO, 2008b). Among the report's recommendations for action, improved access to (public, universal) health insurance was prominent (see Box 2.16). Indeed, over the past decade, acceleration of health spending in many developed countries has led governments to search for alternative financing structures, notably through increased private expenditures. However, some of the policy instruments used to reach those goals, such as restricting eligibility criteria for public insurance and increasing reliance on unregulated private health insurance or cost sharing arrangements, may have had the unexpected effect of erecting additional

Box 2.16 Policy interventions to curtail health inequalities

Factors affecting health include *health-related behaviours* (smoking, alcohol abuse, diet, physical activity), which require individual action to reduce inequalities in health prevention; *psychosocial factors* (psychosocial stressors) that might be linked to higher prevalence among lower income groups due to tighter lifestyle restrictions; *environmental determinants* (social support, social integration), where more affluent individuals will inevitably have better access to health production factors, thus translating into better health; *material factors* (housing conditions, working conditions, financial problems); *access to health care* (easy access to high quality services) where the organization of the health system can determine the extent to which individuals are able to access health care in the event of need; and *attitudes towards the distribution of health and health care*. Although most European countries have explicit public health policies that address these areas, countries vary in their aversion to health inequalities, which might explain why some countries have higher inequalities than others (Costa-Font and Hernández-Quevedo, 2012).

barriers to health coverage. Moreover, because the impact of these policies is generally not randomly distributed in the population, these transformations have raised concerns about their effects on both population health and inequalities in health (Quesnel-Vallée *et al.*, 2012). Wagner *et al.* (2011) argue for the need to expand health insurance coverage, so that all households can have access to needed care without risking financial hardship. Based on the importance of pharmaceuticals in treating acute and chronic illnesses, and because of their contribution to high out-of-pocket health care expenditures, coverage of essential medicines should be an early consideration as countries move from user fees to pooled prepayment mechanisms.

Health status disparities linked to SES are probably the result of a complicated mix of factors suggested by three distinct theories. The first, *natural and social selection,* contends that one of the key determinants of social class is health status. This theory assumes that persons with poor health, high-risk behaviour and social pathologies naturally concentrate in the lower social class. If good health is indeed necessary in order to pursue life goals and affords one the opportunity to succeed in meeting them, it should not be surprising to find that persons in poor health would tend towards a lower SES. Although this might explain the disparity at the margins, however, it is not generally seen as a major explanation.

A second theory, the *structuralist,* attributes class differences in health to structural factors such as the production and consumption of wealth.

Lower SES persons generally exist in less healthy environments, both at home and work. For example, a recent study concluded that there is widespread evidence that the poor in the USA, UK, and perhaps other countries as well, face a disproportionate burden of environmental risks (Huggins, 2002). They face more exposure to air pollution, poor water, ambient noise, sub-standard housing and overcrowding. In contrast, higher SES persons enjoy healthier homes, safer appliances and vehicles, and less hazardous jobs.

The third theory, a *cultural and behavioural* one, sees disparities in health among social classes as the result of differences in behaviour. Often the culture of the lower classes leads to multiple high-risk behaviours that, in turn, lead to poor health. Smoking, alcohol and drug abuse, violence, sedentary lifestyles, obesity, poor diet and other unhealthy behaviours are disproportionately present in lower SES groupings. Many observers have concluded that this last theory is the most explanatory, but most conclude that it must be accompanied by the structuralist theory because the behaviour occurs within this broader social context. As noted by Mechanic, SES is 'perhaps the single most important influence on health outcomes, in part through its direct influence, but more importantly, through the many indirect effects it has on factors that directly shape health outcomes' (1994: 149). These indirect factors are most apparent when one examines two components of SES: income and education.

Income has been found to be a critical variable in determining health status at two levels. At a cross-national level, research consistently shows that the distribution of income has more to do with the health of the population than does the level of medical spending. The best health results are achieved in those societies that minimize the gap between the rich and the poor and that place heavy emphasis on the values of equity. Wilkinson (1997) suggests that healthy, egalitarian societies are more socially cohesive, they have a stronger community life and they suffer fewer of the corrosive effects of inequality. He also found that approximately two-thirds of the variation in mortality rates *within* the populations of developed nations is related to the distribution of income. This includes the UK where, despite universal access to health care, mortality rates among the working-class population increased as income distribution widened in the 1980s (Wilkinson, 1992). In contrast, Japan has the most equal income distribution and the highest life expectancy despite relatively low levels of health care spending (Kawachi *et al.*, 1999).

At the individual level as well, low income is consistently related to ill health. Low-income families are more likely to assess their health status as 'poor'. Low-income persons are significantly more likely to have preventable hospitalizations than high-income persons, with one study finding that the lowest-income group was four times as likely to be hospitalized as the highest-income group (Angell, 1993). The most likely explanation of these disparities is to be found in some combination of the theories discussed above, but its implication for health policy is significant. The impact of any efforts to constrain health care costs will affect most severely those groups that are not only most likely to need the care but also least likely to have other options. Despite greater need, larger proportions of the poor have difficulty in gaining access to health services that might avert poor health.

Some suggest that, given the strong correlation between rates of uninsured people and lower rates of preventive care across US states, chronically uninsured or unstably insured children and adults lack basic access to care for extended periods of time, putting them at higher risk of morbidity and mortality over time (Schoenbaum *et al.*, 2011). While other observers suggest that the poor performance of the USA on various health outcomes relative to other developed countries is primarily related to population differences and not health system performance, Muennig and Glied (2010) found that the risk profiles of Americans generally improved relative to those of many other nations, but that their 15-year survival continues to decline.

Not surprisingly, given its close association with income, education is also significantly related to health status. For instance, although Mackenbach *et al.* (2008) found 'striking differences' among countries in the magnitude and even the direction of these inequalities, in Europe as a whole, smoking and obesity are significantly more widespread among people in lower education levels. In their study of low- and middle-income countries, Ferri *et al.* (2012) found an important 'latent independent protective effect' of education even upon late-life mortality. Given the much higher absolute mortality rates among older people, efforts to ensure universal access to education should confer substantial health benefits for generations to come. Similarly, in their study in East Asian countries, Hanibuchi *et al.* (2010) found that class identification exhibited the strongest association with self-rated health. Moreover, individuals with less education have more frequent short-stay hospitalizations, a higher occurrence of chronic conditions with more limited activity due to such conditions, and significantly lower self-assessment of their health. One study found that of all indicators, education had the strongest and most consistent relationship with health and was the single most consistent predictor of good health (Winkleby *et al.*, 1992).

Health status, then, is intimately related to various measures of SES, particularly education and income (Marmot and Wilkinson, 1999; Wilkinson and Pickett, 2006). These factors are critical in understanding the social and cultural context of health and require considerably more research on how they operate. The interactive model of health care attributes poor health outcomes to a broad range of social factors that are bound up in the SES construct. Although SES might have a direct impact on health, it is more likely that it operates indirectly through other factors. In addition to inequitable access to primary care, health promotion and disease prevention efforts, other critical factors include unemployment, violence, poor diet, breakdown of family support structures and inadequate housing.

Unemployment can influence health by reducing income level and standard of living. Moreover, the importance of work to one's well-being, over and above the financial aspects, is well documented (Hummelgaard *et al.*, 1998). The unemployed have lower self-esteem and experience significant psychological stress that is linked to higher levels of both subjectively and objectively assessed levels of physical and mental ill health. Heightened unemployment rates are associated with heightened death rates. A recent study concluded that 'increases in the unemployment rates in European Union countries are related to deteriorated health as measured by elevated mortality rates over the following 10 to 15 years' (Brenner, 2001: 3). Interestingly, the relationship was strongest in the UK, Sweden, Germany and Finland. Suicide and deliberate self-harm as well as smoking and alcohol and drug abuse are more prevalent among the unemployed, particularly the unemployed youth. At the community level, death rates have been found to increase during times of economic depression and joblessness and to decrease during times of economic growth (Barwick, 1992). Although the full dynamics are unclear, the assumption that employment is crucial to both mental and physical health is supported by a broad array of studies. Reduction of unemployment, therefore, has significant health benefits for the population as well as the individual (Kim *et al.*, 2012).

The family has traditionally played an important role in integrating health-promoting routines into the daily lives of its members. It has also served as an important facilitator of self-esteem and a social setting that provides critical contributions to psychological and physical development. While reality has often fallen short of this ideal, the decline first of the extended family and more recently the nuclear family has had adverse effects on health. Studies consistently find that marriage is associated with lower levels of mortality, better overall health status and healthier behaviour patterns (Stanton, 2003). A study from the Netherlands, for instance, concludes that married people have the lowest morbidity rate, while the divorced show the highest (Joung *et al.*, 1994). Another study from the UK found that even when the effects of smoking, drinking and other unhealthy activities were controlled for, married men had a 9 per cent lower risk of dying as compared to unmarried men (BBC News, 2002). Although the reasons for this are unclear, a likely factor is the 'social support' of having a wife or husband nearby. Another explanation is that both single men and women tend to have less healthy lifestyles including sleep deprivation, poor diet and work habits, and to be more prone to loneliness and depression. Family relationships, however, in whatever form do appear to encourage good health practices and provide strong social links that reduce the likelihood of ill health. Thus, one would expect that, other things being equal, health outcomes would be better in those countries like Japan and Taiwan where close family structures remain a more resilient feature of society.

The context of health care

This chapter has placed health care in a more expansive context for each of our countries. We submit that one cannot understand the dynamics of a health care system without understanding the political and legal institutions and practices of the country and the cultural and historical environment from which it emerged. The size and mix of the population, its ethnic, racial and religious composition, and the level of economic equality, all help shape the health care system of a country. Each of our countries has its own character, a certain combination of features that sets it apart. Although far from an in-depth analysis of each country, this overview demonstrates that each provides a distinct setting for the emergence of a health care system over time. Interestingly, in their analysis of 92 countries covering the 1970 to 2005 period, Bergh and Nilsson (2010) found that economic globalization has a robust positive effect on life expectancy, even when controlling for income, nutritional intake, literacy, number of physicians and other factors, that holds even when the sample is restricted to low-income countries. 'For economic globalization, evidence suggests it is, indeed, good for living' (2010: 1200).

Chapter 1 suggested that there are strong forces that might be leading to a convergence of policies across countries. In this brief overview of the context of health policy in ten countries, it is obvious that although they are all affluent, developed countries, they bring with them a divergent set of structural and value systems that will be useful for comparative purposes in the following substantive chapters. While these factors certainly cannot explain all the differences or similarities among these countries, they help delineate some of the anomalies that will arise out of the more in-depth analysis of these health care systems in the following chapters.

Chapter 3

Funding, Provision and Governance

Health care is often thought of as a system. A health system is a highly complex entity and consists of a range of sub-systems. Among these, the sub-systems of *funding, provision* and *governance* are central for understanding health policy comparatively.

The sub-system of *funding* is concerned with raising financial resources and allocating monies to the providers of health care. Health care can be funded from a range of sources, from taxes and social insurance contributions to private insurance premiums and out-of-pocket payments by patients. Funding, however, is about more than the technicalities of raising and allocating financial resources; funding is also a pointer to power, and control of funding is a major resource in health policy. The sub-system of *provision* focuses on the delivery of health services. Health systems provide a range of services, and patients have varying levels of choice when using health services, such as among individual doctors or different care settings. The delivery of health services is in the hands of different types of providers including public and private, profit or non-profit, hospitals. The mix of providers makes the provision of health care more or less publicly integrated. The sub-systems of funding and provision form the basis of the sub-system of *governance*. Governance describes the modes of coordinating health systems and their multiple actors. Governance is underpinned by tensions between public and private as well as between the centre and localities. As governments tend to play an important role in health systems, governance can also be thought of as government capacity or authority.

In a comparative context, health systems are often grouped under specific typologies of health systems, as discussed in Chapter 1. The typologies present models of funding, providing and governing health care in the form of distinct ideal types (Burau and Blank, 2006). The implicit assumption within many typologies is that certain models of funding are directly associated with certain models of provision. For example, the funding of health care from taxation is said to make for public provision of health care. As the analysis below shows, this is the case in the health systems in some countries. In others, however, individual health systems combine different models of funding and provision, and even rely on a mix of several models of funding or provision. This directs the attention to the country-specific political contexts in which health systems are embedded and that were introduced in Chapter 2.

For example, in Britain and Sweden, where health care is predominantly publicly funded and provided, government looms large in the governance of health systems. At the same time, the specific features of health governance also reflect the fact that the wider political system and health governance in Britain is much more centralized than in Sweden. Similarly, New Zealand's NHS favours a more hierarchical, integrated approach, with clear lines of accountability, and central government capacity to define objectives and monitor developments (Ettelt *et al.*, 2012). The factors that lead to differences among countries coexist with common pressures across health systems including ageing populations, advances in medical technology and increasing demands from patients.

This chapter provides an overview of the funding, provision and governance of health care and shows how they are shaped by country-specific contexts as well as by universal pressures. An important aim will be to assess the relative usefulness of the typologies of the different types of health systems.

Comparing funding of health systems

Funding offers a good starting point for looking at health systems comparatively. Funding provides a first indicator of the relative size of health systems and the role of governments in health systems. Not surprisingly, there is variation among these countries. Table 3.1 ranks the countries according to their per capita expenditure on health care. The USA ranks first and spends over eight times as much per head as Taiwan, which is the lowest spender at $950. However, this is not typical of the entire range because these two countries are outliers. The upper midrange is represented by the Netherlands, Germany, Sweden and Australia, which spend between US$5,056 and US$3,670 per capita on health care. Britain, Japan and New Zealand are in the lower midrange and spend an average of $3,163, while Singapore stands at $2,273.

The picture is similar when looking at health care expenditure as a percentage of GDP in Table 3.2. The majority of countries spend between about around 9 per cent of their GDP on health care. The clear exception is the USA at 17.6 per cent, followed by the Netherlands at 12.0 per cent and Germany at 11.6 per cent. Health spending has increased since the 1970s, although more dramatically in some countries than in others. For example, health spending in Sweden increased from 7.5 to 9.6 per cent between 1975 and 2010, while in the USA it more than doubled over that same period of time.

Table 3.1 ***Per capita expenditure on health care in US dollars, 2010***

United States	8,233
Netherlands	5,056
Germany	4,338
Sweden	3,758
Australia	3,670
United Kingdom	3,433
Japan	3,035
New Zealand	3,022
Singapore	2,273
Taiwan	950

Sources: Data from OECD (2012b); Singapore (World Health Organization, 2012c); Taiwan (Bureau of National Health Insurance, 2008). Figures for Japan and Australia are from 2009.

Table 3.2 ***Changes in health care expenditure as a percentage of GDP, 1975–2010***

	1975	*1980*	*1985*	*1990*	*1995*	*2000*	*2005*	*2010*[a]
Australia	6.5	6.3	6.6	6.9	7.4	8.3	8.8	9.1
Germany	8.4	8.4	8.8	8.3	10.1	10.3	10.7	11.6
Japan	5.7	6.5	6.7	6.0	6.9	7.7	8.2	9.5
Netherlands	7.0	7.4	7.3	8.0	8.3	8.0	9.2	12.0
New Zealand	6.7	5.9	5.1	6.9	7.2	7.7	8.9	10.1
Singapore	n/a	n/a	n/a	2.8	n/a	2.9	3.8	4.0
Sweden	7.5	8.9	8.5	8.2	8.0	8.2	9.2	9.6
Taiwan	3.8	4.8	n/a	5.5	5.7	5.9	6.3	6.4
United Kingdom	5.5	5.6	5.9	6.0	6.9	7.2	8.2	9.6
United States	7.9	8.7	10.0	11.9	13.3	13.2	15.2	17.6

n/a = not available.
[a] The figures for Australia and Japan are from 2009 and Taiwan is from 2008.

Sources: Data from OECD (2008, 2012b); Singapore (World Health Organization, 2012c); Taiwan (Bureau of National Health Insurance, 2008).

Besides the overall level of funding, the sources of funding give an initial indication of the kinds of health system with which we are dealing. Table 3.3 shows that most health systems are predominantly publicly funded. As before, Singapore and the USA are the clear outliers with only 36.3 and 48.2 per cent of spending, respectively, coming from public sources. For the remaining countries, public expenditure as a share of

Table 3.3 *Changes in public expenditure on health care as a percentage of total expenditure on health care*

	1975	*1980*	*1985*	*1990*	*1995*	*2000*	*2005*	*2010**
Australia	73.6	62.6	70.6	66.2	65.8	67.0	67.0	68.5
Germany	79.0	78.7	77.4	76.2	81.6	79.7	77.0	76.8
Japan	72.0	71.3	70.7	77.6	83.0	81.3	82.7	80.5
Netherlands	67.9	69.4	70.8	67.1	71.0	63.1	62.5	n/a
New Zealand	73.7	88.0	87.0	82.4	77.2	78.0	77.4	83.2
Singapore	69.9	68.0	n/a	n/a	n/a	26.0	38.5	36.3
Sweden	90.2	92.5	90.4	89.9	86.6	84.9	81.7	81.0
Taiwan	n/a	44.4	n/a	46.1	n/a	63.8	62.5	n/a
United Kingdom	91.1	89.4	85.8	83.6	83.9	80.9	86.9	83.2
United States	40.9	41.2	39.6	39.4	45.3	43.7	45.1	48.2

* The figures for Japan, the Netherlands and Australia are from 2009.
n/a = not available.

Sources: Data from OECD (2008); Singapore (Ministry of Health, 2008); Taiwan (Bureau of National Health Insurance, 2008).

total health care expenditure ranges from 62.5 per cent in the Netherlands and Taiwan to 83.2 per cent in Britain. Looking at the figures from the early 1970s onwards, continuity is the most striking feature, although there have been interesting changes in some countries. In Japan, New Zealand and the USA the share of public funding rose between a little over 7 per cent and well over 9 per cent, while Taiwan's move to its NHI in the mid-1990s increased the public share from 44 to 63 per cent. In contrast, Sweden and Britain saw a fall in the percentage of expenditure from public sources. Singapore demonstrates an even more dramatic decrease in public funding as it moved to the Medisave scheme, thus theoretically shifting to an individual funding base (see Box 1.3).

With the exception of the USA and Singapore, therefore, the health systems considered here are predominantly publicly funded. However, a closer look at the exact sources of funding reveals important differences. Table 3.4 distinguishes between public expenditure by governments and compulsory social security schemes, and private expenditure from out-of-pocket payments, private insurance and other private funds. Government expenditure can come from general taxation or earmarked taxes, whereas out-of-pocket payments are payments made directly by patients themselves. Out-of-pocket payments come in a variety of forms. As part of social or private insurance, patients may have to cover part of the cost of medical treatment (co-payments).

Table 3.4 *Sources of funding as a percentage of health care expenditure, 2009*

	Public funding		*Private funding*		
	Government[a]	*Social security*[b]	*Out-of-pocket payments*	*Private insurance*	*Non-profit institutions*
Australia	69.0	0.0	19.4	8.2	0.4
Germany	6.8	70.5	12.3	9.6	0.4
Japan	8.6	71.6	16.3	2.5	0.0
Netherlands	8.5	76.9	5.7	5.3	1.3
New Zealand	73.3	9.7	10.6	5.0	1.4
Sweden	81.6	n/a	17.2	0.2	0.2
Taiwan	8.4	67.0	21.0	n/a	4.0
United Kingdom	83.4	0.0	9.6	3.3	3.9
United States	5.8	43.3	12.3	34.7	3.7

[a, b] The figure for the UK is from 2002.
n/a = not available.

Sources: Data from OECD (2008, 2012b); Taiwan (Bureau of National Health Insurance, 2008).

Alternatively, patients may have to pay a fixed amount before the insurance company gets involved (deductibles). Out-of-pocket payments may also occur as a result of self-medication. This includes over-the-counter prescriptions and medical services not covered by health insurance.

Looking at the public sources of funding, it is striking that countries seem to rely principally either on social security, as in the case of Germany, Japan, the Netherlands and Taiwan, or on government funding, as in the case of Australia, New Zealand, Britain and Sweden. As for private funding, most countries rely on out-of-pocket payments by patients, although the percentage ranges from 12.3 per cent in Germany to 21.0 per cent in Taiwan. The exception is the USA, where private insurance is the main source of private funding. Considering the earlier figures on public expenditure, it is not surprising that the sources of health care funding are more diverse in the USA. Here, 6 per cent of health care expenditure comes from government funds, 43 per cent from social security, 35 per cent from private insurance and 12 per cent from out-of-pocket payments. The reasons for these differences in the sources of funding are analysed in more detail in the following sections.

National health services and the commitment to public funding

National health services are the archetype of a publicly funded health system. Health care is predominantly funded from taxation and is available to every resident in the country. Public funding results in universal access.

Britain is a classic example of this type of public funding and significantly, co-payments are low. For example, in 2010 over 80 per cent of funding came from public sources, most of it from general taxation (OECD, 2008, 2012b). In contrast, co-payments by patients accounted for about only 9.6 per cent of funding. The same applies to funding from private insurance. Although the market for employment-based private insurance schemes expanded dramatically in the 1980s in response to tax incentives, it has since levelled off (Baggot, 2004). Significantly, private insurance accounted for only 3 per cent of total health expenditure in 2010 (OECD, 2012b) and in 2008 covered 10 per cent of the population (Boyle, 2011). An important reason for taking out private insurance is to compensate for the perceived low quality of NHS services and for the long waiting lists for elective surgery.

The universality typical of national health services leads to the socialization of funding, although it is never complete (Freeman, 2000). Whereas over 80 per cent of funding in Britain (and New Zealand and Sweden) now comes from public sources, at times national health services have relied to a greater extent on private sources of funding. As illustrated in Table 3.3, for example, in New Zealand the percentage of public health expenditure had fallen over the last 20 years and dropped below that of Britain and Sweden. In 2005, about 77 per cent of health expenditure was public, down from 80 per cent in 1980 (New Zealand Ministry of Health, 2008), but by 2010 public funding was back over 83 per cent. Furthermore, out-of-pocket payments accounted for about 11 per cent and private health insurance 5 per cent of total health care spending in New Zealand in 2009.

In contrast, other countries are actively looking to support the expansion of private health insurance. Australia is a case in point. Here, private insurance accounts for 8.2 per cent of total health care expenditure while 19.4 per cent comes from co-payments by individuals (OECD, 2012b). About 45 per cent of the population has private insurance but this represents a substantial decrease in private insurance from over 80 per cent in 1970 and 64 per cent just prior to the introduction of the universal health insurance Medicare in 1984 (Doorslaer *et al.*, 2008). In light of this steady decline, Australia has taken measures to increase the population coverage of private health insurance, reduce pressure on public hospital waiting lists and services, and support and improve the viability of the insurance industry. In 1999, under the PHI Incentive Scheme, anyone purchasing private insurance received a 30 per cent subsidy, paid either as a tax rebate or as a reduced purchase price of insurance. Then, in July 2000, Lifetime Health Cover was introduced which applied a base premium to those purchasing insurance up until the age of 30 (Bertelsmann Foundation, 2003b).

Public funding through social insurance

Social insurance is another form of public funding. It is a hybrid and combines two very different principles of organizing health care: the insurance is paid for by independent institutions but is publicly mandated (Freeman, 2000: 54f). Taiwan, with its national insurance plan, is an exception in that there is a single plan under governmental control. In contrast to private insurance, social health insurance is based on the principle of social solidarity. Contributions are paid as a percentage of the salary rather than according to the specific health risks of the individual and are often shared by employers and employees. This represents a redistributive policy between high and low risk patients as well as between high and low earners. Dependants of employees (i.e., non-earning spouses and children) are also covered, thus in effect ensuring universal coverage of the population.

The pioneer among its kind was the German health system. Health care is funded by contributions paid more or less equally by employers and employees as a fixed percentage of the monthly salary. The contributions are uniform and set by government and are complemented by an additional flat rate fee paid by employees only and set by individual insurance funds (Gesundheitsreform, 2007; Mosebach, 2006). Membership is compulsory for everyone with annual earnings below a certain ceiling, which is 48,000 euros (Busse, 2008). Social health insurance is administered by private, non-profit funds, which operate under public law. Employees earning above the ceiling and the self-employed also have to be covered by an insurance plan, but can choose to stay with social health insurance or join a private health insurance scheme. However, only 9 per cent of the population are covered by this private insurance. Other sources of private funding are co-payments. Co-payments for drugs were introduced in 1977 and have increased regularly, comprising 28 per cent of expenditure on drugs by 1999 (Wendt *et al.*, 2005). With greater cost pressures, co-payments in other areas were added and rose considerably in the late 1990s (Busse, 2008) and in 2005 made up 13 per cent of the total health care expenditure. In sum, this makes for a heightened focus on individual responsibility (Carrera *et al.*, 2008).

Compared to national health services, social insurance funds are generally characterized by a closer interface between the public and the private sectors, but in some countries the role of the latter is much more marked. For example, in Taiwan social insurance accounts for 67 per cent of total health expenditure, while direct patient co-payments account for 21 per cent. Similarly, in Japan all 5,000 plus insurance plans are (to varying degrees) characterized by co-payments of between 10 and 30 per cent of charges that are designed to constrain demand (Tatara and Okamoto, 2009). The emphasis on individual responsibility is partly offset by government subsidies for the community-based insurance scheme and the pool for health care for the elderly. Overall, insurance contributions account for 72 per cent of health expenditure, national and local government subsidies for 8.6 per cent and co-payments by patients for 16 per cent in 2009 (OECD, 2012b).

Private insurance and the emphasis on individual responsibility

Countries that predominantly rely on private insurance put considerable emphasis on individual responsibility. However, here too individual responsibility is never complete and private funding generally coexists with public funding, particularly for designated groups such as the poor and elderly. The USA is the archetypal example of this system of funding and is characterized by high complexity. Outside of programmes for the elderly and some disabled (see Box 3.1) the US health system remains largely market-based. Private insurance covers 58 per cent of the population and accounts for approximately one-third of total health expenditure (Centers for Medicare and Medicaid Services, 2009b). It is primarily provided by thousands of principally for-profit insurance companies, with the exception of Blue Cross-Blue Shield and a few other non-profits. Virtually all insurance is purchased through group policies by employers (it is very costly for individuals to purchase insurance), with many large employers being self-insured. In most states, employers are not required by law to offer coverage to their employees and increasing numbers do not, although tax considerations encourage them to do so. An additional 13 per cent of total health spending comes from co-payments or other private sources. This private insurance coexists with a social insurance system for the elderly that covers 25 per cent of the population (Bitton and Kahn, 2003). Other public expenditures such as veterans' hospitals comprise 12 per cent of total health care spending. Importantly, an estimated 45 million people have no insurance coverage, although the Affordable Care Act promises to reduce this by half (Hacker, 2011).

Box 3.1 Medicare in the USA: public insurance in a private system

Medicare is a public insurance for the elderly with over 43 million beneficiaries, administered by the federal government and consisting of three parts. Part A is compulsory and covers hospital care funded through social security taxes paid by all working citizens. Part B is voluntary and covers other costs including doctors' bills and outpatient hospital treatment. It is funded by monthly premiums paid by enrollees and substantial federal subsidies. Under the traditional programme, which covers 86 per cent of Medicare beneficiaries, payments to hospitals, physicians and other providers are determined by complex prospective payment systems that provide the programme with a high level of control over the price component of total spending, but not much leverage over the volume of services. The remaining beneficiaries are enrolled in the Medicare+Choice programme, under which private health plans are paid a monthly capitation payment for each enrollee based on the amount Medicare spends per beneficiary in the geographic area served by the plan. Under this system, the total payment by Medicare to plans is fixed, and each health plan establishes its own methods for administering benefits and paying providers within parameters established by federal regulation. In 2003, the Medicare Prescription Drug, Improvement and Modernization Act became law and created Medicare Part D, implemented in January 2006, to provide drug coverage to the elderly, through private, stand-alone drug plans (Centers for Medicare and Medicaid Services, 2009b).

The importance of private insurance is not the only indicator of the emphasis on individual responsibility. This can also be reflected in the ways in which private insurance is organized. For example, in Singapore, the corresponding savings scheme relies on risk pooling that is even more limited than in ordinary private insurance schemes that prevail in the USA. At the centre of the health system is Medisave, a compulsory savings scheme, which is managed centrally by the Central Provident Fund (CPF), Singapore's mandatory pension fund. Under the scheme, each employee and self-employed person puts aside a percentage of monthly income into a Medical Savings Account (MSA) to meet future health care expenses (Asher *et al.*, 2008; Okma *et al.*, 2010). Importantly, although mandatory, this insurance scheme puts individual responsibility centre stage and medical risks remain largely individualized (Lim, 2004). It largely rejects a cross-generational subsidy and instead is moulded around the life cycle where each person builds up her/his own reserves toward their own ill health (Reisman, 2006). More specifically, solidarity is confined to the immediate family and accounts are only transferable to one's spouse, children, parents and grandparents. The very limited redistribution, together with ceilings on contributions, also significantly limits the scope of Medisave, as does the reluctance of individuals to deplete their savings.

In order to help people with long hospital stays pay their bills, in 1990 Medisave was augmented with two voluntary catastrophic insurance programmes, MediShield and Eldershield for the elderly. Approximately 2.7 million people in Singapore have taken medical insurance in the form of MediShield or private Shield plans within the CPF umbrella (Reisman, 2006). Since these plans are not mandatory, risk pooling in Singapore is very limited as compared to social insurance systems. In 2005, MediShield underwent reform designed to broaden the pool to healthier members, restructure private insurance plans and reduce the sizeable pool of uninsured since approximately 440,000 people were not covered by either MediShield or private plans, mainly self-employed people or dependent spouses, who were largely elderly (Lin, 2006).

However, even a health system that puts individual responsibility centre stage in terms of funding has to acknowledge the existence of health market failures. In Singapore, for example, there is the Medifund, a government endowment fund built on surpluses each year that serves as a safety net to provide financial assistance to individuals who, despite the subsidies and payments from their MSAs and the MediShield scheme, cannot pay their medical bills (Okma *et al.*, 2010). However, this does not change the overall picture of the centrality of individual responsibility. Despite the view that this '3-M' system is the centrepiece of Singapore's health care financing system, it presently accounts for less than 10 per cent of national health care expenditure. The rest is made up of employer benefits, government subsidies, and out-of-pocket payments accounting for approximately 60 per cent of total expenditure (Asher *et al.*, 2008).

Control of funding and pressures for reform

As Figure 3.1 suggests, funding is about raising resources from a range of sources (such as taxes, social insurance contributions, private insurance premiums and out-of-pocket payments) and allocating these resources to the providers of health care. Health care tends to be funded by a mix of public and private sources, reflecting predominant types of funding and other, country-specific factors. For instance, in one third of OECD countries, 30 per cent or more of the population are covered by some sort of voluntary private health insurance in addition to the coverage provided by the universal health care system (Kiil, 2012). National health services, with their commitment to universality of access, get the majority of their funding from taxes. Britain and Sweden are classical examples of this type of publicly funded health system while Australia and New Zealand

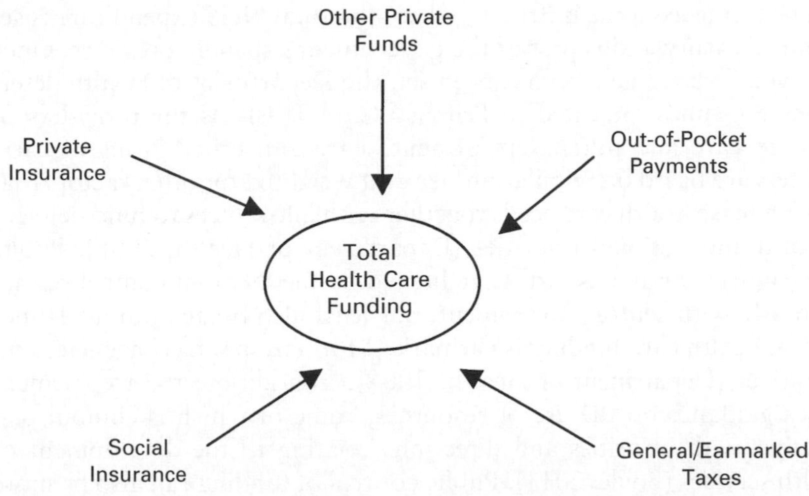

Figure 3.1 *Sources of health care funding*

combine tax funding and elements of private funding with over 20 per cent of funds coming from private insurance and out-of-pocket payments.

Social insurance systems are hybrids, and, except in Taiwan, money is raised from independent insurance funds that are publicly mandated and founded on the principle of social solidarity. Germany (together with Japan and the Netherlands) continues to be the classic example of this type of funding: social insurance contributions account for the majority of health care expenditure, although even here there are increasingly elements of private/privatized funding (Gerlinger, 2010). The latter is even stronger in Taiwan, where social insurance coexists with strong elements of private funding from out-of-pocket payments. Finally, health systems where private insurance dominates place individual responsibility first and rely more heavily on private funds. In Singapore, a highly individualized compulsory savings account is predominant, whereas the USA relies on a mixture of private and public insurance.

As noted earlier, however, funding is about more than raising and allocating financial resources. How funds are raised and allocated is also a pointer to power. Different types of funding result in different types of control, and different types of control lead to different types of pressures for reform. Public funding means public control (Freeman, 2000: 44). Public control, therefore, can be expected to be strongest in national health services, which are chiefly funded by taxes. Taxes place control over funding in public hands, leading to concentration rather than fragmentation and allowing for the control of (global) budgets.

The prime example is Britain, where the total NHS expenditure is set by the Treasury and is part of the government's spending reviews. Once the overall spending level has been set, the Department of Health determines the funds allocated to Primary Care Trusts as the providers of primary care and purchasers of acute care and other forms of care. Budgets are based on population size and weighted for other factors that may increase health care needs together with allowances to fund delivery of local and national priorities (Department of Health, 2008). Public control over funding is further tightened by the fact that control resides primarily with central government, not least also because about 10 per cent of health care funding is earmarked for national level agencies and initiatives (Department of Health, 2008). In addition, the Department issues guidance on the use of resources, some of which is compulsory, together with priorities and directions relating to the development of health services (Boyle, 2011). Public control of funding can also be more decentralized as in Sweden, where public control rests with the county councils (Anell *et al.*, 2012). On specific occasions this may be complemented by central intervention, underlining the national character of the health system. For example, on two occasions the national government has limited the level of taxes that can be raised by county councils (Glenngård *et al.*, 2005).

In national health services, problems of controlling total expenditure are practically unknown. However, public control of funding comes at a price (Klein, 2001). Inevitably, the interests of government as the payer of health care will be reflected in its approach to raising and allocating funds, and cost efficiency and containment are likely priorities (Fattore, 1999). And, to paraphrase Moran (1999: 61), a uniquely generous entitlement philosophy often goes hand-in-hand with parsimonious practice.

Instead, the central challenge of a national health system is to meet the growing demands for health care within a fixed and tight budget. The pressure escalates when patients become less deferential and more demanding and the heightened mismatch between supply and demand manifests itself in long waiting lists for elective surgery. For example, a WHO study ranked the British NHS 18th in the world because of its lack of responsiveness to patients (Laurance and Norton, 2000). Centralization of control adds to the politicization of health care expenditure. Britain is a case in point and here responsibility for the negative consequences of inadequate funding often falls back on central government (Ham, 2009). Health care reforms over the last 20 years can be read as attempts to make limited resources go further and have focused on increasing micro-efficiency and competition. These have included the British NHS going through several waves of major reorganization (Ham, 1999; Klein, 2006; Paton, 2007; Boyle, 2011). Although competition promises to provide more and/or better health services without spending more money (Freeman, 1998, 2000), there are limits to this approach to reform as developments in Britain testify; the country became a victim of its own success in terms of cost containment. Starting in 2000 the government increased spending on the NHS to match international spending levels. Here, an external review into the funding of the NHS provided powerful leverage for a sustained increase in NHS funding (Ham, 2009). Between 1999 and 2005 this led to an annual growth rate 7.3 per cent above inflation and as Klein (2006: 409) notes 'this is more than double the average in previous decades and unprecedented in the history of the NHS'.

In contrast with national health services, public control of funding is weaker in health systems that rely on social insurance and this typically manifests itself in problems of controlling total health care expenditure. A classical case is Germany where health reform has long been seen as an attempt to halt the 'cost explosion'. As a percentage of monthly salaries, social insurance contribution rates make health care expenditure highly visible (Moran, 1999: 74). However, contribution rates have come under pressure not only from rising expenditures but also from falling funding. An increasingly lower proportion of GDP is used for wages, reflecting larger profits by employers and wage increases below productivity as well as high levels of unemployment; also, there is a greater share of wages that is either exempt from contribution or that exceeds the maximum ceiling up to which contributions have to be paid (Amelung *et al.*, 2003; Gerlinger, 2010). This has been exacerbated by unification, to the extent that shortfalls in funding are now the main reason for the financial problems of the health system (Busse and Howorth, 1999: 331). Traditionally, power over funding has been decentralized and fragmented. In part, this is typical of the organizational complexity of social insurance systems but, in the case of Germany, it is compounded by federalism. Until the mid-1990s, there were over 1,000 different insurance funds, each raising its own funds and setting its own contribution rates. Health care resources were allocated from the bottom up and doctors were free to decide on the treatment of patients. Moreover, the federal government was limited to setting (and altering) the framework in which the insurance funds and providers operated.

However, even social insurance schemes allow for some control of funding and, indeed, this seems to be a common trend when looking at recent reforms across countries. For example, Japan has a long tradition of successful public control, with all insurance funds and providers strictly regulated by the government and all health care payments made on the basis of a national fee schedule (see Box 3.2). Moreover, and similar to Taiwan (Cheng, 2003), all billing and payment is centralized through the payment fund of National Health Insurance, which reviews all bills submitted and has the power to reduce payments to minimize

Box 3.2 Japan: low costs, high usage

In Japan, fees for all health care services are set every two years by negotiations between the Health Ministry and physicians. The negotiations determine the fee for every medical procedure and medication, and fees are identical across the country. If physicians attempt to game the system by ordering extra procedures to generate income, the government can lower them at the next round of fee setting. For example, the fee for MRI was lowered by 35 per cent in 2002. As the result of this strict fee structure, costs in Japan tend to be quite low compared to other developed countries. For instance, in 2009 an MRI of the neck region cost only US$98 in Japan compared to about $1,500 in the USA. On the other hand, and partly as a consequence, utilization is much higher in Japan. Japanese patients like medical technologies such as CT scans, and they receive MRIs at a per capita rate eight times higher than the British and twice that of Americans. Japan also has three times as many hospital beds and over four times as many hospital visits per capita than the USA. Due to a large number of people visiting hospitals for relatively minor problems, shortage of medical resources can be an issue in some regions. The problem has become a wide concern in Japan, particularly in Tokyo where it was reported that in 2007 over 14,000 emergency patients were rejected at least three times by hospitals before getting treatment (Tatara and Okamoto, 2009).

fraud. Similarly, in the Netherlands, the (income-related) contribution rates for the two social insurance schemes are set by central government. In addition, private health insurance has also been subject to extensive regulation such as requirements for pooling and a standard insurance package for high-risk employees. The recent reforms continued this trend and integrated private insurance into a single, universal social insurance scheme (Maarse and Meulen, 2006; Rosenau and Lako, 2008; Schäfer *et al.*, 2010; for an overview of similar development in Germany see Leiber *et al.*, 2010; Rothgang *et al.*, 2010).

Systematic and effective public control of funding is weakest in health systems that rely on private insurance. The USA is a case in point. Rising health expenditure has been a major problem and the USA continues to be the most expensive health system of all industrialized countries. As seen earlier, the USA now spends over 17 per cent of its GDP on health care, almost double the average of industrialized nations. It is not only the predominance of private funding that makes public control of expenditure difficult, but also the fragmentation of insurance funds and provider organizations, together with the federalist structure in the USA. The US health system is an amalgamation of over 1,500 private insurance companies and managed care organizations; over 700,000 doctors, a majority of which are specialists in private practice; over 5,700 acute care hospitals (with 5.2 million employees) and 15,000 long-term care facilities (American Hospital Association, 2009). Moreover, the public sector health system includes 3,141 counties that operate community hospitals and clinics; the 50 states which retain the primary constitutional roles of protecting the health of their respective residents and the training and licensing of medical personnel; and finally the federal government which funds Medicare and the joint federal-state Medicaid programme as well as specialized veterans' and research hospitals.

In the 1980s, the government attempted to control Medicare/Medicaid spending by initiating diagnosis-related groups (DRGs), a system under which each category of treatment has a scheduled payment. Furthermore, in order to constrain private sector costs the government encouraged the creation of HMOs and other managed care systems. Other attempts to control cost growth have included a combination of selective provider contracting, discount price negotiations, utilization control practices, and risk-sharing payment methods. After the levelling-off of health care expenditures following the initiation of DRGs and managed care in the late 1980s to mid-1990s, costs rose rapidly, again far exceeding general inflation rates. This is especially the case for Medicare/Medicaid where, despite DRGs, real growth is now approaching double figures annually, despite passage of the Affordable Care Act.

The country examples above focus on direct public control of funding, but more indirect controls also exist and Singapore offers an interesting example. Here, public control is directed at influencing individual citizens' demands for and consumption of health care resources. The controls are so successful that in 2000, the WHO ranked Singapore as the most effective health system in Asia and sixth in the world, despite spending only 3.1 per cent of its GDP on health care (*Straits Times,* 2000). Public control of demand and consumption has several elements: (1) as part of the MSA system individuals are encouraged to use their savings parsimoniously; (2) the government uses education programmes designed to keep health care expectations modest; and (3) the government encourages family responsibilities for care of elderly and ill members (Duff, 2001: 147). The soft elements of public control are combined with elements of hierarchical regulation. Participation in the Medisave scheme is compulsory and caps on contribution rates, together with very high co-payments, have given government tight control of expenditure. The highly centralized political structure of Singapore and widespread public approval of the regime ensures that government control is largely effective (Ham, 2001; Lim, 2004).

Health services and patient choice

Health services are first and foremost medical services, reflecting the prominence of doctors in the delivery of services and the allocation of health care resources. As Table 3.5 suggests, medical health services can be distinguished according to the specificity and the locality of care delivered (see also Chapter 1). Primary care is typically less specialized than secondary care. This distinction corresponds to different localities of care delivery. Typically, primary care services are delivered in ambulatory settings (such as doctors' practices or health centres) whereas acute care services are delivered in (inpatient) hospital settings or in outpatient departments of hospitals. In contrast, chronic care services have traditionally been less medically oriented and are delivered in a range of settings, from people's homes to day centres and nursing homes.

As Table 3.6 suggests, in the majority of these health systems inpatient care accounts for the single largest share of health care expenditure, followed, more or less narrowly, by outpatient care. Interestingly, the difference between expenditure on inpatient and outpatient care expenditure varies considerably among countries. The Netherlands and Taiwan spend significantly more on inpatient care than on outpatient care, whereas in Germany and Japan, the difference in health care expenditure is less. However, all countries are characterized by almost universal abandonment of home health care services. This will be addressed in more detail in Chapter 6.

Patient access to different types of health care varies between countries, reflecting different levels of patient choice. Choice can mean different things, such as the ability to choose a generalist or a specialist doctor as the first point of contact or the ability to choose among different hospitals and ambulatory care settings. A broad distinction can be drawn among complete choice, extensive choice and the GP model, where choice is restricted. The level of patient choice reflects the way health

Table 3.5 *Types and settings of health services*

	Ambulatory settings	*Hospital settings*
Primary Care	Services provided by GPs working in their own practices or in health centres.	Services provided by GPs in long-term care nursing homes.
Acute Care	Services provided by specialists working in their own practices or health centres.	Services provided by specialists on wards or in outpatient departments in hospitals.

Table 3.6 *Expenditure on medical services as a percentage of health care expenditure, 2009*

	Inpatient care	*Outpatient care*	*Home health care services*
Australia	35.1	n/a	0.0
Germany	28.6	29.4	6.3
Japan[a]	32.2	33.9	2.4
Netherlands	35.0	18.6	4.5
New Zealand	27.7	33.9	9.9
Sweden	28.5	42.0	4.0
Taiwan	39.6	34.1	n/a
United States	18.9	50.6	2.8

[a] Figures for Japan are from 2008.
n/a = not available

Sources: Data from OECD (2011a); Taiwan (Bureau of National Health Insurance, 2008).

services are organized, but also explicit decisions about the appropriate level of patient choice.

Taiwan offers virtually unlimited choice, which reflects the combination of a publicly funded NHI and the absence of a formal referral requirement. Thus patients are free to choose any NHI-contacted hospital to receive inpatient or ambulatory care. As a result, the health care service market in Taiwan is highly competitive, even more so than in the USA, and in practice all Taiwanese hospitals, regardless of ownership, behave as private businesses and keenly compete for patients. In 2002, there were 610 hospitals comprised of 23 medical centres, 71 regional hospitals, 41 district teaching hospitals, 344 district hospitals and 131 non-accredited hospitals, primarily small, privately owned hospitals (BNHI, 2008). In addition there were 17,618 clinics for Western medicine, dentistry, and Chinese medicine, the latter providing about 10 per cent of primary care consultations. Patients, however, tend to prefer larger hospitals, and their expansion has been at the expense of many small-scale hospitals.

Next to Taiwan, Singapore offers the widest choice in our countries, but one that is restricted by the availability of sufficient private funds. Patients with an active Medisave (MSA) account are free to go directly to the hospital (private or public) of their choice and choose the level of subsidy they receive in public hospitals. In relation to primary care services, patients are free to choose between private practices and government-subsidized health centres (Box 3.3). MSAs can also be used to buy private insurance or MediShield coverage (54 per cent did in 2005, Asher *et al.*, 2008). Paradoxically, the high level of individual responsibility also limits choice when it comes to expensive or long-term care, because few patients are wealthy enough to afford such care and exercise free choice. Also, once a person's or family's MSA is exhausted, he or she must depend on the Medifund, under which choice as to both providers and class of hospital care is limited. Even those who accumulate the required minimum sum of S$30,000 in their MSA upon retirement at age 55 are likely to find it insufficient to meet their hospitalization bills. One study found that only 17.9 per cent of elderly patients were able to depend on their own account (Reisman, 2006). Thus, in the end, the high level of individual responsibility constrains the choice of those persons who are most dependent on the health system and who have depleted their MSA. Although Medisave contributes to the 'cultural rhetoric' of personal responsibility for health care, Barr (2001) argues that at its core the Singapore system of health funding represents a 'strict rationing of health services according to wealth'.

The health systems in Germany and, to a lesser extent, Sweden also offer extensive individual choice. In Germany, patients are free to choose any doctor working in ambulatory care, but require referral for hospital care. This leads to extensive choice as both generalists and specialists work in office-based settings. In Sweden, patients can choose between using a health centre or going directly to a specialist outpatient department in a hospital. However, in the case of the latter waiting times tend to be longer and co-payments are higher. Interestingly, patient choice has been extended over the last two decades. Since the 1990s patients can choose between public and private health centres; they can seek a second opinion or treatment from alternative hospitals if the care offered is not appropriate; and in some counties, patients have free choice where they

Box 3.3 Liberalization of Medisave use in Singapore

Although the Medisave scheme was originally designed to fund inpatient care, as of 2006 patients suffering from specific chronic conditions can pay their outpatient bills using MSA. This major departure for Singapore's health care financing system reflects the government's acknowledgement that outpatient costs, especially for patients with chronic diseases, can be very high and pose a financial problem to many patients. Patients are now allowed to use up to S$300 of their MSA a year or draw on any or all of their family members' MSAs for approved outpatient treatment. In addition, the use of MSAs under this scheme is subject to a deductible and a cash co-payment of 15 per cent on each outpatient bill in excess of the deductible is set. This reflects the government's concerns that the policy will create a future problem by allowing MSAs to become prematurely depleted (Bertelsmann Foundation, 2006).

seek medical treatment. In 2009, patient choice was further broadened; in fact, it became mandatory as did the right of accredited private providers to open practices (Anell, 2010). Significantly, however, each county has developed its own model, reflecting a 'soft-law-in-the-shadow-of-hierarchy-approach' to policy making (Fredriksson *et al.*, 2012). Taken together, this reflects a strong commitment to equity and quality and contrasts with Britain and the Netherlands, where patients' choice often has been curtailed in the name of efficiency (Saltman, 1998: 164).

The GP model offers the lowest level of patient choice. Patients have to register with a general practitioner (sometimes in their area) and it is the GP who refers patients to specialist out- and inpatient services in hospitals. This gives GPs a strong gate-keeping function. The GP model is widespread among health systems in industrialized countries and this even applies to countries like Australia, New Zealand and the Netherlands, which are committed to individualism, as reflected in significant components of private funding. A possible explanation is that patient choice is expensive and therefore likely to be restricted, especially in times of cost containment. This can also account for the fact that in the USA one of the main characteristics of HMOs was to introduce a gate-keeping role for GPs, thus limiting the wide choices of specialists inherent in the traditional insurance system. As noted earlier, not surprisingly, this led to widespread condemnation of HMOs by US patients and doctors.

Recently the Australian National Health and Hospital Reform Commission proposed voluntary enrolment with a 'health care home' that can help coordinate, 'guide and navigate access to the right range of multidisciplinary health services' (2009: 6). In their comparison of seven countries, Schoen *et al.* (2007) found that already a very high proportion (88 per cent) of Australians reported that they had a doctor or GP who they regularly see. Under New Zealand arrangements, which unlike Australia provide incentives for patient enrolment, however, only 8.3 per cent of patients reported no affiliation with a single primary care provider (Jatrana and Crampton, 2009). Another multinational study reported that 69.8 per cent of UK patients but only 8 per cent of US patients had their regular physician for six years or more (McRae *et al.*, 2010).

The boundaries between different types of choice have become more blurred over recent years and it seems countries are moving towards each other (Thomson and Dixon, 2006). For example, Germany, with its long tradition for extensive choice, has introduced measures to limit choice, mainly to curb expenditure. From 2004, insurance funds have to offer their members the option of subscribing to a gate-keeper scheme in return for a bonus. Significantly, however, the scheme is voluntary, reflecting the strongly entrenched nature of choice. Countries which operate with a GP system seem to be going in the opposite direction, reflecting especially New Public Management reforms, which redefine patients as consumers in markets of regulated competition (for examples see the section below on 'Models of contracting health services'). For example, in Britain there is now patient choice in relation to elective care (Bevan and Ven, 2010; Boyle, 2011).

Welfare mixes in the provision of health care

Health systems allow for different levels of patient choice, reflecting the ways in which heath services are organized as well as specific decisions about the appropriate level of patient choice. This partly corresponds to the principles underpinning different types of health systems. The principles of equity, social solidarity and individual responsibility also inform the welfare mix in the provision of health care: that is, who the providers of health care are (see Box 3.4).

The differences in welfare mix apply primarily to hospitals, whereas the situation in ambulatory care is more uniform. In most countries, doctors working in ambulatory care are independent practitioners, who either practise privately or who are contracted to provide publicly funded medical services. Reflecting their independent status, doctors are typi-

Box 3.4 Welfare mix: mixed meanings and policies

As a *concept* 'welfare mix' refers to the diverse ways in which health services can be provided. Welfare mix is concerned with the division of labour between the public, private, voluntary and informal sector. Inasmuch as the provision of health care is always mixed to a greater or lesser extent, welfare mix is also a *descriptor* of how services are delivered in individual health systems. Finally, as a *political programme* welfare mix challenges the notion that public provision is always best (Evers and Svetlik, 1993). By some, welfare mix is seen to serve better the needs of increasingly diverse societies. Others argue that a more mixed provision of health services is more cost efficient. Different health systems typically have different welfare mixes. Public funding through taxes often accompanies public ownership, leading to a highly publicly integrated provision of health services. Social insurance combines social solidarity with a commitment to individualism/subsidiarity. Public and private providers tend to exist side-by-side, creating complex and less well-integrated structures of health provision. The same is often true for health systems that predominantly rely on private insurance. In both social and private insurance systems, the welfare mix in health care provision comes naturally, whereas in national health services the welfare mix has been closely associated with market-oriented reforms.

cally paid on a capitation or a fee-for-service basis (see Chapter 5 for details).

The provision of hospital care has traditionally been least mixed in national health services, where public hospitals provide the majority of beds and where private hospitals are few. In New Zealand, for example, there are 80 public hospital facilities, which operate under the direction of 21 community-focused and elected District Health Boards (DHBs), the regional administrative tier of the Department of Health (New Zealand Ministry of Health, 2008). Public hospitals derive their entire income from government funding agencies. A few private hospitals, primarily Southern Cross, provide acute health care services and costs are met by individuals or by private insurance. Significantly, only a few DHBs have contracted with private hospitals to provide services (see Box 3.5 for summary of recent changes in New Zealand).

As part of New Public Management reforms and their focus on the virtues of market mechanisms, however, the provision of health services has become more blurred in countries with national health services. For example, in Britain, health reforms since the late 1990s have set renewed focus on the private sector and aim to increase its role in the NHS. This includes independent treatment centres for specialist operations, private GP practices, the continuation of contracting out of ancillary services such as medical supplies, and the so-called Private Finance Initiative (Taylor-Gooby and Mitton, 2008). The initiative, which uses private money and expertise as part of funding public sector projects, has been

Box 3.5 New Zealand reforms of 2009

The New Zealand Government's 2009 Ministerial review of the health system re-stated a series of frequently voiced problems facing its health system. Widespread inefficiencies involved with 21 separate administrative systems (the DHBs) for such a small population, each responsible for planning and funding services locally that leads to routine duplication, lack of coordination and considerable interregional service inequities. The 81 Primary Health Organizations (PHOs) have perpetuated the problem, with many being too small or ineffective, and also meant both DHBs and PHOs are often planning independently for common populations. Furthermore, with devolution of funding structures, there has been no national mechanism for the bulk purchase of equipment and a lack of national coordination around issues such as information technology, payroll and human resources. The Minister of Health has directed the number of PHOs to be halved through mergers and many PHOs will be replaced by the government's planned Integrated Family Health Centres, which are intended to offer a wide range of medical and health services including day-stay surgery. Meanwhile, the first DHB merger was formalized in May 2010, with others likely to follow (Gauld, 2010).

extended to major hospital projects and there is now also a corresponding initiative in primary care. Building on these initiatives, the most recent reforms from 2012 introduce a system of centralized licensing of all providers based on universal criteria. This is envisaged to provide a springboard for including more private providers in the mainstream provision of the NHS and thereby to foster competition (Department of Health, 2012d).

Recent developments mean that countries with national health services are moving closer to the welfare mix that has traditionally existed in social insurance systems. In the Netherlands, over 90 per cent of hospitals are private, non-profit organizations (Exter *et al.*, 2004). Historically, this has allowed accommodating traditional divisions of Dutch society into distinct religious and political segments, precisely by giving private initiative a prominent role in the delivery of health services (Maarse, 1997: 136). Similarly, in Germany the high degree of welfare mix reflects the notion of subsidiarity, whereby public provision is a matter of last resort and the health system typically built on existing provision structures, rather than completely overhauling them (Bäringhausen and Sauerborn, 2003).

Market-based health systems are also characterized by high levels of welfare mixes and, as compared to social insurance systems, private for-profit hospitals play a more prominent role. For instance, in the USA there are 5,708 registered hospitals. Of these, 213 are federal government hospitals and 1,111 state and local government hospitals compared to 2,913 private non-profit community hospitals and 873 for-profit hospitals (American Hospital Association, 2009).

Models of contracting health services

Health systems are about funding and provision, and the two can be linked in different ways. In national health services, funding and provision have traditionally been integrated in public hands. In social insurance systems, by contrast, funding and provision are separate and contracts provide the key link between payers and providers. Private insurance systems operate in a similar way, although contracts are not subject to direct public regulation. The last two decades, however, have seen intriguing changes in many countries. National health services have experimented with the public contract model, often in an attempt to introduce market-style dynamics into their health service. Likewise, competition has been an important element of reform in social insurance systems, altering the nature of the more established public contract model. The public contract model, with its separation between public funding bodies and providers who relate to each other through contracts, is now the dominant model of organizing and reforming health services (OECD, 1992). Interesting variations exist in relation to the degree of government control of the contract process (Verspohl, 2012). For social insurance systems, Hassenteufel *et al.* (2010) suggest that the translation of quasi-market mechanisms into national contexts has been associated with the reassertion of the regulatory authority of governments; this reflects the work of a small group of 'programmatic actors' in government ministries.

Among the national health services, Britain has gone furthest with the implementation of a public contract model (Boyle, 2011). Primary Care Trusts are the purchasers of health care. They are corporate bodies that operate under the general direction of a chairperson appointed by the Secretary of State and receive funds from the Department of Health. In contrast to insurance funds, Primary Care Trusts enjoy less autonomy as they are in effect 'creatures of statute' (Paton, 1997: 23). The same applies to hospitals, which are non-profit trusts within the NHS. Their room for manoeuvre has been further curtailed by an extensive system of national priorities and tight performance management (Baggott, 2004). An exception is the so-called 'foundation hospitals' introduced in 2002, which enjoy greater autonomy in relation to retaining surpluses and recruiting their own staff. Primary Care Trusts negotiate and complete service agreements with other providers, but the contracts are not legally enforceable. Compared to insurance funds, the role of Primary Care Trusts goes beyond paying for services since they, together with health authorities, are responsible for ensuring that the heath needs of the population are met.

The public contract model was introduced in the early 1990s under the banner of an 'internal market', but has subsequently evolved into a system of managed competition with strong elements of planning and regulation (Harrison, 2004). Policy developments under New Labour have been ambivalent. Initially, the government emphasized collaboration, whereas recent years have been characterized by a return to stronger elements of competition, but based on quality rather than price (Paton, 2007). This has gone hand-in-hand with an emphasis on patient choice, which is now extended to all providers (Allen and Hommel, 2006) and the development of greater plurality of provision (including private provision, see above) coupled with payment by results, based on a national tariff for so-called Health Resource Groups (Hunter, 2008). The public contract model is to change yet again, following a major health reform by the coalition government in 2012, whereby commissioning becomes the responsibility of smaller, GP-based Clinical Commissioning Groups (Department of Health, 2012a; Dixon, 2012). At the same time, the oversight of commissioning activities becomes more centralized; this is mostly the responsibility of one regulatory agency at the national level, while the strategic health authorities at the regional level are abolished. On the provider side, all hospitals will be turned into foundation trusts and there will be a centralized system of licensing all providers that is likely to lead to the incorporation of more private providers into the mainstream provision of the NHS.

Developments over the last decades also indicate that the introduction of the public contract model is strongly filtered by country-specific contexts. For instance, in Sweden as an example of a national health service the purchaser–provider split was never introduced comprehensively, clearly reflecting a strong degree of decentralization. County councils are responsible for the funding and provision of health care and are also free to develop their own management systems (Anell *et al.*, 2012). In 1994, for example, only 14 out of 26 county councils had experimented with different models of the purchaser–provider split, a decision that reflected local traditions (Anell and Svarvar, 1998 710). There are similar variations in relation to the extent of patient choice, which is embedded in soft law regulations by the national government (Anell, 2010; Frederiksson and Winblad, 2008). Also, the emerging market was very different from that in Britain and New Zealand; in Sweden competition was combined with patient choice, thus limiting the extent to which purchasers could selectively contract with providers (Jacobs, 1998: 12f.). Saltman (1998) suggests that this reflects a strong commitment to equity and quality compared to Britain, for example. Subsequently, there has been a move away from the competition-based model and towards a model combining more long-term contracts with regionally-based cooperation (Harrison, 2004; Harrison and Calltrop, 2000). This occurred against the background of problems with the implementation of the previous reforms, changing governing coalitions and new policy priorities that were less well served by market mechanisms.

A typical example of the inclusion of market elements in the social insurance variant of the public contract model is the Netherlands (Schäfer *et al.*, 2010). Following a major health reform in 2006, its social health insurance is administered by private, non-profit and for-profit insurance funds, which operate under public law. The insurance funds can choose which providers (i.e., hospitals and doctors working in ambulatory care) they contract with, although the government defines the statutory standard care package. At the same time, insurance funds have been reluctant to use selective contracting, which among others reflects concerns by patients that 'selected providers' are indeed committed to providing the best possible care for patients (Boonen and Schut, 2011). The Statutory Health Insurance Board also has important supervisory functions, especially concerning the management of the statutory standard care package, as well as in relation to payments from the risk equal-

1499

YBP Library Services

BLANK, ROBERT H.

COMPARATIVE HEALTH POLICY.

4TH ED. Paper 373 P.
BASINGSTOKE: PALGRAVE MACMILLAN, 2014

AUTH: UNIVERSITY OF CANTERBURY. COMPARATIVE
SURVEY OF VARIOUS DEVELOPED COUNTRIES.

ISBN 1137023562 **Library PO#** FIRM ORDERS

			List	41.00 USD
8395 NATIONAL UNIVERSITY LIBRAR			**Disc**	5.0%
App. Date 10/15/14	SHHS	8214-08	**Net**	38.95 USD

SUBJ: MEDICAL POLICY--CROSS-CULTURAL STUDIES.

CLASS RA394 DEWEY# 362.1 LEVEL ADV-AC

YBP Library Services

BLANK, ROBERT H.

COMPARATIVE HEALTH POLICY.

4TH ED. Paper 373 P.
BASINGSTOKE: PALGRAVE MACMILLAN, 2014

AUTH: UNIVERSITY OF CANTERBURY. COMPARATIVE
SURVEY OF VARIOUS DEVELOPED COUNTRIES.

ISBN 1137023562 **Library PO#** FIRM ORDERS

			List	41.00 USD
8395 NATIONAL UNIVERSITY LIBRAR			**Disc**	5.0%
App. Date 10/15/14	SHHS	8214-08	**Net**	38.95 USD

SUBJ: MEDICAL POLICY--CROSS-CULTURAL STUDIES.

CLASS RA394 DEWEY# 362.1 LEVEL ADV-AC

ization fund. In short, there is some competition between providers and this is complemented by competition among purchasers, since patients have free choice of insurance funds and complementary health coverage. However, consumer choice is embedded in a delicate balance with government intervention (Maarse and Meulen, 2006). Further, consumer choice remains de facto limited. Whereas one fifth of the population switched insurance funds immediately after the introduction of the reform, this figure has stabilized around about 5 per cent in subsequent years (Brabers *et al.*, 2012). Also, the use of choice seems to be mainly motivated by cost rather than quality. In addition, the number of insurance funds has decreased following the reform (Okma and de Roo, 2009).

In other countries with social insurance systems, the public contract model has retained its original form. For example, in Japan the public contract model has remained relatively state-centred. All providers, public or private, are contracted under the uniform fee system, which the government's Central Social Medical Care Council negotiates with representatives of providers, payers and public interest groups (Tatara and Okamoto, 2009). Under this tightly controlled reimbursement system, where all billing is centralized and no extra billing is allowed, Japan has been relatively successful in maintaining control over costs without instituting the market-based reforms seen in other systems. The communitarian-oriented culture of acceptance in Japan and the aversion to intensive medical intervention has certainly helped in this regard. Similarly, in Taiwan the Bureau of the National Health Institute (BNHI) is the sole purchaser of health care services and has established strict payment schemes for services for all contracted providers (Okma *et al.*, 2010).

Health governance between centre and locality

As we have seen, health systems are about the funding and provision of health care. Health systems are funded from a variety of sources that result in different levels of public control. Health systems consist of a range of services that are delivered by different providers to which patients have different levels of access. The diverse ways in which funding and provision are organized lead not only to different policies and pressures for reform, but also to different politics, different relationships between central and local government, among government and provider organizations/payers, and among payers and providers themselves.

Governance, for its part, does include the regulation of areas such as medical practice and pharmaceuticals, but it is broader than that. It is also concerned with modes of coordinating health systems and their multiple actors (Freeman, 2000). Governance is underpinned by two sets of tensions: between public and private (i.e., between the state and the market); and between centre and locality. Government looms large in most health systems and governance can be thought of as government authority/capacity. Government authority/capacity is reflected in the degree of institutional integration in health systems: that is, in the power of the national government (executive integration), in the extent of government authority over private interests such as doctors, hospitals and insurers (public integration), and in the extent to which policy-making authority is concentrated at national rather than regional or local levels (central integration) (see Freeman, 2000). Executive and public integration are discussed in the next section. This section focuses on central integration – the relationship among the different levels of governance.

Some health systems are more decentralized than others, reflecting the respective political systems in which they are embedded. However, over the last two decades many health systems have attempted to decentralize governance. This indicates convergence, but offers equally strong indications of persistent differences, not least in terms of dissimilar types of decentralization. Here, Saltman and Bankauskaite (2006) distinguish between fiscal, administrative and political decentralization. Illustrations of variations in the type of decentralization can be seen in the health systems in Sweden and Britain. In both countries, health care is publicly funded and provided, resulting in health systems that are characterized by a high degree of public integration and control. At the same time, important differences exist in relation to the levels of governance.

In Sweden, responsibility for funding and provision rests with the county councils, leading to decentralized health governance. Sweden has a strong tradition of sub-central government and, importantly, a type of sub-central government that defines itself by democratic decision making (Håkansson and Nordling, 1997: 194). In addition, health reforms since the 1950s have systematically decentralized responsibility for health care to the regional level of counties (Saltman and Bergman, 2005). This contrasts with Britain where the publicly funded and provided health service is embedded in a highly centralized political system. The centrality of central government is compounded by a tradition that sees local government first and foremost as a provider of services. Not surprisingly, the NHS has been described as a 'command and control system' (Moran, 1999).

The differences in the degree of central integration can also help to explain differences in moves towards decentralization. In Britain, administrative decentralization is paramount and occurred as part of the introduction of a quasi-market in health care that was inspired by the new public management paradigm. (The present analysis focuses on developments in England and therefore the political decentralization following devolution in Scotland and Wales is of less interest.) The actors at local level are Primary Care Trusts and hospital trusts and, at regional level, health authorities which are not only creatures of central government, but also continue to operate within a highly hierarchical system of health governance. Indeed, central control has increased following the introduction of the internal market and most prominently the management of performance has become tighter as part of a more explicit 'quality turn' (Harrison, 2004). Not surprisingly, the autonomy of trusts and health authorities is confined to managerial responsibility.

The complex division of labour among different levels of governance has highlighted problems of accountability (Iliffe and Munro, 2000: 322). However, the relative balance between central and local levels is not static as developments under the previous New Labour government illustrate. Under the heading of 'new localism', primary care trusts had extensive responsibilities and received over 85 per cent of the NHS budget (Klein, 2006). Hospitals were able to apply for foundation status which gave them greater autonomy, including to raise funds, and patients had free choice of provider (Hunter, 2008; Peckham *et al.*, 2008). Similarly, the health reforms introduced by the coalition government in 2012 have several elements of decentralization (Department of Health, 2012a, b, c): the new Clinical Commissioning Groups are smaller than Primary Care Trusts and enjoy greater autonomy; the same applies to hospitals which are to become foundation trusts. Yet both commissioners and providers are to be held accountable at the national level by regulatory agencies. Taken together this certainly makes for a complex interplay between centralization and decentralization (Peckham *et al.*, 2008). Indeed, Klein (2010) suggests that the current dynamics within centre–periphery relations reflect salient tensions inherent in the NHS since its foundation, namely between equity and efficiency on the one hand and democracy on the other.

The case of Britain contrasts with Sweden, where political decentralization occurred in the early 1980s when county councils were given complete control over funding and delivery of services (Anell *et al.*, 2012). Since the beginning of the 1990s this has been complemented by additional measures as part of moves to deregulate and privatize the health system (Frederiksson and Winblad, 2008). Here, decentralization was a genuine devolution of power that built on traditions of sub-central government, and not simply a refocusing of central control as in the case of Britain. This further strengthened the directly democratic character of managerial decision making (Saltman, 1998: 164). However, there are limits to sub-central autonomy and the central level has become increasingly involved. At policy level, specific action programmes have resulted in more direct intervention in service delivery and at the level of supervision the National Board of Welfare now has more extensive powers to regulate provider organizations, based on national priorities and quality standards (Bejerot and Hasselbladh, 2011; Saltman and Bergman, 2005).

Funding from social insurance results in institutional complexity and often limits the degree of central integration of health systems. For example, in Germany a statutory, joint self-administration of insurance funds and providers is at the centre of health governance and this form of corporatism operates at different levels. At the local level, providers and insurance funds relate to each other through contracts, which specify the services to be provided and the prices to be paid, including the financing mechanisms. However, local contracts are embedded in a complex system of framework agreements at state and federal level (again between providers and insurance funds) and these, in turn, are embedded in federal legislation, the Social Code Book. Over recent years, these types of collective contracts have been complemented by specific contracts with individual providers, such as treatment centres comprised of ambulatory care specialists. Here, the insurance funds contract directly with providers without the involvement of the providers' collective organization. This development is part of the introduction of competitive elements in the health system and Gerlinger (2010) suggests that we are thus seeing a liberalization of contract law.

Corporatism adds further institutional complexity. Corporatism is a particular approach to policy making and has several aspects to it (Schwartz and Busse, 1997: 104). In the health care context, corporatism hands over certain powers of the state to corporatist self-governing institutions, including insurance funds and provider organizations. As corporatist institutions, they have mandatory membership and enjoy the right to raise their own financial resources as well as the right to negotiate and sign contracts with other corporatist institutions. In Germany, institutional complexity is underpinned by corporatism as a form of procedural subsidiarity and is compounded by federalism, which taken together results in decentralized health governance, that in many ways also limits the capacity for radical policy change (Altenstetter and Busse, 2005). Nevertheless, corporatism does not stand still (Gerlinger, 2010; Rothgang *et al.*, 2010). The introduction of competition is associated with the expansion of state intervention, including wide-ranging and detailed procedural management, an increasingly restrictive financial framework and tighter framework of statutory regulations. Interestingly, this is coupled with the strengthening of corporatism at the national level, where the powers of the Central Joint Committee have been considerably extended.

However, decentralized health governance can coexist with strong elements of centralism, as the Netherlands and Japan illustrate. In the

Netherlands, the central government enjoys important powers in relation to the regulation of competition, including setting the income-dependent insurance contribution rate, the management of payments from the equalization fund and the definition of the basic health insurance package (Schäfer *et al.*, 2010). Crucially, corporatism is also confined to the national level (Lieverdink and Made, 1997: 132). This more centralized form of corporatism is underpinned by a decentralized, yet unitary, political system, where municipalities and provinces often act as implementation agencies for national policy programmes. Similarly, Japan combines central government control with strong elements of decentralization. Health governance is highly decentralized across 47 regional prefectures and thousands of municipalities, and provides a mixture of delivery levels reflecting a basic principle underlying national policies (Tatara and Okamoto, 2009). Despite this, the central government maintains strong control over all aspects of health care through the rigid and centrally controlled fee structure.

Finally, levels of decentralization are not necessarily universal across the entire health system, but can also vary between different sub-systems. In Australia control over health funding is more highly centralized than control over provision. Over the past two decades, Australia has moved to centralize effective funding control through Medicare (Duckett, 2004b; Rix *et al.*, 2005) and this has reduced substantially the proportion of funding derived from private sources. Moreover, there has been a 'strong centralising tendency' regarding funding within each of the Australian States and Territories in recent years (Dwyer, 2004). This contrasts with Australia's strong tradition of decentralization and individual state autonomy in the provision of health care services that has included a robust and powerful private sector.

The authority of governments in health policy

Looking at the roles of centre and locality in health governance provides a powerful indication of the complexity of health systems and the importance of political contexts for shaping health systems. Ultimately, health governance always happens at different levels: health systems as *systems* require direction from the centre while the provision of health care inevitably involves localities. However, the relative importance of different levels varies among health systems as well as among different sub-systems within the same health system. The variation among and within systems reflects how health care is provided as well as specific political contexts. For example, health governance is highly centralized in Britain, whereas it is more decentralized in the USA. This reflects the fact that the British central government is at the centre of the public funding and provision of health care, whereas in the USA mixed funding and provision naturally decentralizes governance. The differences between the two countries also point to the importance of political contexts. As the comparison with Sweden shows, however, public funding and provision alone do not make for centralized governance, but a unitary, centralized political system plays an important role. Similarly, decentralized health governance in the USA is underpinned by federalism. Differences among systems coexist with differences within the same health system. Japan and the Netherlands are a case in point: both countries combine centralized governance of funding with decentralized governance of provision.

Executive and public integration provide further evidence of the complexity of health systems. The power of national governments and the power of governments over private interests are closely related and offer key indications of the relative authority of governments in health policy. This issue has been implicit throughout the chapter when discussing the sub-systems of funding and provision. The basic assumption is that public funding and provision result in public control – that is, government authority – because the government is the principal public actor in health policy. Public control of funding can be measured in terms of the extent of public funding, the relative importance of taxes and social security as different types of public funding, and the power of government to control funding. Public control of provision can be measured in terms of the share of public provision of health care. On this basis, Figure 3.2 characterizes the health systems in different countries.

The summary of the modes of governance and the extent of government authority in different countries demonstrates the sheer diversity of

		Public Control of Provision		
		High	**Middle**	**Low**
Public Control of Funding	**High**	Britain Sweden New Zealand		Japan Netherlands Taiwan
	Middle	Australia	Germany	
	Low	Singapore		USA

Figure 3.2 *Public control of funding and provision of health care*

health systems. Health systems are all confronted with pressures from ageing populations, advances in medical technology and periodic economic down turns, and these pressures often manifest themselves in pressures to control and contain costs. However, the institutional contexts of health systems and the capacity of governments to address these pressures continue to vary considerably among countries. For example, public control of funding and provision is high in Britain and Sweden, whereas it is low in the USA.

Significantly, the picture is more complex than the typology of health systems introduced in Chapter 1 would suggest. The typology assumes that certain models of funding are directly associated with certain models of provision to the extent that high public control of funding goes hand in hand with high public control of provision and vice versa. This is true for health systems in some countries such as Britain, Sweden, Germany and the USA, which are closest to the ideal types of national health service, social insurance system and private insurance system, respectively. In the health systems of the remaining countries, government authority differs between the sub-systems of funding and provision. For example, Japan, the Netherlands and Taiwan combine relatively strong (central) public control over funding with relatively low public control over provision, reflecting the predominance of non-public providers. This makes government authority over funding comparable to Britain and Sweden, but in relation to provision government authority is closer to the USA.

Differences and similarities are specific to individual sub-systems of health care and as such point to the importance of country-specific political contexts. Examples of country-specific political contexts include the semi-federal political system in the Netherlands that often helps to concentrate authority in the hands of central government and the legacy of a private insurance system combined with federalism in Australia that weakens government authority over funding to some extent. However, acknowledging the uniqueness of individual health systems does not mean abandoning cross-country comparisons; instead, it requires removing the blinders of ideal types of health systems and exploring what Moran (1999) calls the 'political embeddedness' of health systems. Chapter 4 continues this quest by examining the implications of these health system characteristics for the actual allocation of health care resources in these countries.

Chapter 4

Setting Priorities and Allocating Resources

Chapter 3 demonstrated that health systems display variation in the sub-systems of funding, provision and governance that impact on health policy and health care. It also revealed that these sub-systems are dynamic and that many of them have undergone significant changes in recent decades. In order to better understand their impact on health care, it is important to go beneath the institutional and structural dimensions and examine the goals, objectives and priorities of each health system. This chapter also examines the criteria that health care systems use to allocate medical resources and the ramifications of these policies for their respective populations.

The goals of health policy

A successful policy is founded on goals and objectives that should be clarified early in the policy-making process. Two levels of goals are discernible. The first are broad stated goals that often function symbolically and are more in the realm of political rhetoric than reality. The second are specific programmatic goals that frame a particular policy. Both are critical in evaluating the success or failure of a policy. Although some goals can be specified and appraised with accuracy, others are more amorphous; generally, the broader the goal, the more difficult it is to measure. Analysis becomes even more problematic when the goals themselves conflict, when they are defined differently by the various participants, or when they shift over time. In spite of these problems, it is critical to examine the stated goals of health policy.

Ideally, a successful health policy in a democracy would provide high quality services for all citizens on an equal basis. Moreover, it would be an efficient system with little waste and duplication and high levels of performance in all sectors. In addition to the goals of universal access, quality and efficiency, other objectives might include maximizing the choice of patients, ensuring high accountability of health care personnel and guaranteeing rapid diffusion of the newest medical technologies. As will be discussed in Chapter 7, goals might vary as to whether the health

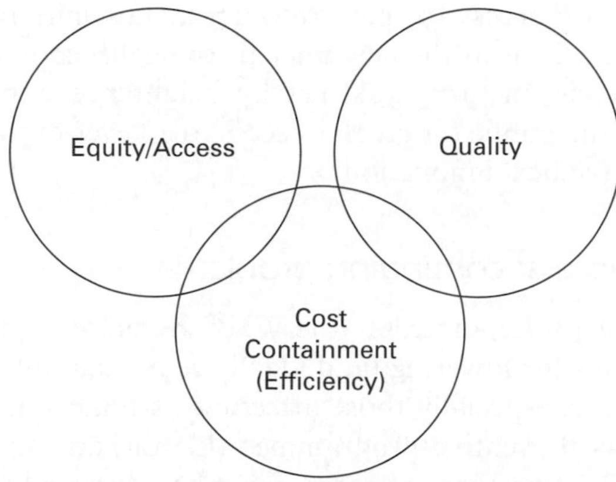

Figure 4.1 *Competing goals of health care*

of the population or the health of individual patients is foremost. Although, as discussed below, the goals of health care are countless, Figure 4.1 displays the three goals at the centre of health policy.

For several decades following World War II, the predominant goals of health policy initiatives in all developed nations were *equity* or *access* and *quality* of health care. Even though the actual policies varied significantly, the goals of access and quality shaped health care priorities. In large part, the disparity among countries could be explained by how much emphasis each nation put on subsidiary competing goals of freedom of choice for consumers, autonomy of health care providers and insurers and assorted notions of common good or solidarity. The actual mix of these policy goals has been shaped by the distinctions in national cultures, politics and institutional structures discussed in Chapter 2. In the USA, for instance, with the strong emphasis put on individual freedom by both patients and the health care community, universal access and equity were never given the prominence they enjoyed in other countries. In contrast, New Zealand and the UK, with their stronger collectivist roots and tradition of common good, enthusiastically embraced comprehensive national health services to deliver on the central goals of universal access and free care at the point of service.

Despite variation regarding universal coverage, health policy in all developed nations in the post-war period placed priority on ensuring all citizens had access to an expanding array of medical interventions. New hospitals were built and many beds were added to existing structures, significantly expanded investments were made in medical education and biomedical research, the supply of medical personnel was increased and the boundaries of medicine extended by the emergence of many new medical specialities. Furthermore, new institutional mechanisms were initiated to ensure access to these resources, thus initiating the era of technological medicine as the new nucleus of health care. This post-war boom of medicine, in turn, was met by heightened expectations and demands from the public for greater access to an ever-expanding arsenal of more costly medical innovations.

Equity and access: continuing problems

In its World Health Report 2000, the WHO reiterates equity as a pressing goal and calls for lowering (and ideally removing) all existing barriers to health care, especially those affecting its financing and access to care, as well as preventive programmes (Costa-Font and Hernández-Quevedo, 2012). Two types of access must be addressed by health policies: financial access and physical or geographical access. Financial access can be met by restructuring health care funding and provision so as to provide universal access to at least a minimal level of health care for all citizens based on need. This entails either creating systems of direct public financing and provision of services or governmental regulation and coordination of private sickness funds with guaranteed coverage for those patients who fall through the gaps in the private system (Box 4.1). Some, such as Germany and the Netherlands, chose to strengthen health systems that pre-dated World War II while others, such as the UK and Sweden, set up new systems to meet these goals. Except for the USA, which chose not to establish a national system, all countries examined here have been largely successful in achieving universal levels of access, despite divergence in the means used to achieve that goal.

Until now, the USA is the only democracy that has not come close to achieving universal access. Estimates of the uninsured range from 40 to 50 million persons, with additional millions underinsured. After a year-long, contentious battle over health reform, the Patient Protection and

Box 4.1 What are equity and access?

According to Mooney (2009), there is an obsession with quantification in economics with the result that when analysing equity, in practice 'use' has been substituted for 'access'. The problem of defining access has, thereby, been circumvented. This has taken the pressure off trying to research access per se. It must be remembered that what is meant by equity and access are partly culturally determined. The continued efforts of health economists to treat equity as some universal construct are misplaced. The lack of effort to look at equity more broadly than health care equity is troubling. To be pursued in practice, equity in both health and health care need a shift in resources, but this will be opposed by those who exercise power over decision making in health care and in society more generally.

Affordable Care Act (ACA) was signed into law by President Obama on 23 March 2010, with the principal goal of addressing this longstanding deficiency in equity (Jost, 2011; Kersh, 2011; Jacobs, 2011; Gruber, 2011). This Act, along with the Healthcare and Education Reconciliation Act of 2010 (signed into law on 30 March), constituted the health care overhaul of 2010.

At its core, the ACA represents an ambitious attempt to provide some measure of equity in what has become the most unequal health care system in the developed world. Although the Act will not be fully implemented until 2014, the ACA frontloaded some of what were thought to be the more popular aspects. As illustrated in Box 4.2, the changes initiated by the ACA are significant, although they fall well short of the transformation originally envisioned by those who favoured a 'public option' to compete with private insurers (Hoffman, 2010). Moreover, this 'patchwork' reform faces severe challenges before it is fully implemented (Marmor and Oberlander, 2011). Most controversial has been the individual mandate that requires all Americans to carry health insurance by 2014. In a highly divisive case, the US Supreme Court upheld the mandate as constitutional, much to the dismay of critics (*National Federation of Independent Business v. Sebelius*, 567 U.S (2012)).

Box 4.2 Key provisions of Affordable Care Act of 2010

- Implements guaranteed issue and community rating nationally so that insurers must offer the same premium to all applicants of the same age, sex and geographical location regardless of pre-existing conditions.
- Introduces minimum standards for health insurance policies and removes all annual and lifetime coverage caps.
- Mandates that some health care insurance benefits will be 'essential' coverage for which there will be no co-payments.
- Requires all non-exempt individuals to purchase health insurance or pay a fine to broaden the insurance pool and deter healthy individuals from buying insurance only after they become ill.
- Expands Medicaid eligibility across all states to include all individuals and families with incomes up to 133% of the poverty level.
- Provides subsidies on a sliding scale for low income persons and families above the Medicaid level and up to 400% of the poverty level if they purchase insurance via an exchange.
- Provides improved benefits for Medicare prescription drug coverage.
- Creates health insurance exchanges in each state to offer a marketplace where individuals and small businesses can compare policies and premiums and buy insurance.
- Fines companies that employ 50 or more people that do not offer health insurance if the government has to subsidize an employee's healthcare.

Box 4.3 Undocumented and uninsured in the USA

The increase in undocumented immigration between 1999 and 2007 contributed to an increase in the number of uninsured people in the USA. During this period, the number increased from 8.5 million to 11.8 million, leading to an estimated additional 1.8 million uninsured (Zuckerman *et al.*, 2011). These uninsured and undocumented immigrants were estimated to represent 27 per cent of the overall increase of 6.9 million uninsured people during this period. They accounted for one in seven of the uninsured in 2007, up from one in eight in 1999. These undocumented immigrants will not be eligible for public insurance or any type of private coverage obtained through exchanges under the ACA. Unless other policy actions are taken to provide for their coverage, or their immigration status is changed, they will eventually constitute a bigger percentage of the uninsured population (Zuckerman *et al.*, 2011). As a possible policy response to this, Cortez (2011) argues that cross-border health insurance plans that utilize foreign medical providers can be much less expensive than traditional, domestic-only plans and offer a feasible alternative for the residually uninsured. Moreover, they are likely to appeal to immigrants and others that are neither eligible for public plans nor able to afford private ones.

Although the ACA does offer benefits for many poorer Americans and is predicted to reduce the number of uninsured by some 15 million (but see Box 4.3), among the biggest winners are the pharmaceutical companies and the private insurance industry. Early in the process, the President made a secret deal with the drug companies (Light, 2011). In exchange for their active support, they were assured the reforms would not allow wholesale price negotiations or unauthorized importation of drugs that could significantly reduce corporate revenues. Likewise, in order to garner support of the insurance companies, the increased costs of covering people with pre-existing conditions, the imposition of minimal standards and the removal of coverage caps was offset by the promise of the mandated infusion in 2014 of tens of millions of younger, healthier individuals into the private insurance pool. Moreover, the Act does not give the federal government much regulatory power to prevent premium increases by insurance companies (Light, 2011; Mariner, 2010).

Despite assurances from the President that persons with insurance would not lose benefits or pay higher premiums, initial public support for reform quickly turned to opposition. By early 2011, in part driven by large increases in insurance premiums that year, public opinion polls found disapproval ratings between 50 and 70 per cent, although those calling for its repeal moderated somewhat after the 2012 election (Kludt, 2012). Moreover, a survey of big employers found that overall they expected their health care costs to escalate and planned to share the burden with employees via higher premiums and out-of-pocket limits (Hobson, 2011). Many workers, therefore, face not only higher premiums but also increased co-insurance and higher deductibles, and possible new surcharges (Andrews, 2010). One unanticipated consequence of the Act is that many companies began reviewing the costs of continuing to provide employee health care benefits and are considering paying the fine and dropping coverage because they feel it hurts them competitively. As a result, it is estimated that there could be a net 10 per cent reduction in access to employer-sponsored health benefits affecting potentially 10 million people (Tully, 2010). Many firms, both large and small, see the availability of coverage to employees through exchanges as giving them the opportunity to discontinue health benefits without leaving their employees unprotected as they had been before ACA. Moreover, there are strong forces driving employers to hire part-time or individual contractor workforces to avoid the escalating costs of providing health care benefits.

Although, unlike the USA, other countries have universal coverage, they too face a problem of equity of access related to the presence of a tiered system in which persons with ample resources obtain services that are either unavailable or constrained in the public system. For instance, New Zealand has a two-tier health system with elective surgery provided by both publicly funded state hospitals and by private hospitals. According to Derrett *et al.* (2009), despite the introduction of a prioritization system aimed at increased equity and fairness, the provision of elective surgery remains inequitable. Moreover, the argument that private provision for better off patients reduces the burden on the public system, thus allowing better access for the poor, has not been supported by the New Zealand case.

Ironically, there is greater public awareness of these discrepancies in the countries with national health services that have made the strongest claims for financial equity. For instance, while universality is at the centre of the British NHS, often it is up to health authorities to decide which services to fund, thus opening the way to local variation, also referred to as the 'postcode lottery'. Waiting lists also limit access to elective surgery and buttress the tiered system. An indication of the highly political nature of the issue is that one of the key pledges the Labour Party made before coming into office in 1997 was to reduce waiting lists. Since then the government added targets for waiting times for numerous specific treatments (Baggott, 2004: 197ff) some of which were removed by the incoming government.

The second type of inequity became especially problematic as health care came to be increasingly specialized and capital intensive. Geographical inequities in health care, although initially reduced by regional reallocation schemes, remain challenging. Isolated, rural communities are consistently undersupplied in terms of skilled medical personnel and facilities in health systems as diverse as New Zealand and Taiwan. In many countries, the disproportionate number of physicians located in urban centres is promoted by the insufficient number of patients in many rural areas needed to justify huge technological investment. Simply put, health professionals go where the patients are, resulting in a concentration of health care facilities in core urban populations and significant inequities in access to specialized care (Stukel *et al.*, 2005). Moreover, Semansky *et al.* (2012) argue that, historically, policy makers have designed reforms with more populous urban areas in mind and have not adequately considered rural contexts that differ from urban regions in terms of population density and geographical and topographical barriers that can hinder access to services.

Although most countries have created incentives to attempt to correct geographical imbalances of physicians, financial inducements and other policies have not resolved the problem (this is discussed in more detail in Chapter 5). For instance, Germany has one of the highest numbers of doctors (see Table 5.1) but they tend to be concentrated in urban areas. In 1993 the freedom to set up practice anywhere was replaced by manpower planning based on community needs, and the number of additional doctors per speciality and region was limited. Although the main aim of this policy was to limit the absolute number of doctors, one of its side effects was to make rural regions more attractive to new doctors (Burau, 2001). More recently, the regulation of the number of doctors in ambulatory care has become less standardized. Instead it is up to regional associations of insurance fund doctors to fine tune supply and geographical distribution of doctors working in ambulatory care (Ozegowski and Sundmacher, 2012).

Despite the overall success of the Taiwan NHI, Kreng and Yang (2011) conclude that a disproportionate amount of health care resources are allocated in North Taiwan, resulting in geographical disparity due to unbalanced allocation. Furthermore, large-scale hospitals are congregated in metropolitan regions, thus limiting access to health care services for patients in rural areas. Not surprisingly, individuals residing in less urbanized areas are less likely to use outpatient services compared to those residing in highly urbanized areas (Lin *et al.*, 2011).

An important barrier to establishing physical equity is the fact that the delivery of health care services to rural areas is significantly more expensive on a per-case basis, in part because of the high cost of capital equipment needed to supply state of the art medical care. As a result, many specialized services can be provided efficiently only in urban regional centres with a critical mass of population. This problem is especially acute in Australia, New Zealand, Sweden and the USA, where a significant minority of the population live in remote areas. Even when patients from isolated geographical locations have equal financial access to the same level of medicine as their urban brethren, travel costs, relocation costs and costs in wasted time produce substantial inequities in effective access. Only in the highly concentrated population of Singapore is this not a problem.

Responsiveness has been identified as one of the intrinsic aspects of equity in health care systems. Robone *et al.* (2011) found that responsiveness is positively associated with health care expenditures per capita and educational development and negatively associated with overall public sector spending. From a policy perspective, improvements in responsiveness may require higher spending levels and the expansion of non-public sector provision, perhaps in the form of increased patient choice. A related equity issue is the increased global market for patients in the form of medical tourism (Cortez, 2008b). For example, more than 374,000 foreign patients sought treatment in Singapore in 2005, four out of five in private clinics and hospitals (Okma *et al.*, 2010). Moreover, growth in the number of foreign patients has been averaging 20 per cent annually because of the stepped-up efforts by Singapore Medicine, a government/industry partnership established in 2003 to turn Singapore into a leading medical hub. Pocock and Phua (2011), however, contend that the rise of medical tourism in Southeast Asia is problematic and raises concerns about its potential impact on health systems, namely the exacerbation of existing inequitable resource distribution between the public and private sectors. They argue that unless properly managed and regulated, the financial benefits of medical tourism for health systems may come at the expense of access to, and use of, health services by local consumers.

Quality care: what is it?

The goal of high quality health care, a hallmark of the 1950s and 1960s, has also proved challenging. The main difficulty in defining 'quality' is that we lack an objective means of measuring what 'quality' health care is (Steinberg and Luce, 2005). International comparisons seldom address this factor because it is much easier to compare cost figures, usage figures and other readily quantifiable factors, although in 2001 the OECD Health Care Quality Indicator (HCQI) Project was initiated to collect internationally comparable data reflecting the health outcomes and health improvements attributable to medical care delivered in OECD countries (see Kelly and Hurst, 2006). The Project goal is to track health care quality by developing a set of indicators to provide international benchmarks of quality and give national policy makers an opportunity to compare the performance of their health care delivery systems against a peer group. Moreover, the Commonwealth Fund, in developing a set of criteria for evaluating health care systems, defines high quality by an inclusive range of indicators such as provision of preventive care services, management of chronic diseases, care coordination, patient-centred care, low instance of medical errors and low preventable death rates (2009).

Even within individual countries, however, quality is rarely monitored systematically because there is little agreement on what criteria should be used. Unfortunately, quality is often equated with the latest diagnostic technologies and with specialist services. This emphasis is deceptive because it assumes that quality can be measured simply by counting the number of diagnostic machines, medical specialists and intensive medical interventions (see McClellan and Kessler, 1999). Quality as defined by technology is also of dubious value when compared to health outcomes (see Box 4.4). Moreover, when quality is defined this way it is likely to clash with the goal of access, which by necessity requires limitations on what levels of care are provided. While the goal of universal access presupposes some minimal level of care for persons in need, it cannot sustain unlimited amounts of resources expended on high-technology interventions for the few. Despite these dilemmas, quality, along with equity, was the most articulated goal of health policy until the mid- to late 1970s and remains a critical objective.

Box 4.4 Does more high-technology medicine improve health outcomes?

Findings from numerous studies confirm that the US health care system makes more extensive use of high technology than other countries. For instance, a study comparing care for heart attack patients in 17 countries showed that, while treatment in all countries has become more intensive, the USA has a pattern of early adoption and fast diffusion of new technologies. By contrast, other countries showed either a late start/fast growth pattern of technological diffusion (Australia and Belgium) or a late start/slow growth pattern (the UK and Scandinavian countries). The patterns of diffusion for new, very high-cost drugs were similar to those for intensive procedures (Docteur *et al.*, 2003: 23). Despite this pattern, however, the USA consistently rates below the top 20 nations in health outcomes. One study found that the USA ranked near the bottom of industrialized nations for the survival rates of infants, despite high spending on neonatal care (Tanner, 2006). Similarly, the Commonwealth Fund Commission on a High Performance Health System (2009) ranked the USA dead last on all three indicators of healthy lives. Other studies have found that Americans aged 55 to 64 are much sicker than their British counterparts (Banks *et al.*, 2006) and that Canadians are healthier than their USA counterparts on almost every measure of health (Lasser *et al.*, 2006). Despite massive spending on the newest technologies, Americans have higher rates of diabetes, hypertension, heart disease, stroke, lung disease and cancer than other Western nations.

Cost containment: strategies of constraint

In the 1970s escalating costs, in large part fuelled by the open-ended goals of access and quality, were aggravated by a global recession and oil crisis. One result was an unmistakable shift in emphasis from access and quality to cost containment in order to constrain unbridled health care spending. Ageing populations, boundless technological expansion and heightened public expectations solidified this goal in the 1990s. Moreover, its prominence was encouraged by the ideological shift towards neo-liberalism, which eschewed the welfare state and placed emphasis on efficiency of the market. Ironically, the emphasis on cost containment and system efficiency has forced evaluation of quality (an effort that was conspicuously absent when quality was the preeminent goal) by requiring that priorities be set in distributing health care resources in terms of value for money.

No country escaped the conspicuous shifts towards improving productivity, maximizing efficiency and incorporating management procedures into health care that occurred in the 1990s onwards. Moreover, to date, reform efforts in most Western countries, with the notable exception of the USA, have been effective to the extent that they have at least slowed the rate of increase of health care spending as a proportion of GDP (see Table 3.2). In contrast, while the ACA promises to produce a more equitable health care system in the USA, it is less likely to constrain the escalating costs because it failed to enact meaningful cost controls (Jacobson *et al.*, 2011). In fact, it is quite likely to increase costs primarily since the major thrust of the Act, as reflected in its title, was to expand access to health care, not to limit heath care. In part, this emphasis was an understanding on the part of the Obama Administration that any mention of cutting benefits for the insured to fund the uninsured would be seen as rationing and strongly opposed by the public. Despite their attempts, however, projected savings in Medicare were viewed by the elderly as a threat and potential 'take back', thus explaining the low support among the elderly for the health overhaul.

Cost containment strategies differ significantly across health systems. Objectives can be to slow the rate of increase in costs, to prevent costs from rising in real terms, or more rarely to actually reduce the costs of health care in real terms. The health care sectors to which a particular cost containment strategy is targeted also vary depending on whether health services are financed by the government on a direct budget basis, through public contracts with independent providers such as physicians paid on a fee-for-service basis or hospitals paid per item of service provided, or by the private marketplace. As seen in Chapter 3, countries with national health services, such as Sweden, the UK and New Zealand, as well as several without, such as Singapore, Taiwan and Japan, exercise direct budgetary control, while countries such as Australia, Germany and the Netherlands rely more on the second, contractual-based approach. Finally, the USA depends upon a less effective mixture of approaches, including those based in the marketplace. The capacity for successful cost containment policies, therefore, fluctuates considerably from one country to the next.

Sweden is a good example of a country with a national health service that has effective controls and where the general rule of 'public funding makes for public control' applies. However, in contrast to Britain and New Zealand, control over funding is decentralized, since health care is predominantly funded from taxes raised by the regional tier of government, the county councils (Glenngård *et al.*, 2005). 'Macro-level' measures of cost containment vary, because county councils decide on the rate of regional taxation, the majority of which goes to health care. Besides this, global budgets play an important role and county councils may allocate funds to districts using needs-based global budgets. Similarly, county councils or districts may fund health centres and hospitals using global budgets in conjunction with other forms of payment. In recent years, resource allocation models have become more mixed and combine fixed per-case payments with price/volume ceilings and quality components. The only true 'macro-level' measure of cost containment is when central government decides to control total expenditure by putting limits on taxation, as it did during the harsh recession in the early 1990s (Harrison, 2004).

Cost containment strategies can operate either by reducing *demand* for, or controlling the *supply* of health care. Additionally, they can be carried out through a direct, regulatory edict or through indirect incentive systems aimed at providers and patients. Furthermore, depending on the system, major efforts can be initiated and implemented either by public agencies – national, state or local – or by the private sector. In general, European countries emphasize macro-management strategies such as global budgets to control their health systems, while the USA, with its abiding fear of centralized control, opts instead to utilize financial incentives to influence the use of health care services. However, even in Europe this is changing with moves to micro-manage some aspects of medical care.

Demand-side strategies

Demand-side cost containment relies primarily on strategies designed to reduce consumer demand by increasing patient consciousness of the costs of providing care. Usually this is accomplished by requiring some form of cost sharing by the users of health care, either through user charges as a flat rate per unit of service (e.g., $50 per hospital night, $20 per doctor visit, $20 per prescription), some proportion of the cost (e.g., 20 per cent of outpatient costs, 30 per cent of inpatient costs), or some combination of these. Out-of-pocket costs are normally applied at the time of use with the explicit goal of discouraging user demand and, by extension, acting indirectly on physicians to reduce services on the knowledge that the patient must share in the cost. Another approach is to require deductibles or excesses (e.g., the first $100 per condition) that the consumer must pay, thereby allegedly discouraging demand.

The form of demand-side strategies varies significantly across countries. In Germany, for instance, co-payments are the most common form of out-of-pocket payments and have a long tradition, particularly in relation to drugs. Since the early 1990s, however, they have increased considerably and in 2002 represented 12 per cent of total expenditure on health care (Busse and Riesberg, 2004: 73). With increasing cost pressures, co-payments in other areas have been added, including charges for inpatient days in hospitals, rehabilitative care facilities, ambulance transportation and dental treatment. Indeed, Carrera *et al.* (2008) conclude that developments emphasize the role of the individual in contributing to the sustainability of health financing and thereby strengthen personal responsibility at the expense of solidarity. The most recent health reforms are a case in point, and since 2007 health insurance funds can offer lower contribution rates to those members who are willing to accept a fixed co-payment on all treatments, or who have made no use of the health insurance over the preceding year (Gerlinger, 2010). In 2003, Japan increased the co-payment rate of all care for patients insured by the Employees' Health Insurance from 20 to 30 per cent to put it in line with that of the National Health Insurance (Bertelsmann Foundation, 2003a).

In contrast, in the Netherlands out-of-pocket payments have traditionally played a marginal role and only co-payments for eyeglasses have been a long established feature of the Dutch health system, reflecting entrenched expectations that all health care should be free at the point of use (Maarse and Paulus, 2003). However, this is different for the exceptional medical risks scheme that accounts for almost half of total co-payments (Exter *et al.*, 2004: 48). Furthermore, under the new unified social health insurance programme for acute risks people have to pay a flat-rate premium directly to their sickness fund (Schäfer *et al.*, 2010). The flat-rate premiums are set by individual insurance funds and are the key component for insurance funds to compete for customers who have free choice of insurance fund. Significantly, with the introduction of the new unified insurance in 2006, the flat rate premium has risen, whereas income-related contributions have been lowered (Bartholomée and Maarse, 2006). Moreover, insurance funds charge patients a compulsory flat-rate co-payment on all health expenditure (except general medical services). Importantly, the co-payment can be waved, if patients choose a preferred provider or follow preventive programmes.

Initially Taiwan's NHI did not have co-payments, but in response to rising expenditures, it adopted a co-payment system, although it waives cost-sharing obligations for veterans, low-income persons, those living in remote mountain areas or on offshore islands and persons with diseases/injuries identified as serious by NHI regulations (Chang *et al.*, 2005). For each outpatient care visit, an insured person must pay a co-payment of NT$50 (US$1.50) to NT$210 (US$6.00), depending on the type of facility visited. For inpatient care, there is also a co-insurance rate of 10 per cent to 30 per cent depending on the length of stay, with payment capped at 10 per cent of per capita income. The co-insurance rate for drugs is 20 per cent, with personal payment for drugs capped at NT$200 (US$6.00) per visit. Furthermore, NHI beneficiaries are required to make a co-payment of 10 per cent of hospitalization costs with an upper limit of NT$24,000 (US$725) per admission, although those with a low-income certificate are exempt from co-payment. Hospitals are allowed to bill patients directly for medical materials not covered by the NHI such as private or double rooms (Cheng *et al.*, 2006).

Out-of-pocket payments in Sweden exist in the form of direct, small patient fees that are paid for receipt of medical attention (for an overview see Anell *et al.*, 2012: 63). The payments are a flat rate and are set by the county councils; however, the national Parliament sets ceilings on the total to be paid by patients annually (Burstrom, 2004). There are separate co-payments for drugs that are set by central government and are uniform across the country. In Britain, out-of-pocket payments take the form of co-payments. Prominent areas of cost sharing include: drugs, where co-payments have risen sharply over time; dental services, where patients have to cover 80 per cent of the costs up to a maximum; and ophthalmic services that have been widely deregulated (Baggott, 2004; Boyle, 2011; for a good European comparison of cost sharing arrangements, see Ros *et al.*, 2000).

A major assumption of demand-side cost containment measures is that use of services will decrease when market incentives are implemented that make a patient bear part of the costs (see Box 4.5 for reverse case). Studies have found that cost sharing through either supplementary insurance or deductibles does, indeed, reduce health spending. The European Observatory on Health Care Systems (1999: 41) cites a study in the UK showing that, despite the existence of widespread exemptions, changes in prescription charges can have a noticeable impact on the number of prescriptions dispensed. It estimated that even the modest increase in prescription charges from £3.75 to £4.25 per item in 1993 resulted in a reduction of 2.3 million prescriptions. Correspondingly, the Rand Corporation Health Insurance Experiment in the USA found that outpatient spending was 46 per cent lower among individuals enrolled in health plans that required 5 per cent co-insurance compared with those

Box 4.5 The politics of co-payments

Between 1996 and 2001 out-of-pocket payments in Australia increased by 52 per cent, the second highest increase among OECD countries. In response, the government introduced the Medicare Safety Net under which patients are eligible to claim 80 per cent of their out-of-pocket costs after reaching an annual threshold. This safety net is an uncapped programme financed out of general tax revenues, but there is concern that it will have untoward impact on providers who can now set fees at their own discretion and be fully paid on a fee-for-service basis. Prior to the introduction of the safety net, competitive pressure among provider groups limited fee rises, but now these competitive pressures will ease because patients no longer bear the full impact of the fees. Moreover, while it is impossible to predict if the 20 per cent co-payment feature will be enough to prevent consumption of unnecessary medical care, as patients face lower out-of-pocket charges, they may actually consume more health care services (Bertelsmann Foundation, 2004a).

in free care plans, with the 25 per cent co-insurance plans producing even larger savings. Likewise, outpatient spending was 30 per cent lower and inpatient spending 10 per cent lower under individual deductible plans, while cost sharing reduced adult hospital admissions by up to 38 per cent as compared to free plans (Peterson, 2006).

Despite these findings of apparent cost savings, there are questions as to how genuine the benefits of a demand-side approach are in the long run, particularly if patterns of inefficient usage remain (Box 4.6). In their study of US seniors, Costa-Font and Toyama (2011) found that while user fees reduced the use of inappropriate medications, expected

Box 4.6 Overuse of emergency rooms

A major problem in some countries is the overuse of more costly ER and specialist care for primary care matters. For many years now, primary care in the USA has been in decline and patients have adapted by seeking care elsewhere when they get sick. For instance, of the over 350 million annual visits for acute care, 22 per cent are managed by GPs, 10 per cent by internists, 13 per cent by pediatricians, 20 per cent by office-based specialists and 28 per cent by hospital emergency departments (Pitts *et al.*, 2010). Similarly, nearly 15 per cent of all ER visits in Taiwan are non-emergency and an additional 20 per cent would have been emergency-preventable with primary care (Tsai *et al.*, 2011). According to Pitts *et al.* (2010), one of the biggest barriers to providing acute care in primary care practice is that many GPs have packed schedules, making 'same day' scheduling, much less treatment of walk-in patients, extremely difficult. It is faster and simpler to refer these patients to a specialist or the nearest ER even though that is considerably more expensive for the health system as a whole.

prescription quality improvements from co-payments are small. Furthermore, in their study of the impact of increasing co-payments on the utilization behaviour of elderly patients, Huang and Tung (2008) found that the increase in co-payment significantly decreases visit frequency, but that this in some cases can delay needed treatment and reduce the adequacy of health care provision to the elderly.

An important question, then, is whether the reduced use of medical resources resulting from co-payments leads to lowered levels of health for those individuals who forgo treatment due to cost considerations. In the Rand study, access to more services did not result in better health among consumers who were young, middle income and in good health. In contrast, access to more services did result in better health outcomes among the poor and those persons with initial clinical indicators of poor health. In other words, while many healthy people can reduce care without adverse health consequences, when ill people forgo needed services, health outcomes suffer. Part of this difference, however, might be explained by the fact that relatively young, healthy and affluent consumers are able to carry supplemental insurance to cover charges, thus undercutting the strategy of cost sharing. Unless prohibited from doing so, those using insurance resources will counteract the apparent cost savings.

Other demand-side approaches to cost containment include the exclusion of certain types of coverage or the reduction of reimbursement for specific services. Moreover, some systems such as Australia and the USA allow extra billing while others have either prohibited or strictly limited extra billing because of its impact on equity and its overall inflationary effect. While Germany, Japan, the Netherlands, Sweden and the UK allow no extra billing by office-based doctors working in ambulatory care, a clear example of extra billing is France. As in many other countries, doctors in ambulatory care are self-employed, independent practitioners, and they are paid on a fee-for-service basis. The majority of doctors contract with the social insurance system, but up to a quarter depart from the negotiated fee schedule in favour of extra billing, referred to as 'sector 2' (Freeman, 2000: 52). Patients are reimbursed by statutory social insurance according to the national fee schedule, regardless of whether they choose a doctor who charges higher fees. Although they must pay for the extra billing themselves, over 90 per cent have additional non-statutory insurance to cover extra billing and other co-payments (Freeman, 2000).

On the whole, demand-side approaches are hampered by their adverse impact on access and their inequitable financial burden across groups in society. While the problems of inequity they raise hypothetically can be reduced by providing subsidies or a safety net for those unable to pay or by providing exemptions to the co-payments (e.g., New Zealand's policy on GPs), this entails a complicated administrative and monitoring system that in turn adds to costs. According to the OECD, 'it is doubtful whether anything other than modest charges (with exceptions for poor and high users) will be either equitable or efficient' (1992: 139).

Supply-side strategies

Supply-side cost containment measures are generally more effective than demand-side measures, especially when they entail the imposition of direct, central controls on payments to providers. In commenting on seven European countries, for instance, the OECD concludes that there is a 'strong suggestion that any cost-containment that was achieved came through direct action on the supply side such as the introduction of global budgeting or central regulation of fees and charges' (1992: 148).

Other than the USA, most countries emphasize strategies that control the supply side by strengthening the hands of insurers and/or by imposing direct, central controls on payments to providers and on the capacities of their health systems (see Table 4.1). For instance, during the 1980s, the Netherlands introduced a system of global budgeting to replace the daily rates paid to hospitals, thus joining the UK and New Zealand which already had mechanisms for capping hospital expenditures (Hurst and Poullier, 1993). Also, since 2002 Taiwan's NHI has operated under a global budget (Cheng and Chang, 2007). Similarly, in 2005 Singapore implemented a global budget policy for public sector hospitals and health care institutions (Bertelsmann Foundation, 2005a). Public health sector hospitals and health care institutions, including polyclinics, which provide primary health care, are given a fixed budget regardless of the number of patients they treat.

Additional instruments of regulatory cost containment are fee and price controls, control over capacity of the system and control over wages and salaries. The most direct supply-side strategy is to tighten

Table 4.1 ***Supply-side strategies***

Global budgeting	*Centralized control*	*Move to ambulatory and home care*
Singapore	Germany	Germany
New Zealand	Japan	New Zealand
Netherlands	Netherlands	UK
Sweden	Singapore	Australia
Taiwan	Taiwan	
UK	USA (Medicare DRGs)	

controls over reimbursement or enforce payment schedules. This is easiest to accomplish in an integrated system where the government has the capacity to set global budgets. Sweden and the UK are classic examples of integrated health systems where government sets global budgets, in the former case at the regional level. In Britain, the total expenditure of the NHS is set by the Treasury and is part of the government's three-yearly general spending review. Once overall spending has been set, the Department of Health determines the funds allocated to Primary Care Trusts. In contrast, hospitals are funded through contracts. Cost-volume contracts were long predominant but have now been replaced by commissioning based on national tariffs for specific Health Care Resource Groups (Baggott, 2004; Boyle, 2011). Here Primary Care Trusts rely on standard contracts developed by the Department of Health. As such, the UK is based on a system of cost-per-case payments.

The situation in Sweden is more complex as funding arrangements vary among county councils. Some county councils use global budgets to pay hospitals and health centres, while others have introduced a purchaser–provider split. For example, contracts with hospitals are often based on fixed, prospective per-case payments that are combined with price/quality ceilings as well as quality components (Anell *et al.*, 2012). However, overall the mechanisms for allocating financial resources have become more mixed.

Another approach is that of Germany where cost containment policy means limiting insurance funds' expenditure to a level where it matches income so that contribution rates remain stable (Carrera *et al.*, 2008). To achieve this, the 1990s have seen the introduction of sectoral budgets or spending caps based on historic spending patterns rather than any needs-based formula as in the UK (Gerlinger, 2010). Some of the budgets limit the expenditure of individual funds while other budgets do not impose these kinds of limits. At the level of the individual hospital, this has coincided with the abolition of the full-cost cover principle and, initially, the introduction of fixed budgets calculated for each hospital; these have subsequently been replaced by a system of fixed payments per case, the so-called 'diagnosis-related groups' (DRGs). Furthermore, since 1989 fixed regional budgets exist in ambulatory care. This means that the fees for individual services are not fixed, but vary depending on the total budget negotiated with the insurance fund and the total volume of services delivered within the regional association of insurance fund doctors. There are also ceilings for the amount of refundable services per doctor that in effect functions as a budget.

Global budgets for hospitals are more effective than price or volume controls alone because they cannot be avoided by raising volume when prices are fixed or raising prices when volume is fixed. Usually, discretion is given to local managers to spend within the prospective budget. Budget caps work provided there is the political will to enforce them, but they can be politically risky because they make the central government liable for the failure of micro-decisions. In other words, global budgets allow hospitals to blame government policy makers for shortfalls in service due to inadequate funding levels. Because hospitals consume the majority of health spending, this single approach is effective; however, budget caps become less effective when the government grants additional funds to those hospitals that overspend and require supplements to their budgets in order to keep operating. According to the OECD, the analysis of per capita health expenditure across all OECD nations suggests that hospital global budgets reduce total national health expenditures by about 13 per cent (1992: 141).

One problem with global budgets is that they might achieve cost containment by forcing hospitals to cut corners, thus providing a lower quality of care. Because they do not readily distinguish as to the quality or intensity of care, there are often no rewards for *good* economical treatment. Chang and Hung (2008), for instance, conclude that the implementation of the global budget in the Taiwan NHI improved cost containment but at the expense of quality. Although they suggest this problem can be minimized through close auditing of quality and a more effective monitoring and review system, global budgets, in themselves, are not sufficient to protect consumers because their focus is on lowering the costs per case. In terms of the goal of containing costs, however, any form of prospective payment will succeed by relating rewards to planned workload and encouraging awareness of cost per case. In contrast, any system with open-ended retrospective reimbursement for hospitals such as traditional private insurance in the USA will have higher expenditures per capita (Lamm and Blank, 2007).

Although global budgets are more easily implemented if there is one central authority, single-source funding is not essential. Germany and the Netherlands, for example, have been successful in securing cost control in systems composed of many payers. Germany has accomplished this by the combination of restraining the payment to providers and centralizing control of funding (Carrera *et al.*, 2008). The 1990s saw the partial introduction of a system of prospective payments in hospitals that in 2000 culminated in the gradual introduction of a comprehensive system of DRGs. In ambulatory care, a maximum ceiling for fees per doctor was introduced, coexisting with fixed sectoral budgets. At the same time, the autonomy of insurance funds in raising and allocating funds has been curtailed. Following the most recent reforms from 2009 (Leiber *et al.*, 2010), the government sets income-related contribution rates that are uniform across insurance funds. The government also determines the formula for allocating financial resources to individual insurance funds as well as the level of additional funding raised by individual insurance funds through flat-rate contribution rates.

In the Netherlands, cost containment has been achieved by a combination of integrated control over funding and measures of spending control. The income-related contribution rates for the two social insurance schemes are set by central government. The additional flat-rate premium raised by individual insurance funds is also subject to regulation and may not, for example, vary on the basis of gender, age or health risks (Maarse and Meulen, 2006; Schäfer *et al.*, 2010). This has been complemented by regulated competition, both among insurance funds for employees and among providers for selective contracting with insurance funds, as well as by micro-level measures to increase efficiency.

Similarly, Japan has been quite successful in controlling a vast network of private insurance funds and local providers by instituting a strict uniform fee structure and prohibiting extra billing. In 2003 Japan began to introduce a diagnosis-based hospital reimbursement system as a financial incentive for university hospitals to decrease inpatient costs by capping the cost per day for each inpatient by disease category (Bertelsmann Foundation, 2003a). The disparate policies of these countries show that control over medical spending can be accomplished without centralized global budgeting. Although direct price and quantity controls may be less effective than global budgets or direct caps, they can be applicable to all segments of health care, including pharmaceuticals, and thus are potentially more comprehensive.

Lacking the centralized regulatory control over health care found in other countries, the USA implemented a prospective payment system in the mid-1980s in the one area it could control, the Medicare programme. As noted in Chapter 3, DRGs were introduced to constrain costs of Medicare spending by setting prospective limits per diagnostic category on a fixed schedule. It was hoped that the private sector would follow this lead to reduce overall costs, but this did not eventuate. There is evidence, however, that this approach alone cannot constrain costs in the long run even for Medicare and that it has resulted in a 'revolving door' through which patients are simply readmitted for a new DRG when the previous one runs its course (Blank, 1997: 142). For instance, while hospitals under the DRG system initially were found to have reduced costs per day by 9.8 per cent and average length of stay by 6.5 per cent, the effect on total costs was offset by an 11.7 per cent increase in admission rates (Culyer *et al.*, 1988). In the late 1990s after the one-time savings from managed care began to dissipate, health care costs in the USA resumed their escalation, surging to nearly 15 per cent annually.

Other supply-side approaches include controls over construction of hospitals, the purchase of expensive equipment and the number of medical students entering particular specialities. Encouragement of outpatient over inpatient facilities and a reduction in the oversupply of acute hospital beds are also likely to reduce costs, as is the shift from more expensive hospital beds to nursing homes or home care (see Chapter 6). The changes in Germany are an example of a move towards this strategy. Traditionally, the monopoly of office-based doctors over the delivery of ambulatory care has hindered the development of outpatient facilities. However, in the face of cost pressures, hospitals are now allowed to offer day surgery, pre-admission diagnostic procedures, and post-discharge treatment. Furthermore, the role of the outpatient departments of university hospitals in the provision of highly specialized care has been recognized through special contracts with insurance funds. Despite these changes the position of specialists in ambulatory care remains strong.

Meanwhile, in the Netherlands there has been a reduction in the capacity for inpatient care while day surgery has expanded (Exter *et al.*, 2004). This shift went hand in hand with increasingly tight government regulation of hospitals. For example, the Hospitals Facilities Act regulated the number of hospital beds and specialist units. Moreover, all major investments in hospitals need the formal approval of the Minister of Health if any added facility is to be reimbursed through social health insurance (Maarse, 1997). Interestingly, central planning for hospitals was abolished in 2008 (Schäfer *et al.*, 2010).

Throughout the 1990s, Sweden saw a substantial decline in the number of hospital beds that was more drastic than in other countries (Glenngård *et al.*, 2005: 62). At the same time, the position of ambulatory care was strengthened. The 1995 Primary Care Act acknowledged primary care as a separate level of care and defined it as the foundation of health care. Furthermore, between 2007 and 2010 there were several reforms to strengthen primary care through the introduction of compulsory patient choice and by opening primary care to private providers (Anell, 2010). This is significant, because compared to other European countries primary care in Sweden has traditionally been less developed. Moreover, concurrent with the reduction in the length of hospital stays, the number of patient visits in primary care has increased over recent years (Anell *et al.*, 2012: 88). Nevertheless, in contrast to most counties, in Sweden primary care does not have a formal gate-keeping function and patients have direct access to specialists.

Major cost containment efforts in Taiwan have been directed at pharmaceutical expenditures that constitute about 25 per cent of the entire NHI budget. The government has introduced many strategies including: price adjustment based on prices of international products or existing drugs; delegation of financial responsibility to regional bureaus; co-payment for outpatient drugs; generic grouping; a global budget payment system for clinics and hospitals; and reduction in the flat daily payment rate of the drugs for clinics. Lee *et al.* (2008) found that a global budget alone without other direct financial incentives would not be able to control expenditures on drugs. They concluded that the most effective strategies were generic grouping, reduction of the flat payment rate and delegation of financial responsibility. Chen *et al.* (2007), however, found that while generic grouping significantly reduced the daily expense of the three classes of drugs they studied, in response to this price adjustment policy hospitals tended to greatly expand the volume of drugs prescribed, thus undermining the capacity of this strategy to constrain overall pharmaceutical expenditures.

As in other countries, at least at a rhetorical level, there has been a movement away from hospitals in the UK. Instead, ambulatory care settings seem to hold the promise of both tailored and cost-effective care (Saltman *et al.*, 2006a). Both points are particularly relevant in the context of the British NHS where patient demand often remains unmet and where successive governments have been interested in making existing funds go further. This is epitomized in the vision of a 'primary care-led' health service where GPs have become key players, not only in the provision, but also in the organization of health services. Following the purchaser–provider split in the early 1990s, GPs were given the option of becoming 'fund holders' and receiving funds to purchase a range of diagnostic and elective procedures. The health reforms under the New Labour government in 1997 built on these developments and GP practices became so-called 'Primary Care Trusts'. As part of these trusts, GPs were responsible for the commissioning of all health care services in their locale while retaining responsibility for the provision of ambulatory health care services. The most recent reforms in 2012 very much keep with the focus on primary care and commissioning is now in the hands of generally smaller, and GP-led, Clinical Commissioning Groups (Department of Health, 2012c).

A final supply-side strategy to cost containment is the creation of competitive market conditions under which the more efficient providers thrive and the relatively more costly ones are driven out of existence. One such approach entails separating the funding and provision functions and thus, it is assumed, opening up competition among providers. In the UK internal market, introduced in the early 1990s, for instance, self-governing public hospitals, together with private-sector hospitals, were envisaged as competing for contracts with the health authorities that funded secondary health. Because of the heated controversy surrounding moves to incorporate marketplace mechanisms, it is important to look at the role of market in health care in more depth.

The government and the marketplace

Fuelled by ideological shifts towards neo-liberalism, one trend over the last few decades across Western democracies is the inclusion of market or quasi-market mechanisms in public health systems in order to provide incentives to improve efficiency (Ranade, 1998; Cortez, 2008b). According to neo-liberalism, public sector monopolies provide few incentives for system efficiency and, in fact, are likely to contain perverse incentives that in effect punish efficiency (see Heywood, 2002). Instead, it argues, one must turn to the marketplace to instil efficient use of resources. Despite this paradigm shift, however, evidence suggests that a totally free market in health insurance can produce neither equity nor efficiency (Wells *et al.*, 2007). Even in the USA, clearly the most market-oriented system considered here, the government exerts considerable regulatory influence over the workings of the market though, despite this effort, it remains the least successful country for controlling costs.

Generally, governments can take one of two main routes in regulating health care systems, although as Saltman (2002) suggests the two approaches often exist side by side. The first approach involves regulation in the more conventional sense of setting constraints on the public and non-public sector. This detailed command-and-control type of activity is generally designed to supplant or override market forces and institutions. This can be brought about by specifying coverage of insurance policies, regulating membership and premiums, controlling the quantity and quality of prices, mandating set fee structures and schedules, fixing wage rates, or controlling planning capacity. For example, as noted above, in Japan over 5,000 independent insurance plans and predominantly private providers are highly regulated by the government through the universal fee structure, centralized billing and payment, standard co-payments and prohibition of extra billing.

The second approach, generally termed pro-market or pro-competitive, places more emphasis on the promotion of control by the health care community itself. The aim here is to maximize autonomy for insurers, providers and consumers through the operation of traditional marketplace principles. The government's role is to provide a balance among the assorted stakeholders as it does in other areas of the economy. Under a pure market model, the health care system is, in effect, a large business that, if left alone to operate according to the principles of supply and demand, will best serve the consumer public. For reasons discussed below, no system embodies the pure model, and even in the USA, providers, especially hospitals, face close scrutiny and indisputable constraints as a result of regulation by local, state and national government.

The reason why a pure market approach cannot work is that health care contains none of the self-selecting mechanisms needed to check market excesses. In order for an efficient, market-based health care system to function, several conditions are essential. First, all decisions must be that of the consumer. Second, consumers must know the value

Box 4.7 Distortions in the health care market

The market for health care contains many distortions, including: (1) the asymmetry of information between physicians and patients; (2) the clinicians' dual role as patient agent and independent business owner who profits by ordering or providing medical services; (3) the effect of insurance in reducing the apparent cost to patients, thus leading to the 'price-wedge' distortion or 'moral hazard'; (4) tax subsidies that have a similar effect on consumers' decisions to buy insurance; and (5) the monopoly power bestowed on certain professions and, in some countries, on health insurance plans that constrain competition (Wells *et al.*, 2007).

and costs of the goods they are contemplating purchasing. Third, consumers must pay the full cost and receive the full value of the goods they choose to buy.

Importantly, not one of these conditions is present in the market for health care services (see Box 4.7). First, no medical decision is solely that of the patient. Although some discretion is possible, ultimately the individual patient's choice is heavily conditioned and inhibited by providers. Second, most patients have a difficult time judging the value of the care they get. As a result, health care professionals have enormous sway in deciding both the type and cost of care provided. The specialized knowledge required for the dispensation of health care, in conjunction with the emotional and often urgent nature of medical decisions, undercuts the patient's ability to be a rational shopper. Furthermore, it does not follow that more informed consumers of health care shop for lower cost. In fact, evidence suggests that more information often leads to higher costs because informed patients tend to be more demanding in terms of drugs, tests and treatments (Ubel, 2001).

The major reason that patients are unlikely to be frugal consumers as assumed by marketplace models, however, is the failure to meet the third condition. Third-party payment, whether public or private, ensures that the consumer who receives the value pays only a fraction, if any, of the costs (Ubel, 2001: 32). Without controls, however, health insurance, either social or private, is accompanied by overconsumption because neither the patient nor the physician has much incentive to economize when an amorphous third party is paying the bill. *Moral hazard* is a term used by economists to refer to the behavioural changes that occur when people are put in a position to spend or risk the funds of others rather than bear the cost themselves (Havighurst, 2000). The bottom line is that unless there are strong incentives not to do so, people will generally want more when someone else is paying for the service (see Box 4.8). Nevertheless, it should be noted that, although he does not dispute the reality of moral hazard, Nyman (2008) argues that the preoccupation

Box 4.8 How moral hazard works

You have just finished a meal with a group of six of your friends at a fancy restaurant, and the waiter rolls by with a cart of desserts at a price of £7 each. You are hesitant to order because you are full and do not think you can get £7 worth of pleasure from the dessert. Then in a flash of absolute brilliance, you remember that you are splitting the bill seven ways, meaning the cost of the dessert to you will be only £1. Surely you will be able to get a pound's worth of pleasure? So you go ahead and order. Unfortunately, your friends, reasoning the same as you, all order a dessert too. As a result, each of you pays the full price for a dessert that none of you would have spent £7 on. 'Health care insurance, like the single check in a restaurant, distributes expenses across many people, creating an incentive to buy health care services that cost more than they are worth, a phenomenon health economists refer to as moral hazard' (Ubel, 2001: 31).

with it is misplaced and that a portion of it actually generates a welfare gain in reducing downstream costs.

The moral hazard problem is by no means unique to private insurance, and in fact is inherent in any third-party payment system. However, without strict controls and a restructuring of traditional market functioning, both equity and efficiency will be lacking. Pure market solutions are destined to fail in the long run because they serve to reaffirm claims to unlimited resources by those persons who can afford it or have coverage. Although there are steps that can be taken by governments to modify the market (e.g., move from retrospective to prospective payment systems), adequate regulation requires inclusion of bureaucratic controls in order to shape the diverse demands of the health care marketplace. While this does not negate a role for the market, alone it is insufficient to deal with the peculiarities of health care. A major intention of moves towards managed care in the USA and elsewhere is to curb this moral hazard by limiting services that the insured person can use at the plan's expense.

Other mechanisms designed to rein in moral hazard are co-payments, discussed earlier, and medical savings accounts as found in Singapore. Proponents argue that the medical savings account (MSA) model has the potential to constrict health spending by exposing consumers to greater cost sharing. The theory is that if people are given the opportunity to accumulate their own funds to pay for health care, they are more likely to think twice before using health services since the cost will be drawn from their personal account. As a result, MSAs have received considerable interest across a variety of types of health systems and have even been discussed as an option for European systems (Thomson and Mossialos, 2008). In the USA, the Health Savings Account provisions of the 2003 Medicare Prescription Drug, Improvement, and Modernization

Act provided generous tax breaks for individuals who established such accounts when coupled with a qualified high-deductable health insurance plan. As of January 2008 over 6 million privately insured Americans had participated (Glied, 2008). In addition to Singapore and the USA, about 15 other countries have either adopted or considered MSA programmes to reduce the moral hazard and shift some responsibility for risk bearing to the individual. Despite these efforts, its appeal to consumers in the USA has been muted and some observers conclude there is little to recommend them to European policy makers. 'Since MSAs are essentially a variant of cost sharing, their introduction could set in motion a process of de-insurance that may increase choice for some, but is also likely to jeopardize important health policy goals' (Thomson and Mossialos, 2008: 4). In other words, what might work in Singapore will not necessarily work in other cultural and political settings.

In addition to the asymmetry of knowledge and power between patients and health care professionals, the inability of health care consumers to judge the value of the services they receive and the general failure of marketplace mechanisms to produce efficiency, risk spreading through insurance is essential but also highly problematic. Although private insurance can spread the risk and the burden of payment, private insurers have an incentive to exclude, or at least raise the premiums of, high-risk individuals. Typically, private health insurance is most economical for people who are healthy, while most health care is consumed by sick people unable to obtain affordable private insurance in the marketplace. Income redistribution based on market principles is, thus, not possible without intervention that negates the very principles of supply and demand. To some extent, then, a social insurance mechanism is needed to resolve this problem.

There are ways of controlling the non-public sector, however. As noted earlier, although Japan's health care system is dominated by the private insurance sector and providers compete for patients, all sectors are strictly regulated through a centralized national fee schedule. While universal coverage guarantees access to available health care, in large part the uniform fee schedule has been successful in restraining total health care expenditures and has a critical role in setting allocation priorities. It serves as an allocation mechanism by providing a financial incentive structure for the provision of selected services (i.e., primary care) by setting the fee allowed higher than the actual costs. In contrast, it can discourage medical applications deemed undesirable by setting the allowable fees lower than the actual costs. For Ikegami (1992: 691), the schedule is a 'powerful tool' for promoting certain services and thus shaping the distribution of health care resources.

In addition to Japan, other countries actively intervene in private health care markets with detailed regulations of the command-and-control type. The Netherlands has gone as far as integrating private health insurance into a unified, compulsory social insurance, where private insurers (on par with the other insurance funds) are mandated to provide basic insurance at set income-related premiums. In contrast, in the UK, where private insurance plays only a supplementary role, there is little regulation of the private insurance market, while in the USA regulation is widespread but largely uncoordinated, confusing and historically ineffective in controlling costs. Although many traditionally public health systems have undergone reforms aimed at increased reliance on market or quasi-market mechanisms, in all cases governments have maintained firm control. Germany, the Netherlands, New Zealand, Sweden, Taiwan and the UK have introduced or strengthened competition among the providers in their health systems without sacrificing cost control and universal coverage.

In Sweden, New Zealand and the UK, the so-called 'purchaser–provider split' was introduced as an effort to mimic market mechanisms and to stimulate competition among providers. In the UK, the initial internal market with its emphasis on regulated competition was transformed into a public contract model that aimed to build on long-term cooperation (Ham, 2009). For example, contracts were replaced by long-term service level agreements and purchasers became commissioners, that is, organizations that are concerned not only with paying for services but also with planning. In contrast to the UK, the introduction of the purchaser–provider split has been much less widespread in Sweden, reflecting the high degree of decentralization in the health system.

Meanwhile, in Germany and the Netherlands, the introduction of market mechanisms has mainly focused on competition among purchasers rather than providers: that is, the insurance funds (Gre *et al.*, 2002; Lieverdink and Made, 1997). This was brought about by allowing employees a free choice of insurance fund, thus breaking with the tradition of occupation-based health insurance. In Germany, the insurance funds compete for employees on the basis of the additional, flat-rate contribution rate raised by individual insurance funds (Leiber *et al.*, 2010). This contribution rate supplements an income-related contribution rate set by government that applies across different insurance funds. To mitigate the unequal distribution of health risks, the funds from this contribution rate are pooled centrally and allocated on the basis of a risk adjustment mechanism.

Ironically, Australia has taken measures to bolster private insurance in light of the steady decline in the proportion of the population with insurance for private hospital treatment since the 1980s. In order to increase the population coverage of private insurance, reduce pressure on public hospital waiting lists and services, and support and improve the viability of the private insurance industry, Australia introduced a series of measures under the Private Health Insurance Incentive Scheme. In 1999, anyone purchasing private insurance received a 30 per cent subsidy, paid either as a tax rebate or as a reduced purchase price of insurance. Then, in 2000, Lifetime Health Cover was introduced, which applied a base premium to those purchasing insurance up until the age of 30. Those who have continuous private health insurance cover from age 30 continue to pay the base rate. Those joining after 30 pay an age- related premium calculated at 2 per cent on top of the base premium for every year of age, up to the age of 65. Thus the government's solution to the private health insurance problem was to secure a reduction in the cost of premiums (the 30 per cent rebate), limit the out-of-pocket costs faced by the insured patient (the introduction of no-gap policies) and encourage younger people to join and maintain their fund membership through Lifetime Health Cover (Bertelsmann Foundation, 2003b).

Although cost containment, accompanied by market mechanisms, became a central tenet of health policy reforms of the 1980s and 1990s, it has proven to be an elusive and disputable goal. To the extent that cost-containment measures weaken the promotion of the health of the population, they provoke disapproval. On the other hand, it is evident that without successful initiatives to constrain costs, health care systems face severe funding crises. Because of these counter-pressures, priority setting in health care undoubtedly will prove to be an even more incendiary issue in the future than it is currently. Central to this is the concept of rationing medicine.

Allocation and rationing: the need to set priorities

'All health care systems face problems of justice and efficiency related to setting priorities for allocating a limited pool of resources to a population' (Sabik and Lie, 2008: 1). As pressures emerge to expand basic care coverage to encompass access to intensive curative regimes, the goal of universal coverage is threatened. The core issue facing all countries, then, is how to accommodate these important, but often conflicting goals. Weale (1998) likens this dilemma to what logicians call an inconsistent triad: a collection of propositions, any two of which are compatible with each other but which, when viewed together as a threesome, form a contradiction. 'Perhaps we can have only a comprehensive service of high quality, but not one available to all. Or a comprehensive service freely available to all, but not of high quality. Or a high quality service freely available to all, but not comprehensive. Each of these three possibilities defines a characteristic position in the modern debate about healthcare costs and organisation' (Weale, 1998: 410).

While most Western countries have opted to ensure universal coverage but limit the range of health care services, the USA has a system that offers high-technology, comprehensive care, but without access to all. Those with first-rate insurance coverage enjoy ready access to specialized medicine with considerable freedom of choice, but at the cost of equity in the health system. Critics of national health systems argue that free availability comes only at a cost to quality, choice and rapid technological diffusion. Weale (1998) suggests that while the third option – sacrificing some comprehensiveness in order to achieve at least a core range of high quality services available to all – was a possibility when drugs were few and treatments simple, that is no longer so. It is simply not possible to meet the needs of all citizens without compromising goals. To a large extent, this is what allocation, rationing and priority setting are all about – balancing the competing goals and demands facing the health system. In the end, this frequently entails making hard choices among equally admirable goals. That also explains why priority setting in health care is such a politically charged topic in all countries (Sabik and Lie, 2008).

Allocation decisions are needed at three levels: allocation to health care; allocation within health care; and rationing at the individual level. The first level, macro-allocation, requires a decision as to how much of its resources a society is willing to devote to health care: 5 per cent of GDP, 10 per cent, 15 per cent, or an unlimited amount? It addresses what priority society places on spending for medical care as compared to education, housing, social welfare, national security and so forth. To what extent does increased allocation of resources to medical care improve the health of the population if the funding must come at the expense of these other areas? In other words, what are the 'opportunity costs' of putting additional resources into health care? (See Chapter 7 for expanded discussion of this issue.)

Once society makes this determination, it must decide how these resources are to be allocated among the myriad categories of spending within health care, to particular forms of treatment and to specific disease categories. Should priority be placed on preventive medicine, health promotion and primary care, or on more intensive high-technology medicine? Should treatment of diseases of the elderly or care of young mothers and children be given higher priority? Similarly, should precedence be placed on extending life or improving quality of life; the marginally ill or the severely ill; high-incidence diseases or rare diseases; AIDS or cancer or heart disease? At some stage, allocation within health care requires consideration of tradeoffs that can be more or less transparent, centralized or decentralized, fair or unfair, but always controversial.

Finally, assuming that society is unable or unwilling through its allocation policies to meet the health care needs of all persons due to limited

Box 4.9 Rationing is essential in tax-funded health systems

It has become commonplace for decisions made by the UK's National Institute for Health and Clinical Excellence (NICE) to be greeted with public outrage (Harrison and McDonald, 2007). It comes as little surprise that the Institute's rejection of five appeals against its guidance restricting the use of four drugs for Alzheimer's disease has been branded 'blatant cost cutting' by the Alzheimer Society. But this reaction says less about NICE's decision-making process than it does about the divide between patient expectations of the health system and understanding the necessity for rational spending. Public-opinion surveys in the UK repeatedly show overwhelming support for a universal health system, but it is clear from reactions to decisions such as that of NICE that individuals do not connect the NHS ideal with the necessity for some form of rationing to make the best use of limited funds. Is this simply a misunderstanding? Not quite. One big barrier to resolving this problem is the government's unbending commitment to the mantra of patient choice. By encouraging patients to demand more from health services, it effectively ignores the fact that a tax-based system means that some kind of rationing is essential (*The Lancet*, 2006).

resources, rationing decisions at the individual level are unavoidable (Lamm and Blank, 2007). The ubiquitous nature of scarcity driven by the trends discussed in Chapter 1 makes it certain that the demands of individuals and groups will exceed the available resources, thus requiring the rationing of these resources (see Box 4.9). Collectively, it is impossible for doctors to offer all technologically feasible and clinically beneficial medicine to all patients (Weinstein, 2001). As noted by Fleck (2002), there can be no health reform without health care rationing and no fair health reform without health care rationing for all.

Rationing is generally defined as the denial of a treatment to an identifiable patient who would benefit from it. This could be any type of treatment, but most often it is an expensive procedure or drug. Whatever specific form it takes, rationing always results in the situation where potentially beneficial treatment is denied on cost grounds. Given that rationing is necessary, the question becomes one of how to implement it. How do we assure legitimacy and impartiality without compromising success? Furthermore, if resources are to be focused on the provision of 'appropriate' health care, who should define it and how can it be determined? And, what are the criteria for rationing – total lives saved, life-years saved, or quality-of-life years saved? Because there are no unequivocal answers and because rationing is so entangled with problems of cost containment and efficiency, its implementation is always exceedingly divisive.

Table 4.2 *Forms of rationing medicine*

Form	*Criteria used*
Physician discretion	Medical benefit to patient Medical risk to patient Social class, gender, ethnicity or mental capacity
Competitive marketplace	Ability to pay
Private insurance	Ability to pay for insurance Group membership Employment
Social insurance	Entitlement Means test
Legal	Litigation to gain access and treatment
Personal fundraising	Support of social organizations Skill in public relations Willingness to appeal to public
Implicit rationing	Queuing Limited manpower and facilities Medical benefits to patient with consideration of social costs
Explicit rationing	Triage Medical benefits to patient with emphasis on social costs and benefits

Source: Adapted from Blank (1997: 93).

Although the term rationing provokes strong emotions, all health systems ration medicine because none can provide unrestricted health care resources for all their citizens (Ham and Robert, 2003; Maynard and Bloor, 2001). Furthermore, despite intensified pressures on health care systems today, rationing has always been a part of medical decision making. Table 4.2 illustrates the range of ways in which health care can be rationed. Whether imposed by an attending physician, a market system where price determines access, a triage system (see Box 4.10) where care is distributed on the basis of benefit as defined by the medical community, or a queue system where time and the waiting process become the major rationing mechanisms, medical resources have always been distributed according to criteria that inherently contain varying degrees of subjectivity. Moreover, in many instances, rationing principles can be grounded in a value context that results in an inequitable distribution of resources based on social as well as strictly medical considerations.

Box 4.10 Medical triage

Triage, meaning 'choice' or 'selection', is used when many patients simultaneously need medical attention and medical personnel cannot attend to all. The rule is to first treat persons whose condition requires immediate attention without which they will progress to a more serious state. Others, whose condition is not as serious and who are stable, are deferred. This sort of triage is often necessary in busy emergency departments. A second sort of triage is indicated in disasters where the most seriously injured may be left untreated even at risk of death if their care would absorb so much time and attention that the work of rescue would be compromised. As applied to rationing, triage means that some patients will not be treated if the use of resources on them would be futile and would divert resources from those patients who would benefit more.

Although a combination of these types of rationing is present in all countries, each health care system places emphasis on particular forms. Countries with national health systems have an easier time using more explicit rationing mechanisms through their control of the supply of resources. This is because they usually have not explicitly defined their services, as is common in social and private insurance systems where the member has, in effect, a contract for specific services. In national health systems, the services are purposely kept vague by the government so as to provide more room for manoeuvre. Also, in countries with socially determined health budgets, constraints in one area can be justified on grounds that the money will be spent on higher-priority services in another area. By contrast, in the fragmented US system or Singapore's individual responsibility system it is considerably more difficult to refuse any services for specific patients because there is no certainty the funds will be put to better use elsewhere. The lack of a fixed budget, either for government funding or overall national health care spending, makes it impossible to say where money 'saved' from rationing will go, but it does not mean that rationing does not exist (Box 4.11).

Not surprisingly rationing is more complex in social insurance systems where legislation and/or contracts explicitly spell out the coverage. In principle, this makes rationing easier as it merely involves excluding certain treatments and procedures from the list of reimbursable services. An obvious lever is the assessment of medical technology discussed below. In the Netherlands, for example, the coverage of social health insurance has come under scrutiny and homoeopathic drugs have been excluded, while the standard dental package has been considerably reduced. However, the explicit way in which coverage is defined also makes rationing more difficult because it makes any exclusion of services highly visible and therefore potentially costly in political terms.

Box 4.11 Rationing in the USA: haphazard and uncoordinated

Americans resist direct, explicit limitations on medical care, but rationing occurs in less obvious ways on many levels. It begins with coverage decisions over the scope of benefits and eligibility, while at the programme level decisions are made about reimbursable providers and institutions. Related decisions include the use of formularies and payment tiers, gatekeepers to specialized services, access to primary care doctors and specialists and other managerial choices that influence coverage, access and treatment. Rationing also occurs at the direct service level when clinicians make decisions on patient priorities, time for each, need for referral and more or less expensive interventions. Other types of rationing that are not transparent to the public include: denial of access and services; rationing by selection based on subjective assessments of likely benefit or patient status; rationing by deflection when patients are sent elsewhere to avoid responsibility for care; rationing by deterrence when people are confronted by unresponsive phone systems, rude personnel and long waiting times; rationing by delay that makes it difficult to schedule an appointment in a timely fashion; rationing by dilution by offering less content in the service than is reasonable or needed; and rationing by termination when people in distress are told that no more can be done for them and they should not return. The inclination to see rationing solely as distribution of an unavoidably scarce resource misses the numerous policy and service decisions that determine what care people receive (Mechanic and McAlpine, 2010).

Supply-side rationing is traditionally practised by national health services and depends upon setting strict limits on medical facilities, equipment and personnel. Rationing in both the Netherlands and Germany has focused on measures such as reducing the number of hospital beds, setting sectoral budgets and contribution rates, and restricting the increase in the number of doctors. In these systems the availability of resources inevitably affects clinical decisions, with, as noted in Chapter 3, GPs often serving as gate-keepers and deflecting patients from overloading the system.

In contrast, market-oriented systems depend on *demand-side* rationing which is even more contentious. The USA, for instance, begins with excess hospital capacity and an oversupply of accessible specialists. As a result, the system has the capacity to perform any available procedure, including those that the public system does not cover. Persons with adequate insurance or resources are unlikely to accept artificially imposed constraints on their access to medical specialists. Moreover, demand-side rationing in this environment is susceptible to constant personal appeals for coverage and is difficult to sustain politically.

Taiwan	UK	Germany	Japan	Australia	USA
Sweden	New Zealand	Netherlands		Singapore	

No Price Rationing — **High Price Rationing**

Figure 4.2 *Degree of price rationing*

An overlapping distinction is between *price* and *non-price* rationing (see Figure 4.2). Price rationing is commonplace in the USA where health care resources are denied only to persons who cannot afford them or who have inadequate third-party coverage. In contrast, non-price rationing, which is characteristic in public health systems, depends on limiting the availability of certain health services, and thus denies medical resources even to persons who have the means to afford them. Of course, one option open to patients in countries with strict non-price rationing is to go elsewhere (medical tourism) for treatment and pay for it out-of-pocket (Cortez, 2008a). Another option is to use the private sector if one is available domestically.

Another aspect of rationing is that some forms can be carried out only by government action while others fail to distinguish clearly between public and private sector choices. As one moves to the more explicit forms of rationing at the bottom of Table 4.2, a more systematic government role is required and thus it is no surprise that these types are found primarily in national health systems. Other forms of rationing, such as public relations and market, often occur outside the public sphere. A related question regarding the government role in rationing centres on where it is carried out: Are these decisions made by government, by a department or ministry, by regional health authorities, or by individual hospitals? Are these decisions highly centralized or decentralized, bureaucratized or ad hoc?

Rationing has also been proposed as a means of guaranteeing every citizen a basic level of health care and excluding from coverage treatments outside this package. The explicit tradeoff here is between universal access to those services deemed basic on the one hand and unequal access to the full range of technically feasible services on the other. In many countries, a *basic* level of health care focuses on primary care and excludes high-technology services such as organ transplants, fertility treatments and cosmetic surgery. However, when basic care is broadened to include unrestrained access to intensive and expensive curative regimes, it undermines the goal of universal coverage. Health systems such as Britain, New Zealand and Japan are more successful in providing universal coverage and maintaining lower per capita costs than the all-embracing US system, but only so long as they curb accessibility to high-technology medicine. Once they try to provide levels of medical care similar to the USA, they lose this advantage.

One approach to rationing, then, is to define a set of funding priorities or list of core services to be funded (for an overview see Sabik and Lie, 2008). In 1992, New Zealand set up the Core Services Committee with the objective of implementing a comprehensive core services strategy to ration health services. The Committee promulgated four principles for assessing a service: benefit; value for money; fairness; and consistency with the community's values and priorities (New Zealand Core Services Committee, 1992). After extensive public consultation and research on a range of specific treatment regimes, however, the Committee concluded that a specific list of funding priorities with exclusion of specific treatment categories was untenable and opted instead to continue services already funded. Exclusion of treatment categories was not only politically explosive, but also raised questions of fairness and did not account for variation among specific patients within each category.

Another approach was offered in the 1991 Dunning Committee report advising the Dutch government on priorities in social health insurance (Ham, 1997b: 51). Similar to New Zealand, the Committee proposed a comprehensive approach that would include health technology assessment, the use of guidelines for the adequate provision of care and the identification of criteria for prioritizing patients on waiting lists. The aim was to provide politicians with tools to decide on a basic health care package. Such explicit priority setting was considered necessary in order to continue guaranteeing access to essential care for all. Interestingly, however, after publication of the Committee's report, initiatives have focused on assessing the cost-effectiveness of health technologies (and developing guidelines) rather than on choices between services (Ham, 1997b: 54). Again, this reflects professional and public resistance to the removal of certain services, such as contraceptives, from public funding (similarly, see Sabik and Lie, 2008).

The Swedish Parliamentary Priorities Commission, which reported in 1995, was distinctive not only in its cross-party membership but also in its emphasis on ethical considerations of priority setting (Ham, 1997b: 51). As such, the Commission offered different ways of thinking about priority setting to front-line practitioners and decision makers. The primacy of ethical considerations meant that human dignity was more important than the principle of need or solidarity, whereas cost efficiency was subordinate to all three principles. In contrast to the Netherlands and the UK, in Sweden human dignity and the rights of the individual were central. 'Applying this approach meant that discrimination based on age, birth weight, lifestyle and whether illnesses were self-inflicted would not normally be allowed' (Ham, 1997b: 59).

Unlike the Netherlands and Sweden, the UK has not conducted a national inquiry into priority setting. This reflects the fact that in the UK priority setting happens at the local level of the health authority (Locock,

2000). In response to a comprehensive review by a parliamentary committee, however, the government articulated its view on the issue. While explicit exclusion of services from the NHS was seen as unnecessary, it was felt that resources should be concentrated on the most effective type of treatments. This plea for 'evidence-based medicine' has been echoed by developments in health technology assessment, particularly the creation of the National Institute for Clinical Excellence (NICE) in 1999 that, interestingly, is perceived by some to constitute explicit, national rationing (Syrett, 2003). At the same time, with its focus on national standards and transparency, NICE offers a counterweight to the predominant practice of local decisions on provision and coverage of service (Landwehr and Böhm, 2011).

Perhaps the most detailed prioritization system was adopted in the US State of Oregon in the 1990s. Oregon generated a list of prioritized health care services in order to extend Medicaid services to all persons on public support. The criteria used to rank over 700 diagnostic and treatment categories included the cost of the procedure, its potential to improve quality of life and the number of years the improvement is expected to last. In order to measure cost-effectiveness of treatments, a Quality of Well Being (QWB) scale defined 24 distinct states of health. One thousand individuals were surveyed and asked to assign a numerical score to each of these states of health, from a scale of zero (as good as dead) to 100 (perfect health), and each of these states of health was assigned an overall numerical weight. These QWB scores were used to calculate the cost-effectiveness, and thus the priority ranking, of the condition-treatment pairs (Mendelson *et al.*, 1995). The result of this process was a series of 'league tables' of condition–treatment pairs ranked in descending order of priority. Under the implementation of the Oregon Plan, the procedures to be funded in a given year depend on the total amount budgeted by the state legislature, thus explicitly tying specific treatments to levels of health care funding.

Rationing by exclusion has been criticized as price rationing because those patients with the ability to pay can often obtain the services in the private market or elsewhere while those who do not must do without. Other problems include 'co-morbidity inconsistencies', when one condition is included and the other not, and 'diagnostic creep', where doctors manipulate diagnoses to ensure they fall within the funded list (see Mullen, 1998). Core service or other prioritizing schemes also can lead to political pressures to add dramatic lifesaving interventions for individuals, especially for those previously covered services eliminated from the list.

Although not as transparent as these attempts to prioritize health care services, the universal fee structure of Japan has a clear prioritizing function through its control over the diffusion of new technologies. More expensive innovations are discouraged because the charge allowed for a new treatment is computed by comparing it to the cost of the nearest existing treatment. Therefore, while one might explain the low rate of organ transplantation in Japan by cultural veneration of the dead or dislike of invasive technologies (Miller and Hagihara, 1997), expensive medical interventions are also discouraged by the government's strong role in fixing prices. Rationing decisions are made through the incentive structure determined by societal priorities as reflected in the fee levels. Moreover, the government ensures equity in financing among the multitude of private and public plans and equality of service since providers are always paid the same amount for a service no matter what insurance plan the patient has, even if on public assistance. Although the system has problems with multiple diagnoses and increased volume to make up for fee constraints, overall Japan has created an effective system for eliminating the necessity of making patient-specific rationing decisions at the individual level.

In Germany, priority setting is both implicit and explicit (Busse, 1999; Landwehr and Böhm, 2011). In comparison to the Netherlands and Sweden it is implicit, in that there has been no formal review of the issue. At the same time, priority setting is quite explicit in that it is part of the contractual and fee negotiations between providers and insurance funds. For example, broad priorities can be expressed by defining the coverage of social health insurance through a positive list (as in the case of care by non-physicians) or through evaluating the effectiveness of new as well as existing diagnostic and therapeutic methods. Fine-tuning of priorities is also possible through defining the relative value of an individual treatment as part of the fee schedule. For example, changes in the fee schedule in ambulatory care have reduced reimbursements for more technically oriented specialists and rewarded generalist office-based doctors (Rosenbrock and Gerlinger, 2004).

These diverse efforts at rationing represent rather primitive initial attempts to face systematically the problems of setting health care priorities within the context of scarce resources. Although none of these efforts has been fully successful, they have helped lay the groundwork for fair and workable rationing approaches. Explicit priority-setting efforts will have to withstand pressures for dramatic, often lifesaving, interventions for specific individuals identified as needing them and face claims that a narrowed core services agenda will magnify the inequities between those with private insurance and those without. According to Klein (2005), the legitimacy of any rationing scheme depends on better, more evidence-based methods of analysis. Moreover,

> Given conflicting values, the process of setting priorities for health care must inevitably be a process of debate . . . which cannot be

> resolved by an appeal to science and where the search for some formula or set of principles designed to provide decision-making rules will always prove elusive. Hence the crucial importance of getting the institutional setting of the debate right . . . the right process will produce socially acceptable answers – and this is the best we can hope for. (Klein and Williams, 2000: 25)

In order to attain legitimacy, rationing processes need to command the confidence of a public who do not know, or care, about the technical aspects but want assurance that decisions reflect social values and are taken in ways that are transparent.

Rationing by lifestyle and age

Any rationing of health care resources is complicated because, as noted in Chapter 1, the distribution is skewed towards a very small proportion of the population. With the growth of sophisticated curative treatments, health care spending became concentrated in a relatively small number of patients in acute care settings. Typically, these high users of health care are likely to be persons with chronic medical problems who are repeatedly admitted to the hospital. This small fraction of patients exerts

Table 4.3 *Lifestyle and self-inflicted diseases*

Lifestyle	*Self-inflicted diseases*
Alcohol abuse	Cirrhosis of the liver, encephalopathy, foetal alcohol syndrome, accidents, violence
Cigarette smoking	Emphysema, chronic bronchitis, lung cancer, coronary artery disease
Drug abuse	Suicide, overdose, malnutrition, infectious diseases
Overeating	Obesity, hypertension, diabetes, heart disease, varicose veins
High fat intake	Arteriosclerosis, diabetes, coronary artery disease
Low-fibre diet	Colorectal cancer
Lack of exercise	Coronary artery disease, hypertension
High-risk sexual behaviour	Sexually transmitted diseases, AIDS, cervical cancer

Source: Adapted from Leichter (1991: 77).

disproportionate leverage on medical resources by repeated use of hospital facilities. In addition to the elderly, high users of health care are predominantly identified as persistently ill individuals, many of whom have unhealthy lifestyles and are non-compliant. A few risk factors, including alcohol and drug abuse, cigarette smoking, obesity, sedentary lifestyles and unhealthy diets, are particularly evident among high users of medical care (see Table 4.3). In addition to having more frequent episodes of ill health, patients with these behaviours require greater repeated hospitalizations for each episode, thus increasing the 'limit cost' of the illness.

Over the last half century, data on the major causes of mortality have reflected a shift from infectious diseases to degenerative chronic diseases linked to individual behaviour (Nolte and McKee, 2011). Today, behavioural causes account for nearly 40 per cent of all deaths in the USA (Mokdad *et al.*, 2004) and even more in other countries like Taiwan where the estimate is over 50 per cent (Wen *et al.*, 2008). As illustrated in Table 4.4, two factors, smoking and obesity, alone account for 35 per cent of the 2.4 million deaths in the USA. Moreover, it has been estimated that 50 to 90 per cent of all cancers are promoted or caused by various personal and environmental factors. 'Better control of fewer than ten risk factors . . . could prevent between 40 and 70 per cent of all premature deaths, a third of all cases of acute disability, and two-thirds of all cases of chronic disability' (Sullivan, 1990: 1066). Likewise, as will be discussed in Chapter 7, the impact of obesity on health care spending is substantial and growing rapidly (Thorpe *et al.*, 2004a).

Table 4.4 *Causes of death in the USA, 2000*

Cause	*Estimated number of deaths*	*Percentage of total deaths*
Tobacco	435,000	18.1
Diet/activity patterns	400,000	16.6
Alcohol	85,000	3.5
Microbial agents	75,000	3.1
Toxic agents	55,000	2.3
Motor vehicles	43,000	1.8
Firearms	29,000	1.2
Sexual behaviour	20,000	0.9
Illicit use of drugs	17,000	0.7
Total	1,159,000	48.2

Source: Adapted from Mokdad *et al.* (2004).

These data raise serious implications for rationing. First, they suggest that any efforts to reduce health care costs must be directed at high users simply because they collectively consume such a high proportion of funds. 'There are serious limitations to the effectiveness of any cost containment strategies that focus on the 90 percent of the population that collectively accounts for only one-third of the total US health care spending' (Berk and Monheit, 2001: 17). Second, they demonstrate that considerable redistribution of societal resources is necessary if these individuals, many of whom are poor and/or on benefits, are to get the many health services they need. Third, they raise vital questions concerning the extent to which society can afford to support individuals who knowingly engage in high-risk behaviour. This is a particularly salient issue when these services include long-term, expensive interventions such as intensive care and organ transplantation.

Due to the high costs risky behaviours generate, health systems are under heightened pressure to become more actively involved in personal lifestyle choices. Whether out of concern for fairness, paternalism, strict economics or a blame-the-victim mentality, momentum has increased for aggressive efforts to effect changes in individual behaviour deemed dangerous for health. This is clearly evident for smoking and drinking. Attempts to prohibit smoking in public places and discourage its use through high taxes and to remove the drinker from the highways are being approached with near missionary zeal in many countries. Anti-obesity programmes are likely to follow (see Chapter 7).

What should be done, however, when efforts to change behaviour fail and we are faced with patients who need treatment for self-imposed illness? Should smokers get heart transplants or by-pass surgeries? Should alcoholics who drink themselves into liver failure be candidates for liver transplants? If so, should they go to the top of the organ waiting lists if they are the most urgent cases? Is it fair for those who try to live healthy lives to pay the enormous costs of those who do not? In other words, can it ever be fair to ration medical resources away from those individuals who cause or contribute to their own ill health? The answers to these questions, of course, are in part to be found in the cultural frameworks discussed in Chapter 2, but they also reflect the economic realities of limits.

In an age of scarce resources in which medical goods and services are rationed, the debate over lifestyle choice will increasingly focus on the extent to which this choice ought to influence rationing decisions. More than any other issue surrounding the rationing of medical resources, this aspect of lifestyle promises to be the most poignant. When should lifestyle criteria be expressly entered into the rationing equation? Who is responsible for establishing the criteria? What impact will this selection process have on the practice of medicine? What limits, if any, are there on

Box 4.12 How much is too much?

Gregory 'X' is a 'frequent flyer', a label that many emergency rooms give to their regular visitors. Developmentally disabled and unwell in large part because he refuses to take his blood pressure medicine, between 1996 and 2001 he called '911' and was taken to the emergency room by ambulance over 1,200 times. His emergency room visits, ambulance rides and hospital stays have cost taxpayers over $900,000, with no end in sight. According to the staff, Mr X enjoys his notoriety and the treatment he receives, which he takes for granted – 'last year they told me my bill was a quarter-million dollars. I said so what? I'm sick. Take care of me.' Is there a moral obligation to treat such patients indefinitely or should society set limits? If so who should implement these limits (Foster, 2001)?

the care of persons who continually harm themselves? (See Box 4.12 and consider what decision you would make in this case.)

Another highly controversial aspect of rationing centres on the disproportionate use of health care resources by the elderly, especially those over age 80 (Reese *et al.*, 2010). The most common argument against considering age in making health care decisions is that such rationing amounts to age discrimination and is unfair because of the past contributions made to society by the elderly (Evans, 1997). In other words, society owes the elderly their 'just rewards'. Critics also reject economic arguments that greater savings are made from denying care to the old because younger people are relatively more productive to society or that more life-years are gained by giving preference to younger people. Moreover, opponents contest the view that elderly patients are less able to benefit from treatment and reject chronological age as a useful gauge of benefit, arguing that all patients should be assessed for treatment equally on the basis of their physiology alone (Churchill, 2005).

In contrast, the 'fair innings' argument maintains that it is just that those people who have already had more than their fair share of life should not be preferred to the younger person who has not been so favoured. Is it unfair to deny the young the opportunity to become old while allowing those who are already old to become older? Williams (2000) suggests that we should not object to age being a criterion used in the prioritization of health care, because the alternative is too outrageous to contemplate – namely, that we expect the young to make large sacrifices so that the elderly can enjoy small benefits. 'This vain pursuit of immortality is dangerous for elderly people: taken to its logical conclusion it implies that no one should be allowed to die until everything possible has been done. That means not simply that we shall die in a hospital but that we shall die in intensive care' (Williams, 1997: 820).

Likewise, Callahan (1990) argues that even with relatively ample resources, there are better ways to spend our money than on indefinitely extending the life of the elderly beyond the 'natural lifespan'. According to Callahan, a natural life span is one in which life's possibilities have on the whole been achieved and after which death may be understood as a sad, but nonetheless relatively acceptable event. To this end, we must abandon the notion that we should try endlessly through medical progress to revise old age and instead accept ageing as a part of life, not just another medical obstacle to overcome. See Box 4.13 regarding kidney transplants and decide for yourself what is fair.

The maldistribution of health resources in favour of the elderly will escalate in part because more-intensive technologies and drug options continually increase the range of potential interventions and thus the relative costs of high users. More important, however, is the quantity of health resources required by an ageing population. It is a fact of life that the older we become, the more health resources we consume. The elderly use more acute care, are hospitalized about twice as often, stay longer in hospitals and are much more likely to be readmitted to the hospital. In the USA, nearly half of all ICU patients are over age 65, and the cost of ICU care for a patient over age 65 is three to five times more per day than the cost of resources utilized for the average acute-care admission. Those age 65 and over comprised about 13 per cent of the US population in 2002, but they consumed 36 per cent of total personal health care

Box 4.13 Age, health and fairness in rationing kidney transplants

The current system for allocating kidney transplants to adults with end stage renal disease in the USA has emphasized fairness according to a single principle: the longer a person has waited for a kidney, the more priority he or she has to receive one, with no consideration as to life expectancy before or after receiving a transplant. Thus, higher priority could be given to an 80-year-old on dialysis with diabetes mellitus and extensive vascular disease who has waited longer than a more recently listed 30-year-old with no comorbidities (Reese *et al.*, 2010). Although this system worked reasonably well when the number of older adults needing transplants was small, epidemics of obesity, diabetes mellitus and hypertension have led to rapid growth in the number of older adults with kidney failure. As a result, the waiting list for kidney transplants more than doubled from 30,000 candidates in 1997 to over 83,000 candidates in 2009, while the proportion of recipients aged 65 and older increased from 6.5 per cent to over 16 per cent, with many centres accepting patients in their 70s or 80s (Reese *et al.*, 2010). Is it fair to take age and health into account when rationing scarce organs, given that many younger, healthier people will die as a result of not doing so?

expenses. The average health care expense was $11,089 per year for elderly people but only $3,352 per year for those aged 19–64. 'Similar differences among age groups are reflected in the data on the top 5 per cent of health care spenders. People 65–79 (9 per cent of the total population) represented 29 per cent of the top 5 per cent of spenders. Similarly, people 80 years and older (about 3 per cent of the population) accounted for 14 per cent of the top 5 per cent of spenders' (Stanton and Rutherford, 2005: 3).

Average per capita expenditure, then, is approximately four times higher for the elderly than the non-elderly, and, more importantly, the rate of increase in such spending for the elderly is nearly three times that of the non-elderly (CDC, 2007). Ironically, because of medical improvements and technologies that prolong life, chronic disease requiring frequent medical care has become an increasing drain on scarce medical resources. People who in earlier times would have died of one illness are often kept alive to suffer long-term decline in quality of life (see Box 4.14). Furthermore, because of the concurrence of multiple and often chronic conditions, the cost of prolonging life at older ages is higher than at younger ones, increasingly so since the introduction of antibiotics has reduced the incidence of death from illnesses such as pneumonia.

The debate will go on, but with the ageing of the baby boomers, unless something is done to change the skewed spending pattern, this burgeoning cohort will consume an inordinate proportion of health care resources. Simply put, health care costs cannot be controlled without using age as a criterion in rationing simply because the elderly are the prime users of technologies that increase the costs of medicine. Although logically the elderly offer a prime target for rationing, given their political influence attempts to explicitly ration medical care on grounds of age are

Box 4.14 Keeping elderly alive but at what cost

The cost of caring for ageing US citizens by 2030 will add 25 per cent to the nation's overall health care costs unless they actively work to stay healthy and preventive services are provided to help them (CDC, 2007). Even if improved lifestyles and medical technologies are able to reduce the major causes of premature death, we will be left with a growing elderly population whose additional years of life may be dominated by non-fatal but highly debilitating conditions such as arthritis, osteoporosis and Alzheimer's disease (Stanton and Rutherford, 2005). The result could be longer life but worsening health, thus an actual decline in active life expectancy. Under these circumstances, health care becomes Sisyphean, where we conquer one disease only to throw ourselves into the arms of another disease as we attempt to fill this fiscal black hole by using resources that are desperately needed by other generations (Lamm and Blank, 2007).

unlikely in many countries. Although using age as a factor in rationing has been most widely condemned in the USA, however, in other countries such as the UK old age 'is a criterion for rationing health resources and it occurs at all levels of the National Health Service' (Williams, 2000: 198).

Whatever one's view on whether the elderly are getting their fair share of the health budget or if they ought to get less than younger people because they have had their fair innings (or fair share earlier in life), there is no denying that the ageing population is a major problem for the distribution of health care resources and, in fact, in the redistribution of all societal resources. It is also clear that the problem will get progressively worse, particularly in countries like Australia, New Zealand, Taiwan and the USA that currently have relatively young but ageing populations, and that existing priorities in health policy will be challenged. Any debate over setting limits to medical technologies and rationing health care must address the intergenerational redistribution of resources as well as the implications of any policy changes for the elderly. It is likely that as the issues raised here become fathomed by current younger generations, especially those now under age 30, intergenerational tensions over health care will ensue.

Efforts to control new technologies

As noted in Chapter 1, the proliferation of biomedical technologies is a major force pushing up health care costs in all countries. Although the patterns of introduction, diffusion and rationing of new technologies vary across countries, generally those with centralized funding and controls require that new technologies be accommodated within existing systems of resource allocation. Because tradeoffs must be made between the innovation and current treatment for that particular condition as well as other existing conditions, there is an obvious need to establish priorities. Analysis of marginal costs and benefits and comparison with existing treatments is critical, and a new procedure or drug can be rejected unless there is evidence it will have a major positive impact on health outcomes and/or reduce costs.

In contrast, in market-oriented systems new technologies are seldom rejected even when found to be ineffective and less so if they are efficacious and safe, but unaffordable. Since elimination of ineffective technologies alone is unlikely to restrain costs, countries face difficult decisions that involve sacrificing clinically useful technologies that might work but that collectively could bankrupt the system while contributing very little to the health of the population. In any case, mechanisms are needed to engage in prospective assessment of technologies before they are diffused as well as compel discontinuation of those technologies that

Box 4.15 Lack of systematic assessment

In the USA, assessment of new health policies is rarely systematic and typically undertaken by a haphazard collection of the curious, concerned or adequately funded. Moreover, often the objectivity of the investigators is difficult to assess, and studies are retrospective and include populations that are convenient from a sampling perspective but not relevant to broader policy making. 'Even though the concept of evidence-based decision-making is widely accepted in the clinical world, the approach has not permeated health policy' and this often leads to the 'discovery of unintended consequences years later' (Wharam and Daniels, 2007: 677).

are ineffective, only marginally effective, or effective but too expensive to find social justification.

Bodenheimer and Fernandez (2005) suggest that controlling costs while preserving quality requires a multifaceted approach. In addition to strengthening primary care and disease management programmes and reducing inappropriate care, medical errors and the use of hospital and emergency departments by high-cost patients, we need the dissemination of effective technology assessment mechanisms. Yet, in most countries, the history of health technology assessment (HTA) has been inconsistent and controversial (see Box 4.15). It has been characterized by strong opposition from interests that see it as a threat to their autonomy and, conversely, by reproach from others who feel that it has failed to provide critical assessment and thus stem the dissemination of questionable technologies and procedures.

HTA is well established in Australia, Britain, Sweden, the Netherlands and the USA, whereas in other countries it is still in its infancy (Banta, 2002; for an overview of European countries see Garrido *et al.*, 2008a). MacDaid (2001) offers possible explanations for this. In Germany biomedical and clinical research has been dominant, whereas the status of health services research and economic evaluation has been low. This is exacerbated by reliance on decisions obtained through consensus and expert opinion. The importance of economic evaluation also seems to be related to the strength of health economics training that has a long tradition in the Netherlands, Sweden and the UK.

In the Netherlands, when the implementation of the Dunning Report guidelines for the exclusion of some medical services from social insurance coverage proved too controversial, attention turned to HTA. An initial evaluation of the effectiveness of 126 existing technologies was undertaken as part of the investigative medicine programme run by the Health Insurance Funds Council (Ham, 1997b: 62). In this shift towards evidence-based medicine, emphasis has been placed on the role of professional bodies and specialist associations. Interestingly, as Exter *et al.*

observe, 'since the 1990s, such systematic evaluations . . . are used as an important tool to assist policy-making, including priority setting' (2004: 99). Here it is also indicative that the government created a specific programme to fund evaluation of health technologies. In sum, the Dunning Report has had a long-lasting effect on health policy and indeed its basic algorithm for health priority setting provides the basis for decisions taken on the basic health insurance package (Schäfer *et al.*, 2010: 99).

In 1987, Sweden was the first European country to establish a public agency, the Swedish Council on Technology Assessment in Health Care, which is responsible for promoting the cost-effective use of health care technologies (Garrido *et al.*, 2008b). The Council reviews and evaluates the social, ethical and medical impact of health technologies and then distributes the information to front-line decision makers, including officials in the central government and county councils as well as doctors (Werkö *et al.*, 2001). In addition, the National Board for Health and Welfare has been commissioned to develop evidence-based guidelines for the treatment of selected chronic illnesses. Interestingly, the guidelines come in versions not only for health personnel and patients, but also for policy makers and include guidance in priority setting (Glenngård *et al.*, 2005).

Similarly, in recent years, HTA in Britain has received heightened public awareness with the creation of NICE (Harrison and McDonald, 2007). The Institute is responsible for evaluating new technologies and care guidelines with regard to their clinical and cost-effectiveness at the request of the Department of Health. The Institute's guidance on the effectiveness of specific drugs has attracted particular public attention, among them Beta Interferon for multiple sclerosis sufferers, the flu drug Relenza and new types of drugs for breast cancer patients. The establishment of NICE accompanied the development of the National Service Framework, which set out patterns of care for specific diseases, disabilities and patient groups and the establishment of the Commission for Health Improvement which, in turn, is responsible for monitoring and improving standards at the local level (Harrison and McDonald, 2008).

The Australian Health Technology Advisory Committee advises the government on the costs and effectiveness of targeted medical technologies. The Committee has representatives from the federal and state governments as well as the medical profession, insurance funds, hospitals and consumers. The Australian Institute of Health and Welfare also established a health technology division to monitor technological developments and advise the government on whether and under what conditions technologies should be used in Australia. Of the specific major areas studied, including MRIs, organ transplant procedures and laparoscopic surgery, recommendations have led to the introduction of these

Box 4.16 Evidence-based medicine in Australia

In 1998 a formal process to provide evidence-based medicine with regards to the introduction and use of new medical procedures was implemented in Australia. As part of this process, an expert panel, the Medical Services Advisory Committee (MSAC), was created to make recommendations to the Minister of Health as to which new medical services and technologies should be included on the Medicare Benefits Schedule (MBS). The MBS in turn sets a scheduled fee for medical services for which the Commonwealth government will pay. In order for a medical procedure to get funding to cover the fee for a medical practitioner, the procedure must have an MBS Item Number and be evaluated by contractors employed by the Medicare Benefits Branch (O'Malley, 2006; Gallego *et al.*, 2011).

new techniques on a controlled basis (Palmer and Short, 2000). Additionally, in 1998 the Medical Services Advisory Committee was established to screen new medical procedures and services (see Box 4.16).

In the USA, assessment of medical technology has been pervasive in both the private and public sectors, but there has been little cooperation, coordination or even exchange of data among the many assessment endeavours. This situation led the American College of Physicians to conclude that the USA 'has no effective policies to restrain the spread of technology' (2008: 60). In a major study, the Institute of Medicine (IOM) likewise concluded that the USA must strengthen its capacity to assess clinical services (IOM, 2008). It recommended that Congress establish a National Clinical Effectiveness Assessment Program to develop standards and processes to provide 'systematic, reliable and unbiased information on clinical effectiveness' (see Box 4.17). It argued that although

Box 4.17 IOM call for a National Clinical Effectiveness Assessment Program

According to the Institute of Medicine, Congress should direct the secretary of the Department of Health and Human Services (DHHS) to designate a single entity to ensure production of credible, unbiased information about clinical effectiveness. The Programme should: (1) set priorities for, fund and manage systematic reviews of clinical effectiveness; (2) develop a common language and standards for conducting systematic reviews of the evidence and for generating clinical guidelines and recommendations; (3) provide a forum for addressing conflicting guidelines and recommendations and (4) prepare an annual report to Congress. The secretary of DHHS should also appoint a Clinical Effectiveness Advisory Board to oversee the Programme. Its membership should be designed to minimize bias and include representation of diverse public and private sector expertise and interests (Institute of Medicine, 2008).

numerous stakeholders, policy makers and government entities have proposed that new investments be made in comparative effectiveness research, more attention is needed to assure that health care decision makers can discern which evidence is valid and under what circumstances. To that end, the IOM recommended that the Program appoint an independent Priority Setting Advisory Committee to develop and implement a process for identifying high priority areas that merit systematic evidence assessment. It should be noted that such efforts have been proposed frequently in the past with little long-term success in the highly fragmented private/public environment of US health care.

In part because of the historical lack of effective national guidance in the USA, and driven by rapidly mounting Medicaid costs, individual states have begun to 'reevaluate their once-limited role in the assessment of medical technology' (Mendelson *et al.*, 1995: 84). In a few states, detailed assessments are being conducted on selected technologies. Leading the way are Minnesota's Health Technology Advisory Committee, Washington State's Health Services Effectiveness Advisory Committee and the Oregon Medical Technology Assessment Program.

As noted earlier, HTA in Germany has tended to lag behind other countries and until recently was focused on the licensing of pharmaceuticals and medical devices (Perleth *et al.*, 1999). Beyond that, the assessment of medical technology is linked to the coverage specified in contracts with health care providers. In the case of ambulatory care, where regulation has developed furthest, the federal committee of doctors and insurance funds decides on the effectiveness of new technologies to be covered by health insurance as well as re-evaluate existing technologies based on the criteria of benefit, medical necessity and efficiency. As assessments are sector-specific, overall the system of HTA has been fragmented (Busse, 1999) although developments in recent years mark a more systematic approach (Burau, 2007a; Sauerland, 2009). Examples are Disease Management Programmes for selected chronic illnesses that are based on evidence-based clinical guidelines and connected to mechanisms of financial reimbursement and the new Institute for Quality and Efficiency that in many ways resembles NICE in the UK and is responsible for evaluating clinical guidelines and providing information on quality.

To date, the inclusion of quality management in Taiwan has been limited although there is increasing discussion of clinical guidelines and evidence-based medicine. While the BNHI has initiated a variety of quality monitoring and assurance programmes, including the Fee-for-Outcomes (FFO) approach and the construction of hospital quality indicators (Cheng, 2003), in comparison to other countries examined here, Taiwan has lagged behind in this area. Moreover, HTA has been limited in Taiwan and the NHI has not made significant efforts to shape the diffusion of the latest sophisticated high-technology medicine (Lu and Hsiao, 2003). Again, the ardent belief in the medical model, combined with the strong profit motive of providers in Taiwan, has resulted in the proliferation of new medical technologies with little substantiation as to whether they actually improve health.

In summary, HTA has become more critical in priority setting as the scarcity of resources increasingly conflicts with intensified demands and pressures for the dissemination of innovative techniques. Evidence-based medicine is currently a catch phrase for efforts to resolve health care dilemmas and provide a foundation for the allocation and rationing of health care resources, but it continues to lack clear definition and commitment in most countries.

Information technologies in medical practice

Another emergent debate over technologies in health care centres on the role of health information technologies (HIT) that facilitate the comprehensive management of health information across computerized systems and the exchange of this information among consumers, providers, government and quality entities and insurers. To date, most policy attention within HIT has focused on electronic health records (EHRs), which represent a systematic use of digital health information about individual patients or populations (Jha *et al.*, 2008).

EHRs have been touted by some as the most promising instrument for improving the overall quality, safety and efficiency of the health delivery system and moving an archaic, disjointed and inefficient system into the 21st century (Chaudhry *et al.*, 2006). Proponents argue that broad and consistent utilization of EHRs (and HIT in general) will moderate costs, improve quality, reduce medical errors, increase administrative efficiency, decrease paperwork and expand access to affordable care. Moreover, many public health benefits, including early detection of infectious disease outbreaks and improved tracking of chronic disease management and evaluation of health care, could accompany the use of HIT (Davis *et al.*, 2009). In contrast, critics of EHRs argue that the start-up costs in time and money are prohibitive and raise concerns over privacy and confidentiality and other potential unintended consequences of digital records. As a result, adoption of HIT and, especially, systems for sharing information across providers has been slow and erratic across countries (Schoen *et al.*, 2007).

New Zealand was among the first countries to adopt HIT, particularly in primary care, where it has one of the highest international rates of use. Although GPs moved quickly into EHR use in the 1990s, until recently HIT in general has lacked government leadership or coordination (Gauld *et al.*, 2012). As a result, most physician groups are unable to share records with one another and interoperability with hospital systems and after-hours facilities is limited. In 2009, however, the national IT Health Board was created to coordinate developments, including nationally consistent portable electronic patient records, with an aim for all New Zealanders to have access to a basic set of web-based health information by 2014. The IT Health Board also produced the National Health IT Plan in 2010 to facilitate a fully integrated health system and works with a range of agencies, including private vendors whose activities such as working towards common standards are coordinated under the aegis of the New Zealand Health IT Cluster (Thomson *et al.*, 2011).

Through the use of reimbursement, incentives and locally-led commissioning from private providers, EHRs are also used in all GP practices in the UK NHS (Gauld *et al.*, 2012). Despite this, as in New Zealand the use of HIT in secondary care is sporadic, largely because of huge cost overruns and delays in implementing a nationwide NHS HIT programme deployed in 2005. The goal was to have 60 million patients in a centralized electronic health record by 2010, but because of numerous setbacks and widening criticism, it was terminated as a sentinel programme in 2011, although EHRs in physicians' offices remain.

In Germany, there has been a high uptake of relatively sophisticated HIT in primary care settings, including that used for disease management and referrals, although interoperability between hospitals and primary care settings remains limited. There is no national strategy for HIT, but the electronic health card introduced in 2011 is to be fully implemented in 2014. Patients will decide whether their medical data are saved on the card or not. Similarly, in the Netherlands, all GPs use EHR for health recording and for administrative purposes. Drug prescription, communication with specialists and performance measurement are facilitated by EHR systems, although, to date, hospitals have comparatively low levels of EHR use and poor interoperability (Gauld *et al.*, 2012). A National IT Institute for Healthcare was created to improve this situation and coordinate future developments, although in November 2011 the planned national electronic patient record system was tabled for the immediate future.

Australia has been active in the development of lifetime EHRs for all its citizens and has a near universal use of them in GP practices and more limited usage in the hospital sector. The national strategy on health information is managed by the Australian Health Ministers' Advisory Committee, with accords in place among governments and other key agencies on developing, collecting and exchanging data to improve the health of the population and the delivery of health services (Thomson *et al.*, 2011). In conjunction, health system performance indicators are being adopted and monitored. Moreover, an intergovernmental strategy on HIT was approved and the National E-Health Transition Authority (NEHTA) created to improve the quality and efficiency of health care. Under the Healthcare Identifiers Act of 2010, a unique 16-digit health care identifier is being assigned to each health care consumer and provider to improve communications in discharge, tests, referrals and prescriptions. Another major national EHR initiative, Personally Controlled Electronic Health Record (PCEHR), is due to be available nationally by 2013.

Singapore has a comprehensive HIT system that began as an effort to develop hospital administrative systems for admissions, discharges and billing processes. This was supplemented in 2004 with an Electronic Medical Record Exchange (EMRX) to provide an electronic platform for the sharing of medical documents, which, in turn, led to the advent of EHRs designed to permit the eventual integration of diverse sub-systems. Singapore also developed the Integrated Care Services (ICS) webportal to connect acute hospitals, primary care providers and the public with step-down services including nursing homes and chronic disease facilities. A distinctive feature of Singapore's HIT services is a personal health record (PHR), which incorporates hardcopy personal health books that provide individuals with ownership of their health records and promote better continuity of care both at the institutional level and at home (Lim, 2006).

Taiwan has four major systems of HIT. The foundation of Taiwan's NHI system is digitized patient records and claims, which are closely linked to the other three elements: online claim submissions, the BNHI virtual private network (VPN) and the smart IC card (Long and Chang, 2012). The incentive for Taiwan's providers to digitize their patient records and claims is that with online claim submissions and reviews they can receive reimbursement from BNHI more quickly. Moreover, the online claim submission saves substantial administrative costs on both sides. These first three components are connected through the VPN and comprise Taiwan's NHI management information system that allows BNHI to carry out real-time monitoring of utilization. There is evidence that this system contributes to reduction of duplications in diagnostic procedures and laboratory tests, as well as duplication or contraindications of prescription drugs (Chi *et al.*, 2012).

Despite a number of initiatives over the past decade, HIT is not widely used in Japan other than for billing purposes. In 2010, the government announced the New IT Strategy to encourage its use. The Strategy has four parts: (1) develop patient electronic medical records that can be accessed by all providers; (2) develop HIT and telehealth platforms to help link patients with doctors and nurses in underserved areas; (3) create a platform that can monitor pharmaceutical prescriptions and adverse events in real time; and (4) create a claims database of all conditions and interventions to facilitate assessment of community needs and development of interventions (Thomson *et al.*, 2011). In spite of these initiatives, there continue to be many political and cultural barriers to widespread HIT adoption in Japan.

According to a study by RAND Health, the US health care system could save more than $81 billion annually, reduce adverse health care events and improve the quality of care if it were to widely adopt HIT (Hillestad *et al.*, 2005). Despite calls for action by the Institute of Medicine and an Executive Order from President Bush in 2004 that established a ten-year plan to expand HIT, most medical records are still stored on paper, meaning that they cannot be used to coordinate care, systematically measure quality, or reduce medical errors. As of 2009, less than a third of physicians' offices had high functionality EHRs and less than 2 per cent of hospitals had comprehensive EHR systems (Thomson *et al.*, 2011). In order to stimulate investment in HIT, the 2009 American Recovery and Reinvestment Act provides financial incentives of up to $27 billion over six years for physicians and hospitals tied to the attainment of benchmarks for the 'meaningful use' of HIT (Thomson *et al.*, 2011). Moreover, the President's Council of Advisors on Science and Technology concluded that the move to EHRs is critical to cost containment efforts (Executive Office of the President, 2010). EHRs also figured prominently in the Affordable Care Act as noted by then Office of Management and Budget Director Peter Orszag in describing the Obama Administration's strategy: 'In order to help contain cost growth over the long term, we need a new health care system that has digitized information...in which that information is used to assess what's working and what's not more intelligently, and in which we're paying for quality rather than quantity' (Charlie Rose–Peter Orszag Interview, 2009).

Trends in priority setting

National policies on priority setting are a pertinent area to test the concept of convergence (discussed in Chapter 1) since the predominance of public funding means that resources are limited, thus making priority setting inevitable. Table 4.5 summarizes our findings that reconfirm the interrelationship between convergence and embeddedness suggested by Saltman (1997). Using Bennett's (1991) distinctions between convergence by policy goals, policy content and policy instruments, our analysis shows that there is some convergence, but it is restricted largely to the procedural aspect of policy goals and does not appear to extend to content and instruments. Despite signs of convergence at the ideational level, policy content and the preferred policy instruments for implementing such policy continue to vary widely across these countries. By and large, countries continue to adopt different strategies to deal with similar problems.

Table 4.5 ***Substantive and procedural aspects of health policy convergence***

	Procedural aspects of health policy convergence		
Substantive aspects of health policy convergence	*Policy goals*	*Policy content*	*Policy instruments*
Rationing/ priority setting	An issue in all countries, but limited agreement on its meaning.	Much variation. Demand vs supply, price vs non-price rationing.	Wide variation though some moves towards more centrally controlled instruments.
Increased dependence on marketplace	An issue in all countries, highly controversial in many countries.	Most countries have adopted some market features but there is no clear convergence.	Wide variation even among national health and social insurance systems.
Cost containment strategies	An important goal in all countries, but even at this level its importance relative to universal access and equity varies.	Some moves to co-payment, provider-payment mechanisms, etc., but persistent differences in weight given to demand vs supply.	Considerable variation and mixes of policy instruments used to contain costs.

Source: Adopted from Blank and Burau (2006).

While there has been a shift in goals in all countries towards cost containment, the disparate emphases on an array of demand- and supply-side approaches display significant diversity across these countries. Also, while the inclusion of efficiency or cost containment as a goal appears universal, there remain wide disparities among the countries as to the degree of access and equity in their respective health care systems. Similarly, although all countries have integrated some aspects of the market into their systems through recent reforms, the wide variation in both form and degree argues against the conclusion that they are converging to a market-driven health system. Far from it! Unlike the USA, other countries continue to maintain relatively robust regulatory controls over market forces.

Regarding the allocation and rationing of health care resources, about the only perceivable convergence is that it is increasingly evident in all countries that medicine must be rationed because, in the light of endless technological possibilities, no country can serve all the health needs of their population to the fullest. Countries with global budgets or other supply-side controls are likely to depend on non-price rationing mechanisms and make tougher choices at the macro-allocation level. In contrast, countries that rely more heavily on price rationing forgo setting broad limits, thus losing any semblance of equity or systematic rationing policy. The result is that rationing in national health systems differs greatly from that in social insurance systems and, especially, market-dominated systems.

It should also be noted that health policy is not static and that movement in one direction is often followed by a move in the opposite direction as political fortunes change or the public responds negatively to a change. Any discussion of convergence risks underestimating the political dynamics inherent in health policy. For instance, New Zealand was widely cited in the early 1990s when it initiated strong market reforms as an example of NHS convergence towards a market system, but most of these reforms were repealed by later governments.

In the end though, all countries must face the issue of rationing of health resources for the high users of medicine, including the elderly and individuals who engage in multiple high-risk behaviours. Evidence suggests that there is little consensus in our countries as to whether or how to do this. Finally, because the diffusion of medical technologies is such a critical factor in cost containment and central to any debate over rationing (it is generally expensive technologies or drugs being rationed), the preliminary efforts at HTA outlined here must be strengthened. The process must be made more transparent concerning the explicit tradeoffs required when a decision is made to fund expensive new technologies: where specifically will the money come from, and what other programmes might be cut? This leads us back to medical professionals who, as we shall see in the next chapter, continue to wield considerable power and have a substantial stake and interest in cost containment, rationing and health policy in general.

Chapter 5

The Medical Profession

The power of the medical profession stems from the fact that health care is largely defined as medical care. Doctors are responsible for diagnosis and as such define patients' health care needs. Doctors also provide treatment, but more often than not this involves (either directly or by referral) other health practitioners, such as medical specialists, nurses, physiotherapists, laboratory technicians or dieticians (see Box 5.1). This puts doctors in a key position regarding the allocation of health care resources. Health systems, health policy and politics cannot be understood without doctors and vice versa. Doctors often enjoy considerable power and are seen as the archetypal example of a profession. Autonomy and dominance are at the heart of medical power and refer to the ability of doctors to make autonomous decisions concerning the contents and the conditions of medical work (see also Box 5.2).

Inasmuch as doctors are embedded in specific sub-systems of funding, provision and governance, professional autonomy will always be contingent and relative, and this also points to the complex relationship between doctors and the state. Significantly, professional autonomy and power are part of the implicit contract between doctors and the state (Burau *et al.*, 2009). The state grants professional autonomy in return for

Box 5.1 Nurses in health systems

Among the other practitioners involved in the provision of health care, nurses play a particularly prominent role. Traditionally, nursing has been conceptualized as a 'semi-profession', reflecting the relative dominance of the medical profession in health systems. In contrast, later feminist analyses have set focus on nursing and its 'professional projects' in its own right (Witz and Annandale, 2006). This has been echoed by studies, which have stressed that the health division of labour is not necessarily fixed, but instead dynamic and in flux and in fact more resembles a 'negotiated order'. Like doctors, nurses predominantly work in hospitals and the strong specialization of medical treatment has resulted in a wide range of specialisms for post-degree training, including intensive care nursing, child care nursing and operating theatre nursing. Nurses also work outside hospitals: in primary care settings as practice nurses in GP practices, and in community settings as home nurses for the elderly or public health nurses.

Box 5.2 Understanding professions

The understanding of professions has changed over time. Early approaches defined professions by specific traits (such as formal knowledge, long training and high social status) and by a positive role in society. However, these approaches have been criticized for taking the self-image of professions at face value and for remaining largely uncritical. Instead, later approaches focus on the social organization of power. Freidson (1994) for example defines professions as being primarily concerned with attaining and maintaining control. Control consists of autonomy (that is, control over the professions' own work) and dominance (that is, control over the work of others). Medical power is highly complex and has both an individual and a collective dimension, comprising the freedom of individual doctors to practise as they see fit as well as the activities of doctors' professional organizations. Here, Light (1995) further distinguishes among clinical and fiscal autonomy, practice and organizational autonomy, and organizational and institutional control. Elston (1991) adds cultural authority to her understanding of medical power. Cultural authority refers to the dominance of medical definitions of health and illness. At the same time, analysing professions across different countries has become an important concern for recent studies on the organization of expertise (Burau *et al.*, 2004). This builds on earlier historical analyses that emphasized the diversity of the phenomenon called 'professionalism' and exposed the Anglo-American centredness of many ideas about professions. For example, Johnson (1995) suggests that professions and the state have tended to be perceived as separate entities, which then relate to each other as autonomous professions and interventionist state. This makes it difficult to understand professions in Continental and Nordic countries, which have traditionally been 'state interventionist'.

doctors providing services central to the legitimacy of modern states. Medical practice, by virtue of the specialized knowledge on which it is based, also gives legitimacy to the (potentially problematic) allocation of health care resources. However, inherent in this interdependent relationship between doctors and the state is tension, such as that between medically defined need and the finitude of financial resources. For the medical profession, the challenge is 'to manage the relationship with the state so as simultaneously to appropriate public authority without surrendering to public control' (Moran, 1999: 99).

What are the implications for understanding doctors in the context of health systems and policy? Power emerges as a central theme, as does the complex nature of medical power. Far from being absolute, the power of doctors is relative and varies between different specialities, points in time and countries. This comparative analysis highlights how medical power is contingent upon the specific sub-systems of funding, provision and governance. At the same time, the power of doctors is intrinsically changeable as it is linked with states and their agendas. Analysing how health care reform affects doctors and their power is crucial. Equally, as much as doctors are entangled with health systems, changes in the regulation of medicine also give an indication of wider changes in health systems (Moran, 1999).

This chapter explores the issues of embeddedness, power and change in relation to the role of the medical profession. The first section provides an overview of the medical profession using OECD statistics. The second section locates the practice of doctors in the context of the health system, while the third directs attention to recent reforms and how they have affected doctors. The fourth section examines how doctors are paid and what this says about the relative power of doctors. This is followed by an analysis of the political organization of doctors and the role doctors play in the policy process. The concluding section summarizes relations between doctors, health policy and the state.

Who doctors are

Doctors are often thought of as a homogeneous group. The notion of profession suggests a cohesion that allows for dominance and autonomy. This corresponds to the idea that medical professionalism is a universal phenomenon (see Box 5.1). However, even a cursory look at statistics reveals considerable diversity among doctors across and within countries, for example in terms of the number of specialists or the percentage of female doctors. The analysis of statistics naturally remains on the surface, but as an overview it provides a useful starting point for comparison. Through highlighting similarities and differences, statistics raise 'why' questions which demand more detailed analysis. The number of doctors presented in Table 5.1 provides a first indication of the diversity that exists across countries.

In many countries, the trend in the number of doctors per 1,000 inhabitants since the early 1960s tells a familiar story of welfare state expansion together with a shift towards curative, specialized medicine. In the majority of countries, the number of doctors has more or less doubled. Beyond the commonality of growth over time, the current number of doctors ranges from 1.5 doctors per 1,000 inhabitants in Taiwan to 3.8 in Sweden. The remaining countries fall into roughly four groups: Singapore and Japan with approximately 2 doctors per 1,000 inhabitants; New Zealand, the UK and the USA with about 2.5 doctors per 1,000 inhabitants; Australia with slightly more than 3 doctors per 1,000 inhabitants; and Germany and the Netherlands with 3.7 doctors per 1,000 inhabitants. The variation is significant and, while there is no ready explanation for it, it may reflect differences in the levels of health

Table 5.1 *Number of practising doctors per 1,000 inhabitants, 1980–2010*

	1980	*1985*	*1990*	*1995*	*2000*	*2005*	*2010**
Australia	1.8	1.9	2.2	2.5	2.5	2.8	3.1
Germany	n/a	n/a	n/a	3.1	3.3	3.4	3.7
Japan	1.3	1.5	1.7	n/a	1.9	2.0	2.2
Netherlands	1.9	2.2	2.5	n/a	3.2	3.7	n/a
New Zealand	1.6	1.7	1.9	2.0	2.2	2.1	2.6
Singapore	n/a	n/a	n/a	1.4	n/a	1.5	1.8
Sweden	2.2	2.6	2.9	2.9	3.1	3.5	3.8
Taiwan	n/a	n/a	n/a	1.3	1.3	1.5	1.5
United Kingdom	1.3	1.4	1.6	1.8	1.9	2.4	2.7
United States	n/a	n/a	n/a	2.2	2.3	2.4	2.4

* The figures for Australia are from 2009 and the figures for Taiwan are from 2007.
n/a = not available.

Sources: Data from OECD (2008, 2012b); Bureau of National Health Insurance (2008).

care expenditure. It might also reflect government restrictions on the number of doctors in the form of limits on the number of medical students or the number of doctors who are allowed to establish practices outside hospitals.

The disparity in the number of doctors also disguises regional variations in the distribution of doctors. This is particularly pertinent in large, unevenly populated countries. Australia is a case in point. There are no legal restrictions on the ability of doctors to establish a practice wherever they wish in Australia. This has resulted in a geographical maldistribution of doctor–patient ratios that are much higher in the capital cities than in the remainder of each state, especially among specialists in the most rural areas (Palmer and Short, 2000: 196). Successive Commonwealth governments have attempted to address the shortage of doctors in the bush, but the imbalance in their distribution has proven persistent, in part reflecting lifestyle choices of doctors (Davies *et al.*, 2006).

Day *et al.* (2005) found that recent changes in bulk billing have done little to ameliorate geographical inequities. In May 2009, the Commonwealth government announced reforms to help address major workforce shortages in rural and remote health services, including cash incentives to encourage doctors to work in some of Australia's most isolated communities. Under the new system, a doctor relocating from a major city to a regional centre could receive a grant. If that doctor moved to a very remote area the grant could be considerably higher. Retention payments will also be linked to remoteness, with bonus payments for doctors working in some of Australia's most inaccessible locations set to have their packages almost double from $25,000 to $47,000 a year. Moreover, restrictions on overseas-trained doctors will be lifted sooner if they move to rural areas to practise and more locum relief will be available for doctors in 'difficult locations'. It is estimated that at least 17,000 additional health professionals, including 1,800 doctors, are needed urgently in rural and remote Australia just to ensure basic access to health care (FarmOnline, 2009).

The situation is similar in the USA. Approximately 20 per cent of the US population resides in rural areas while less than 9 per cent of US physicians practise there (Association of American Medical Colleges, 2008). Despite incentive programmes, remote areas find it difficult to retain doctors. The fact that the USA is heavily skewed towards specialities compounds this problem since family practice doctors are the most common rural physicians. In fact, the more specialized a physician is, the less likely he or she will practise in a rural area (National Rural Health Association, 2009). The NRHA reports that 2,157 geographic regions designated as health professional shortage areas are in rural areas, compared with 910 in urban settings. The numerical increase in the number of physicians in the USA has not resulted in a proportional increase in physicians practising outside urban areas and has not alleviated geographic maldistribution.

The BNHI in densely populated Taiwan encourages health care providers to serve in remote areas through higher reimbursements or waivers of military service obligations. The government also runs a programme that pays for the studies of medical students who agree to work for six years in an isolated area or at a special medical facility. Currently, over 1,000 doctors who participated in this programme are working at clinics and medical institutions on outlying islands and in rural and mountainous areas (*Republic of China Yearbook*, 2008). Despite these efforts, large disparities still exist especially in the rugged and isolated mountainous districts.

Countries differ not only in terms of the number of doctors but also the diversity of the medical profession itself. One feature of this diversity is the fact that doctors are increasingly female to the extent that, as Table 5.2 shows, in the majority of countries well over a third of doctors are women. This can be attributed both to cultural and economic developments that have changed the position of women in society and to more specific state-initiated measures that have strengthened the position of women doctors (Riska and Wegar, 1995). For example, the end to discriminatory practices has helped to increase the number of female medical students, as has the establishment of new medical schools with

Table 5.2 *Female practising doctors, as a percentage of practising doctors, 2007*

Australia	33.8
Germany	39.7
Japan	17.1
Netherlands	36.0
New Zealand	37.8
Sweden	43.1
United Kingdom	40.6
United States	30.1

Source: Data from OECD (2009a).

their emphasis on community and primary care medicine. In Japan, however, women doctors account for less than 20 per cent of all doctors. The traditional dominance of males in the medical profession in Japan has been resistant to change, although an increasing number of young women have entered medicine in recent years, and the proportion of women is significantly higher among younger doctors. The reason for the smaller proportion of female doctors in the USA (30.1 per cent) is less clear, but it might be linked to the fact that medical education in the USA tends to be considerably longer than in other countries (4 years of medical school after 4 years of university). Also, the strong emphasis on medical specialities instead of general practice might be less attractive to potential women candidates who prefer the latter.

Another indication of the diversity of the medical profession is the division between generalist and specialist doctors. As Table 5.3 illustrates, in most countries there are significantly more specialists than generalists. One possible explanation is that in specialist practice and acute care the medical model of health and illness can excel. The ratio is even higher in Sweden and Taiwan, where the number of specialists per 1,000 inhabitants is five to six times that of generalists. In the case of Sweden, this reflects the fact that hospitals have long been dominant in the provision of health care, with patients having direct access to specialists in outpatient hospital departments. In contrast, the provision of ambulatory care has been patchy.

Data for Japan are unavailable in part because, unlike Western countries, in Japan the generalist–specialist distinction is almost meaningless. Thus, OECD data combines specialists and generalists. By tradition all physicians are doctors of medical science and trained to become a specialist, but once they complete their training only a few continue to practise their speciality, with most leaving the large hospitals to practise

Table 5.3 ***Numbers of generalist and specialist doctors per 1,000 inhabitants***

	Generalist doctors	*Specialist doctors*
Australia	1.43	1.35
Germany	1.48	2.03
Japan	n/a	n/a
Netherlands	0.47	1.01
New Zealand	0.76	0.79
Singapore	1.00	0.63
Sweden	0.60	2.56
Taiwan	0.20	1.30
United Kingdom	0.72	1.77
United States	0.96	1.46

n/a = not available.

Sources: Data from OECD (2009b); Taiwan Medical Association (2004).

in small community hospitals or open their own clinics without any formal retraining as a general practitioner. Significantly, there is no nationally recognized or formal system of speciality training or registration; rather numerous academic societies have established their own certification systems. Both physicians and nurses are licensed for life in Japan with no requirement for license renewal or continuing medical or nursing education, and no peer or utilization review (Thomson *et al.*, 2011).

One problem facing many countries is the difficulty of ensuring an adequate supply of trained doctors to service growing and ageing populations within the context of an expanding array of medical technologies, compounded by an ageing medical profession. One response has been import of medical professionals, particularly doctors and nurses, from less developed countries, thus exacerbating health care resource gaps in their home countries (see Box 5.3). This problem is often most pronounced in the primary care workforce (Harris *et al.*, 2011) because medical students are drawn to specialities or sub-specialities which typically offer greater compensation, prestige and regular working hours (Davis *et al.*, 2009).

According to Schwartz (2011), the USA is heading towards a severe primary care workforce bottleneck due to decreased production and accelerated attrition. Demand will be fuelled by the 80 million Americans retiring over the next 20 years and the expanded insurance coverage for

Box 5.3 New Zealand workforce reforms

Past inattention to workforce development has meant that New Zealand has faced an ongoing health workforce crisis: it is the highest importer in the OECD of foreign born and trained doctors and among the highest of nurses and, at the same time, has lost many younger health professionals (largely to Australia). Moreover, some hospitals and rural areas rely heavily on highly paid locums, driving up their costs and raising questions about service sustainability (Gauld, 2010). In order to address the loss of New Zealand-trained professionals overseas, a voluntary bonding scheme was introduced in February, 2009, to reward medical, midwifery, and nursing graduates who agree to work in hard-to-staff communities and specialties with higher vacancy rates and locum use. The government has also increased the availability of medical and nursing school places with more doctors and nurses expected to join the workforce in coming years. DHBs are increasingly working collaboratively to ensure sustainability of and access to specialist services in smaller towns and regions (Thomson *et al.*, 2011).

32 million Americans in the Affordable Care Act. Meanwhile, the primary care workforce is shrinking. A third of GPs will leave medical practice over the next decade as baby boomer physicians retire. As a result, by 2016 the number of adult primary care physicians leaving practice will exceed the number entering. However, the projected shortfall includes surgeons as well (Sheldon, 2011). For instance, while demographic needs have increased dramatically, in 1981, 1,047 surgeons were certified by the American Board of Surgery and by 2008 that number had dropped to just 909. Addressing these national shortfalls without further disrupting the global workforce will be a challenge in the coming decades.

Types and settings of medical practice

In many ways medical practice goes to the heart of what doctors are about. It is here that doctors relate to patients and make decisions about the allocation of health care resources. This occurs at the micro-level of individual clinics, doctors' surgeries and ward rounds but it is also embedded in the respective health system. The sub-systems of funding, provision and governance frame the practice of doctors. The settings of medical practice describe the institutions in which medicine is organized and relate to what Moran and Wood (1993) call the 'regulation of market structures'. This section focuses on the settings where different types of doctors work and the implications this has for the power of the medical profession.

Table 5.4 ***Types and settings of medical practice***

	Ambulatory settings (in either solo or group practice)	*Hospital settings*
Generalist/ specialist practitioners[a]	*Generalists only* Australia, Britain, Netherlands, New Zealand, Sweden, Singapore, Taiwan	*Mostly specialists* Australia, Britain, Germany, Netherlands, Singapore, Sweden, Taiwan, USA
Private/public practitioners	*Mostly public* Sweden	*Mostly public* Australia, Britain, New Zealand, Sweden, Singapore
	Mostly private Australia, Britain, Germany, Germany, Japan, Netherlands, New Zealand, Singapore, Taiwan, USA	*Mostly private* Japan, Netherlands, *Public and private* Germany, Taiwan, USA

[a] It is difficult to include Japan in this category as there is no clear distinction between generalist and specialist practitioners.

As Table 5.4 illustrates, hospitals and ambulatory practices are the typical settings for doctors. Ambulatory settings can be further distinguished into solo and group practices. Different settings are closely associated with different types of medical practice (ambulatory settings with general practitioners and hospitals with specialists), although there are exceptions. As discussed in Chapter 3, in the majority of countries, patients have direct access to GPs, but need a medical referral to see specialists. In contrast, there is more diversity in terms of the public/private distinction, reflecting the public/private mix of the health systems in which medical practice is embedded.

Hospital doctors are either public or private practitioners, depending on the ownership of the hospital. As providers of specialist care, hospitals are complex organizations that rely on the division of labour across a wide range of health practitioners. This means that specialists depend to a great extent on the work of others when they practise in hospital settings. As complex organizations, hospitals also need management structures to coordinate the different parts of the labour process. In addition to being an organizing force, hospital managers personify the rationality of economics, which has come to the fore over concerns about cost pressures and containment. Not surprisingly, potential and real conflicts between managers and doctors have become a prominent issue, and highlight the contingency of medical power.

The introduction of market mechanisms and corresponding managerialist reforms are the key here. For instance, in New Zealand before the health reforms of the 1980s and 1990s, hospital boards were run by triumvirates composed of medical staff, nursing staff and administrators, with medical staff predominant on most boards. In large part, the reforms were an effort to wrest control from these boards, which critics felt were self-serving, inefficient and unconcerned with cost control. Beginning in 1983 with the government's setting of hospital budgets and culminating in the replacement of hospital boards with Area Health Boards in 1989, a series of steps was taken to create a structure for hospitals that would enable them to 'avoid capture by the medical community' (Blank, 1994). The continual erosion of the influence of the medical community over decision making and the shift in authority to managers and outside consultants has been a contentious issue that at times has resulted in near open warfare between the parties. Moreover, since the introduction of capitation funding for general practice, regulatory control of general practice fees has become increasingly intense, to the discomfort of many GPs who have yet to adjust to the political implications of increased public funding of their services (Dovey *et al.*, 2011).

As developments in other countries suggest, there are also limits to the managerialist approach and, for example, Britain has seen the revival of elements of professionally based management since the late 1990s, but under changed conditions. In his assessment of recent reforms, Hunter (2008) argues that the medical profession is no longer exclusively seen as a problem, but also part of the solution. It is indicative that a medical specialist appointed junior minister was chairing a review of NHS reforms; he proclaimed that future change should be clinically and locally driven. In this respect primary care trusts and the notion of practice-based commissioning were already a focal point for the type of organizational change envisaged by the review. Indeed, this is confirmed by the most recent health reforms in 2012, which introduce GP-led Clinical Commissioning Groups.

The situation is different in smaller ambulatory settings where doctors tend to work as independent, private practitioners. Solo practice, the traditional way in which doctors have worked, provides the greatest independence, while group practices are more likely to circumscribe independence. For instance, the independence associated with solo practice is especially pronounced in Japan where doctors operate out of so-called 'clinics', a majority of which have some inpatient accommodation, where they exercise discretion on admission and discharge (Ikegami, 2007). Clinics can keep a patient for up to 48 hours and are legally defined as having fewer than 20 beds. Doctors working in ambulatory settings do not have access to hospital facilities, although most doctors have some degree of specialization. Like Japan, in Taiwan, most general practice clinics are solo practices; less than 20 per cent are partnerships or group practices. Until the advent of the NHI made the practice illegal, physicians both prescribed and dispensed prescriptions in their offices.

In contrast, in other countries most primary care doctors work in group practices. The significance of group settings is particularly apparent in Sweden where doctors work in multidisciplinary health centres where their role is not necessarily paramount. This reflects the fact that the provision of health care has long been dominated by hospitals (Harrison, 2004) and that the initiative to set up health centres came from political-administrative circles (including the Ministry for Health and Social Affairs) not the medical profession (Garpenby, 2001). According to Ham (2010), however, there is substantial evidence of the value of multidisciplinary team work in primary care with much of the responsibility for the management of chronic diseases resting on nurses working as part of the team.

However, operating in a group setting can also strengthen the position of doctors as demonstrated by the emergence of regional independent practice associations (IPAs) of ambulatory care doctors in New Zealand and Australia. The IPAs act as collective negotiators, contract and fund holders for doctors who are overwhelmingly generalists. In New Zealand, for example, IPAs emerged largely as a pre-emptive response by GPs to a perceived threat by regional purchasers that contracts would be introduced for publicly financed primary care services, thus undercutting the tradition of fee-for-service private practice (Smith and Mays, 2007). Although developments in contracting and alternative methods of funding and managing services were initially either resisted or treated with caution by the majority of GPs, early successes in contracting, in budget holding for pharmaceutical and laboratory services and in establishing new services led to a progressive recruitment of IPA membership (Ashton, 2005).

In 2001, the New Zealand government introduced its Primary Healthcare Strategy aimed at strengthening primary care, improving access and reducing inequalities in health through development of 80 Primary Healthcare Organizations (PHOs), which are non-governmental, not-for-profit organizations contracted by their local DHB to manage capitation budgets devolved under contract and to purchase/commission a range of primary health services for their enrolled populations. Patients are encouraged to enroll with their general practice, and are then part of the enrolled population for the PHO to which the medical practice belongs. By 2009, nearly 95 per cent of the population was enrolled in one of the PHOs and most general practices are now part of a PHO (New Zealand Ministry of Health, 2009). An important feature of PHOs has been the engagement of GPs in health planning, resource allocation and broader health system decision making in a way that is consistent with their own professional aspirations and in the direction of wider health system goals of public health (Gauld, 2008).

Similarly, in Taiwan Primary Community Care Networks (PCCNs) were the product of recent primary care health reform initiatives. A PCCN consists of a group of clinic physicians whose medical jobs are categorized as family care. In turn, the clinics have to cooperate with at least one hospital for their patients' secondary or tertiary care (Lin *et al.*, 2010).

Regardless of the relative size of the practice settings, the status of independent contractors is likely to give doctors in ambulatory settings considerable autonomy. Nevertheless, it is in specialist practice that the medical model with its emphasis on acute illness and specialist knowledge can excel, making hospitals the most prestigious setting within which doctors work. A notable exception is Japan, which places heavy emphasis on preventive medicine and primary care in ambulatory settings. The relatively low number of doctors per capita in Japan is at least partly due to government policies fixing limits on the number of new entrants in medical schools and the number in each speciality.

In the majority of countries, hospitals are the only places in which specialist doctors practise. Examples of the few exceptions that exist are Germany and the USA. In Germany, hospital work is seen as transitional and is used as a springboard to set up a specialist practice in ambulatory care. In the USA, many specialists practise in ambulatory settings. However, as a result of managed care, demand for GPs is growing because of their increased use as gate-keepers and to encourage the use of primary care doctors in lieu of more expensive specialists (see Box 5.4). These moves have generated opposition by a US public which is used to being able to consult a specialist directly rather than having to be referred by a GP (Lamm and Blank, 2007).

Box 5.4 Primary care models in the USA

In the USA, the 'patient-centered medical home' model, in which a patient can receive targeted, accessible, continuous, coordinated and family-centred care by a personal physician, has gained particular interest as a means of strengthening primary care. Another movement generating considerable momentum among both public and private payers is the creation of 'accountable care organizations' (ACOs), which are networks of providers, including hospitals and physicians, that agree to take responsibility for providing a defined population with care that meets quality targets. In exchange, they share in the savings that constitute the difference between actual and forecasted health care spending for their population (Thomson *et al.*, 2011).

The practice of doctors is embedded in the specific context of hospitals and ambulatory care and their relative position in the sub-systems of funding, provision and governance. This is a truism but nevertheless highly relevant to understanding medical practice. In the case of Germany, for example, hospitals have traditionally been less well integrated in health governance, reflecting not only the mix of public and private non-profit providers, typical of social insurance systems such as those found in Japan and the Netherlands, but also the absence of a system of self-administration. Instead, health governance has been fragmented into contracts between individual hospitals and insurance funds, and into coexisting competencies between the federal and state governments. The fragmentation of health governance (also typical of other federalist countries such as Australia and the USA) strengthened the position of the provider side and left hospitals and hospital doctors relatively untouched by health reforms in the 1980s (Schwartz and Busse, 1997). However, this has been changing and the practice of hospital doctors is now much more strongly integrated in and controlled by joint self-administration (see Burau, 2007b). The funding of hospitals has moved away from prospective payments to payments based on DRGs, also flanked by extensive measures of quality assurance (see Sauerland, 2009). The Joint Committee as the key body of the joint self-administration now has a separate sub-committee on hospital care. The sub-committee consists of representatives from the hospital association, doctors and insurance funds, and is responsible for maintaining and extending the catalogue of hospital services covered by the health insurance and for deciding on measures of quality assurance.

The situation is different in national health services, which have traditionally been characterized by a greater degree of public integration. Britain is a typical example of a system where the degree of integration of ambulatory care has actually increased since the early 1990s. As part of the introduction of the internal market, many GPs chose to become 'fund holders' and were given budgets to purchase diagnostic procedures and elective surgery for their patients. GPs thereby extended their managerial responsibilities beyond their own practice and moved closer to the mainstream of NHS management. The reforms under the New Labour government from the late 1990s took this development a step further. General practices became part of Primary Care Trusts, which were responsible not only for the provision of primary care but also for the commissioning of all other health services within a certain area (Peckham and Exworthy, 2003), which developed into a comprehensive system of 'practice-based commissioning'. GPs worked within an organization that is directly funded by and accountable to government. The Minister for Health appointed the chief executives of Primary Care Trusts and the Trusts were subject to government guidance in the same way as hospital trusts. For example, Primary Care Trusts had to follow the National Service Framework that includes guidelines about appropriate care for individual patients and preferred service models (Checkland, 2004). This is complemented by the new GP contract introduced in 2004, which offers substantial additional rewards in return for meeting specified performance requirements, and by the specification of clinical models discussed in more detail below. From the perspective of the relative integration into the NHS, the new Clinical Commissioning Groups continue the trend, although under the banner of a greater room for manoeuvre for local/clinical decisions (Department of Health, 2012e). In short, government control over medical work in primary care has increased, pointing to the contingency of medical authority (Harrison and McDonald, 2008; Hunter, 2008).

Reforming medical practice

Positioning doctors in the context of health systems provides a sense of the type of settings where doctors work. More importantly, this also gives an insight into the relative permeability of medical practice when it comes to reform. Considering the centrality of doctors in the allocation of health care resources, any reform will, directly or indirectly, affect the practice of doctors. Measures to control expenditure at the macro-level have progressively been complemented by measures to control the allocation of health care resources at the micro-level, and it is these measures that can be expected to affect doctors most directly (Burau *et al.*, 2009). Reforms directed at the micro-level have included changes to how doctors are paid (discussed in the next section), restrictions on available treatment and quality management measures such as medical audit, clinical standards and, more recently, evidence-based medicine.

In any publicly funded health system, available treatment is naturally restricted in terms of both the range and the volume of services. By virtue of being contract based, social insurance systems such as those in Japan, Germany and the Netherlands have traditionally spelled out more explicitly what services are covered while the commitment to comprehensive coverage has remained vaguer in national health services. In Germany, for example, the Social Code Book Five defines the scope of social insurance, which is complemented by the more specific provisions of self-administration. In contrast, national health services are based on the duty of government to provide services as opposed to the right of patients to receive them. As Harrison (2001: 279) observes in relation to the British NHS, '[t]his enables governments to "cash limit" (that is, cap) increasing proportions of the annual NHS budget'.

Concerns about cost pressures and containment, together with the move to a public contract model in national health services, have, however, put the issue of restricting treatment high on the political agenda. This is well illustrated by New Zealand's attempts to define core services discussed in Chapter 4. Such a process can be highly controversial in political terms and here evidence-based medicine potentially offers a new source of legitimacy. However, political conflicts remain prominent as the example of the National Institute for Clinical Excellence (NICE) in Britain illustrates (see Box 4.9). As Harrison and McDonald (2008) observe, the focus of the Institute has clearly moved from being a vehicle for influencing clinical practice to offering national appraisals of (cost) effectiveness of clinical decisions and subsequent authoritative advice on their availability under the NHS. As the high profile case of treatment of multiple-sclerosis relapse shows, the political legitimacy of NICE is limited and in the end the government decided to sidestep the Institute and the rules of evidence-based medicine (Harrison and McDonald, 2007). In contrast, market-based systems like those in the USA and Singapore are unlikely to set limits on treatments that a patient might want as long as they have the personal resources or insurance to cover the costs.

Even in national health services the explicit exclusion of treatment is notoriously controversial among patients and doctors because such measures directly constrain medical practice. In contrast, doctors (by exercising clinical freedom) have traditionally been secret accomplices in the rationing of health services (Harrison, 1998). By providing a medical rationale for the necessity of treatment in individual cases, doctors have given legitimacy to implicit rationing. Nevertheless, the alliance between doctors and the state has become fragile, reflecting more assertive and demanding patients and government challenges to medical autonomy as well more general cost concerns. In the case of Britain, for example, the national contract previously stated only that GPs had to provide their patients with 'all necessary and appropriate care'. In contrast, the latest contract from 2004 is more specific and lists the type of services GPs have to provide and also includes specific quality outcomes, the achievement of which is rewarded with extra payments (Baggott, 2004; Boyle, 2011).

The emergence and magnitude of quality management in recent years has to be seen against the background of controversies surrounding the explicit restrictions on available treatment and potentially challenges existing mechanisms for regulating medical work (see Box 5.5). Quality management promises to square the circle between restricting treatment and ensuring the quality of health care, while at the same time allowing for (and even using) medical judgement (Harrison, 1998; Klazinga, 2005). This solution is politically attractive because it diffuses blame for potentially unpopular decisions away from government while safeguarding the autonomy of doctors over clinical decision making.

Box 5.5 Professional self-regulation of medical work

Professional self-regulation has been the traditional approach to setting and ensuring standards of medical practice, and involves licensing and (by implication) education and training. Further, self-regulation is a key indication of the 'professionalism' of doctors and is at the centre of the regulation of competitive practice in medicine (Moran and Wood, 1993). A typical example of professional self-regulation is the General Medical Council in Britain, which is responsible for keeping a register of doctors and for regulating their education, training and professional standards. The regulatory ideology underpinning the GMC has traditionally been rather narrow and isolationist and the Council has tended to focus on protecting doctors from market competition on the one hand and from interference from the state on the other (Moran, 1999: 103). Similar arrangements exist in Australia, Germany and the USA. However, as recent scandals in Britain have demonstrated, these arrangements are not necessarily successful at securing the quality of medical work and have led to policy reform (Fenton and Salter, 2009). In other countries, by contrast, professional self-regulation is less prominent and here the bodies regulating medical work are government agencies that include doctors, but not exclusively so. In Sweden, for example, the Medical Responsibility Board, a government agency that assesses and decides on complaints and instances of malpractice, consists of members drawn from different stakeholders in the health service, including county councils, municipalities, the unions of health professionals and the public, all of whom are appointed by the government.

In some countries like Britain and New Zealand, the prominence of quality management has coincided with a move away from purely market-based reforms. In both countries, health reforms of the late 1980s and early 1990s were built on a belief in the superiority of the market and business style management. In contrast, quality management redirects attention to medical practice, though one that is expected to adhere to explicitly defined standards. In the other countries, the introduction of market mechanisms itself has stimulated the development of mechanisms of quality management. As Herk *et al.* argue in the case of the Netherlands '[t]he increasing importance of health insurers as negotiating partners of the providers put[s] increasing weight on measurable quality, on quality indicators, which could be objectified and specified in contracts' (2001: 1726). Initial legislation on quality goes back to the mid-1990s, but following limited implementation the government put renewed emphasis on quality and in 2004 introduced new, compulsory measures supervised by the Inspectorate of Health Care (Exter *et al.*, 2004; for an overview see Klazinga, 2008, Schäfer *et al.*, 2010).

The medical audit has been a long-standing quality management measure. As an instrument to systematically evaluate clinical care and increase the accountability of doctors, it has been heavily promoted by many governments. However, as Herk *et al.* demonstrate in their comparative study of the Netherlands and Britain, medical audit demonstrates 'the capability of the [medical] profession to maintain autonomy through re-negotiated mechanisms for self-control' (2001: 1721). As part of this process, professional controls have become more formalized and the freedom of individual doctors more circumscribed by collegial regulation through peer review.

The case of the Netherlands is indicative here. The professional organizations of doctors took the lead in developing medical audit in the late 1970s and this helped the medical profession maintain control. Doctors are well represented on the board of trustees of the Institute for Quality Assurance in Hospitals, and while medical audit has become compulsory, doctors have remained responsible for its organization. The system of site visits as the predominant form of medical audit emerged in the late 1980s (Lombarts and Klazinga, 2001). This was a time of increasing public concerns over health care expenditure and related questions about the (economic) autonomy and accountability of hospital doctors. Here, doctors 'traded' peer-controlled quality assurance in exchange for the government not interfering with the income of specialists. External peers, under the auspices of the specialist scientific societies, conduct the site visits. Being doctor-led and doctor-owned, the results of individual reviews remain confidential and the implementation of recommendations is left to the group of specialists itself. As Dent (2003) suggests, the development of clinical guidelines tells a similar story. The Netherlands was one of the first countries to adapt and widely implement clinical guidelines, although importantly clinical guidelines have mostly taken the form of consensus guidelines combined with peer review.

This type of doctor-led medical audit may also take a more individualized form. For example, in New Zealand, doctors on general registration must work under the general oversight of a doctor who holds vocational registration in the same branch of medicine. An overseer is similar to a mentor and assists a doctor in his or her continuing education and audit. Doctors report to the Medical Council, the professional self-regulatory body, every year as part of their annual practising certificate application and each year some will be audited to ensure they are meeting requirements. This enhanced rigour of regulation, combined with the transfer of the disciplinary function from the Council to a separate tribunal, were major innovations of the Medical Practitioners Act 1995. Despite this auditing, overall quality improvement efforts in New Zealand have been patchy, without coordination or sufficient emphasis, and, despite considerable funding increases since 2000, data show limited productivity improvements in terms of medical procedures and patient service access (Gauld, 2010).

Box 5.6 Australian Primary Care Collaborative Program (APCCP)

The national APCCP is a large-scale coordinated programme of rapid change management to improve service delivery in general practices across the 4,300 general practices in Australia. The Divisions of General Practice are designated as the local organizers of collaboratives. The Programme's initial objective is to involve 600 general practices, representing 20 per cent of the practices in each geographical location. It is being funded under the Primary Care Providers Working Together component of the Focus on Prevention funding package and is managed or commissioned by the Primary Care Quality and Prevention Branch of the Australian Department of Health and Ageing. The National Primary Care Collaboratives aim to improve care in national priority disease areas, provide greater integration among providers in the primary care sector, and focus on prevention through better chronic disease management and accessible primary health care (Bertelsmann Foundation, 2004c).

In other countries, doctors have been less successful in exclusively controlling medical audit. For example, in Australia, medical acts in each state provide the principal control over the practice of medicine and conduct of medical audit, and are administered by state medical boards that are similar to boards in the USA (Box 5.6). Furthermore, in the early 1990s legislative action was taken to facilitate the monitoring of doctors in specified areas by the Health Insurance Commission under the Medicare programme. Doctors who are suspected of excessive ordering are referred to the Medical Services Committees of Inquiry, although the test of whether a particular treatment is acceptable falls on local medical community standards which vary considerably across states (Palmer and Short, 2000: 195ff.).

In some ways, clinical guidelines are the natural extension of medical audits because audits assume the existence of standards of good practice against which performance can be judged. Significantly, guidelines have become increasingly evidence-based, and 'emphasis shifted from professional consensus to systematic evidence or from professional endorsement to authority derived from science' (Herk *et al.*, 2001: 1728). From the perspective of doctors, evidence-based medicine is ambivalent (Berg *et al.*, 2000). Evidence-based medicine promises to strengthen the scientific nature of medicine by reducing unwarranted variation in diagnostic and therapeutic practice. At the same time, guidelines encourage a standardized approach to practice and as such limit the leeway for professional judgement. Reflecting this ambivalence, Harrison (2002) suggests that clinical guidelines are part of a 'scientific-bureaucratic' model of medicine that gives primacy to knowledge derived from research and distilled into guidelines of best practice. Developments in Britain and

Sweden illustrate not only the shift to clinical guidelines, but, importantly, also the variety of rationales for introducing them.

In Britain, setting, measuring and improving quality standards was one of the priorities of the last Labour Government. At the centre was a system of 'clinical governance' designed to set and monitor clinical standards (Fenton and Salter, 2009). As part of this system NHS managers were responsible for clinical quality, putting particular emphasis on cost-effectiveness. This built on systems of medical technology assessment developed throughout the 1990s but, in contrast to its predecessors, the government established a set of institutions that supposedly ensures professional compliance (Harrison, 2002; Harrison *et al.*, 2002: 13). As discussed earlier (see Box 4.9), NICE plays a central role in this and is responsible for evaluating new technologies and care guidelines with regard to their clinical and cost-effectiveness. As such, conflicts between medical and economic rationality are embedded in the Institute's work (Butler, 2002; Syrett, 2003). The Institute can rule against treatment that is proven clinically effective on the basis that the costs to the NHS are disproportionate to the long-term benefits. Technically, doctors can choose not to follow NICE guidance, although in practice this will be difficult. The establishment of NICE in 1999 must be seen in conjunction with the development of the National Service Framework which sets out patterns of care for specific diseases, disabilities and patient groups, and the establishment of the Commission for Health Improvement (and since 2009 the Care Quality Commission) which is responsible for monitoring and improving standards at local level (Boyle, 2011; Fenton and Salter, 2009; Harrison and McDonald, 2008).

In Sweden, by contrast, the development of quality standards was initially underpinned by the intention to counterbalance the increasing decentralization of the health system. The debate on quality assurance was initiated in the mid-1980s by a government agency, and the National Board for Health and Welfare emerged as one of the key actors in quality management. The Board became responsible for collecting data on health outcomes and good practice and intensified its monitoring of health care personnel and health care providers. For the government, quality management became a 'new means of influencing and monitoring health care' (Garpenby, 1999: 409). Significantly, and in line with the emphasis on consensus building, national agencies only provide general guidelines, leaving considerable space for doctors to develop strategies independently at the local level (Garpenby, 1997: 197). Recently, however, there has been greater focus on nationwide initiatives and since 2006 performance indicators have been applied more systematically in collaboration with the National Board of Health and Welfare (Anell, 2008). This is part of a heightened concern for transparency arising from debates about variations in quality especially in relation to hospitals

(Blomgren, 2007; for similar developments in relation to quality registers see Bejerot and Hasselbladh, 2011). At the same time, although doctors do not have any formal representation on the relevant government agencies and consultation committees, the Medical Quality Council, a body set up by doctors, serves as a pool for recruiting individual doctors into these agencies and committees.

Not surprisingly, and in contrast to the UK and Sweden, clinical guideline development in the USA has been highly decentralized and involves many public and private organizations including medical professional societies, patient advocacy groups, insurance payers and government agencies. Moreover, the current processes underlying guideline development are often vulnerable to bias and conflict of interest, thus the quality of clinical practice guidelines is often poor and not based on scientifically validated processes (see Box 5.7). According to the Institute of Medicine (2008), there is no infrastructure or process for encouraging the development of objective, trustworthy clinical advice. It recommends that Congress direct the US Department of Health and Human Services to designate an entity with the authority, expertise and funding necessary to set priorities for evaluating clinical services, to conduct systematic reviews of the evidence available on these priorities and to promote the development and use of standards-based clinical practice guidelines.

Medical care is at the centre of health reform, reflecting the centrality of doctors in the definition, provision and allocation of health care resources. Macro-level reforms have increasingly been accompanied by micro-level reforms that affect the practice of doctors more directly.

Box 5.7 Quality controls in Japan lag

The Japan Council for Quality Health Care (JCQHC), established in 1995, undertakes a number of activities related to improving quality throughout the health system. They include creating clinical guidelines, hospital accreditation and tracking complaints made to medical safety support centres. However, the JCQHC has no regulatory power to punish poorly performing providers and there is little in the way of regulation regarding quality improvement. Hospital accreditation in Japan is voluntary and undertaken largely as an improvement exercise rather than as a way to penalize poor providers; roughly one-third of hospitals are accredited by the JCQHC, which does not disclose names of hospitals that have failed the accreditation process. Thus, despite the JCQHC, formal policies and structures for monitoring and promoting quality remain relatively underdeveloped in Japan. Information on quality is rarely collected or reported, and few mechanisms exist to encourage quality-improvement activities. Policies that establish incentives for quality and efficiency, while still in the beginning stages, are being developed and implemented (Thomson *et al.*, 2011).

However, the picture that emerges here is ambivalent. Doctors are certainly under greater pressure to account for their practice, but the turn to quality provides an opportunity for doctors to appropriate measures of control. In many ways, quality management marks the rebirth of medical practice, although under different, more closely defined terms.

Paying for medical care

How doctors are paid is not merely a technical issue; in fact, systems of remuneration are important pointers to power and are at the centre of the regulation of doctors (Moran and Wood, 1993). Power here refers to the privilege of doctors to be rewarded according to the medical treatment they provide. Systems of remuneration can either sustain or constrain this privilege, which in part can also account for variations in payments across countries (for an overview, see Fujisawa and Lafortune, 2008; Jegers *et al.*, 2002). The fee-for-service system, under which doctors are paid for the individual services rendered to patients, supports this type of medical privilege most extensively. In contrast, with payment by salary there is little connection between the services rendered and the payment received by doctors. Between these two extremes is payment based on capitation, whereby doctors are paid according to the number of patients registered with their practice. Typically, hospital doctors receive a salary, whereas office-based doctors are paid on either a fee-for-service or a capitation basis. In addition to systems of payment, another indication of medical power is the role of doctors in the determination of fee schedules and payment structures.

As Table 5.5 illustrates, the payment of doctors is characterized by variation and includes unexpected cases, such as salaried office-based doctors in public health centres (in Singapore) and hospital doctors paid on a fee-for-service basis (in Japan, the USA and in private hospitals in Singapore). Significantly, however, in most cases pay is not directly related to the volume of services, and even where this is the case, there are limitations on payments. If power refers to the privilege of doctors to be rewarded according to the medical treatment they provide, medical power is restricted.

Concerns for cost containment are likely to direct the attention to systems of remuneration, especially in countries (including Australia, Germany, Japan, Taiwan and the USA) where doctors are paid according to the volume of services provided. Classical examples of the fee-for-service system are Germany and the USA, which also illustrate its problems. In Germany, the Uniform Value Scale (*Einheitlicher Bewertungsmasstab*) lists the services that are reimbursed by health insurance funds, together with their relative weights for reimbursement, which are measured in points. Since 2009, the monetary value of each point is fixed and there are top-ups for high quality care (Fujisawa and Lafortune, 2008). This constrains the total expenditure on ambulatory care, although not the incentive to maximize the volume of services at the level of the individual practice.

Nevertheless, the fee-for-service system in Germany remains problematic from the perspective of cost containment and has undergone several changes in recent years. Fee negotiations take place within legally set limits and doctors may be subject to utilization review, either randomly or if their levels of service provision are significantly higher than those of their colleagues. This has been accompanied by measures to change the system of payment itself, including rewards for particular specialities (GPs in particular) and specific services (e.g., counselling rather than medical testing), together with blanket payments for certain sets of services.

The undesirable consequences of a fee-for-service system can be compounded by other factors. In Taiwan, for example, the combination of high levels of patient choice and cultural patterns that favour medical visits and pharmaceutical use has led to over-usage. Outside of hospitals the NHI pays providers on a fee-for-service basis, with patients free to choose among providers (see Box 5.8). Because NHI coverage is extended to virtually all physicians in all specialties, patients are in the

Table 5.5 ***Types of payment for different types of doctor***

	Predominantly salaried	*Predominantly capitation payments*	*Predominantly fee-for-service payments*
Ambulatory care doctors	Singapore (public)	Britain Netherlands New Zealand Sweden	Australia Germany Japan Netherlands Singapore (private) Taiwan USA[a]
Hospital doctors	Australia Britain Germany New Zealand Singapore (public) Sweden Taiwan		Japan Singapore (private) USA

[a] The USA is undergoing a shift due to HMO movement but is still fee-for-service based.

Box 5.8 Informal payments to doctors

One pattern that sets Taiwan apart from other developed countries is that Taiwanese physicians see almost twice as many patients per week as their US counterparts. As a result, Taiwan has the highest average number of outpatient visits per capita in the world at 14 per year (over 26 for those over age 65). For generations, patients in Taiwan have developed a physician usage culture that includes consulting physicians for minor ailments, visiting many physicians to find one that will do what the patient wants, and finding and using the most popular doctor, even when he or she does not specialize in what the patient needs. A unique cultural factor is the practice of patients giving informal payments to physicians to get better service. In their study, Chiu *et al.* (2007) found that both before and after the introduction of the NHI, Taiwanese newspapers portrayed informal payments as appropriate means to secure access to better health care. Although the NHI reduced patients' financial barriers to care, it did not change deeply held cultural beliefs that good care depended on the development of a reciprocal sense of obligation between patients and physicians. Although illegal, physicians may also encourage the ongoing use of informal payments to make up revenue lost when the NHI standardized fees and limited income from dispensing medications.

position to pick and choose. Even after the introduction of measures to prevent duplication of services, the patient habit of doctor shopping persists. Moreover, medicines are prescribed in almost all visits and constitute over 25 per cent of the entire national medical expenditure (Wen *et al.*, 2008). Taiwanese expect to get free or almost free medicines, on the average three to four kinds per visit. They may take them later or just hoard them for security reasons.

A different approach to constraining expenditure in the fee-for-service system is the so-called system of 'bulk-billing' adopted by Australia with the introduction of Medicare in 1984/85. In Australia, doctors' fees are not regulated. Under the bulk billing system of payment, however, a GP can choose to bill the government directly and receive 85 per cent of the scheduled fee, thereby avoiding administrative costs and delay. This also ensures that services are effectively free to the patient at the point of service. However, if the GP chooses not to bulk bill or chooses to charge patients a co-payment, the patient pays the bill and is reimbursed by Medicare for 85 per cent of the scheduled fee (Thomson *et al.*, 2011). Although the proportion of bulk billing increased steadily until the mid 1990s, it has declined significantly since 2000 (Swerissen, 2004). In response to concerns about the fall in the bulk-billing rate, the Commonwealth government proposed a 'Fairer Medicare', later implemented as 'Medicare Plus'. This package introduced a participating practice scheme under which GP practices that agreed to charge a no-gap fee to concessional patients were eligible for increased Medicare rebates for these patients.

Controlling doctors' pay in a fee-for-service system is further complicated if the health system is characterized by weak public and central integration. A case in point is the US, where ambulatory-care doctors are paid through a combination of methods, including fee-for-service payments, discounted fees paid by private health plans, capitation rate contracts with private plans, public programmes and direct patient fees. However, the growth of HMOs and other managed-care schemes has resulted in changes in the methods of payment away from fee-for-service reimbursement. HMO doctors may be salaried, paid a fee for service, or paid a capitation fee for each person on their list. A variation of the HMO is the Preferred Provider Organization (PPO) in which a limited number of providers – doctors, hospitals and others – agree to provide services to a specific group of people at a negotiated fee-for-service rate that is lower than the normal charge.

By contrast, in other countries ambulatory-care doctors are paid predominantly on a capitation basis, allowing for much more direct control of doctors' remuneration. New Zealand is typical here, and indeed the country moved to capitation payments relatively recently, illustrating the advantages of this type of payment from the point of view of access. In New Zealand, capitation payments coexist with sizeable co-payments, but as noted earlier this is changing. GPs are now grouped under PHOs, which are not-for-profit organizations funded on a capitation basis that contract with DHBs to provide a comprehensive set of preventive and treatment services for their enrolled populations. Historically, government subsidies were paid on a fee-for-service basis targeted to low-income and high-risk people, but because the subsidy levels were not sufficiently tied to inflation and because GPs retained the right to set their own levels of co-payments, it resulted in a significant cost barrier to GP services for some people. In an effort to remove or reduce this cost barrier, in 2002 the government introduced the Primary Health Care Strategy to ease access to general practice services and transform publicly funded primary health care payments from targeted welfare benefits to universal, risk-rated insurance premium subsidies (Howell, 2005).

For many years, Sweden was an example of one of the few countries where the majority of ambulatory-care doctors were public employees and paid a salary. This manifested the high degree of public integration of the health system, and doctors were firmly positioned in what is a very politically controlled health system (Garpenby, 2001: 263). In this respect Dent (2003: 53) suggests that medical professionals in Sweden appear more like civil servants than autonomous professionals. However, private providers of ambulatory care have also existed, particularly in major cities, and their numbers increased after the introduction of patient choice for family doctors in the early 1990s (Harrison, 2004; Harrison and Calltrop, 2000). The providers are private in that their facilities are privately run, although the majority have contracts with county councils. In 2003, a third of health centres and practitioners worked in privately run facilities (Glenngård *et al.*, 2005). Health reforms since 2007 have further opened up primary care for private providers, who in many counties now can operate on par with public providers (Anell, 2010). This has also had knock-on effects for the remuneration of doctors working in ambulatory care, which has moved away from salaries and towards more mixed systems, combining capitation payments, payment by visit and pay for performance (depending on the individual county).

Unlike ambulatory-care doctors, hospital doctors tend to be salaried employees, although in many countries they have the right to treat private patients who represent an alluring source of added income since services are often paid for on a fee-for-service basis and remuneration tends to be high. In Britain, for example, the right to practise privately was the condition on which hospital doctors agreed to become part of the NHS when it was set up in 1948. Hospital doctors were initially opposed to a tax-funded health service, instead advocating the extension of the existing health insurance system, but they were won over by a number of concessions. Besides private practice and pay beds, they received large increases in salaries for those receiving distinction awards. This led the then Minister of Health to remark that he had 'stuffed their [the hospital doctors'] mouths with gold' (quoted in Ham, 1999: 11). Indeed, in the most recent contract from 2003 there is no longer any limit on earnings from private practice and not surprisingly the British Medical Association (BMA) described the contract as a 'victory' (Boyle, 2011: 118).

There are some countries where hospital doctors are paid on a fee-for-service basis, but these are notable exceptions. In the Netherlands, for example, medical specialists have traditionally been independent practitioners who have 'bought' the right to practise in a hospital and who practise in partnerships. As such, they contracted directly with patients and insurance funds and were reimbursed on a fee-for-service basis separately from hospitals. However, this changed in 2000, after which doctors began to receive a lump sum directly from the hospital in which they practise. As a result, specialist medical services are now an integral part of the hospital contract and budget (Harrison, 2004), thus potentially providing leverage for hospital managers to exercise greater control over the practice of medical specialists (Trappenburg and Groot, 2001). This trend has continued and since 2008, the remuneration of medical specialists has been part of the hospital-wide system of payment based on DRGs (Schäfer *et al.*, 2010).

Table 5.6 ***The involvement of doctors in systems of pay determinations***[a]

	Salaries	*Capitation/fee-for-service payments*
Set by government	Britain (with review body as intermediary); Singapore (for doctors in public health facilities); Taiwan (hospitals)	Australia (de facto); Britain (with review body as intermediary); New Zealand (de facto); Taiwan (fixed-fee schedule)
Negotiated between doctors and payers of health services	Australia Germany New Zealand Sweden	Germany Japan Netherlands (government approval required)
Set by doctors		Singapore (for doctors in private health facilities)

[a] The USA has been omitted from this table as the system of pay bargaining is too fragmented.

The involvement of doctors in the process of determining pay is another indication of medical power. As Table 5.6 illustrates, there is some variation here. However, in large part salaries and capitation/fee-for-service payments are negotiated between doctors and the payers of health services, although there may be some restrictions, as in the Netherlands. Even where the government alone decides, the decision may be based on a broad range of evidence, as in Britain, or be limited in scope, as in Singapore. Significantly, doctors enjoy considerable power relative to pay determination compared to other groups of employees, although they can rarely act alone.

In the case of salaries, the process of pay bargaining involves pay negotiations where medical power depends on the relative strength of unions and employer organizations, together with the overall economic climate. An interesting exception is Singapore, where doctors working in public health facilities are paid on the basis of the civil service pay scale, which is set by government with little input from the medical community.

The situation is more complicated in the case of capitation and fee payments, as they are the basis for many rounds of future remuneration. Negotiations of this type generally require extensive bargaining to reach an agreement. Countries operate different kinds of decision systems, ranging from payments set by government and negotiated with doctors to payments set by doctors themselves. Britain provides an interesting example of the first variant where the government determines capitation payments and allowances for GPs and salary scales for hospital specialists, although the Minister for Health normally takes into account the recommendations of the Review Body on Doctors' and Dentists' Remuneration, which is an independent agency financed by government. The government appoints the members of the Review Body, usually with the approval of the BMA. The recommendations of the review body are based on demands submitted by the professional organizations and the government as well as other input, such as the budget plan and the evaluation of statistical material (see, e.g., Department of Health, 2009). With the introduction of the new GP contract in 2004, the scope of the Review Body has been more restricted and the so-called 'target intended average income' applies only to a limited number of doctors (Fujisawa and Lafortune, 2008).

By contrast, in other countries doctors' organizations have more direct influence and negotiate directly with the payers of health services. For instance, the Japanese Medical Association (JMA) nominates all five doctors who sit on the fee-scheduling body and negotiates fees with the Health Ministry's Health Insurance Bureau. The influence of doctors is bolstered by the fact that '[i]n effect, those on the provider side must work through the JMA since 'hospitals, pharmaceutical companies, and other important actors are not directly represented on the council' (Ikegami and Campbell, 1999: 63).

In other countries, the negotiation process has become curtailed in recent years. In Germany, for example, where control over funding has become more centralized the autonomy of negotiations between doctors and insurance funds has become constrained (Rosenbrock and Gerlinger, 2004; Rothgang *et al.*, 2010). This began with the introduction of legally fixed regional budgets for ambulatory medical care that replaced negotiated budgets after 1992. The regional budgets have now been replaced with a maximum ceiling for fees per doctor. Similarly, doctors in Taiwan have been critical of being left out of the reimbursement shaping process. As a result, there is considerable tension within the medical profession over NHI reimbursement rates and a feeling that savings are being made 'on the backs of doctors' (Chang *et al.*, 2005: 38).

The organization of doctors' interests and access to the policy process

Issues around the practice and payment of doctors often concern medical practitioners as individuals. In contrast, the political organization of doctors' interests directs attention to doctors as a group and how doctors

		Access to policy process	
		As outsiders through lobbying	*As insiders through corporatism*
Organization of doctors' interests	*Cohesive*	Australia, Britain, Japan, New Zealand, Singapore, Sweden, Taiwan	
	Fragmented	USA	Germany, Netherlands

Figure 5.1 *The organization of doctors' interests and access to the policy process*

relate to the policy process. The interests of doctors can be organized in different ways, through specialist scientific societies, professional associations or trade unions. An important indicator of power is the degree of cohesion (or fragmentation), that is, the extent to which a group of doctors speak with one voice, or at least with different voices complementing each other. This has become increasingly challenging as distributional struggles between diverse groups of doctors have intensified under pressures of cost containment. At the same time, countries offer dissimilar points of access to organized interests, reflecting the specific characteristics of the respective political and health systems. The power of doctors to a great extent depends on how a state is organized and on how powerful it is.

As Figure 5.1 suggests, in most countries the political organization of doctors is relatively cohesive, with one organization acting as the main agent of doctors' interests. This normally goes hand-in-hand with a high membership among doctors. However, in some countries divisions between different types of doctors have led to the fragmentation of the political organization of doctors. These divisions affect the distribution of financial resources and intensify under policies designed to contain costs. The relative collective strength of doctors coexists with varying degrees of access to the policy process, which, as noted in Chapter 2, embody one indicator of how the power of the state is organized.

In most countries, doctors have to rely on lobbying the government from the outside. As Britain demonstrates, the extent of influence varies over time and the cohesion of interest organizations is only one factor; instead the government's chosen approach to policy making plays an important role. At the same time, lack of cohesion is not necessarily a bar to influence, as the USA, Germany and the Netherlands demonstrate. The considerable influence of doctors in the USA reflects not only the economic power of the medical sectors, but also the weakness of the state in health governance. Germany and the Netherlands, to a lesser extent, are unusual in that doctors are an integral part of health governance and as such often have privileged access to the policy process. Being insiders gives doctors considerable influence, although this may come at the price of becoming agents of cost containment.

In the majority of countries the political organization of doctors shows a considerable degree of cohesion. This reflects a number of country-specific factors, including the type of political system and the size of the country. Cohesion is expected to be most likely in small unitary countries such as New Zealand, Singapore and Taiwan. New Zealand, for example, has one primary medical association that has a high level of membership among doctors. The New Zealand Medical Association (NZMA) is a voluntary organization that claims membership of about 70 per cent of the country's doctors. As such, the Association has a broader-based membership than many national medical associations. As well as being a membership-based organization, the NZMA also acts as an umbrella for many other medical and health organizations and maintains formal links with affiliates, including the Royal Colleges and speciality organizations, and acts as the primary representative of the profession in dealings with the government (New Zealand Medical Association, 2013; Marshall, 2003).

Even in larger unitary countries the organization of doctors' interests can be cohesive. Britain is a case in point. The BMA is at the centre of the political organization of doctors' interests and more than 80 per cent of doctors are members (European Observatory on Health Care Systems, 1999: 22). The BMA acts in a dual role as a professional organization and as a trade union. As a professional organization, it promotes medical education and professional development, whereas as a trade union it represents doctors' economic interests. This de facto monopoly puts the BMA in a strong position in principle, but also requires that it caters to a diverse range of constituencies within the medical profession. Here, conflicts between GPs and hospital consultants have been particularly prominent within the BMA (Giamo, 2002).

Likewise, as Sweden demonstrates, a more decentralized political system is no bar to a cohesive organization of doctors' interests. More than 90 per cent of doctors are members of the Swedish Medical Association (SMA) (Garpenby, 2001: 261). The Association acts as a type of umbrella organization and the specific interests of its membership are channelled through seven professional organizations and 28 local bodies. The SMA coexists with a range of scientific societies and while the Swedish Society of Medicine is the largest, with over 60 per cent of doctors being members, the smaller specialist societies are more influential actors (Garpenby, 2001: 264). The Medical Association and the Society of Medicine have different responsibilities, although in relation to some issues the two organizations compete with each other (Garpenby, 1999).

In comparison, the political organization of doctors can also be highly fragmented. The USA represents a clear case of fragmentation between generalists and specialists that has been exacerbated by federalism and the sheer size of the profession. Although less than half of all practising doctors are members of the American Medical Association (AMA), it remains a very powerful political lobby group with significant influence in Washington, DC, and the state capitals. However, many speciality medical groups have been established which concentrate on their own interests, often in conflict with the AMA. There are literally hundreds, if not thousands, of medical associations at the local, state and national level in the USA, and although the AMA is the single most influential, the voice of the medical community is considerably more disjointed than in other countries.

The organization of doctors' interests may be divided, not only between different types of doctors, but also between different types of organization. For example, in Germany the *Marburger Bund* is the main professional organization and trade union for hospital doctors, but the situation surrounding ambulatory-care doctors is more complicated. The vast majority of these doctors cannot exclusively rely on private practice and instead have to provide services under social health insurance. However, this requires joining one of the regional associations of insurance fund doctors (*Kassenärztliche Vereinigungen*) that assume an intermediate position between doctors and the state (Rosenbrock and Gerlinger, 2004). As public law bodies, the associations have the statutory responsibility of ensuring the provision of ambulatory care and organizing the remuneration of doctors, including control functions such as assessing the economic efficiency of the performance of individual doctors. At the same time, they represent the interests of doctors when the associations negotiate contracts and fees with insurance funds. The tensions inherent in this dual role have become more prominent and intensifying distributional struggles have made it more difficult for the associations to integrate the conflicting interests of their membership (Burau, 2001, 2009). The distributional struggles result from a combination of the increasing number of doctors, falling income and more extensive government control. The heightened conflicts have also negatively affected the division of labour between the associations of insurance fund doctors and the two lobbying organizations for ambulatory-care doctors. At the same time, the position of the associations of insurance fund doctors has also been weakened because insurance funds can now contract directly with individual groups of doctors (Gerlinger, 2010).

The relative cohesion of the political organization of doctors is only one measure of collective power of the medical profession. A complementary measure of power is the role of doctors in the policy process, and different health and political systems provide distinct degrees and types of access. This demonstrates how the power of doctors is tied to the power of the state. In most countries, doctors' organizations have access to the policy process as outsiders, mostly through lobbying and limited informal consultation.

Countries with tax-funded health services embedded in a centralist and a federalist political system, respectively, illustrate the ups and downs of the influence of doctors. Here, the relationship between the medical profession and the state has traditionally been close. However, access to the policy process has principally consisted of lobbying and informal consultation. In Britain, for example, the fragility of this type of access became apparent in the late 1980s. Reform efforts in part were aimed at weakening the role of the profession in the governance of health care and this affected the influence of doctors in health policy, resulting in a widening rift between government and doctors. Significantly, the medical profession was practically excluded from the policy review that led to a major reform in the early 1990s (Harrison, 2001). Similarly, Hunter (2008) and Kay (2001) see the conception and implementation of the GP fund-holding scheme and its subsequent redefinition as practice-based commissioning as an indication of the weakened influence of the medical profession. This stands in sharp contrast to the former corporatist settlement that was characterized by a strong insider role of doctors in government (Giamo, 2002).

In contrast, the strength of the health care industry combined with a policy process that is typically driven by lobbying and one where winning is largely manifested in blocking change can help to sustain the position of the medical profession. The USA, where the medical profession seems to have been more successful at maintaining its traditionally compelling influence over health policy, is a case in point. The medical sector is consistently ranked among the best organized and financed sectors in influencing politicians at the national and state levels by the Congressional Quarterly Service.

In contrast, in corporatist systems, corporatism means that doctors are an integral part of health governance and this often gives them access to the policy process as insiders (see Giamo, 2002; Kuhlmann, 2006). However, as the example of Germany shows, even as insiders the influence of doctors is variable. Together with the insurance funds, doctors form an organization of self-administration, which is responsible, not only for negotiating contracts, but also for implementing health care legislation. Here, the Joint Committee is important and its responsibilities include defining the benefits catalogue, clinical guidelines and measures of quality assurance (see Busse and Riesberg, 2004). The role of doctors in the health system is highly institutionalized and codified in

Social Code Book Five. In addition, the federal structure of health governance offers doctors multiple points of access. Significantly, however, doctors are involved in a public role granted to them by the state, and are not first and foremost involved as representatives of private interests. This can lead to the kinds of conflict of interest discussed above and can constrain the collective power of doctors.

Over the last decade the federal government in Germany has expanded the scope of self-administration while at the same time circumscribing its activities. For example, the Joint Committee is now responsible for evaluating the medical efficacy and economic efficiency of existing treatments. Issuing such guidance may be subject to a timetable, with the possibility of a unilateral decision by the Ministry. Thus, the pendulum has swung from autonomous negotiations towards hierarchical decisions by the state (Burau, 2007a; Luzio, 2004; Rothgang *et al.*, 2010; Wendt *et al.*, 2005). The government has defined more precisely the substantive issues to be decided and has set deadlines by which time agreement has to be reached. Doctors have become key agents of cost containment precisely because the system of self-administration is adaptable and depoliticizes the implementation of potentially problematic policies (Giamo and Manow, 1999: 978). Yet, recent years have been characterized by a greater scepticism about the capacity of the Associations of Insurance Fund Doctors. Since it is now possible to complete contracts with specific groups of doctors instead of the Associations, there has been open discussion about abolishing them (see Greß *et al.*, 2004).

Doctors, the state and health policy

Doctors are deeply embedded in health systems, and since the state looms large in health systems and policy, doctors inevitably have a close relationship with the state. This means two things: medical power will always be contingent on the state, but states cannot do without doctors. Light's (1995) notion of 'countervailing powers' offers one way of understanding the close, but above all changeable, relationship between doctors and the state. As discussed here, medical power oscillates between highs and lows. Highs of medical power (dominance) produce imbalances and provoke countervailing powers originating from the state, third-party payers and patients. This in turn and over time weakens medical dominance and strengthens the power of the state.

In his discussion of the Foucauldian notion of 'governmentality', Johnson (1995) goes one step further and suggests that doctors and the state are inextricably linked through the process of governing. Johnson (1995: 9) observes that '[e]xpertise, as it became increasingly institutionalized in its professional form, became part of the process of governing'. It is impossible to distinguish clearly between doctors and the state: the state depends on the independence of doctors to secure its capacity to govern provision, reflecting the need of states to assert their agency in times of concerns about costs. This has noticeably changed the institutional context within which doctors work, but, importantly, has not necessarily reduced their power (Moran, 1999).

Chapter 6

Beyond the Hospital: Health Care in the Home

Care outside hospitals has traditionally been the poor relation of health systems. Health systems are concerned first and foremost with the provision of medical care and focus on acute illness. Doctors are the key professionals shaping the delivery of health care and hospitals are the primary location. The emphasis is on *curing* as opposed long-term *caring*. Less acute, more long-term health care is typically characterized by considerable diversity in terms of the range of services, the user groups, the localities of service provision and the professionals involved.

Care outside hospitals includes basic care to help with daily living, mobility and self-care; medical and nursing care to help with physical and mental health problems; therapy, counselling and emotional support to promote well-being; and other social, educational and leisure activities (Tester, 1996). User groups are equally diverse and reflect the support required at different stages of the life span, ranging from severally ill infants to people at the end of life. Other beneficiaries include people with mental illness and disability, physical disability, drug-related disorders and progressive illness (Means *et al.*, 2003). Care outside hospitals is also located in different settings, such as residential care and nursing homes, day hospitals and sheltered housing, as well as people's own homes. The professionals involved are equally diverse and include community nurses, mental health nurses, care assistants, home helps, counsellors and physiotherapists.

The diversity of care outside hospitals reflects the varied yet interlocking needs of people who require long-term care (Rummery and Fine, 2012). Diversity makes care outside hospitals interesting, but also difficult to define, analyse and compare. At the same time, care services are often locally specific and even tailored to particular individuals and it is difficult to identify the typical, let alone to generalize. For example, in their comparative analysis of community care policies in Finland and Britain, Burau and Kröger (2004) highlight the distinctively local nature of policies together with the importance of local politics. Antonnen *et al.* (2003b) go even further and suggest that because of the interchangeability with informal care, the use of formal care services is highly individualized and does not follow any systematic patterns. Furthermore, although care services outside hospitals are central to the health of individuals, they can be remote from the health system. In the context of our comparative analysis of health policy we therefore need to focus on a specific aspect of care outside hospitals, and notably an aspect of care that is closely related to health systems.

This chapter focuses on home care for older people. Older people represent the largest user group of care outside hospitals and in the face of ageing societies have attracted considerable attention in health policy terms (Olivares-Tirado *et al.*, 2011; Hieda, 2012). Home care for older people is also closely related to health systems, as demonstrated by the involvement of nurses. Tester (1996: 76) describes home care as 'any type of care and support offered to older people in their homes, whether ordinary or specialized settings, by formal and informal carers'. Home care involves a wide range of activities, from basic physical and mental care to counselling, support for informal carers and offering information. With home care the underlying disease is of secondary importance and instead help with basic activities of daily living is the focus. It encompasses a wide range of tasks and cuts across boundaries between health and social care, and between formal and informal care. It also involves nurses rather than doctors and, most importantly, principally women as informal care givers. Indeed, unpaid care givers deliver the majority of home care; it is estimated that formal care represents only one-fifth of the total help older people receive (OECD, 2005b). This further contributes to the marginal position of home care in health systems. This chapter focuses on home health care: the health care aspects of home care and the services provided by home nurses. However, given the nature of home care it is important to explore the interfaces with other aspects of home care, particularly informal care, but also social care.

Although health systems continue to focus on curing acute illness, interest in home care is growing and it is becoming a higher priority on the health policy agenda in many countries (Stenger and DeVoe, 2010; Ryburn *et al.*, 2009; Kröger, 2001). It is indicative that the comprehensive Health Project by the OECD included a study of 'long-term care for older people' (OECD, 2005a). This change reflects demographic as well as cost pressures. Similarly, the OECD has also recently published reports on healthy ageing (Oxley, 2009), the long-term care workforce (Fujisawa and Colombo, 2009), and on paying and providing long-term care (OECD, 2011c), among others. Moreover, as the number of older (and very old) people increases, both in absolute terms and as a proportion of the total population (for data see Chapter 1), so does the need for long-term care. Combined with falling birth rates, this also means a greater need for formal care, since the pool of potential informal carers becomes smaller.

Unfortunately, this increase in the need for long-term care comes at a time of intense concerns about costs and efforts to contain the public spending on health care as discussed in Chapter 4. At the same time, the diversity of home care services makes it difficult to predict the effects on expenditure and to adapt policy initiatives accordingly (Saltman *et al.*, 2006b). However, for many observers home care promises to square the circle between demographic and cost pressures (Duff, 2001). This is based on the assumption that care in the home is much less costly than that in high-tech hospitals and labour-intensive nursing homes. Substituting care in the home for institutionally based care is also said to provide better quality care because it allows for more autonomy and flexibility. As noted by Ryburn *et al.*: 'Governments are increasingly aware that the provision of home care services results in an overall improvement in the quality of life and maintenance of a basic standard of living for many frail older adults in the community, and that it may reduce or delay high intensity, high-cost services such as residential care or hospital admission' (2009: 225). Moreover, home care settings make it easier to combine formal and informal care arrangements. The shift in priorities also reflects the disparaging views towards the institutionalization of older people that emerged in the 1970s (Jenson and Jacobzone, 2000).

There is no shortage of political debate about the value of care in the home and the appropriate balance between individual and collective responsibilities (Haynes *et al.*, 2010). However, it is less certain what is happening beyond the level of political rhetoric and at the level of policy. As Haverland and Marier (2008) argue, old age policies generally are tricky; they often involve redistributive welfare programmes, which require a sense of collective responsibility, yet there is an increasing division between the younger and the older generations. The question of policy developments is also interesting from a comparative perspective because home care policies are pushed by demography and costs, but are shaped by country-specific factors. Key factors include how the funding and provision of health care is organized, where health systems draw the boundary between health and social care, and cultural assumptions about the appropriate relations between the generations and between women and men, what Pfau-Effinger (2004) calls 'gender cultures'.

Analysing the policies of home care is not only topical, but also offers novel perspectives on health policy and systems. Home care highlights the complex interrelationships among different sectors of health care provision and between health care and other welfare services, as well as between formal and informal health care (Miller *et al.*, 2010; Ranci and Pavolini, 2013). This compellingly demonstrates the multifaceted embeddedness of health care raised in Chapter 1. Home care (as well as public health discussed in Chapter 7) also demonstrates that many services now central to health are at the margins of health systems.

Finally, home care makes for an interesting study of the politics of health care because the medical profession is less directly involved: other actors are pushing reform agendas here.

This chapter provides an analysis of home care and home care policies for older people. A first section examines the size and importance of home care through an analysis of available data. The subsequent section looks more closely at the provision of home care and how its organization and level of provision are shaped by the type of health system within which it is embedded. Provision is closely tied to the funding of home care, which is discussed next. The relative security and generosity of funding are favourable conditions for the growth and development of home care as a distinct sector of health care provision. Another important factor is the relative strength of policies that explicitly support the substitution of formal home care for both institutionally based care and informal care (Kröger, 2005).

The fourth section looks more closely at the interface between formal and informal care and the underpinning cultural expectations about the role of women in care giving. This linkage is important because, as mentioned above, the majority of home care continues to be provided by unpaid care givers. Under the banner of a greater welfare mix, the objectives of reforms are to integrate care givers more explicitly into formal care arrangements and to support care givers through payments and related benefits. The final section of this chapter compares and contrasts key trends in recent policy initiatives on home care and evaluates the extent of change. Has home care merely been redefined by acknowledging the importance of informal care and externalizing costs into the community (Duff, 2001)? Or have there been serious attempts at substituting formal home care for informal and institutional care?

Home care statistics

Compared to other sectors of health systems, international statistics on home care are meagre and often non-existent. This paucity of data illustrates the marginal position of home care in health systems. Diverse, sporadic and often non-public sources of funding make it difficult to capture in one single figure how much is spent on home care. Also, the organization of home care is often highly decentralized, making it more difficult to gather standardized figures across different localities, let alone different countries. As a result, the statistics discussed here are incomplete and often not directly about home care. Thus, in order to get a sense of the degrees of de-institutionalization, the analysis looks at trends in institutionally based care, for which more statistics are available. However, the question as to whether de-institutionalization has

Table 6.1 ***Estimated spending on long-term home care as a percentage of total health expenditure, 2010***

	Total spending	*Public spending*
Germany	4.6	0.4
Japan	0.5	0.0
Netherlands	3.9	1.4
Sweden	3.5	3.2
United States	0.39	0.17

Source: Data from OECD (2012b).

been followed by the development of formal home care services remains unresolved.

Total spending on long-term care in Table 6.1, which includes home and institutionally based care, gives a first indication of the relative size of this sector of health care provision. The majority of countries spend very little on long-term care, between 0.39 per cent of the total expenditure on health care in the US and 4.6 per cent in Germany. Moreover, it is likely that most goes to institutionally based care, which is more expensive than home care.

The percentage of 65-year-olds and over receiving formal home care in Table 6.2 offers a more direct indication of the relative size of home care

Table 6.2 ***Population aged 65 and over in different care settings as a percentage of the total population****

	In institutions	*Receiving home care benefits*
Australia	5.5	14.7
Germany	3.9	7.1
Japan	3.2	5.5
Netherlands	2.4	12.3
Sweden	7.9	9.1
United Kingdom[a]	5.1	20.3
United States[b]	4.3	2.8

* Various years 2006–2010
[a] Figures for UK from 2004
[b] Figures from US from 2004

Source: Data from OECD (2012b).

Table 6.3 ***The growth of institutionalization rates of people aged 65 and over*** **(%)**

Australia[a]	-0.4
Austria[b]	-0.2
Norway[c]	-0.2
Sweden[c]	1.5
United States[d]	-0.2

[a] Figure refers to growth between 1995 and 2003.
[b] Figure refers to growth between 1996/1997 and 2000.
[c] Figure refers to growth between 1991 and 2000.
[d] Figure refers to growth between 1973/1974 and 1999.

Source: Data from OECD (2005b).

services. In the Netherlands and Sweden an average of over 10 per cent of older people receive formal help at home. In other countries between 2.8 per cent (USA) and 7.1 per cent (Germany) receive formal home care services. Although only a fraction of older people receives formal help in all countries, the variation is striking. With the exception of the USA, the percentage of older people receiving formal home care is greater than the percentage living in institutions, thus highlighting the importance of home care for older people.

The growth of institutionalization rates in Table 6.3 offers a more detailed picture of how the relative importance of institutionally based care has been changing over time. With the exception of Sweden, growth rates are negative and are about 0.2 per cent. In most countries, then, fewer people now live in institutions. In part, this reflects policies explicitly aimed at de-institutionalization. However, as Table 6.4 indicates, this does not mean that the number of long-term care beds has fallen. In the majority of countries, the number of beds per 1,000 people has increased over the last two decades; indeed, they have more or less doubled. In short, in most countries institutionally-based care continues to be important.

Irrespective of the inconclusive trends in the provision of institutionally based care, the spending on other types of services for the elderly and disabled has increased significantly. Table 6.5 lists per capita public expenditure on day care, rehabilitation, home help services and other services in kind. Despite inconclusive trends in the provision of institutionally based care, spending on other types of services for the elderly and disabled seems to have increased.

Analysis of these extremely limited available statistics has given a first impression of home care in our countries. In terms of both funding and

Table 6.4 ***Number of long-term care beds per 1,000 people, 1995–2010***

	1995	*1998*	*2000*	*2003*	*2005*	*2010a*
Australia	4.1	4.2	4.5	4.8	5.2	7.7
Germany	3.7	n/a	n/a	8.6	9.2	10.3
Japan	0.8	1.5	1.8	2.1	2.3	5.6
Netherlands	3.6	3.7	3.7	3.8	4.0	10.4
New Zealand	n/a	n/a	n/a	n/a	n/a	8.0
Singapore	n/a	2.1	2.1	n/a	2.3	n/a
Sweden	17.2	16.0	16.9	16.2	15.2	14.2
Taiwan	n/a	n/a	1.9	n/a	2.0	1.8
United Kingdom	3.6	3.8	3.5	3.1	2.9	8.7
United States	n/a	5.5	5.4	5.4	5.3	5.4

n/a = not available.
[a] Figures for Australia and Germany from 2009

Sources: Data from OECD (2012b); Singapore Ministry of Health (2008); Bureau of National Health Insurance (2012).

provision, home nursing is marginal in all countries, in some more so than in others. At the same time, there is little evidence of a systematic move away from institutionally based care. In some countries institutionalization rates have fallen, but in most the number of long-term care beds has increased. Nevertheless, more public money is being spent on alternative services for older people such as day centres and home helps.

Table 6.5 ***Per capita public expenditure on services for the elderly and disabled (US$)***

	1983	*1988*	*1993*	*1998*	*2003*
Australia	n/a	n/a	n/a	4	n/a
Germany	2	6	38	129	157
Japan	n/a	n/a	n/a	4	10
Netherlands	27	37	118	68	n/a
United Kingdom	13	26	n/a	n/a	n/a
United States	18	34	84	120	131

n/a = not available.

Source: Data from OECD (2006).

Providing home health care

Home care is embedded in health systems and, as such, its provision is closely related to that of health systems. However, as the poor relation, home care is often not fully integrated in the institutional fabric of health systems, thus creating distinct features in the provision of services. More broadly, this relates to the respective boundaries between health and social care services and the relative integration between the two services. The degree to which this is the case is an interesting question from a comparative perspective.

The provision of home care reflects the level and security of funding but is also influenced by other factors. This includes policies explicitly aimed at substituting formal home care for institutionally-based care and informal care, together with cultural expectations about the role of the family in care giving, discussed in more detail later in this chapter. Substitution policies refer to a set of policies that are intended to replace institutionally-based care with care in the home and related settings. Motivations are both financial and humanitarian. These policies have focused on de-institutionalization (see OECD, 2005a), although any effects are partly offset by the increasing number of older and very old people (Jacobzone *et al.*, 1999). Policies have focused less explicitly on developing non-institutional care settings, often resulting in additional demands on women as informal carers (Jenson and Jacobzone, 2000). When assessing the provision of home care, it is important to look at how services are organized and who provides these services. Again, both aspects give an indication of the degree to which home care is integrated in health systems and influence the level of service provision.

Considering the diversity of health systems, it is not surprising that the provision of home care services shows wide variation (see Figure 6.1). Only in Britain and Sweden are home nursing services provided publicly and firmly integrated into the health system. This situation is typical of national health services, which are characterized by a high degree of public integration (see Chapter 3). However, this does not

Predominant Type of Provision

		Public	*Non-profit*
Level of Provision	*High*	Sweden	Netherlands
	Low	Britain	Australia, Germany, Japan, New Zealand, Singapore, Taiwan, USA

Figure 6.1 *The provison of home health care*

necessarily guarantee a high level of service provision. For instance, in Britain targeting and shifting responsibilities to less well integrated social care services away from the NHS has undermined the traditional entitlement for home nursing (Glendinning, 2013). The push towards a more mixed provision of services has paradoxical consequences, because the fragmentation of services not only requires more coordination, but also makes it more difficult. Trudie Knijn (2000) in her analysis of the Netherlands identifies this as one of the central tensions underlying contemporary market reforms. This contrasts with Sweden, for example, and here a crucial factor is that home health care is embedded in a gender culture that combines ideas of universal access to services with ideas of individual independence from the family as a source of financial and care support.

However, private, non-profit providers can also be part of a universal system of service provision, resulting in a high level of this provision. In the Netherlands, for example, this reflects a long-standing commitment to home care, together with service provision which combines health and social care as well as secure funding (this last element is discussed in the following section). This is the exception to the rule and in many other countries, the provision of home care is highly mixed and less well integrated into the health system, thus reflecting either a strong legacy of informal care (as in Germany, Japan, Singapore and Taiwan), health systems with a strong liberal element (as in Australia and the USA) and/or weaker demographic pressures (as in New Zealand). However, with ubiquitous demographic and cost pressures, some countries have adopted more explicit policies. In response, some have extended their social insurance to cover home care, whereas others have introduced a tax-funded home care programme.

Sweden is the paradigmatic case of a country where the level of service provision is high and where the public provision of services dominates. Home care is embedded in a national health service, which makes for strong public integration. This also reflects a strong commitment to the primacy of formal care services over informal care that resonates with a gender culture where universal access to formal care is seen as a central means to secure the independence of individuals, both as potential employees and care recipients. Yet, this coexists with a high degree of decentralization, and some suggest that the wide differences at local level make it more appropriate to talk about a multitude of 'welfare municipalities' rather than a single welfare state (Trydegård and Thorslund, 2001). Moves towards devolution since the early 1990s have exacerbated this trend (Ciarini, 2008; Rauch, 2006). Not surprisingly, the organization of services is characterized by diversity. In half of the localities, county councils have delegated the responsibility for home nursing to municipalities (National Board of Health and Welfare, 2000). This results in highly integrated service provision since municipalities also provide other long-term nursing services in institutional settings together with social-care-oriented home help services. In the other half, county councils continue to organize home care as part of primary care services.

As the international statistics discussed earlier indicate, Sweden has a high percentage of older people receiving formal home help. Services for older people with long-term care needs have long been well developed and social preferences for home care, together with the need for de-institutionalization, were recognized very early (see Anell *et al.*, 2012; Gough, 1994; Trydegård, 2000). However, recent financial constraints combined with an emerging ideology of 'welfare mix' have put a strain on the system (for a more detailed case study see Burau *et al.*, 2007). Private providers have come to play a significant role in the delivery of home care and between 1993 and 2010 the number of publicly-funded hours of home care delivered by private providers increased from 2 per cent to 19 per cent (Meagher and Szebehely, 2013: 59f). The targeting of services also disguises an overall reduction of service levels. Home-based care services have become concentrated towards very old people and towards older people living alone; that is, in older people who need help most. As a consequence, the number of older people receiving extensive help has increased significantly, while the overall percentage of older people receiving home care has fallen (Ciarini, 2008; Trydegård, 2003). These changes illustrate a gradual move away from universal welfare policies and contrast with earlier reforms (Meagher and Szebehely, 2013), while the overall commitment to tax funding, female employment and universalism remains unchanged (Lyon and Gluckmann, 2008; Theobald, 2003).

High public integration can facilitate but does not necessarily safeguard high levels of service provision, as the case of England demonstrates (Glendinning, 2013). Home nursing services are provided publicly with GP-led Primary Care Trusts responsible for organizing the provision of services. The Primary Care Trusts are intended to commission home help services and this should help to better integrate the provision of home-based care services across the health and social care divide. However, the level of service provision is low, not least reflecting lower overall spending on health care in the UK compared to other countries (see Chapter 3), as well as the hollowing out of entitlements to tax-funded home nursing. Instead, home-based health care over the last decade has focused on acute care needs, while other care needs have been redefined as social care for which older people have to pay depending on the local authority areas (Lewis, 2001). As a consequence, substitution policies that could have helped expand the provision of home nursing services have been weak, if not non-existent. The same applies to social-care-oriented services where speedier discharge of older people from hospitals and the reduction of long-term care facilities has not been matched by comparable public funding to stimulate the development of home-based services (Gibson and Means, 2000; Glendinning, 1998). More broadly, this reflects a gender culture where, in contrast to Sweden, family care is only partly to be shared with the state. As a result, the availability of social care service is uneven (Brodhurst and Glendinning, 2001).

In short, public provision makes for publicly integrated home care. However, a similar degree of integration in the health system can also be achieved with a more mixed provision of services, which is dominated by non-profit providers. For instance, in the Netherlands, the provision of home care is in the hands of non-profit organizations, the regional Cross Associations. Only one organization operates in any one area and provides skilled nursing services, personal care and prevention (Tester, 1996). In the past, separate organizations existed for home nursing and home help services, but in the early 1990s the two began to merge with the aim of increasing the efficiency of service delivery (Kerkstra, 1996). Integrated provision of services coincides with a high overall level of service provision, which is comparable to Sweden and which reflects a long-standing commitment to formal care services dating back to the late 1960s (Knijn, 1998). Interestingly, the Netherlands also had a higher proportion of people living in institutions than any other European country and it was only in the 1980s that policies focused more explicitly on substitution (Loo *et al.*, 1999).

In contrast, in many other countries a predominantly mixed provision of home care services coincides with low levels of integration of services in the health system as well as low levels of service provision. Germany (together with Japan, Singapore and Taiwan) is a classical example of a country where the development of home care services has been impeded by a deeply embedded gender culture that gives preference to informal care. The principle of subsidiarity defines home care first and foremost as the responsibility of the family (for an overview see Doyle and Timonen, 2007). The introduction of long-term care insurance in Germany has only partly changed this. Security of funding coexists with basic coverage, which is cash limited and not needs based, and there is an explicit emphasis on informal care in the form of cash benefits for informal care givers (Theobald and Hampel, 2013). Fee-for-service payments also encourage the provision of services that are closely tailored to the conditions under which services are reimbursed by insurance. As a result, services often remain highly segmented, circumscribed and inflexible (Theobald, 2004). Having said that, the end of the monopoly of the five main non-profit providers has led to the escalation of alternative providers (46 per cent privately owned) providers, which increased from 4,300 in 1992 to 11,800 in 1999 (Cuellar and Wiener, 2000: 19). In

2009, 61.5 per cent of providers were for-profit, although they tend to serve fewer users (Theobald and Hampel, 2013: 128). This has resulted in greater diversity in the provision of home care, if not necessarily significant increases in the level of service provision (Theobald, 2012). At the same time, sharp separations among health and social care, acute care and rehabilitation, and ambulatory and hospital care continue to exist (Theobald, 2004). Policies have been concerned more with closing gaps in the provision of long-term care, not specifically with home care as such (Boom, 2008). Instead, support for informal care has been strongest and most explicit.

The development of home care services can also be impeded by strong liberal elements in the health and welfare system. In Australia, for example, the historical emphasis on private funding and the heavy role of charitable agencies in providing care for older people, combined with the provision of health care by the states and not the Commonwealth, resulted in a highly fragmented provision of home care (Someya and Wells, 2008). However, this situation changed with a series of steps in the early 1980s culminating in the introduction in 1985 of the Home and Community Care Program (HACC), an intergovernmental programme that subsidizes a range of community services to support people in their own homes. The aims of HACC are to provide a 'comprehensive, coordinated and integrated range of basic maintenance and support services' for frail elderly people and their care givers in order to enable them to be more independent, thus enhancing their quality of life and preventing their inappropriate admission to long term residential care (Australian Department of Health and Ageing, 2006a). The types of services funded include nursing care, allied health care, meals, personal care, transport, respite care and counselling. Some services charge a small fee depending on ability to pay and the number of services used but this varies from state to state.

Despite HACC, a national conference concluded that 'rampant bureaucracy' meant Australia's home care programmes for the elderly were in dire need of an overhaul. Experts and advocates agreed that caring for the elderly in their homes needed to be simplified and better funded. They criticized the buck-passing between the Commonwealth and the states and suggested that the system would be run better by either one, but not both (Wroe, 2003). In response to such criticism, in 2004 the Ministry released *A New Strategy for Community Care – The Way Forward* that outlined the Australian government's vision for streamlining Commonwealth-funded programmes and providing a more consistent and coordinated community care sector (Australian Department of Health and Ageing, 2006b). The Australian government and state/territory governments jointly fund the Aged Care Assessment Program (ACAP) to conduct client assessments in relation to five dimensions of need: physical, psychological, medical, cultural and social. The core objective is to comprehensively assess the care needs of frail older people and to assist them to gain access to the most appropriate types of care, including approval for government-subsidized residential and community care services.

However, the legacy of strong liberal elements remains present, even when there are moves towards greater public involvement. For example, under the national 'Ageing in Place' programme in New Zealand, home care services are increasingly publicly subsidized (Miller *et al.*, 2008). As a result, government home support expenditure more than doubled between 1995/6 and 2002/3 (New Zealand Ministry of Health, 2003: 40). The government partially or fully subsidizes a wide range of home care services, particularly those that depend upon professional expertise such as nursing. At the same time, eligibility and level of service are determined by needs assessment, although since 2005 asset testing is being gradually phased out (Miller *et al.*, 2008). This is typical of a care regime that combines very limited universality with means testing and where privately paid and charitable services complement family care. In relation to the last aspect, it is also indicative that there are additional community support services that are not publicly funded, such as transportation, which are also often provided free of charge to persons in need. The main source of funds for these services is the Lottery Grants Board that provides funds to not-for-profit organizations.

Funding home health care

The ways in which home care is funded are significant in two respects: security of funding, together with the relative level of public funding, are important factors shaping the provision of home care services. Funding arrangements also give an indication of the extent to which home care is an integral part of a health system.

The funding of home care ranges from taxes and social insurance contributions to out-of-pocket payments and private insurance. The first two provide secure funding, whereas out-of-pocket payments are a much less reliable source of funding. The funding of home care is typically highly mixed since funding from public sources is often insufficient, and a substantial amount of home care is funded from private, out-of-pocket payments. The importance of non-public sources of funding is even greater if the indirect costs incurred by unpaid care givers are taken into consideration. At the same time, diverse approaches to funding create different types of access. In countries with tax funding, patients tend to have direct access to services. In contrast, in countries with social insurance funding patients often need a medical referral to access services.

Table 6.6 ***Funding home health care***[a]

Predominantly tax-based funding	*Predominantly social insurance contributions*	*Predominantly private funding*
Australia	Germany	Singapore
Britain	Netherlands	USA
New Zealand	Taiwan (NHI)	
Sweden		

[a] Japan is difficult to categorize as home health care is funded by taxes and social insurance contributions to equal extents.

As Table 6.6 shows, there is considerable variation in relation to the funding of home care that reflects the respective health systems. In contrast to medical care, public funding of home care often only provides basic coverage that must be supplemented by substantial amounts of out-of-pocket payments and/or unpaid informal care. The degree to which this is the case is influenced by the broader gender culture and the relative state support for formal care services more generally. In Britain, New Zealand and Sweden, tax funding of home nursing (and home help services in Sweden) is embedded in a health system that is universal in its orientation. This leads to generous entitlements in principle. In Australia, home care is also tax funded, but this is part of a health system with strong private elements and entitlements are means-tested (Someya and Wells, 2008).

Social insurance funding in Germany, Japan, the Netherlands and Taiwan makes home care an earned right, although individual benefits are often needs based. Integrated funding of health and social care (as is the case in Australia, the Netherlands and Sweden) can add further security to funding arrangements. In contrast, the USA and to a lesser extent Singapore rely heavily on private funding (Teo *et al.*, 2003). This undermines the security of funding for individuals. At the same time, entitlements to tax-funded home care have been reduced as services have been targeted to the very needy (as in Sweden) or defined as means-tested social care (as in Britain). This reflects both financial pressures and an ideological turn towards welfare mix. Nevertheless, other countries have seen the introduction of tax-funded programmes covering home care (as in Australia and the USA) and even the introduction of new additions to social insurance (as in Germany and Japan).

In some countries with national health services, public provision of home nursing coincides with tax funding; Britain and Sweden are typical examples. Taxes may be combined with complementary sources of funding such as out-of-pocket payments, which in Sweden constitute 10 per cent of expenditure (National Board of Health and Welfare, 2000: 6). Tax funding represents a high degree of public integration and security of funding, although the levels of funding vary among countries and over time. In Britain, for example, home nursing services are part of the NHS and, as such, are funded out of general taxation and are free at the point of use. Although this implies generous entitlements in principle, in practice the use of home nursing services is restricted, reflecting the tight cash limits under which the NHS operates. Over the last decade, more and more services have been defined as social rather than health care, and, depending on the local authority, as such they incur charges. Combined with targeting of services by local authorities, this means that older people increasingly have to rely either on their own funds or on the help of families and friends in order to pay for services and stay in their own homes (Baldock, 2003; Glendinning, 2013). Brodhurst and Glendinning (2001) suggest that this strategy produces a considerable reduction of citizenship rights in what was a universal system until the early 1980s.

Within this context, devolved governing structures may offer possibilities for policy change. A case in point is Scotland, which in 2002 established a social right to home care. In addition to home nursing, patients now also have access to free personal (social) care, which covers personal assistance and hygiene, together with simple treatments. The only condition is that patients be over age 65 and that their care needs have been assessed (see Marnoch, 2003). The introduction of free home care is an example of the emerging health care federalism in the UK and distinct health policies in Scotland since, under the 1997 devolution legislation, the Scottish Parliament can pass its own laws on social issues and also raise some, albeit limited, additional taxes (Woods, 2004).

In other countries, tax funding is embedded in a health system with strong elements of private funding and this makes for a great variety of sources of funding. For example, in Australia, the HACC, which covers home nursing and home help services, was initiated only in 1985. Its services are means tested. The HACC, an integral part of a set of changes known as the Aged Care Reform Strategy, was the product of a 1982 Commonwealth inquiry which recommended that the entire system of aged care support be overhauled and more home care services provided to enable people to stay in their own homes (Jenson and Jacobzone, 2000: 59). Nevertheless, funding for home care remains a combination of public, private, charitable and individual funding, as the testing of assets is used for home care support. Also, public funding is a complex combination of different sources.

HACC is a joint Commonwealth, state and territory cost-shared programme with the Commonwealth contributing 60 per cent and the states and territories providing 40 per cent. While the Commonwealth and state/territory governments jointly allocate funds to HACC regions based on agreed targets for service outputs, the sub-national governments are solely responsible for its administration, for allocating funds to services within regions and for the day-to-day operation of the programme. In 2007–08, 225 per 1,000 persons aged 65 and over received HACC services (Department of Health and Ageing, 2008). The HACC also funds a wide range of non-profit organizations (Australian Department of Health and Ageing, 2006a). Under HACC, palliative care services are provided by government and non-government providers to people in their own homes, community-based settings such as nursing homes, palliative care units and hospitals. The impact of HACC represents a sweeping shift in the balance from nursing home to hospice and home-based care. Between 1985 and 1990, for instance, while Commonwealth expenditure on nursing home care increased by 9 per cent, the corresponding increases in expenditure for home care and hospices were 95 per cent and 127 per cent, respectively (Australian Department of Health and Ageing, 2003).

The public funding of home care has traditionally been less well established in social insurance systems, reflecting an implicit focus on the working population, together with an often strong communitarian orientation that reveres self-help by individuals and communities (see Chapter 2). Here, the principle of subsidiarity underpinning German social policy is indicative. The principle of subsidiarity holds that social, political and economic activity is undertaken at the lowest appropriate level of social organization (Freeman and Clasen, 1994). This principle is the cornerstone of Catholic social teaching, which has been very influential. Subsidiarity assigns primary responsibility for welfare to the individual and to the family and resonates with a gender culture that builds on part-time caring by women and full-time paid employment by men. Furthermore, welfare is funded through social insurance and is provided as an earned right rather than on the basis of need. In terms of the provision of formal services, priority is given to non-governmental, non-profit organizations. Not surprisingly, the introduction of social insurance for home care has been a relatively recent phenomenon in Germany as well as Japan (for a more detailed case study of Japan, see Burau *et al.*, 2007).

In 1989, faced with a fast-growing elderly population and the problem of social hospitalization, the government in Japan instituted the Gold Plan to expand services for older people. One goal of this Plan was to facilitate access to care services by contesting the assumption that home care is to be provided by family alone and by shifting resources from hospitals to social support services, such as home nursing and social care (Tatara and Okamoto, 2009; Yamashita, 2011). Two criticisms of the policy were that it was not matched by government attention to the quality of care and that it failed to sufficiently reimburse home health care

(Kobayashi and Reich, 1993). As a result of these shortcomings, the Gold Plan was expanded in 1997, when Japan enacted the Public Long-term Care Act, which marked a clear shift towards funding a comprehensive programme of long-term care, both health and social care.

Under Japan's Ten-Year Strategy to Promote Health Care and Welfare for the Elderly (The New Gold Plan) that came into effect on 1 April 2000, municipalities are the insurer while the central government, the prefectures and medical care insurers provide multiple layers of support (Ikegami, 2007; Imai and Fushimi, 2012). Half of the cost of long-term care insurance administered by the Financial Stability Fund is borne by the premium payments of the insured and the other half is funded by public funds. Of the public funds, the ratio among the national government, prefectures and local municipalities is fixed at 2:1:1. In addition, the national government pays towards compensating for financial gaps among municipalities, which occur because of the differences in the ratio of subscribers of advanced elderly age to their abilities to bear the burden (Japan Ministry of Health, Labour and Welfare, 2004). To ensure impartiality between service users and non-users, in principle the users are required to pay a 10 per cent co-payment for long-term care, although in the case of the low-income elderly, a maximum amount is set (Tsutsui and Muramatsu, 2007). According to Fukuda *et al.* (2008) between 2000 and 2004 the number of certified care recipients doubled from 1.49 million to 2.97 million. The Japanese LTCI provides only services rather than cash for care and recipients can choose their services and providers. The most popular service is adult day care, with 1.9 million users (6.5 per cent of people aged 65 years and older), benefiting both frail older people and their caregivers (Fukuda *et al.*, 2008).

In 2005, the Japanese government revised the Long-term Care Insurance Act in order to better promote the development of an integrated community care system and the establishment of community integrated support centres in all municipalities (Tamiya *et al.*, 2011). The centres are charged with coordinating health and social care services and organizing formal and informal care. The coordination of the latter turned out to be one of the most significant tasks. As a consequence, formal care through health and social services was merged with informal care provided by non-profit organizations and other forms of voluntary assistance including people known to the receiver, such as family members, friends and colleagues (Matsushige *et al.*, 2012). Continuing threats to the success of the system, however, include dissatisfaction with home-based care, provision of necessary support for family care givers and fiscal sustainability (Tamiya *et al.*, 2011).

However, even under new insurance schemes, the legacy of subsidiarity can be influential. For example, in Germany so-called long-term care insurance is funded entirely by insurance contributions. Another distinct feature is that the insurance includes cash benefits that older people can use to pay informal care givers. This was designed to encourage informal care by the family and wider network (Meyer, 1996) and, despite the freedom of choice, a clear majority of beneficiaries receiving care at home choose cash benefits (Eichler and Pfau-Effinger, 2009). Furthermore, the security of the new funding arrangement contrasts with the limited levels of funding available, and many older people must continue to rely on out-of-pocket payments and/or unpaid care givers (Cuellar and Wiener, 2000: 17; Theobald and Hampel, 2013).

Among the social insurance systems there are also outliers. For instance, in the Netherlands home care is covered by a separate type of health insurance that was introduced in the late 1960s and covers a range of exceptional medical risks (Knijn, 1998). The insurance is compulsory for all employees irrespective of income and is supplemented by central government funds and out-of-pocket payments. This represents a strong element of universalism in a health system in which almost one-fifth of the population is covered by private health insurance. The Netherlands is unusual in that the insurance covers both home nursing and home help services. Integrated funding means that the scope of the insurance is relatively extensive, which in turn has led to a high level of service provision and use of formal services (Coolen and Weekers, 1998: 50). However, concerns about expenditure coupled with a renewed emphasis on subsidiarity and the primacy of self-help in relation to informal care have begun to weaken the universalist orientation of home care in the Netherlands (Visser-Jansen and Knipscheer, 2004).

In contrast, other countries largely rely on private funding of home care. In Singapore, for instance, users are expected to pay for home care services out of their Medisave accounts or through the private or public insurance they can purchase with those accounts (Teo *et al.*, 2003). Health care services for the elderly in Singapore are mostly run by voluntary welfare organizations, although government financial assistance is available. However, even in countries like Singapore, home care has become a concern of policy makers. To address the apprehension over the heightened health needs of the rapidly ageing population, the Inter-Ministerial Committee on Health Care for the Elderly (IMC) was created in 1997 to provide strategies for the provision of health care for the elderly. The IMC has consistently stressed that the elderly are to be cared for in their own homes for as long as possible with institutionalization being a last resort. The government recognizes that these care services can be expensive and provides financial assistance in the form of subsidies to the elderly who lack adequate resources. To ensure that the subsidy goes to those who need it, means testing was introduced in 2000. The subsidy goes directly to service providers to offset the bill for care fees and charges. Services in Singapore today include home medical and nursing care as well as day respite and rehabilitation centres (Singapore Ministry of Health, 2009).

Developments were taken a step further in June 2002, when the government introduced a public long-term disability insurance scheme, ElderShield, to ensure basic economic protection against expenses required in the event of severe disabilities. The ElderShield payouts are set at $300 per month, up to a maximum of 60 months that is considered sufficient to cover a substantial portion of a patient's share of subsidized nursing home charges and defray the expenses of those who choose home care. An ElderShield policy holder is covered for the rest of her life if at age 65 she has paid all the premiums under the Regular Premium Plan or a lump sum premium under the Single Premium Plan. For those who are not eligible for ElderShield or who exhaust their benefits, there is a government assistance scheme that offers means-tested support for up to 60 months per lifetime for those with low monthly household incomes (Singapore Ministry of Health, 2008). Moreover, in October 2000, the Ministry of Health launched a scheme to bring affordable health care to needy elderly people who do not live near to the polyclinics that normally provide affordable health care for them. All Singaporeans over age 60 are entitled to a subsidy of 75 per cent of the fees charged at polyclinics (Mehta and Briscoe, 2004).

Like Singapore, Taiwan traditionally depended on informal, largely family, care givers, but the rapid urbanization and changes in family structures has led to a decrease in the number of family members who can take responsibility for caring for their elders, thus requiring the hiring of carers or entering care facilities (Hsiao and Huang, 2012). In 2008, the government initiated a ten-year, long-term care plan to create a more integrated service delivery system and to lay a foundation for the establishment of a long-term care insurance programme to be implemented in three to five years (Nadash and Shih, 2012). The services it provides encompass care services (e.g., home-based care, daycare), home nursing, rehabilitation services, provision of assistive devices, respite care, meals-on-wheels and transportation services and institutional care. The subsidy for home-based care depends on the disabilities of the senior citizen, not the family income, although the level of subsidies does vary according to income. In addition to cash benefits for seniors themselves, the government provides allowances for informal care givers (although not for migrant domestic helpers) in lower income families. While many of the care giving responsibilities of the family have been taken up by the state, the marketplace and non-profit agencies, however, the family still plays a dominant role in Taiwan (Wang, 2011).

In the USA, as can be expected in a market-based health care system, public sources of funding are marginal, often means-tested and highly fragmented. However, in recent years, largely to reduce costs, Medicare has initiated programmes targeted at home care and encouraging people to stay at home (Sloane, 2005; Wilensky, 2005). All Medicaid beneficiaries are now eligible for home nursing care if they meet certain conditions. Although these conditions vary widely across states, they often require that virtually all assets be liquidated (Miller *et al.*, 2008). For those eligible for Medicaid, however, a fairly wide array of personal care services are obtainable although, again, availability and funding varies extensively by state (see Kitchener *et al.*, 2007 and Grossman *et al.*, 2007). In contrast, services supported by Medicare are more narrowly construed as medical and it does not pay for 24-hour care at home, drugs, meals or home help services. In 2007, the National Commission for Quality Long-Term Care made recommendations for strengthening and standardizing the now disparate elder care across the USA (2007).

There have been a number of initiatives to provide public funding for home care in the USA, the most important of which is the Program of All Inclusive Care for the Elderly (PACE). After more than a decade operating as a federally supported demonstration project, PACE is now recognized as a permanent provider under Medicare and a state option under Medicaid for people over 55 years of age who are frail enough to meet their state's standards for nursing home care. The PACE organization must offer a service package that includes all Medicare and Medicaid services provided by that state as well as additional services including primary care, social services, restorative therapies, personal care and supportive services, nutritional counselling, recreational therapy and meals. Under prospective payment, Medicare/Medicaid pays home health agencies (HHAs) a predetermined base payment adjusted for geographic differences in wages across the country (Stenger and DeVoe, 2010). Thus, the HHA receives a fixed monthly payment for each patient, regardless of the services an enrolee uses. In 2008, there were over 9,000 Medicare certified home health agencies in the USA, with over 3 million beneficiaries (Centers for Medicare and Medicaid Services, 2009a).

The interface between formal and informal care

As the analysis above suggests, home care is a complex policy field. Public funding is often insecure and insufficient and has to be supplemented by out-of-pocket payments. Moreover, publicly-funded services are increasingly targeted at highly dependent older people and in many instances the entitlement to publicly-funded services is being diluted. Furthermore, the level of service provision is often basic and involves a diverse range of providers. As a result, the emphasis on welfare mix competes with the policy goal to integrate services across varied providers and with the boundary between health and social care.

The analysis thus far has focused only on formal home care – the care provided by paid staff with formal training/qualifications. The policy field becomes even more complex when it is realized that the bulk of home care has been (and still is) traditionally provided by family and friends: that is to say, informal, unpaid care givers. Tester (1996), in her comparison of community care in a number of European countries and the USA, estimates that informal care givers provide 75 to 80 per cent of care. With cost containment in health care and inadequate resources to develop home care services, the burden on informal care givers has actually increased in recent years. Substitution policies also mean that home care services are directed at highly dependent older people who would otherwise require institutional care. Significantly, informal care work is still viewed as women's work, and an overwhelming proportion of it is still being carried out by women in family settings (Jenson and Jacobzone, 2000; OECD, 2005b).

Informal care is important in all countries, but there are interesting variations in regard to the underlying cultural assumptions about the relations between generations and between women and men (Pfau-Effinger, 2004). In those countries where family bonds and/or collectivist values are traditionally strong, the care-giving responsibilities of families are extensive. The inverse applies to countries where values of individual independence dominate. Here, it is more accepted that care giving be in the hands of paid professionals, or at least that they complement informal care. These clusters of values and cultural traditions coincide with different types of care regimes (Burau *et al.*, 2007), as shown in Figure 6.2.

Sweden is the classic example of a public service care regime where equality and individual independence are the key and which is character-

		Value Orientations	
		Individual Independence	*Family Responsibility*
Care Regime	*Public Service*	Sweden	Netherlands
	Means tested		Australia, Britain, New Zealand, USA
	Subsidiarity		Germany, Japan, Singapore, Taiwan

Note: Japan and Singapore do not easily fit into (European) types of welfare regime. However, with Germany they share an explicit emphasis on family responsibility.

Figure 6.2 *Value orientations in informal care and welfare regimes*

ized by high female employment (see Rauch, 2006; Trydegård, 2000). Many responsibilities traditionally associated with families, such as care of older people and children, have been taken on by the public sector and formal care has been chosen over informal care. The overall commitment to this principle remains strong, although recent years have seen a much more explicit concern with the role of the family in care giving (Meagher and Szebehely, 2013). In other public service care regimes, the attitude towards the role of women in care giving is more ambivalent and in the Netherlands, for example, ideas of family care coexist with a strong emphasis on formal care. The insurance for exceptional medical risks introduced in the 1960s compensated for weakening traditional divisions in Dutch society (Alber, 1995) and marked the introduction of universalist elements into what otherwise was a conservative welfare state (Knijn, 2001).

In contrast, Britain is an example of a care regime with increasingly strong liberal elements and where means testing tends to prevail (Baldock, 2003; Means *et al.*, 2003). The NHS is an exception to the rule that the public funding and provision of welfare is often minimal, designed as a safety net for those who cannot provide for themselves. While many other welfare services are defined universally, in practice they are often means tested or income related. The responsibility of the individual (and the family) is central, whereas that of the state is residual. In relation to older people, it is assumed that families take on caring responsibilities. Among the means-tested care regimes, Australia is an example of a country that has been most active in the expansion of public support for families. In comparison, the US government is now beginning to accept some responsibility for long-term care of the elderly, although by and large it continues to be the duty of the family to arrange and fund this care through private insurance or personal resources.

Germany is the archetypal example of a subsidiarity care regime that places great importance on the family as an organizing principle of society (Alber and Schöllkopf, 1999). This reflects Catholic teachings on the family. However, Germany is unusual in the explicitness with which demands are made on the family. In this respect the idea of subsidiarity is vital, under which self-help is understood as the responsibility of individuals. If self-help is no longer possible, then it is the responsibility of the family to take over from the individual, followed by voluntary organizations, and, only if all else fails, will the state then step in.

The subsidiarity model is under pressure from demographic developments, though, as the example of Japan (similarly Singapore and Taiwan) illustrates. Traditionally, it has been the case that elderly parents live with their eldest son's family with an arrangement for sharing resources. Moreover, this strong filial duty to care for elderly family members often falls on the daughter-in-law. Thus, in some cases, a woman might be caring for two sets of parents simultaneously. Direct relatives, including children, grandchildren and siblings, may be legally required to provide financial support to maintain their elderly relatives. At the same time, one of the major factors driving reform in home care in Japan is the ongoing decline in the supply of in-family care givers due to the ageing process and the increasing labour market participation of younger women (Jenson and Jacobzone, 2000). In their study of Japan, Matsushige *et al.* (2012), for example, emphasize the relevance of informal care by friends or family for integrated home care and conclude that health policy needs to establish incentives that enable collaboration across the formal–informal division of care.

With home care on the political agenda of many health systems, there has been a corresponding interest in informal care. Expectations of a gap in informal family care as well as research findings concerning the significance of informal care have opened up the political debate (Hochschild, 1995). Home care inevitably involves informal care. The home is where older people live with their spouses and partners, and home is also one of the places where older people meet with friends and family. The spatial interface of personal relationships and home care facilitates the provision of informal care. Policies on home care have acknowledged the importance of informal care (see Burau *et al.*, 2007; Lundsgaard, 2004; Ranci and Pavolini, 2013), and from a comparative perspective the interesting question is what form this formalization takes and how policies define the interface between formal and informal care.

Here, a number of considerations come into play. In times of resource constraints, it seems inevitable that health systems continue to rely on informal care. Compared to formal care, this is the cheaper option, but only if the costs associated with informal care such as lost income and pension entitlements are ignored (Jacobzone, 1999; Jamieson, 1996). Another consideration is that the expansion of formal care might reduce the provision of informal care and even create new, expanded demands for formal care (Jamieson, 1996). This can be either a desirable or an undesirable policy outcome, although studies indicate that substitution is not straightforward. For moderately disabled older people, home-based care is likely to be the best (and most efficient) option, whereas for severely disabled older people, institutional care is more appropriate (Jacobzone, 1999). If anything, this suggests that substitution needs to be tailored to the particular circumstances of individuals (see Low *et al.*, 2000). Moreover, even in countries with relatively high levels of publicly-funded formal care, families continue to play a significant role as informal care givers. For example, even in Sweden an estimated two-thirds of the total volume of home care is provided informally (Johansson, 2000).

Policies on the informal aspects of home care pick and mix considerations about the interface between the formal and the informal in distinct ways, which are shaped by cultural assumptions about relations between the generations and between women and men. At the same time, it is interesting that in recent years many countries have experimented in one way or another with a more explicit integration of informal care into the (formal) health system. Haynes and associates, for instance, conclude that while views about family responsibilities may vary across countries, 'it is logical to suggest that a culture which sees family relationships as important can also be a culture which recognizes the case for state support of the family' (2010: 80). Twigg (1989) has developed a typology for understanding the range of relationships that exist between welfare agencies and informal care givers. She distinguishes among care givers as resources, when they are taken for granted; care givers as co-workers, when they are treated instrumentally to ensure the continuation of their caring activities; care givers as co-clients, when agencies are concerned with the needs of care givers in their own right; and superseded care givers, when agencies aim to replace them with paid formal care staff.

Looking at the interface between formal and informal care, similarities within differences are most striking. Countries vary significantly in terms of their expectations about the role of women in care giving. Sweden and the Netherlands are examples of countries that have traditionally favoured formal care, whereas Japan, Singapore, Taiwan and Germany are examples of coutries that explicitly expect women to take on caring responsibilities. This attitude also exists, but more implicitly, in liberal welfare regimes in countries like Australia, Britain, New Zealand and the USA. However, despite these differences, many countries – with exceptions such as Singapore, Taiwan, New Zealand and the USA – have begun integrating informal care into the formal system of funding home care. In this regard, payments for informal care givers have become vital. Although payments are largely symbolic (rather than reimbursements for a service), they are important indicators of a turn towards welfare societies.

With their traditionally strong preference for formal care, recent developments in Sweden and the Netherlands underline the pertinence of the emphasis on informal care and the move towards a welfare society. As Daatland (1996: 257) observes in relation to Sweden, '[t]he policy rhetoric encourages family care, voluntarism, and welfare pluralism'. For example, in the late 1990s the municipalities received additional funding to increase support for caring relatives that can take a number of forms (Szebehely, 2005). Municipalities can employ informal care givers as care assistants. Alternatively, older people can receive grants to pay informal care givers for the help they receive at home. Nevertheless, the importance of such forms of support remain limited and in 2004 only 0.5 per cent of people receiving formal care services were cared for by informal care givers employed by the municipality (Burau *et al.*, 2007). Having said that, informal care giving has increased as the public supply of some secondary services such as help with domestic work and personal care has fallen; the availability of family care now also plays a part when assessing the need for care services (Ciarini, 2008; Meagher and Szebehely, 2013).

In comparison, the Netherlands adopted a more systematic approach and financial support for informal care givers came as part of the introduction of a personal budget (a cash benefit) in 1995 (for a more detailed case study see Burau *et al.*, 2007). The budget provides care receivers with the opportunity to establish their own care provision including the right to employ a family member. The introduction of the budget has been a part of care service reforms in the 1990s aimed at introducing more market elements, especially choice, into health care (Knijn and Verhagen, 2007). The notions of autonomy and independence resonated with the criticisms of the self-help movement against paternalistic service provision; and carer organizations voted for care budgets as an opportunity to compensate for informal care giving (Kremer, 2005; Tjadens and Duijnstee, 2000). While the initial implementation of the cash benefits has been piecemeal, the number of recipients of personal budgets has increased steadily, for example from 5,401 in 1996 to 123,000 in 2010 (White, 2011: 8). Indeed, the personal budget option has turned out to be so popular that the scheme was temporarily closed to new applicants. Nevertheless, the salient tensions underlying the care regime and rooted in the breadwinner–care taker model that takes women as carers for granted remain present and are even exacerbated. As Outshoorn (2008; similarly, Lyon and Gluckmann, 2008) suggests, informal care has become more clearly the cornerstone of the care regime, with publicly provided care assuming a more residual role.

Considering the conservative orientation of its welfare regime and the explicit emphasis on family responsibility, it is not surprising that in Germany the introduction of long-term care insurance also extended the commitment to unpaid informal care. The demands made on the families of older people are now being addressed by a range of support mechanisms that are meant to help sustain informal care (Theobald, 2004; Theobald and Hampel, 2013). Besides benefits in kind, the insurance offers financial benefits which older people can use to pay their informal care givers and also pays contributions to the pension and accident insurance of informal care givers who qualify. In addition, the insurance offers respite care as an annual benefit for older people cared for by the family. Although the monetary value of the financial benefits is only half that of the benefits in kind, the majority of beneficiaries receiving care at home choose cash benefits (Burau *et al.*, 2007). This reflects the continued strength of cultural norms about the role of the family in care giving (Eichler and Pfau-Effinger, 2009; Wenger, 2001).

By comparison, the emphasis on informal care has typically been implicit in liberal welfare regimes while the explicit support of informal care givers has been weak. Significantly, in Singapore, the USA, Taiwan and New Zealand, public payments to informal care givers do not exist. In the first two countries, this reflects strong private elements in the provision and funding of home care. In Singapore, for example, a strong emphasis on obligations of female care givers plays an important role, as does the fact that individuals in effect control their own health care accounts and can use them for long-term care insurance should they so decide. In the USA, the liberal orientation of the care regime is exacerbated by the high degree of fragmentation in public funding. In Taiwan, as in Singapore, it reflects the focus on family responsibility for care of the elderly. In New Zealand, the relative youthfulness of the population is one possible explanation for the absence of formal support for care givers, although public debate on this issue is increasing.

However, among liberal welfare regime countries there are also examples of schemes paying family members for home care work. Indeed, Australia has a long tradition of this type of payment and the Department of Families, Community Services and Indigenous Affairs administers two allowances for care givers (Australian Department of Health and Ageing, 2006a). The Carer Allowance is an income supplement available to people who provide daily care at home to a family member who has a long-term disability or severe medical condition. It is a non-means or asset-tested, non-taxable payment of small cash benefits to family members who support a person who would otherwise be eligible for admission to a nursing home. In contrast, the Carer Payment is an income support payment for people who are unable to participate in the workforce full time as a result of their caring responsibilities. Carer Payment is subject to income and asset tests and is paid at the same rate as other social security pensions. The level of benefit is quite low, but ensures that carers have an adequate level of income and receive some compensation for their contribution.

In comparison, the corresponding schemes in Britain have been more recent and are embedded in moves to promote consumerism in quasi-markets and more specifically the notion of extending opportunities for choice and control (Glendinning, 2008; more generally Burau *et al.*, 2007). The introduction of 'individual budgets' combines various measures that have emerged from the late 1990s onwards, including direct payments. Over the years, individual budgets have expanded in terms of target groups and since 2003 also include older people (Boyle, 2011).

Policy trends and developments

Home care is full of contradictions. Home care is varied and diverse, yet it is a basic health need across countries. Home care is hardly visible in international statistics, yet it is central to the health of an increasing number of people. Home care funding and provision is often fragmented, yet home care is high on the health policy agenda of many countries. These are some of the salient contradictions in home care. The interesting question is what, if anything, recent policy trends and developments have changed regarding home care.

The provision of home care services is diverse, reflecting a political emphasis on a mixed economy of welfare and competition. Diversity means a greater number and wider range of providers. This requires greater coordination, but at the same time makes coordination (and ultimately integration into the rest of the health system) more difficult. Problems of coordination can be exacerbated by a sharp divide between different types of care (e.g., health and social care in Britain), the absence of national legislation (as in the USA) or highly decentralized governance structures (as in Sweden). Also, diversity of provision does not necessarily translate into adequate levels of provision. This gives credence to the general tenet that in times of cost constraint, diversity of provision often coincides with a targeting of services to those in greatest need (as in Britain and Sweden) or to those without any other means (as in Australia, and for social care in Britain and New Zealand).

At the same time, the funding of home care remains insecure and continues to rely largely on private funding and unpaid informal care. Only in Singapore and the USA does the insecurity of funding arise from the absence of public funding schemes. Many other countries have schemes funded either from taxes or social insurance contributions, but which are restricted because of needs and/or means testing or because the scheme provides only basic coverage (as in the case of long-term care insurance in Germany or home health care in Taiwan). Notwithstanding the continued insecurity of funding and the limits on funding, some countries have witnessed the wholesale introduction of new schemes over the last two decades. In Germany and Japan this took the form of the extension of social insurance and in Australia it took the form of a tax-funded programme. Even in the USA, states participating in the publicly funded PACE programme include a home care component.

Regardless of policy trends in the provision and funding of services, however, home care remains overwhelmingly informal, women's work. Most countries acknowledge the centrality of informal care, although this takes different forms, reflecting differences among care regimes and gender cultures. Policy responses range from the gender-blindness of liberal welfare traditions (USA) and gender-specific expectations in male-dominated, collectivist societies (Japan, Singapore and Taiwan), to the ideology of the welfare society (Sweden), the revival of subsidiarity (Germany), and symbolic payments to care givers (Australia, Britain, Germany and the Netherlands).

Chapter 7

Public Health

Until now the focus of this book has been on health care policy. We have been concerned with hospitals, doctors and other health care professionals and the funding, delivery and governance of health care services. Largely, it has centred on the care of individual patients. Chapter 5 demonstrated the wide range of settings and activities in the delivery of modern medical care. Chapter 6 extended this to integrate health care with non-health arenas by demonstrating that it is not possible to disengage health care from social care. The health of a home care client is as dependent on personal care as it is on medical care, perhaps in many cases more so. Even this more inclusive picture of health care, however, might be criticized for underestimating what are its most important dimensions according to some observers: health promotion and disease prevention, which together are regularly termed public health. Due to the breadth and rather amorphous nature of public health, this chapter is more of an overview of the policy concerns facing our countries than a comparative analysis as were previous chapters. Examples from our countries, nevertheless, are used throughout the discussion to demonstrate the wide scope of public health issues facing all countries.

The biggest advances in human health and longevity in the 20th century were the products of improved hygiene and clean water supplies, vaccines to prevent viral infections and antibiotics to combat bacterial infections. Historically, such endeavours constituted the backbone of public health, although as we will see in this chapter public health is much more expansive today. Simply put, public health is concerned with the health of the community as a whole. Although public health can be defined in many ways, common denotations of the term include health promotion, disease prevention, primary care, community health and population health. Public health encompasses a wide range of activities including the management of diseases that threaten the health of the population, the assessment of the health needs of specific populations and health education and promotion.

Global public health

The move to public health necessitates the inclusion of international organizations into the health care equation. Increasingly, health care has become a global matter as illustrated by many examples ranging from communicable diseases, to obesity, to environmental health. In all areas of public health, national boundaries become less consequential as health threats assume global proportions. Moreover, particularly with infectious disease in the context of rapid and extensive world travel, there is a need for systematic, concerted cooperation by the international community. In public health, therefore, increased attention has turned to the role of international health organizations and agreements among countries to deal with these health perils. International health, or global health, then, is a field of health care with a primarily public health emphasis that deals with health issues across regional or national boundaries. Additionally, public health experts recently have become interested in global processes that affect human health (Keefe and Zacher, 2011; Crisp, 2010; Skolnick, 2011). The impact of globalization on health, for example, illuminates the complex and changing sociological environment within which the determinants of health and disease express themselves.

The most visible of the myriad of international organizations that have a health remit is the World Health Organization (WHO). The WHO is a specialized agency of the United Nations that is concerned with global public health (for details on the WHO see Youde, 2012). The WHO was established on 7 April 1948, is headquartered in Geneva, Switzerland, and is a member of the UN Development Group. The WHO played a leading role in the eradication of smallpox and its current priorities include: communicable diseases, particularly HIV/AIDS, malaria and tuberculosis; the mitigation of the effects of non-communicable diseases; sexual and reproductive health; nutrition, food security and obesity; and substance abuse. The WHO is accountable for the World Health Report, a leading international publication on health, the worldwide World Health Survey and World Health Day.

The World Bank is another major intergovernmental agency tied to the UN that is heavily involved in international health and loaning money to poor countries on advantageous terms not available in commercial markets (Harman, 2012a, 2012b). In addition, three subsidiary agencies of the UN Economic and Social Council are committed to international health programmes. The UN Children's Fund (UNICEF) has made the world's most vulnerable children its top priority and devotes most of its resources to those under age five from the poorest countries. The UN Population Fund focuses on family planning programmes, while the UN Development Programme concentrates on AIDS, maternal and child nutrition and maternal mortality. In conjunction with WHO and the World Bank, it also sponsors the Special Programme for Research and Training in Tropical Diseases.

Box 7.1 International collaborative health research

International collaborative health research is expected to help reduce global health inequities. Although investment in health policy and systems research in developing countries is essential to this process, funding for international research is mainly channelled towards the development of new medical interventions. This imbalance is largely due to research policies in high-income countries that lead them to invest in health research aimed at boosting national economic competitiveness rather than reducing health inequities. This has encouraged a model that favours products that can be commercialized, targets health needs that can be met by profitable, high-technology products and has the licensing of new products as its endpoint. This pattern diverts funding away from research that is needed to implement existing interventions and to strengthen health systems (Pratt and Loff, 2012).

In addition, substantial work in global health is performed by a multitude of non-governmental organizations (NGOs). Services provided by international health NGOs include direct health care, community potable water and alleviation of endemic and epidemic infectious diseases and malnutrition. Examples of NGOs dedicated to global health are CARE, Médecins Sans Frontières (Doctors Without Borders), The International Committee of the Red Cross, the Red Crescent, Oxfam, Partners in Health, Project HOPE and Save the Children. In addition, many bilateral agencies, which are governmental agencies in a single country, provide aid to developing countries. Although the largest of these is the US Agency for International Development (USAID), most developed nations have a similar body. However, this aid usually focuses on research and often fails to address the immediate health problems facing the most vulnerable populations (see Box 7.1).

Global health challenges

Although great strides have been made in conquering health scourges of the past such as smallpox, numerous novel threats to public health continually unfold. They include events such as terrorism, wars and natural disasters (for example, the Great East Japan Earthquake, tsunami and nuclear power plant disaster of March 2011) as well as longer-term health threats like viral and bacterial infections and high-risk behaviours. For instance, in the first half of 2006 among the many WHO Epidemic and Pandemic Alerts and Responses announced were anthrax, avian influenza, ebola haemorrhagic fever, E. coli outbreaks, hepatitis, influenza, meningococcal disease, plague, severe acute respiratory syndrome (SARS), smallpox, tularaemia and yellow fever.

Box 7.2 The growing threat of tuberculosis in Europe

New drug-resistant strains of tuberculosis pose the disease's greatest threat to Europe since World War II. '[O]ur message to EU leaders is: Wake up. Do not delay. Do not let this problem get further out of hand', states Markuu Niskala, secretary-general of the International Federation of Red Cross and Red Crescent Societies. Tuberculosis, a respiratory illness spread by coughing and sneezing, is the world's deadliest curable infectious disease that the WHO estimates killed 1.7 million people in 2004. The high levels of multi-drug resistant tuberculosis in Baltic countries, Eastern Europe, Russia and Central Asia, and the emergence of a new extremely drug-resistant strain known as XDR-TB have led international public health officials to create the 'Stop TB Partnership in Europe'. In Europe, 50 people get sick and eight people die of the disease every hour. The rate of incidence of TB in the Western European countries that comprised the EU before it enlarged in 2004 is 13 cases per 100,000 people every year. That number doubles in the ten newest EU members. It doubles again to 53 in Romania and Bulgaria and yet again to 98 in the former-Soviet republics further east. But migration and EU expansion change things. For instance, TB cases in London have been increasing every year for almost ten years and in some London areas with many immigrants, rates are as high as 100 per 100,000 (Bulman, 2006).

Although many of these diseases are endemic to Third World countries, developed nations are at mounting risk due to immigration, air travel and the global economy. As illustrated by Box 7.2, even diseases that were once presumed to be vanquished have re-emerged on the public health agenda.

Until the mid-twentieth century health care centred principally on public health approaches. Few medical technologies or lifesaving procedures existed and hospitals were primarily charity institutions for those who could not afford a personal physician. Because the leading causes of premature death were infectious diseases such as tuberculosis, typhoid and cholera, attention was focused on ameliorating the conditions under which they spread across populations. To contain the spread of a contagious illness, public health authorities relied on many strategies including isolation and quarantine. Isolation of people who have a specific illness physically separates them from healthy people and restricts their movement to stop the spread of that illness. It allows for the focused delivery of specialized health care to people who are ill and protects healthy people from getting sick. People in isolation may be cared for in their homes, in hospitals, or at designated health care facilities. In most cases, isolation is voluntary, however, governments have broad authority to compel the isolation of sick people to protect the public.

Quarantine, in contrast, applies to people who have been exposed and may or may not be infected but are not yet ill. Separating exposed people and restricting their movements is intended to stop the spread of an illness, and quarantine has proven to be highly effective in protecting the public from disease. Although governments generally have wide authority to declare and enforce quarantine within their borders, often it is problematic politically because of its severe human rights ramifications, particularly when targeting specific social groups, and its potential adverse economic impact. The political nature and dangers of quarantine are well illustrated by reactive calls to segregate AIDS victims in the mid-1980s before the mechanism of HIV transmission was understood.

Protecting the public health also entails a wide range of monitoring and inspection mechanisms designed to prevent the spread of disease through food and water supplies, environmental threats and risky workplaces. As highlighted in Box 7.3, because of the transportation of food across long distances, often across national boundaries, the threat of contaminated food products can occur far from the origin of the product or processing facility and affect widespread populations. The case of 'mad cow disease' in the 1990s and the more recent threat of the spread of bird flu through humans highlight the need for continued attentiveness. Moreover, threats of biological terrorism and the emergence of even more aggressive strains of viruses clearly require proactive vigilance with regard to public health and funding. Public health strategies, then, run the gamut from quarantining individuals suspected of having communi-

Box 7.3 E. coli threats to public health

Less than a week after the US Food and Drug Administration lifted its warning on spinach grown in California, a brand of lettuce grown there was recalled over concerns about E. coli contamination. Pathogenic Escherichia coli bacteria or E. coli can proliferate in uncooked produce, raw milk, unpasteurized juice, contaminated water and meat. The lettuce scare came amid other government warnings that shipments of beef could cause grave health risks including paralysis, respiratory failure and death. Epidemiologists also warned consumers to stay away from some bottled carrot juice after a woman was paralysed and two people in Toronto died, apparently due to botulism poisoning. Although most healthy adults recover within a week without long-term side effects, young children, senior citizens and people with compromised immune systems are vulnerable in extreme cases to kidney damage or death. The outbreaks have sparked demands to create a new federal agency in charge of food safety. 'This recent outbreak must be a wake-up call to get our food safety house in order, because right now it's in pure disarray', according to US Senator Schumer. 'We need to have one agency take charge to ensure the next outbreak isn't far worse' (Konrad, 2006).

cable diseases deemed to be threats to the public health, to regulating the workplace for health and safety, to reducing unemployment and economic disparities, to reducing greenhouse emissions and the depletion of the ozone layer.

The SARS epidemic

Although public health is often viewed as a remote and esoteric field in which people are regarded as mere statistics, the spread of SARS in 2003 highlights the importance of public health and the fact that, since infectious diseases do not respect borders, international cooperation is essential. SARS is transmitted via droplets from infected individuals who, as a result of coughing, transmit the virus to close contacts. Although this epidemic dissipated after several months, during that time it caused a great deal of concern and huge economic costs. SARS began in China but was quickly spread around the world. Although researchers eventually found evidence of the virus in the civet cat that is eaten as a delicacy by some Chinese (Ross, 2003), most SARS victims contracted it after being in close proximity with an infected person. Although the number of persons killed by SARS was small by epidemic standards, it demonstrated how vulnerable to the rapid spread of communicable diseases we are in an age of air travel and concentrated medical facilities where, ironically, many of the victims became infected.

China's handling of the disease was seen by many observers as reprehensible. When the first SARS cases appeared in southern China in March, Beijing denied it and tried to suppress the news, thus allowing the disease to be spread beyond its borders by unsuspecting victims. In contrast, and as might have been predicted given its strong community-centred culture, Singapore instituted an aggressive home-quarantine system in response to SARS. Whereas health officials in Toronto, Canada, simply asked citizens suspected of SARS exposure to self-quarantine, Singapore took more extreme steps to enforce quarantine, including the use of video cameras and electronic bracelets to monitor the movements of those suspected of incubating the disease. It also passed a bill requiring quarantine-breakers to be fined up to $5,000 without being charged in court. The Health Minister also warned that the government might name and shame quarantine-breakers. Although criticized by some Westerners, Singapore's tough approach was praised by the WHO (Greenlee, 2003). In the end, SARS was controlled but only after more rigorous public health policies were adopted. The WHO credited old-fashioned quarantines with breaking the back of the outbreak (Wong, 2003).

Soon after the passing of the SARS story, in early 2004 the media began to report the spread of avian influenza across Southeast Asia.

Although 'bird flu' differs from SARS in that its transmission is from infected birds to humans, public health experts feared that it might mutate to enable it to spread from human to human. Another continuing public health threat is anthrax. Although its manufacture and use as a weapon for bioterrorism has generated the most anxiety, humans can become infected with anthrax by handling animal products or eating undercooked meat from infected animals. Anthrax raises the possibility of investigation of terrorist suspects alongside investigation of the outbreak of the infectious disease and a likelihood of public panic and the inundation of public health officials with reports of suspicious white powder (Howse, 2004).

Global public health resources were again challenged by what began as 'swine flu' in Mexico in April 2009. Within a week cases were identified as far away as Israel and New Zealand. Many flights from, and trade with, Mexico were halted and individuals potentially exposed to the virus were isolated and quarantined in some countries. Renamed H1N1, in part to stop the unnecessary slaughter of millions of hogs that occurred in Egypt and elsewhere, the WHO raised the alert level to a 5 (out of 6), declaring that 'a pandemic was imminent'. Although the virus was less virulent than anticipated, it caused major disruptions and served as yet another forewarning of the potential global threat of infectious diseases and a fear that a full pandemic could be a massive killer in spite of all our advanced medical technologies (Bennett and Carney, 2010). On 19 May 2009 WHO Director-General Margaret Chan repeated her warning that this new virus had great pandemic potential and could pose a grave threat to humanity even though the fatality rate was low with no major outbreaks outside North America and on 10 June WHO for the first time in history raised the alert level to 6, an international pandemic. 'This virus may have given us a grace period but we do not know how long this grace period will last. No one can say whether this is just the calm before the storm'.

Tay *et al.* (2010) describe the ambitious public health control measures implemented in Singapore to contain H1N1 and mitigate its social effects. Containment strategies included the triage of delirious patients at frontline healthcare settings, admission and isolation of confirmed cases, mandatory quarantine orders for close contacts and temperature screening at border entry points. After sustained community transmission became established, containment shifted to mitigation. The 2009 H1N1 pandemic was also the first test of the revised International Health Regulations (IHR) that was adopted in 2005 and took effect in 2007. The new IHR marked a move away from the disease-specific approach of the earlier version to an approach focused on whether a public health event constitutes a 'public health emergency of international concern' (Bennett and Carney, 2010: 303).

One of the by-products of a pandemic is the disruption of the global economy. Mackey and Liang (2012) note that the lack of a formal system to review trade restrictions imposed during international public health emergencies creates disincentives for surveillance and reporting, thereby undermining protection efforts. The 2003 SARS outbreak exposed major weaknesses in global governance that caused uncoordinated public health and economic responses. While the new IHR demonstrated improvement, it fails to allow for management of public health emergencies in a way that balances threats to health and those to economies and trade. As a result, Mackey and Liang (2012) contend that the creation of a joint WHO–WTO committee to adjudicate these conflicts might better achieve that balance.

The continuing AIDS epidemic

Although a 2012 report of the Joint UN Programme on HIV/AIDS (UNAIDS) reported remarkable progress in combating acquired immunodeficiency syndrome (AIDS) (Box 7.4), it remains a critical global health problem with an estimated 34 million persons infected with the human immunodeficiency virus (HIV), which causes AIDS. Each year around 2.7 million people become HIV infected and 1.8 million die of AIDS (WHO, 2012b). Although HIV continues to be a health problem in developed nations, the worst affected region is sub-Saharan Africa, where over one out of five adults are infected in some countries (see Table 7.1). Moreover, since 2001, the number of new HIV infections in the

Box 7.4 UN report on AIDS

In November 2012, UNAIDS reported over a 50 per cent drop in new HIV infections across 25 low- and middle-income countries and a decline of AIDS-related deaths globally by over 25 per cent between 2005 and 2011. It contends that these data show that acceleration of domestic investments in AIDS by the governments of countries most affected is working. More than 81 countries increased domestic investment by at least 50 per cent between 2001 and 2011. Most progress is being made in reducing new HIV infections in children and half of the global reductions in new HIV infections in the last two years have been among newborn children. Impressive gains were also made in reducing tuberculosis (TB) related AIDS deaths in people living with HIV. In the last two years alone, a 13 per cent decrease in TB-related AIDS deaths was observed. In conclusion, the UNAIDS report stated that eradicating AIDS was in sight, owing to better access to drugs that can both treat and prevent the incurable HIV. An aim to eventually end the worldwide AIDS epidemic is not 'merely visionary' but 'entirely feasible', according to the report (UNAIDS, 2012).

Table 7.1 *AIDS rates for adults (15–49), selected countries, 2009*

Swaziland	25.9
Botswana	24.8
Lesotho	23.6
South Africa	17.8
Zimbabwe	14.3
Zambia	13.5
USA	0.6
UK	0.2
All of our other countries are 0.1 or less	

Source: UNAIDS (2010).

Middle East and North Africa was up more than 35 per cent and evidence suggests that the epidemic is spreading rapidly in Eastern Europe and Central Asia, where the number of persons living with HIV increased by 250 per cent in the last decade (Foundation for AIDS Research, 2012).

There are many policies that can be implemented to reduce the impact of AIDS, beginning with the prevention of HIV transmission. Circumventing sexual transmission involves encouraging safer sexual behaviour through delayed first sex, partner reduction, increased male circumcision and condom use. Likewise, the spread of HIV through drug injection can be slowed by outreach work, needle exchange and drug substitution treatment, while transmission from mother to child can be drastically cut through use of medicines and the avoidance of breastfeeding (UNAIDS, 2010).

Although as yet there is no vaccination or cure for AIDS, patients who take a 'cocktail' of antiretroviral drugs daily can expect to recoup their health and live for many years (UNAIDS, 2010). As a result, in most developed countries, AIDS has been redefined as a chronic disease. Although antiretroviral therapy has saved 14 million life-years in poorer countries since 1995, an estimated 6.8 million people are eligible for treatment but do not have access. Moreover, of the 34 million people living with HIV, about half do not know their HIV status: if more people knew their status, they could come forward for HIV services. However, while AIDS prevention and treatment regimens are now well recognized, they have been less successful in reaching key populations including sex workers, men who have sex with men and people who inject drugs (UNAIDS, 2012).

Again, despite recent gains, access to prevention tools such as HIV education, condoms, clean needles and programmes to prevent mother-to-child transmission are inadequate in many countries. Other major obstacles include weak infrastructures and shortages of health workers in the worst affected countries (UNAIDS, 2010). Political or cultural attitudes, such as opposition to condom promotion, sex education and needle exchanges are also significant impediments. Another common problem is stigma and discrimination of people known to be living with HIV who are often shunned or abused by community members and even health workers. In addition to causing personal distress, this social environment discourages people from seeking HIV testing, treatment and care.

AIDS funding has come from individual governments, multinational organizations and private organizations. Over the last two decades, efforts to fight AIDS have accelerated, with increased funding from the USA and other developed countries and heightened spending by affected countries. The USA accounts for 48 per cent of all international assistance for HIV and together with the Global Fund for AIDS, Tuberculosis and Malaria provides the lion's share of investments in HIV treatment (UNAIDS, 2012). However, the amount of funding available remains short of what is needed for a fully effectual response. In 2011, US$16.8 billion was available and the need for 2015 is between US$22 and 24 billion (UNAIDS, 2012). Furthermore, major international organizations, such as the WHO and UNAIDS, do not provide funding but rather coordinate and monitor global HIV and AIDS treatment, care and prevention efforts. The WHO routinely issues guidelines to help countries achieve the highest attainable standards, while UNAIDS monitors the global epidemic through an annual reporting system and the release of annual reports on the global AIDS epidemic and other HIV and AIDS issues.

Regrettably, while infectious disease control is one of the earliest and most important functions of the modern state, it still receives at best only modest attention (Greer and Mätzke, 2012), although recently there has been increased activity in Europe. Martin and Conseil (2012), for instance, provide a useful overview of the current state of policies and laws governing pandemic influenza prevention and control in Europe and the concept of harmonization across European states, including an overview of supranational initiatives and powers created to enhance coordination of national pandemic disease policy. The European Centre for Disease Prevention and Control (ECDC) has been established by the European Union (EU) to act as a hub for disease control, drawing on networks across the continent to achieve what other political systems do with large agencies (Greer, 2012).

The individual and public health

Generally, disease prevention activities focus on the health of communities or populations rather than individuals, but De Ferranti (1985: 67) makes a valuable distinction between patient-related and non-patient-related preventive care. Patient-related approaches are generally defined as primary care, take place in a clinical setting and include immunization, health education between patients and GPs, and cancer, cholesterol and prostate screening programmes. Non-patient-related preventive approaches include such disparate activities as improved sanitation and water systems, promotion of health and hygiene, provision of adequate housing, control of pests, food safety and the monitoring of disease patterns (epidemiology).

Although an integral part of health care, public health – including routine primary care services for well patients, health education, disease prevention, immunization programmes and health promotion activities – consistently receives only negligible shares of health care budgets. OECD countries, on average, spend only 3 per cent of their health care budgets on prevention and public awareness campaigns (OECD, 2005c). In Australia, total public health expenditure comprises less than 2 per cent of the total recurrent health budget (Hilless and Healy, 2001). In the USA, it fares even worse with less than 1 per cent of the health care budget devoted to public health. Despite the AIDS epidemic and the heightened costs of substance abuse, violence and teenage pregnancy, public health spending as a proportion of US health care spending fell by 25 per cent between 1981 and 1993. Furthermore, the effects of the current global economic crisis on the spread and control of communicable diseases are unknown and there are few specific national policies and programmes aimed at mitigating its health impacts (Rechel *et al.*, 2011). Moreover, preventive services as compared to acute care are more susceptible to budget cuts resulting from the economic crisis with services targeted at vulnerable and hard-to-reach population groups at special risk.

Despite recent shifts toward a more public-health-oriented approach in many countries, even the most attentive countries would be well served to put a significantly larger proportion of their health care budgets into such efforts (Ham, 2010; Fry, 2010). Mounting evidence demonstrates that the most significant improvements in health come from public health measures, not curative medicine, even though the latter efforts are the most dramatic and therefore the most readily funded. For instance, while 99 per cent of health spending in the USA goes to medical treatment, it is estimated that this spending prevents only 10 per cent of early deaths. In contrast, population wide, public health approaches have the potential to help prevent some 70 per cent of early deaths through measures targeted at the social, environmental and behavioural factors that contribute to those deaths (Fuchs, 2004).

Framing a public health policy

Despite general agreement that it is more humane and cost-effective to avoid a condition of ill health in the first place than to have to treat it later, modern health systems continue to emphasize curative approaches – treating the ill rather than keeping people healthy. In part this is because the medical community has an intrinsic interest in curative medicine and, as illustrated in Chapter 5, is a dominant force in all systems. In addition, prevention deals with statistical future lives while curative medicine deals with identifiable patients who need help now. When a patient is facing imminent death, the individual, his or her family, and society as a whole are willing to pay heavily for any innovation that offers even a small promise of saving his or her life. In contrast, we are less likely to demand innovations that will save many more lives in the distant future, because while promotion/preventive programmes also ultimately help individuals, it is difficult to identify who they might be. Curative medicine, on the other hand, relates to specific patients in a 'direct, immediate and documentable way' (Baird, 1993: 347). Improving our understanding of how the public health system should be organized is imperative, therefore, because its organizational structure can make a significant difference to the public's health. In view of the sparse resources society is willing to expend for public health, it is essential to have a structure in place that most appropriately and efficiently allocates those resources (Jacobson, 2012).

In spite of convincing corroboration that the most significant advances in the health of populations have come from outside medicine, then, many forces, particularly the medical professions and the health care industry, have strong economic interests in maintaining or increasing funding for treatment (see Box 7.5). In combination with patients (we must remember that virtually everyone is a potential patient) and a public easily swayed by optimistic media coverage, they have aggrandized curative medicine at the expense of public health. Human-interest stories and favourable media coverage inherently follow technological breakthroughs in treatment, not public health efforts. Television dramas exalt those who save individual lives such as trauma teams and surgeons, not public health nurses or epidemiologists.

Together, these forces provide formidable obstacles against a meaningful reallocation of scarce resources from curative medicine to public health strategies. If the goal of the health care system is to improve the health of the population, however, public health programmes, particularly those that effect changes towards healthier lifestyles, are critical. This, in turn, requires a reassessment of the prevailing medical model with its myopic view of health. The public's health, instead, is the product of a complicated mixture of dynamic, adaptive and complex systems

Box 7.5 Confusion over the meaning of 'public health'?

According to MacIntyre (2011), the Australian national health reform agenda appears to have omitted public health. 'A question that has been troubling me since the Australia 2020 Summit and the government's rhetoric on preventive health has been: where does public health fit into national health reform?' Despite huge national investment to avert a crisis in human resources for health, including the creation of Health Workforce Australia, the need for a public health workforce has been ignored. The National Health and Medical Research Council (NHMRC) commissioned the Nutbeam report in 2008 to improve the effectiveness of research funding for public health, but no concrete changes have resulted. 'Having read the various documents on national health reform ... I am left wondering why public health is such a notable omission... I get the sense that the powers that be believe that "public health" and "primary care" are one and the same thing... Perhaps it is as simple as politicians and the public thinking that "public health" means provision of acute health care in public hospitals and through Medicare, but I believe there is confusion even among relatively well informed stakeholders' (MacIntyre, 2011: 38).

of agencies, infrastructure, relationships and interactions, and we must focus on these to learn how to improve health outcomes and reduce health risks in a population (Van Wave *et al.*, 2010; Ehrlich *et al.*, 2009).

Many observers contend that a reallocation towards disease prevention and health promotion would not only enhance health but also save money. As noted by Gostin *et al.*, while there is 'powerful intrinsic value in making health care services accessible', the USA could achieve better health outcomes at a lower cost 'by shifting priorities toward health promotion and disease prevention, mediated principally through primary care and population-based services' (2011: 1781). Likewise, for Mueller, the 'three goals of health policy – cost containment, quality and access – can all be well served by policies related to promoting health' (1993: 152).

Other observers, however, are more sceptical of the savings from preventive strategies (Cawley, 2007). In fact, many studies on programmes for hypertension screening, reducing high blood cholesterol and cancer screening tests demonstrate that the net costs per year of life saved are exceedingly high. A review by the US Office of Technology Assessment reported that of the numerous preventive services it evaluated, only three were potentially cost saving (childhood immunizations, prenatal care for poor women and selected neonatal tests for congenital disorders). Similarly, screening for high blood pressure typically costs more than treating heart attack and stroke victims (Leutwyler, 1995: 124). The low per-unit cost of some population screening procedures easily obscures their true cost, which is the cost of achieving the desired outcome for the few who will benefit. Even though the cost of a single application might be low, if the condition screened for is rare, a huge number of such procedures might be necessary to identify and prevent one case.

The fact that population screening does not always save money should not detract from the need to rebalance health care budgets towards disease prevention and health promotion which encompass a wide range of activities. Moreover, the investment in better health in itself is a worthwhile goal, for example to promote 'healthy ageing', even if the immediate costs are high (Cubit and Meyer, 2011). The rationale behind spending more on public health, then, is the intrinsic value we place on the health it confers on the population, not its monetary savings. Commitment to public health is a measure of concern for the future. Public health, then, is ultimately a question of what kind of society we want, and there is a close connection between democracy, equity and social security on the one hand and good public health on the other (Raphael and Bryant, 2006). Any investment in preventive/promotion programmes shifts benefits from present patients to statistical persons who will enjoy healthier lives in the future because of these investments. Prevention can also compress morbidity by extending a person's healthy years and thereby reducing the individual and social burden of illness. Moreover, by postponing the time at which we become victims of a chronic disease, prevention allows people to live healthier and more active lives, even though it might not necessarily extend their lifespan or save money (Donato and Segal, 2010).

There is one important caveat regarding preventive/promotion strategies that deal with behaviour-linked illnesses that today represent major contributors to ill health. Even though some of the linkages between lifestyle and health remain speculative, to be successful prevention programmes must change people's behaviour. Furthermore, even where evidence of danger is convincing, such as smoking, alcohol abuse, obesity, or even gambling (Adams *et al.*, 2009), there is considerable debate over how effective preventive measures alone can be in changing such behaviour. To effect necessary behavioural changes requires investment of considerable resources for preventive programmes as well as for research to better understand the linkages between social and personal factors. Despite these limitations, health promotion is a definitive element of health care reform and extensive efforts must be made to educate, encourage and motivate essential behavioural changes.

Tenbensel *et al.* (2012) found that since 2003 there has been an increasing interest in initiatives that address health promotion and population health outcomes. Clearly, there are now strong motivations for Western countries to shift priority back towards primary care/

prevention/health promotion activities. Furthermore, ageing populations and the resulting changes in disease structures certainly support movement towards chronic care facilities and less expensive forms of institutional or home care as opposed to more costly hospital care (Cubit and Meyer, 2011). These moves are politically challenging, however, because they are often justified on the grounds of cost-effectiveness and frequently viewed as threats to the medical establishment. Furthermore, they give the appearance of sacrificing the lives of a vulnerable group of identifiable patients for a more nebulous aggregate population. Also, because of the unpredictable nature of disease, few members of the public are able to distance themselves from the plight of individual patients and their need for immediate and often costly support in time of need.

Public health responsibility and funding

While public health continues to be underfunded compared to acute-care medicine, all countries here have wide-ranging public health programmes, although as with other areas of health care, each country brings with it a particular orientation for organizing public health services. For instance, while Singapore has a highly centralized and vigorous public health policy, in most countries at least the non-medical aspects of public health are delivered by locally administered programmes. The major responsibility for public health often falls on states, municipalities or other sub-national units, although in recent years some governments, such as Australia, have attempted to provide central coordination and increased funding to the localities in order to strengthen public health programmes.

Next to Singapore, New Zealand has the most centralized framework for public health, with responsibility vested in the Ministry of Health, but even here many public health activities are carried out through local programmes or District Health Boards. The National Health Committee is an autonomous committee appointed by and reporting directly to the Minister of Health on public health issues. Section 14 of the Public Health and Disability Act of 2000 commissioned the Public Health Advisory Committee as a sub-committee of the National Health Committee (New Zealand Ministry of Health, 2003). Its role is to provide independent advice on public health issues, including factors influencing the health of people and communities, and the promotion and monitoring of public health. The Committee's mandate includes giving advice on what measures would deliver the greatest benefit to the health of the population. It has also conducted extensive research on the social, cultural and economic determinants of health.

In Britain, central government, health authorities and GPs share responsibility for public health (Baggott, 2004). Within central government, public health falls under the remit of the Department of Health, although only since 1997 has there been a separate minister devoted to public health. Primary Care Trusts were until recently responsible for delivering public health and reducing health inequalities, both within the framework set by the Department of Health. It is indicative that the assessment of the performance of trusts includes indicators of health improvement. Primary Care Trusts took over responsibilities from the health authorities marking the culmination of earlier policy developments. Although GPs have traditionally focused on the demands of individual patients, they have increasingly been integrated in public health initiatives. For example, the GP contract includes financial incentives for GPs to achieve immunization and disease screening targets. Since 2004 this comes in form of performance-related payments as part of the so-called 'Quality Outcome Framework'. Following the most recent health reforms in 2012 and the introduction of Clinical Commissioning Groups, local authorities are now taking over the responsibility for public health at the local level. Here, local authorities will be supported by 'Health and Wellbeing Boards', which bring together a wide range of local actors to coordinate public health initiatives (Department of Health, 2012b).

In contrast to Britain, responsibility for public health in Germany has always been more decentralized, reflecting its federal structure. As in Australia and the USA, public health traditionally has been the responsibility of the states and include activities ranging from environmental health and the monitoring of communicable diseases to health education/promotion and physical examinations of school children (Busse and Riesberg, 2004). The range of services covered varies from state to state, as does the structure of the local public health offices responsible for the delivery of services. However, since the 1970s an increasing number of public health activities, particularly health promotion and disease prevention measures, have become part of social health insurance and responsibility has shifted from the public health offices to ambulatory care doctors. As a result, the provision of public health services has become more standardized because doctors are now legally obliged to deliver public services as part of the benefits catalogue within the health insurance system. However, the focus of ambulatory care doctors on individual patients, together with the fact that many practise single-handedly, potentially undermines the public orientation of measures of health promotion and disease prevention. Significantly, immunization rates in Germany are relatively low by international standards (Busse and Riesberg, 2004: 93). The role of local public health offices is now mainly supervisory, focusing on controlling food safety and drinking water and compiling health statistics (Greiner and Schulenburg, 1997).

Sweden resembles Germany in that the responsibility for public health is decentralized and rests with county councils and municipalities as service providers (Glenngård *et al.*, 2005; Anell *et al.*, 2012), although preventive and population-based measures are more highly integrated into the delivery of primary care services. Health centres employ school nurses to provide health education to children, and doctors provide one-to-one health education on diet and alcohol consumption, operate well-women clinics and immunize children. Complementing this at the national level is the National Institute for Public Health, which is responsible for national programmes of health promotion and disease prevention. As in other areas of health care provision, the National Board of Health and Welfare is responsible for supervising and monitoring what transpires at the level of county councils and municipalities.

Compared to Sweden, the responsibility for public health is even more decentralized in the Netherlands. Following the 1989 Public Prevention Act, some core responsibilities for public health services, including health monitoring and dealing with contagious diseases, have been delegated to local authorities. The activities of local public health agencies are only loosely prescribed, but typically focus on the young, elderly and minority groups and include health promotion and education, vaccination and public health research projects (Maarse, 1997; Schäfer *et al.*, 2010). The considerable autonomy at local level has resulted in substantial diversity in the delivery of public health services (Okma, 2001). In response to concerns about inequalities in access to public health services, a commission was established and in 1998 recommended that local authorities present an annual review of their public health activities. It also recommended that the Ministry of Health define a basic set of services that all local authorities must provide. The activities of the local authorities are overseen by the Inspectorate of Health, which has responsibility for monitoring the quality of health services and health protection measures (Exter *et al.*, 2004).

As in the Netherlands and Sweden, a large share of the responsibility for public health services in Japan falls on local governments and to a lesser extent the county-like prefectures. Each of the municipalities has a division responsible for health and the employment of public health nurses (Nakahara, 1997: 123). In 2005, approximately 3,200 municipalities were reduced to 2,300 in a policy aimed at strengthening the financial basis of local governments and reducing administrative costs (Bertelsmann Foundation, 2005b). In addition to basic environmental services such as water supply and waste disposal, under the Community Health Law of 1994 these primary local governments administer community health programmes, including maternal and child care, immunization, nutrition guidance, health education, health screening and health examinations for those over 40.

As decentralized as the organization of public health is in these countries, it is even more so in the federal systems of the USA and Australia. As noted earlier, the USA is a federal system with responsibility for many functions falling on sub-national units. Moreover, the US Constitution explicitly gives states the authority to protect the health of their residents. Each of the 50 states has a public health agency or department. In addition, there are 3,066 counties that have public health responsibilities as well as tens of thousands of cities, towns and other municipalities, all of which undertake some public health activities, many quite extensive. At the federal level, the Centers for Disease Control and Prevention have primary responsibility for monitoring and policy making in disease prevention, but they must rely on compliance from the state and local agencies to implement their guidelines. Despite many recent federal initiatives, an authoritative report (*The Future of Public Health in the 21st Century*) concluded that much yet needs to be done to provide 'a strong governmental public health infrastructure' that is needed in order to 'protect and promote health and well-being' of Americans (Institute of Medicine, 2002).

Although all sides in the debate over the USA Affordable Care Act (ACA) cited the importance of public health, after legislative bargaining important public health investments were stripped from the final bill, including smoking cessation programmes, reproductive health, HIV prevention and other preventive services, even as major increases were provided for cancer research in the National Institutes of Health. Despite this, Pollack (2011) concludes that the ACA, which establishes a Prevention and Public Health Fund to support preventive services and the public health infrastructure and will require all insurers to cover evidence-based preventive services, will have a positive impact on public health. In contrast, Gostin *et al.* (2011) conclude that while the ACA included promising public health provisions, it failed to make population health a focus of the reform. 'In short, our thesis is that health care reform's core purpose should be to improve the public's health, which is best achieved through cost effective interventions at the population level' (Gostin *et al.*, 2011: 1782).

Public health in Australia too is a tiny, highly fragmented component of the health system that has been funded 'poorly and unsystematically' (Lin and Robinson, 2005). This is not surprising since like the USA and Germany, Australia is a federal system where the states have primary responsibility for public health and the delivery of population health services. However, there have been many recent efforts to increase national coordination. For instance, the Commonwealth Population Health Division has a formal responsibility to keep Australians healthy by helping them avoid illness and injury (Australian Department of Health and Ageing, 2002). In 1996, the National Public Health

Partnership was created between the Commonwealth and states to strengthen collaboration and improve the health of Australians through a national approach to population health. The Commonwealth invests in population health activity through a combination of Public Health Outcome Funding Agreements and direct grants to states/territories and community organizations, as well as through supporting population health activity undertaken by GPs and their divisions. Moreover, the Communicable Diseases Network of Australia and New Zealand coordinates the surveillance of communicable disease and responds to outbreaks. Despite these varied activities, however, Commonwealth support for public health programmes accounts for only about one-third of public health expenditure with the bulk coming from state and local governments.

In Taiwan, public health is a Department of Health, not an NHI, responsibility, with services provided through local agencies. The NHI provides few incentives for citizens to improve their health through behavioural changes, expending about 98 per cent of its budget for medical care and between 1 and 2 per cent on medical screening. Furthermore, because health promotion falls under a governmental budget separate from NHI, there is little integration of medicine and health promotion. As a result, health promotion receives minimal attention from the public and is isolated from the activities of the NHI. Moreover, the extremely heavy workloads of GPs mean that their limited time with each patient offers little opportunity for health promotion. Finally, the private dominance of health care provision has meant that health promotion does not have high priority since it tends not to be a money maker.

Health promotion policies

The health promotion efforts in our countries have varied in their intensity, form and focus and to some extent their approaches and commitment reflects the general health goals predominant in each country. In countries such as Germany, New Zealand and Sweden, where the prevailing culture is more communitarian and egalitarian, health promotion strategies have focused on social factors and are more oriented toward broader approaches to health determinants (see Raphael and Bryant, 2006). In contrast, more individualistic countries such as Singapore and the USA tend to stress individual factors. Another variation is the extent to which health promotion is directed towards the population at large or at specific groups such as smokers, pregnant women or children. Furthermore, some countries have tended to target promotion policies at specific diseases or issues while others have taken more comprehensive approaches. In all cases, health promotion strategies reflect the organizational variation in public health activities in general, with some countries displaying rigorous national programmes and others largely delegating it to assorted sub-units.

Although health promotion is but one aspect of public health, it has received more attention recently as the links between individual behaviour and health have been elucidated. Even those countries that lack well-established health promotion policies realize that promoting healthy lifestyles is not only an effective way of improving the health of their populations, but also a crucial strategy for reining in escalating health care costs, in other words, a key factor in cost containment. Goetzel *et al.* (2007), for instance, present evidence that health promotion and risk reduction programmes can reduce unnecessary health care utilization and yield a favourable return on investment. Not surprisingly, then, countries across the full range of health systems have instituted programmes for health promotion and disease prevention, although their form and comprehensiveness vary greatly.

In Germany, the fragmented structure of public health and its increasing medicalization over past decades have tended to work against a national strategy for health promotion. While health promotion has traditionally been the remit of the states, an increasing range of public health responsibilities have been integrated into the services offered by ambulatory-care doctors (Busse and Riesberg, 2004). At federal level, responsibility for health promotion falls under the Ministry of Health, although the Federal Centre for Health Education is responsible for initiating and coordinating national health promotion campaigns. Significantly, however, the work of the Federal Centre has focused on a number of selected campaigns. Long-term campaigns include AIDS, drugs and sex education, whereas topical campaigns have been concerned with encouraging organ and blood donation.

As in other European countries, Dutch patients have access to a wide range of health services and the availability of publicly mandated insurance schemes makes this access virtually universal. This is complemented by programmes for vaccinations, screening for cancers and pre- and post-natal screening, many of which have expanded over recent years. Recent policy initiatives have focused on promoting healthy lifestyles, reducing alcohol and tobacco consumption and targeting new diseases such as HIV/AIDS, as well as health problems related to socio-economic status (Okma, 2001). The National Contract for Public Health (2001) also stresses the need for cooperation among local and national levels as well as different sectors of health care provision.

By international comparison, Swedish citizens enjoy good health and long life expectancies. However, there have been concerns about health inequalities among certain social groups and, in 1991, a national strategy for public health was published (Whitehead, 1998). The strategy emphasized the importance of cooperation among different levels and coincided with the creation of the National Institute of Public Health, which is responsible for national programmes. In 2000, this was complemented by the publication of national goals in public health, which reiterated the need to reduce health gaps among different social groups (Ministry of Health and Social Affairs, 2001). These developments culminated in a government bill on public health objectives in 2003 that is committed to ensuring social conditions that ensure good health for the entire population (Glenngård *et al.*, 2005). The policy was updated in 2008 and there is now a clearer focus on individual choice and responsibility together with greater emphasis target groups, namely children, young people and the elderly (Anell *et al.*, 2012).

Britain, too, has seen many initiatives in health promotion, but the White Paper, *The Health of the Nation,* in 1992 provided the first national strategy (Baggott, 2004). The White Paper identified priorities for health promotion and also set specific targets in relation to heart disease, strokes, cancers, mental illness, sexual health and accidents. The underlying stance is that individual behaviour is the key factor responsible for poor health. This strong individualist orientation is not surprising considering the New Right orientation of the government at the time and was moderated somewhat after the Labour government came into power in 1997. The revised strategy, encapsulated in the 1999 White Paper, *Saving Lives: Our Healthier Nation*, combines health promotion focused on the individual with an acknowledgement that social factors such as poverty also cause poor health. This led to a greater focus on improving the health of disadvantaged people and narrowing health gaps through health improvement programmes and designated health action zones. A central feature of these initiatives is that they rely on collaboration among a wide range of actors, from central government and health authorities to local government and voluntary organizations and even private businesses. In contrast, some initiatives have again focused attention on the impact of individual behaviour on health improvements. For example, under the 2009 Health and Social Care Bill, a Health in Pregnancy Grant was available to all women who attended the 25th week antenatal appointment with their GP where they were given advice to lead healthy life styles, which Oliver (2008) characterizes as a form of 'libertarian paternalism'. The programme, however, was abolished by the Coalition government.

As a prime example of an egalitarian country, it is not surprising that New Zealand has adopted a broad health promotion approach that emphasizes social factors. In 2002, the New Zealand Ministry of Health launched *Achieving Health for All People*. The purpose of this document is to provide a framework for comprehensive health promotion action under the New Zealand Health Strategy that emphasizes the importance of a population health approach for the improvement of health and the reduction of inequalities. A key theme of this initiative is that 'public health action is not the responsibility of public health services alone, or even of health services as a whole. It is about the organised efforts of society' (New Zealand Ministry of Health, 2003). The Health Promotion Forum is a national umbrella organization representing over 200 groups nationwide that provides national leadership and support for good health promotion practice. The Forum provides advocacy, training and skills development to both member organizations and the health promotion workforce at large and facilitates networking, informed debate and contributions to policy development at regional, national and international levels. In their analysis of the government's attempt to reorient the health sector towards population health, however, Tenbensel *et al.* (2008) question the governmental capacity to adequately address nationally determined population health policy priorities at the local level.

Likewise, Japan launched its broadly based First National Movement for Health Promotion in 1978 and the second wave in 1988. A key measure taken in the first movement was the creation of Municipal Health Centres (MHCs) in every municipality to coordinate health promotional activities. The second wave was dubbed 'Active 80 Health Plan' because its purpose was to promote a prolonged life span of 80 years. After more than 20 years since its inception, these health promotional activities have begun to bear fruit, as reflected in the third wave of the national health promotion movement, 'Healthy Japan 21'. The period covered was between the years 2000 and 2010 with a defined set of goals in health promotion. In this wave, emphasis was placed on the prolongation of the 'healthy life span', meaning a life span without disability. This new focus reflected the problems facing the country with the world's longest life span. In a research project conducted by the Tokyo Citizens' Council for Health Promotion, the implementation of Healthy Town initiatives stressed the importance to citizens of a health-conducive physical living environment; social networks and mutual help; and societal discipline/rules and good access to services (Takano and Nakamura, 2004).

According to Wen *et al.* (2008), the NHI claim that universal access to medical care would solve health problems in Taiwan has perpetuated the medical quest for a quick fix and distracted people, including policy makers, from recognizing the benefits of health promotion. The results of this lack of a focus on prevention under the Taiwan NHI are conspicuous in regard to cancer. At a time when most other causes of death have been declining, the cancer mortality rate in Taiwan has been increasing at about 1.5 per cent a year with the number of cancer deaths more than doubling in 20 years and the 5-year survival rate being poor (Wen *et al.*,

2008). Both oral and esophageal cancer rates have increased, most prominently among men, not surprisingly given that both are known to be caused by smoking and betel nuts which are common among low income males. The lesson is clear that cancer control policy cannot rely solely on treating cancer after it develops, but must focus on promotion/prevention.

Although the delivery of most health promotion activities in the USA occurs at the sub-national level, the US Office of Public Health and Science serves as the health secretary's primary advisor on matters involving the nation's public health and oversees the Public Health Service (PHS). In turn, the Office of Disease Prevention and Health Promotion is mandated to provide national leadership for disease prevention and health promotion through the 'formulation of national health goals and objectives; the coordination of the Department of Health and Human Services activities in disease prevention, health promotion, preventive health services, and health information and education with respect to the appropriate use of health care; and the stimulation of public and private programs and strategies to enhance the health of the Nation'. Although the US public health community has long recognized that policies and programmes that emphasize health promotion are effective both in terms of dealing with health problems and achieving cost savings, many federal programmes have a crisis orientation and do not lend themselves to approaches that require a longer-term perspective (Radin, 2010). To some degree this reflects the ambivalence within American society about public investment in health.

Like the UK, the USA has a very individualist orientation in its health promotion initiatives. As a result, much health promotion is centred on screening and prescription of drugs to reduce cholesterol and high blood pressure. In 2010, the US Department of Health and Human Services unveiled *Healthy People 2020* which sets the national health objectives for the decade, including the creation of social and physical environments that promote good health as well as promoting quality of life, healthy development, health equity and healthy behaviours across life stages. It also highlights the social determinants of health and health disparities, includes education and income objectives and takes a more expansive view of the impact on health resulting from constructed and natural environments. Concomitant with *Healthy People 2020*, the National Health Promotion and Prevention Council provides a vehicle for implementing a 'health in all policies' strategy across government agencies, according to Fielding *et al.* (2012). Although past efforts of this type have fallen short of their potential, it is hoped that *Healthy People 2020* will serve as the foundation for the National Prevention Strategy and facilitate national, state and local prioritization of policy and programme interventions. Similarly, the US Preventive Services Task Force offered recommendations for strengthening preventive efforts (Centers for Medicare and Medicaid Services, 2010).

This heavy emphasis on individual responsibility in health care is also reflected in the ambitious health promotion activities of Singapore. In 1992, Prime Minister Goh Chok Tong launched the National Healthy Lifestyle Programme designed to educate Singaporeans about the importance of leading a healthy lifestyle and to encourage them to participate in regular exercise, eat healthily, avoid smoking and manage stress. The Programme takes an integrated approach that includes creating a supportive social and physical environment to encourage individuals to practise healthy behaviour. Between its inception in 1992 and 2001, the percentage of Singaporeans aged 18 to 69 years who exercised regularly increased from 17 to 20 per cent and those smoking dropped from 18 to 14 per cent (Singapore Ministry of Health, 2008). However, because the diet of Singaporeans has not improved and is still linked to high blood cholesterol and high blood pressure, the 2002 National Healthy Lifestyle Campaign focused on the promotion of healthier food choices (Singapore Ministry of Health, 2008).

While strengthening public health research has become an important objective for international health organizations, there has been less support for public health/health promotion research in Europe. Although all 27 EU countries have strategies for public health, Conceição and McCarthy (2011) found 'little coherence' in public health research programmes. Moreover, while the European Commission has country contact points for both EU research and health programmes, they do not coordinate with national health research programmes.

Despite historic neglect, and, as noted above, largely out of necessity, health promotion is enjoying heightened attention by many governments. This trend would represent going full circle back to the roots of health care if not for the fact that the resources being put into health promotion remain but a minute fraction of what is put into acute care. Also, because health is so tied to lifestyle choice, the success or failure of these health promotion initiatives is heavily dependent on the capacity to alter individual behaviour. Smoking-related illness and an obesity epidemic are driving public health institutions to consider a variety of methods, including broadened use of sin taxes, to influence health behaviours of target groups (Green, 2011). This trend is reinforced by the ongoing global economic crisis that forces governments to consider a variety of methods to generate funds for infrastructure. As a result, public health approaches progressively conflict directly with the notion of the right to live one's preferred life free from government constraint. This tension is starkly illustrated in policies aimed to stem obesity, smoking and alcohol abuse.

Obesity and health

According to the WHO, obesity is increasing at an alarming rate throughout the world. 'In every region of the world, obesity doubled between 1980 and 2008,' says Dr. Ties Boerma, Director of the Department of Health Statistics and Information Systems at the WHO. Today, half a billion people (12 per cent of the world's population) are considered obese (WHO, 2012a). The highest obesity levels are in the WHO Region of the Americas (26 per cent of adults) and the lowest in the WHO Southeast Asia Region (3 per cent). By the same token, the 2006 International Congress on Obesity warned that an 'obesity pandemic threatens to overwhelm health systems around the globe'. The WHO's latest projections indicate that globally approximately 1.6 billion adults (age 15+) are overweight and at least 400 million are obese (WHO, 2009a). TheWHO further projects that by 2015, approximately 2.3 billion adults will be overweight and more than 700 million will be obese. Once considered a problem only in high-income countries, being overweight or obese is now dramatically on the rise in most countries (see Table 7.2). At present, 65 per cent of the world's population live in countries where being overweight or obese kills more people than being underweight (see Box 7.6).

Obesity is defined as a condition of excess body fat (generally the term overweight applies to those persons with a Body Mass Index (BMI) between 25.0 and 29.9 and obese to those with a BMI 30 or above). Obesity is a major risk factor for a large number of debilitating and life-threatening disorders including chronic diseases such as cardiovascular disease (mainly heart disease and stroke) that comprise the world's number one cause of death, killing 17 million people each year. Moreover, it is a major cause of diabetes, which has rapidly become a

Table 7.2 ***Comparative obesity rates, 2012 (% over age 18)***

Country	%
United States	30.6
United Kingdom	23.0
Australia	21.7
New Zealand	20.9
Germany	12.9
The Netherlands	10.0
Sweden	9.7
Singapore	6.0
Taiwan	4.0
Japan	3.2

Source: WHO (2012a).

Box 7. 6 A double burden of disease

According to the WHO, many low- and middle-income countries are now facing a 'double burden' of disease. While they continue to deal with the problems of infectious disease and under-nutrition, at the same time they are experiencing a rapid upsurge in chronic disease risk factors such as obesity and overweight, particularly in urban settings. It is not uncommon to find under-nutrition and obesity existing side-by-side within the same country, the same community and even within the same household. This double burden is caused by inadequate pre-natal, infant and young child nutrition followed by exposure to high-fat, energy-dense, micronutrient-poor foods and lack of physical activity (WHO, 2009a).

global epidemic. The WHO projects that, largely because of obesity, deaths from diabetes will increase by more than 50 per cent worldwide in the next 10 years (2009a). Risk for all of these diseases heightens progressively as a person's BMI increases.

The European Commission has warned that obesity is now 'an urgent public health issue' that requires coordinated action by the EU and member states. It reported that up to 27 per cent of European men and 38 per cent of women are now considered obese and that obesity-related illnesses account for as much as 7 per cent of total health care costs in the EU (Haddon, 2006). In the USA the situation is even grimmer: 60 million Americans 20 years and older are obese and the prognosis is bleak with over 9 million children and teens ages 6–19 being overweight. Lang and Rayner (2005) suggest that the USA is widely accepted as the benchmark for the extent of obesity. A National Health and Nutrition Examination Survey estimated that 65 per cent of adults are either overweight or obese, up from 47 per cent in 1980 and 56 per cent in 1994. Moreover, based on current trends, it is predicted that by the year 2025 levels of obesity alone could be as high as 45 to 50 per cent in the USA (Box 7.7) and between 30 to 40 per cent in Australia, the UK (Box 7.8) and other EU countries (Haddon, 2006).

Of greatest concern is the skyrocketing rate of obesity among young children and adolescents in many countries. Of the 14 million overweight children in Europe, 3 million are considered obese. Worldwide, in 2010 over 40 million children under the age of five were overweight (WHO, 2012a). These data reflect significant upturns in obesity over the last several decades (Lang and Rayner, 2005). For instance, the percentage of overweight children aged five to 14 years in the USA has doubled in the last 30 years, from 15 to 32 per cent. By 2000 it was estimated that 6 million American children were obese enough to endanger their health and this number is mounting. According to Nancy Krebs, an obese adolescent has over a 75 per cent chance of becoming an obese adult (as

Box 7.7 US obesity rates to soar by 2030

If Americans stick to their eating and exercise habits, future historians will look back on the early 21st century as a golden age of svelte. Using a model of population and other trends, a report released by the Trust for America's Health and the Robert Wood Johnson Foundation projects that unless Americans change their ways over half will be obese by 2030. The 'F as in Fat' report highlights the current glum picture of the obesity epidemic, in which 35.7 per cent of adults and 16.9 per cent of children age 2 to 19 are obese. For the first time, the report builds on state-by-state data from the Centers for Disease Control to project obesity rates. In every state, that rate will reach at least 44 per cent by 2030. In 13 states that number will exceed 60 per cent. As a result, the Report projects 7.9 million new cases of diabetes a year, compared with 1.9 million new cases in recent years. There could also be 6.8 million new cases of chronic heart disease and stroke every year, compared with 1.3 million new cases a year now. The increasing burden of illness will add $66 billion in annual obesity-related medical costs over and above today's $147 billion to $210 billion (Begley, 2012).

quoted in McConahy, 2002). Overweight children five to ten years of age are 9.7 times more likely to have two risk factors for type 2 diabetes and 43.5 times more likely to have three risk factors. As with adults, all diseases are exacerbated in children who are obese.

The tracking of obesity from childhood to adulthood is well substantiated and findings suggest that obese children are much more prone to chronic diseases that have a detrimental impact on their health in adulthood. It has been posited that the children of this generation may be the first to die before their parents because of health problems related to weight. According to health expert Jay Olshansky, 'within the next 50 years, life expectancy at birth will decline, and it will be the direct result

Box 7.8 Britain is the fattest country in Europe

Britain's status as the fat man of Europe has been confirmed by a government report showing that many citizens are losing the battle of the bulge and slipping into obesity. Nearly a quarter of men and women in Britain are now obese and according to a Foresight report published in 2007, if nothing is done to deal with the problem, nearly 60 per cent will be obese by 2050. In 2008 the government launched a new strategy to encourage exercise and healthy eating habits in an effort to tackle the obesity 'time bomb' facing the country. It also includes making cooking lessons compulsory in schools by 2011 and reviewing advertising restrictions on unhealthy foods. The government is also investigating whether financial incentives, such as payments or vouchers, could be used to encourage people to lose weight (Creagh, 2008; Mills, 2009).

of the obesity epidemic that will creep through all ages like a human tsunami . . . There has been a dramatic increase in obesity among the younger generation and it is a storm that is approaching' (Reuters, 2005). Similarly, Brian McCrindle, a childhood obesity expert, warns the resulting 'wave of heart disease and stroke could totally swamp the public health care system'. Lawmakers must take a broader view of this 'looming problem' and consider actions such as banning trans fats and direct advertising of junk food towards children (quoted in Reuters, 2005).

Recent studies demonstrate that the social environment and individual behaviour are crucial factors in the obesity epidemic (for a discussion of the many factors, see Sassi *et al.*, 2009). Increases in overweight and obesity are attributable to a number of factors, including a shift in diet towards increased intake of energy-dense foods that are high in fat and sugars but low in vitamins, minerals and other nutrients. For the past 30 years, behavioural changes in Western societies, and more recently Japan, Singapore and Taiwan, have led to the expansion of high-calorie, fast food diets and all-you-can-eat buffets. Reinforcing this shift are trends towards more sedentary jobs and the replacement of physical activity with television, the Internet and video games as primary recreation activities for many families. In addition, today's youth are considered the most inactive generation in history, caused in part by reductions in school physical education programmes and unavailable or unsafe community recreational facilities (Get America Fit, 2012):

> Overweight and obesity are social phenomena. The lifestyle choices leading to overweight and obesity, typically those concerning nutrition and physical activity, as well as the outcomes of those choices in terms of body weight, tend to be shared among members of the same families, social networks and peer groups ...This phenomenon may be at least partly responsible for the very fast pace at which overweight and obesity rates have been rising in recent years. (Sassi *et al.*, 2009: 45)

A complicating factor for policy makers is that the prevalence of obese individuals varies with age, education, income and marital status. Individuals in lower SES groups, as well as those individuals with low educational attainments, are more likely to be obese (Mackenbach *et al.*, 2008; Costa-Font and Hernández-Quevedo, 2012).

Although the cause of obesity is multifaceted and varies according to the individual, it is clear that in many cases, chronic overconsumption of food plays a fundamental role. When this type of overeating becomes compulsive and out of control, it is often classified as a food addiction, a label that has caused much clinical and scientific controversy (Davis and Carter,

2009). Food addiction, which more accurately may reflect addiction to specific components of food, can be described in much the same way as other addictive behaviours (Taylor *et al.*, 2010). Davis and Carter (2009) conclude there is compelling evidence that highly palatable foods eaten in abundance have the potential to cause the same alterations in the brain as conventional substance dependence and thus justify its inclusion as an addiction disorder. Like drugs, foods induce tolerance over time, so that increased amounts are needed to reach and maintain satiety. Likewise, withdrawal symptoms such as distress and depression often occur during dieting, and there is a high incidence of relapse. These symptoms parallel to a remarkable extent those described in the *Diagnostic and Statistical Manual of Mental Disorders,* fourth edition (DSM-IV), for substance abuse and dependence, leading some to argue that food addiction should be considered a psychiatric illness (Volkow and O'Brien, 2007; Davis and Carter, 2009).

In making the argument for overeating as an addictive behaviour, it is clearly not appropriate to include all cases of excessive food consumption. For some individuals, overeating is a relatively passive, habitual event that occurs almost without awareness, in the form of liberal snacking and large portion sizes. For others, however, it can be compulsive and excessively driven. According to Davis and Carter (2009), there is sound clinical and scientific evidence that binge eating disorder is a phenotype particularly well suited to an addiction conceptualization. Neural imaging studies have shown that specific areas of the brain, such as the caudate nucleus, the hippocampus and the insula, are activated by food as well as drugs, and that both cause the release of striatal dopamine (Taylor *et al.*, 2010).

Whatever the ultimate cause, however, obesity has many negative health and social ramifications. Mortality and morbidity rates are higher among overweight and obese individuals than average-weight people. A person who is 40 per cent overweight is twice as likely to die prematurely as a person of average weight. As a result, overweight/obesity is the number two cause of preventable death in the USA and the fifth leading risk for global deaths. Obesity is also a known risk factor for heart disease, stroke, hypertension, sleep apnea, osteoarthritis and some forms of cancer (Thorpe *et al.*, 2004a). At least 2.8 million adults die each year as a result of being overweight or obese. Moreover, in large part due to obesity, there has been a 76 per cent increase in type 2 diabetes in adults aged 30 to 40 since 1990 in the USA (WHO, 2012a). An estimated 80 per cent of type 2 diabetes, 70 per cent of cardiovascular disease, 30 per cent of gallbladder surgery and between 7 and 42 per cent of certain cancer burdens are attributable to overweight/obesity. It is also a major cause of hypertension, osteoporosis, varicose veins and joint replacement surgery (WHO, 2012a).

Box 7.9 Obesity related costs in the USA

Type 2 diabetes ($63.14 billion), osteoporosis ($17.2 billion), hypertension ($3.23 billion), heart disease ($6.99 billion), post-menopausal breast cancer ($2.32 billion), colon cancer ($2.78 billion), endometrial cancer ($790 million), workdays lost ($39.3 million), physician office visits ($62.7 million), restricted activity days ($29.9 million), bed-related days ($89.5 million) (Get America Fit, 2012).

Obesity, then, has negative economic consequences for societies and individuals. The medical care costs of obesity in the USA alone are staggering. In 2008 dollars, these costs totalled about $147 billion (Finkelstein *et al.*, 2009). Regardless of how one calculates the costs, obesity and the conditions related to it comprise an increasing share of health care expenditures and add significant pressures on health systems (see Box 7.9). Moreover, bariatric surgery, mainly stomach banding devices, is one of the fastest growing areas of health spending, particularly in the UK and USA (*Worldwide Market...*, 2007). In addition to its direct costs there are indirect costs for individuals, including ill health and reduced quality of life and for society though loss of productivity due to high rates of sick leave and premature pensions.

Not surprisingly, there has been a spate of studies analysing the costs of obesity and impact on health care systems (Costa-Font and Hernández-Quevedo, 2012; Pelone *et al.*, 2012). In their macro-analysis of the costs of obesity in Europe, Von Lengerke and Krauth (2011), for instance, found that excess per-capita direct costs ranged from €117 to €1,873, depending on cost categories and comparison group (normal weight, non-obese). They warned, however, that while on average higher costs for obese individuals were found across most studies, there was considerable variation within sub-group analyses. They suggest that findings such as higher health care costs in severely obese groups with higher socio-economic status and lower lifetime long-term care costs in obese groups due to reduced life expectancy, may generate hypotheses both on under- and overuse of services (2011). In their systematic review of the direct costs of obesity worldwide, Withrow and Alter (2011) observe that obesity was projected to account for between 0.7 and 2.8 per cent of a country's total health care expenditures. Furthermore, obese individuals had medical costs that were approximately 30 per cent greater than their normal weight peers.

In their study, Wang *et al.* (2011) used a simulation model to project the probable health and economic consequences from a continued rise in obesity in the USA and the UK. These trends project 65 million more obese adults in the USA and 11 million more obese adults in the UK by

2030, consequently adding 6 to 8.5 million cases of diabetes, 5.7 to 7.3 million cases of heart disease and stroke, 492,000 to 669,000 additional cases of cancer, and 26 to 55 million quality-adjusted life years forgone for the USA and UK combined. The combined medical costs associated with treatment of these preventable diseases are estimated to increase by $48 to 66 billion annually in the USA and by £1.9 to 2 billion annually in the UK by 2030 (Wang *et al.*, 2011: 815).

Policies and strategies to combat obesity

Given the variations found in terms of the priority they place on health promotion, one would expect similar disparities across countries in their response to obesity. As noted above, although obesity is a global problem that transcends national boundaries, its prevalence varies significantly from country to country. Moreover, in their content analysis of the submissions to the New Zealand Inquiry into Obesity and Type 2 Diabetes, Jenkin and associates (2011) found 'stark contrasts' between the ways the food industry and public health sectors framed obesity (Box 7.10). Similarly, although there are many approaches to combating obesity, in their survey of obese individuals, Thomas *et al.* (2010: 420) found that respondents favoured interventions that focused on encouraging individuals to make healthy lifestyle changes such as regulation of junk foods, physical activity programmes and public health initiatives. They found substantially less support for interventions perceived to be invasive or high risk (gastric band surgery), stigmatizing (media campaigns) or commercially motivated (commercial diets and gastric banding surgery). Moreover, Maher *et al.* (2010) argue that while obesity is constructed as a broad public health crisis, within this crisis individuals are seen as responsible for their own bodies and body sizes. In terms of childhood obesity, regrettably, one result has been to impute maternal responsibility for the weight of their children, thus deflecting attention from broader social factors.

This section examines a sample of a range of policy strategies and programmes designed to deal with obesity. Because of the magnitude of its problem, the USA has taken the lead, although Australia and New Zealand present good examples of the range of strategies available (including food policy and collective/individualized public health strategies). Singapore offers a rather radical example of compulsion that is unlikely to work in other countries while Japan has taken a more measured approach to the emerging problem. Again, the importance of the cultural context of health policy is readily apparent in these diverse responses.

Although the Australian government took note of the problem in 1995 by convening the National Health and Medical Research Council

Box 7.10 Conflicting views on obesity

While the food and marketing sectors regarded obesity as an economic burden to the health system with its health impacts limited to those who were obese, the public health sector positioned obesity as an epidemic affecting both the overweight and obese. Furthermore, there was disagreement over the main causes of obesity. Specifically, the industry framed obesity as a consequence of poor lifestyle choices attributed largely to lack of knowledge, and cultural or other character deficits. It argued that lack of physical activity rather than increased food consumption was the dominant cause of obesity. In contrast, public health groups saw obesity as a natural response to an environment characterized by the ubiquitous marketing and availability of low cost, energy-dense/nutrient-poor foods: increased consumption of such products was the dominant cause of obesity. On the matter of potential solutions, the industry stressed education as a key strategy to address obesity while public health advocates argued for government regulation of food and marketing industry activities and a revamping of national obesity strategies and policies to address wider determinants of health. Finally, while the industry espoused the individualism of 'market justice,' public health appealed to the communitarian ethos of 'social justice' (Jenkin *et al.*, 2011: 1028).

on the Prevention of Obesity, by 2000, 17 per cent of men and 20 per cent of women were classified as obese, with a further 49 per cent of men and 27 per cent of women overweight, ranking it second in the world behind the USA (Nathan *et al.*, 2005). In response, the National Obesity Taskforce was established to develop a national approach to address the problem and identify initiatives needed to prevent obesity (Lin and Robinson, 2005). By 2005, Australia was able to drop its ranking for obesity to sixth but when those figures are combined with the proportion of overweight people, Australia still ranks fourth in the world behind only the USA, Mexico and the UK. The federal government now aims to halve the number of overweight children by 2015 by expanding the Healthy Schools Program that provides grants for initiatives such as improving school menus and launching a national physical activity campaign aimed at children and adolescents. In the State of Victoria, for instance, the Kids – 'Go for your life' (K-GFYL) initiative is a health promotion programme that aims to reduce the risk of childhood obesity by improving the socio-cultural, policy and physical environments in children's care and educational settings. Membership is open to all primary and pre-schools and early childhood services across the state and member schools and services are centrally supported to undertake the health promotion activities. Once the K-GFYL programme 'criteria' are reached the school/service is assessed and rewarded (de Silva-Sanigorski *et al.*, 2010).

Box 7.11 Fighting obesity in Singapore

More than a decade ago, Singapore decided that the best way to fight the war on expanding waistlines and ballooning health care cost, was to begin with the young. The government created a school-based intervention programme that includes rigorous exercise for overweight children and recommendations on food sold in canteens. Overweight children are separated from their classmates and instructed to exercise more until they lose weight. For example, as a member of a Singapore primary school's 'Health Club' where membership is compulsory for overweight children, Siow does special exercises on top of the normal physical education curriculum. Teachers monitor her height and weight every month. While the school does not put restrictions on what she can eat, teachers meet her parents regularly to recommend healthier ways to prepare their daughter's meals at home. These 'health clubs' reduced the proportion of overweight students from 14 per cent in 1992 to 10 per cent in 2003, but many, like Siow, have not lost weight. If she fails to do so, she is doomed to stay in the programme until she completes her pre-university schooling (Associated Press, 2006).

Singapore has been one of the most proactive, and some might say draconian, countries with a strong commitment to reduce the prevalence of being overweight or obese (see Box 7.11). Since it introduced the 'Fit and Trim' programme in schools, levels of obesity among students have dropped and fitness improved. The government also has initiatives to mobilize its adult population, of which about 6 per cent are obese, to adopt healthier lifestyles. Singapore holds a month-long fitness campaign each September aimed at getting the entire population to eat better and stay active. The theme for the 2004 campaign was 'Fighting Obesity' and it was launched with a mass aerobic workout class of 12,000 people. Moreover, Singapore health authorities are also deliberating nutrition labelling and regulations to reduce trans fat in the food supply (Tan, 2011). Despite these efforts, a continuing trend towards overweight citizens is attributed to a shift in diet towards Western fast foods. In response to studies that show that many Asians have more fat as a proportion of total body weight than Caucasians of the same age, sex and BMI, and in response to the recommendations of the WHO, the Health Promotion Board lowered the BMI score for obesity among Asians to compensate for these differences.

Although the Japanese are not nearly as overweight as Americans (24 per cent as compared to 65 per cent), there is concern over changes in eating patterns. Men in all age groups have grown heavier in the past two decades, with the highest rate of obesity (34 per cent in 2003) among men in their 40s. The government set aside about $600,000 in the 2006–7 Budget to combat childhood obesity (Inagaki, 2006). Moreover, Healthy

Japan 21, a ten-year national plan for health promotion and disease prevention established by the Ministry of Health, Labour and Welfare, covers nine focus areas, including nutrition and physical activity, that explicitly set goals for decreasing obesity in adults and school children. Early detection of overweight students and education on healthy body weight take place in most primary and secondary schools in Japan (Matsushita *et al.*, 2004).

More than half of New Zealand adults are now obese (17 per cent) or overweight (35 per cent). Obesity in New Zealand increased by 55 per cent between 1989 and 1997 and was predicted to increase to 29 per cent of all adults by 2011 if no changes were instituted. In response, the New Zealand Health Strategy targeted the reduction of the rate of obesity as one of the 13 priority areas for population health. District Health Boards (DHBs) are required to report annually on progress towards each of these priority areas. In 2001 a toolkit was promulgated to provide guidance to DHBs on the importance of obesity as a public health issue and the most effective ways to reduce it in their populations. It notes that any effort to reduce the incidence of obesity or prevent any further increases must include key partners outside the health sector including non-government organizations such as Agencies for Nutrition Action, Heart Foundation, New Zealand Nutrition Foundation and Diabetes New Zealand; government agencies such as Child, Youth and Family Services, the Recreation and Sport Agency and the ministries of Youth Affairs and Education; the media; local councils; Pacific health initiatives and church groups and the food and weight-loss industries.

As part of a four-year bid to reduce its escalating obesity levels, in 2006 New Zealand banned fatty, sugary foods and drinks from school shops (Associated Press, 2006). At the launch of the NZ$67 million anti-obesity campaign, then Prime Minister Helen Clark said that over 30 per cent of children are either overweight or obese and that improving nutrition and encouraging more active lifestyles is the first step in fighting this epidemic. Imminent steps include introducing healthy food, drink and exercise policies into all government agencies. A labelling system for food and drinks was implemented for the 2007 school year, and although the government will not regulate to bring about change, school boards are required to develop policies that promote and achieve healthy nutrition and reduce consumption of unhealthy foods and drinks (Mernagh *et al.*, 2011).

Obesity has also become a very acrimonious political issue in the USA (see US Department of Health and Human Services, 2001, 2005). In 2001, the US Surgeon General's Call to Action emphasized the need to create supportive environments which provide accessible and affordable healthy food choices and convenient opportunities for regular physical activity (US Department of Health and Human Services, 2001). In May

2002, a $4.1 million USDA Team Nutrition programme began to teach children healthy eating habits (Kersh and Morone, 2002) and in June of that year the White House implemented the Health and Fitness Initiative to highlight physical activity (US Department of Health and Human Services, 2004).

Unlike other countries, however, policies in the individualistic USA have been aimed more at ensuring that obese patients are not discriminated against by medical professionals and less at encouraging behavioural changes. In fact, there has been considerable emphasis on making allowances for obese patients so as not to make them feel inferior (see Box 7.12). For example, Medicare redefined obesity as a medical problem and approved payment for a wide array of surgical weight-loss procedures for obese elderly patients. As a result, the number of bariatric surgeries has quadrupled since 2000 and is forecast to proliferate in the future (American Society for Bariatric Surgery, 2006). Obesity-related hip and knee replacements are also predicted to grow by 600 per cent in the coming decade. Furthermore, the Social Security Administration allows obesity to qualify for disability income, and, as of 2002, the Internal Revenue Service acknowledged the medical importance of treating obesity, making physician-prescribed weight-loss programmes deductible medical expenses (Shortt, 2004).

One issue that has been simmering in many countries is the extent to which the government should intervene in the food choices of their citizens. For instance, the consumption of sugar-sweetened beverages has been linked to risks for obesity, diabetes and heart disease and some argue that a compelling case can be made for policies to reduce consumption of these beverages (See Box 7.13). Short of outright bans as in New York City, taxation has been proposed as a means of reducing the intake of these beverages and, thus, lowering health care costs, as well as a means of generating revenue that governments can use for health programmes. In the USA, 33 states currently have sales taxes on soft

Box 7.12 Preparing for large patients

As Americans keep getting bigger, hospitals are revamping themselves to accommodate an influx of obese patients. When these patients check into a hospital, they are likely to find themselves in a room with a wider doorway than the 42-inch standard, a bed that holds up to 1,000 pounds and a ceiling lift system to move them to the bathroom. Toilets in such a room are extra-sturdy and mounted to the floor instead of a wall. The obese are more likely to suffer from chronic medical ailments like diabetes and severe joint problems, bringing them into the hospital. As a result, more hospitals are making capital investments to set up separate wings and whole floors for obese patients to keep up with demand (Reuters, 2006).

Box 7.13 Ban on super-sized sugary drinks

In September 2012, New York City passed the first US ban of oversized sugary drinks in its latest controversial step to reduce obesity and its deadly complications. The mayoral-appointed city health board outlawed sugary drinks larger than 16 ounces nearly everywhere they are sold, except groceries and convenience stores. Violators of the ban, which does not include diet sodas, face a $200 fine. Opponents, who cast the issue as an infringement on personal freedom and called the Mayor an 'overbearing nanny', vowed to continue their fight, possibly by going to court in the hopes of blocking or overturning the measure before it takes effect in March. The City Health Commissioner heralded the measure's passage as a major step toward making New Yorkers healthier and said it was likely to be copied elsewhere in the nation – and even the world – as were the city's bans on trans fats and smoking. He said that if the law results in shrinking only one sugary drink per person every two weeks from 20 ounces to 16 ounces, New Yorkers could collectively prevent 2.3 million pounds gained per year which would slow the obesity epidemic and prevent much needless illness (Allen, 2012).

drinks (mean tax rate, 5.2%), but the taxes are too small to affect consumption and the revenues are not earmarked for programmes related to health (Brownell *et al.*, 2012). Although the precise impact of a particular tax cannot be known until it is implemented and studied, research to date suggests that a tax on sugar-sweetened beverages could reduce consumption if the rate was sufficient. In addition, like tobacco taxes, it has the potential to generate needed revenue to prevent obesity and address other costs resulting from the consumption of sugar-rich beverages.

Schools are often identified as a natural site for intervention to improve the diets of students and help prevent excess weight gain and obesity. However, in their New Zealand study, Walton and colleagues (2010) found frequent barriers to improving school food environments and promoting healthy nutrition, including the high proportion of food brought to school from home, the crowded curriculum and limited resources to implement changes. Barriers that varied across socio-economic contexts included the capacity of home and community settings to support healthy diets, the degree to which schools relied on fundraising and a lack of engagement of parents and families with the school food environment.

Although the national level remains the primary focus of public health policies on obesity, increasingly there are initiatives at the international level. In the context of Europe, the Regional Office of the World Health Organization has been particularly active since the late 1990s. Initial consultations among member states culminated in a commitment in

Box 7.14 Obese people denied surgical procedures in a bid to cut costs in the NHS

Three Suffolk primary care trusts have ruled patients with a body mass index (BMI) of over 30 will not get operations like hip and knee replacements. A person of average weight would have a BMI of between 18.5 and 24.9. Dr Brian Keeble, a director of Ipswich PCT, said: 'We cannot pretend that this work wasn't stimulated by pressing financial problems.' Under new guidelines surgery will not be performed unless 'the patient has a body mass index below 30 and conservative means have failed to alleviate patient's pain and disability' (BBC News, 2005).

2000 to create Nutrition Action Plans (Lang and Rayner, 2005). This has been followed by other initiatives, most recently the European Charter on Counteracting Obesity (WHO, Regional Office for Europe, 2006). In contrast, the EU has been consistently less active, not least reflecting the marginal position of health policy in relation to other policy issues within the EU and demonstrating that any policy initiative on obesity must compete for attention with other public health issues such as food safety.

Tobacco policy

Cumulatively, tobacco, alcohol and illicit drugs 'prematurely kill about 7 million people world wide each year and the number is rising' (Reuters,

Box 7.15 Smoking policy in Taiwan

Smoking in Taiwan is regulated by the Tobacco Hazards Prevention Act promulgated in July 2007. Tobacco advertising is banned and smoking is banned in all indoor public places. The Government of Taiwan is planning to extend the smoking ban to cars, motorbikes and pedestrians. Smoking already is prohibited in all educational facilities; libraries, museums, art galleries and other institutions for cultural or social education; medical treatment centres, nursing institutions, other medical institutions and social welfare organizations; governmental agencies and state-owned enterprises; mass transportation vehicles, taxicabs, tour buses, the MRT system, stations and traveller waiting areas; financial institutions and post offices; physical training, sports, or body fitness facilities; opera houses, movie theaters and other entertainment places; hotels, shopping malls, dining and drinking establishments and indoor workplaces shared by more than three persons. Fines have been issued to both individuals and businesses for violations ('Smoking in Taiwan', 2012). The government created a hotline and offers a monetary reward for citizens who submit photos of violators. Individuals found smoking in smoke-free facilities will be fined between NT$2,000 and NT$10,000 (US$67 to US$334).

2005). As a result, most countries have instituted public health measures designed to reduce the incidence of smoking. In January 2009, for instance, Taiwan become the second country in Asia to ban indoor smoking in all public facilities including hotels, restaurants, karaoke bars, Internet cafes and transport stations (see Box 7.15) an approach that has been adopted in many of the other countries examined here. Other strategies include raising the price of tobacco products through taxes, banning certain types of advertising, requiring health warnings on tobacco products and enforcing the minimum purchasing age (for specific country regulations, see www5.who.int/tobacco/).

Other countries, like Singapore, have very restrictive and rigid policies where, as part of the Smoking Regulations 2003, cigarette packets sold in Singapore must carry graphic images of the harmful effects of smoking such as bleeding brains, toothless gums and blackened lungs aimed at making smokers face up to the serious health effects of smoking. Since the launch of the National Smoking Control Programme in 1986, smoking prevalence in Singapore declined from 20 to 14 per cent, one of the lowest in the world (Bertelsmann Foundation, 2004b). More drastically, New Zealand plans to institute a multifaceted programme to become the first tobacco-free country (Box 7.16).

The WHO Framework Convention on Tobacco Control (FCTC) is an international treaty designed to respond to second-hand smoking. It specifies the measures that governments should implement (e.g., advertising bans, taxation, smoke-free policy, health promotion and cessation support). The FCTC came into force in 2005, after being the interna-

Box 7.16 A smoke-free country?

There are smoke-free bars, smoke-free parks, even smoke-free college campuses. But a smoke-free country? In 2012, New Zealand's government squeezed smokers more than ever by announcing a 40 per cent hike in tobacco taxes over the next four years. New Zealand already charges more than 70 per cent tax on cigarettes, compared to 41 per cent on average for China, 45 per cent on average for the USA and 80 per cent for France. Prices there are already among the highest in the world, and by 2016 they will top NZ$20 (US$15) a pack. Officials hope higher taxes and new restrictions will bring the nation of 4.4 million closer to a recent pledge to snuff out the habit entirely by 2025. Other countries have lauded the idea of trying to wean their populace off tobacco, but few, if any, have been willing to put a date on it. Health officials are so serious they recently considered hiking the cost of a pack of cigarettes to NZ$100 (US$75). Although that idea was dismissed, another measure, which will force retailers to hide cigarettes below the counter rather than putting them on display, will come into effect in July, similar to a law in the UK (Perry, 2012).

tional treaty ratified by the largest number of countries at the fastest rate, but by 2008 very few countries were implementing all its measures. In Europe, for instance, implementation is at best incomplete and in most developing countries it is minimal (Wipfli and Huang, 2011). Although Article 8 of FCTC mandates its signatory and accession countries to enforce smoke-free public places through legislative, executive, or administrative measures, only 5 per cent of the world's population benefits from national legislation covering a wide range of public places. Moreover, over half of the world's population is not currently protected from second-hand smoking by any law, even though they live in countries where sub-national jurisdictions have the legal power to restrict smoking in public places (WHO, 2009b).

Many studies suggest that prominent health warnings with graphic pictures will reduce demand for cigarettes, with pictorial warnings on plain packaging producing the greatest decrease (Thrasher *et al.*, 2011; Hammond *et al.*, 2009; Germain *et al.*, 2010). After taxation the other two regulatory changes that concern the tobacco industry the most are homogeneous packaging and below-the-counter sales. According to Mitchell (2010) both would significantly restrict the industry's ability to promote their products, particularly in 'dark' markets, such as Australia, where tobacco advertising is banned. As illustrated in Box 7.17, plain packaging allows manufacturers to print only the brand name in a mandated size, font and place (Freeman *et al.*, 2008).

In line with these WHO guidelines, ground-breaking legislation that all tobacco products sold in Australia must be in plain packaging went into effect on 1 December 2012. In advance of its implementation, tobacco companies launched High Court challenges against the law, saying it infringes their trademark rights and violates minimum obligations for the protection of intellectual property rights under the TRIPS Agreement and the Paris Convention that require World Trade Organization (WTO) Member States to maintain a register of trademarks and establish minimum standards governing the registration of such marks. Trademarks are signs or combinations of signs capable of distinguishing goods or services from other goods or services.

In addition, three legal challenges were mounted at the WTO by the Dominican Republic, Ukraine and Honduras, charging that the Australian laws unfairly restrict trade. Trade diplomats expect the three complaints against Australia will be bundled together before moving to the adjudication stage, with little chance of a settlement before then. Mitchell (2010), however, expects the claims to be dismissed and argues that plain packaging is WTO compliant. She argues that it does not violate any provisions of the TRIPS Agreement or the Paris Convention. It is implicit within the TRIPS Agreement itself, and especially Article 20, that a high degree of domestic regulatory autonomy shall be afforded to

Box 7.17 WHO and plain packaging of tobacco products

Guidelines for the implementation of Article 11 of the FCTC, concerning the packaging and labelling of tobacco products, states that parties should consider adopting measures to restrict or prohibit the use of logos, colours, brand images or promotional information on packaging. This 'plain packaging' should increase the noticeability and effectiveness of health warnings and messages, prevent the package from detracting attention from them and address industry package design techniques that may suggest that some products are less harmful than others. Article 13 of the FCTC requires each party, within constitutional limits, to 'undertake a comprehensive ban of all tobacco advertising, promotion and sponsorship'. Paragraphs 15 to 17 of the guidelines for the implementation of Article 13 refer to the potential for plain packaging to eliminate the effect of advertising and promotion on packaging. Paragraph 16 defines plain packaging as packaging with 'black and white or two other contrasting colours, as prescribed by national authorities; nothing other than a brand name, a product name and/or manufacturer's name, contact details and the quantity of product in the packaging, without any logos or other features apart from health warnings, tax stamps and other government-mandated information or markings; prescribed font style and size; and standardized shape, size and materials' (Conference of the Parties to the WHO FCTC, 2008).

a Member State to enact measures to protect and promote public health. While details of the regulations have not yet been released, the general move towards plain packaging is consistent with the FCTC and should fall within the scope of permissible regulation under Article 20. 'No concern about plain packaging … should prevent the Government from implementing what is an important initiative at the top of the global public health agenda' (Mitchell, 2010: 422).

According to Ueda *et al.* (2011), although the Japanese government ratified the FCTC in 2004, there is yet to be effective national tobacco control. Until 1985, the tobacco industry was a government-run monopoly. Currently, the government is still involved in tobacco advertising and etiquette campaigns and the Ministry of Finance controls 50.2 per cent of Japan Tobacco, the world's third biggest tobacco company. Not surprisingly, unlike other countries included here, non-smoking areas are uncommon even in fast food or family restaurants, although all trains either have non-smoking cars or are completely smoke-free. Cigarettes can be bought in tobacco stores or at an estimated 500,000 cigarette vending machines. Since 2008, a customer must have a Taspo smart card developed by the Tobacco Institute of Japan, the nationwide association of tobacco retailers, and the Japan Vending Machine Manufacturers Association in order to purchase cigarettes from vending machines. In

2003, the Ministry of Health, Labour and Welfare introduced a National Health Promotion Plan to improve national health, including the launch of the Healthy Japan 21 campaign for 2000–10 that was intended to enable people to take positive steps toward improving their health. Alongside these programmes, the Health Promotion Act went into effect in 2003 that establishes targets to prevent lifestyle-related diseases. Prevention of second-hand smoke exposure was one aim, and Article 25 in this law suggested that persons in charge of public places such as schools, gymnasiums, hospitals and theatres take measures to prohibit smoking.

Although systematic comparative estimates on the societal costs of smoking are unavailable, smoking causes a significant number of deaths and smokers generally consume more health care resources than non-smokers. In the USA, for example, it is estimated that 19 per cent of all premature deaths – an estimated 291,000 deaths among men and 229,000 among women – annually from 2002 through 2006 were smoking-attributable (Rostron, 2011). Given that the USA has relatively low levels of smoking, death rates from smoking in other countries are assumed to be similar, if not higher.

Table 7.3 illustrates that smoking rates vary significantly across countries, especially among women. In Singapore, high prices and strict regulations have cut overall smoking rates, but the extremely low rate for women is obviously cultural since male smoking is near the average. Japan and, until recently, Taiwan have had relatively relaxed regulations and by far the highest rates of male smoking. Evidence suggests, however, that laws can make a difference and that public health and education programmes reduce smoking rates (see Box 7.18). Data from ten

Table 7.3 ***Smoking rates, men and women (%), ranked by men, 2012***

	Women	*Men*
Taiwan	5.2	41.1
Japan	8.4	32.2
Netherlands	18.8	23.1
Germany	17.6	26.4
Singapore	3.0	26.3
United Kingdom	20.7	22.3
New Zealand	17.0	19.3
Sweden	15.1	12.8
United States	13.6	16.7
Australia	13.9	16.4

Source: Data from OECD (2013).

Box 7.18 English smoking ban

The number of people who quit smoking through NHS stop smoking services in England in mid-2007 when the ban on smoking in public places came into force was 28 per cent higher than the same period in the previous year before the ban. Nearly 165,000 smokers gave up the habit (National Health Service, 2008). In September 2012, NHS announced the Stoptober campaign to encourage the nation's 8 million smokers to give up smoking for 28 days from 1 October. People who stop smoking for 28 days are five times more likely to stay smoke-free, so smokers who sign up will be given support and encouragement throughout the month.

European countries where rigorous tobacco control policies have been implemented, including Sweden and the UK, show a decrease in the number of tobacco-related deaths in recent years (WHO, 2003). The most effective control measures include high prices on tobacco products, total bans on advertising, support for cessation treatment and policies requiring the creation of smoke-free environments.

In their study of 15 countries, Borland *et al.* (2011) found wide variation in the availability of assistance to stop smoking but overall a higher use of medication than behavioural support. There is also disparity in the provision of advice to patients from health professionals to stop. As a result, WHO (2003) notes that most countries would benefit from clarifying and strengthening anti-tobacco controls. For example, less than 25 per cent of countries in the European Region earmark any tobacco tax revenues for control measures or health promotion, and of those only five allocate more than 1 per cent. However, recent European Union directives and a Framework Convention on Tobacco Control aim to counter the industry's traditional capacity to undermine national controls (WHO, 2003).

A European report on tobacco control policy shows that while smoking rates stabilized at 30 per cent for the region as a whole (38 per cent for men and 23 per cent for women) over the last five years, increases in population meant that the number of smokers rose (WHO, 2003). Most countries show a gap in smoking rates between the lowest and highest socio-economic groups. In some countries, the poorest smoke three times as much as the richest. This report further found that smoking rates among young people across Europe are converging, eliminating former differences according to gender and geography, and that although several countries reported reductions in adult smoking, none showed significant reductions in smoking by young people. In addition, the gender gap has become less significant among teenagers: in 12 countries girls smoked as much as, or more than, boys (WHO, 2003).

Alcohol policy

Like smoking, alcohol abuse can cause severe health problems, and there is 'sufficient evidence to indicate that alcohol is a significant threat to world health' (WHO, 2001). In fact, alcohol contributes far more years of life lost to death or disability than tobacco and illegal drugs combined (WHO, 2001). To date, most countries have not been as rigorous in their attempts to reduce alcohol consumption as they have tobacco, but instead have tended to focus on reducing drinking and driving and other alcohol-related behaviour. Table 7.4 illustrates the range of consumption in our countries. Not surprisingly, wine-producing countries in Europe have traditionally had the highest rates, but since 1995 the trend indicates that the UK (see Box 7.19) is closing the gap (Institute of Alcohol Studies, 2002; Oliver, 2009). Sweden, due to high prices, and Singapore, due to high prices, strict regulations and its emphasis on personal responsibility for health, display the lowest consumption rates. Cultural factors regarding the acceptability of alcohol use also play a role in alcohol consumption.

The most common form of alcohol regulation is the setting of a minimum age for purchase or consumption. Studies have found that such restrictions are effective in reducing motor vehicle crash fatalities (Wagenaar and Wolfson, 1995). At present, Australia, the Netherlands and the UK have set the legal drinking age at 18; Japan, New Zealand and Sweden at 20; the USA generally at 21; and Germany at 16 for beer and wine and 18 for distilled spirits (WHO, 2002). Central to the effectiveness of such preventive efforts is enforcement, which varies considerably both across and within countries.

Table 7.4 *Alcohol consumption, per capita in litres/year (16 and over)*

	1995	*2000*	*2005*	*2009*	*Change*
Germany	11.1	10.5	10.0	11.7	0.6
Netherlands	9.8	10.1	9.7	9.4	–0.4
Australia	9.6	9.8	9.8	10.3	0.7
New Zealand	9.4	8.9	9.4	9.3	–0.1
United Kingdom	9.4	10.4	11.3	10.2	0.6
Japan	8.9	8.6	8.5	7.4	–1.5
United States	8.3	8.2	8.4	8.7	0.4
Sweden	6.2	6.2	6.6	7.3	1.1
Singapore	n/a	2.9	2.2	n/a	-0.7
Taiwan	n/a	3.4	3.3	n/a	-0.1

Source: Data from OECD (2012a).

Box 7.19 Alcohol deaths soar in Britain

The number of middle-aged men drinking themselves to death in Britain has more than doubled since 1991. Deaths among women in the same age group also nearly doubled, fuelling concerns over binge-drinking and rising alcohol consumption. Campaigners said the link between heavier drinking and the rise in alcohol-related deaths was established more than 50 years ago. The number of alcohol-related deaths in 2005 stood at 8,386, compared to 4,144 in 1991. Death rates among middle-aged men more than doubled to 30 per 100,000 of the population, with the highest rate of deaths among men and women in the 55 to 74-age bracket (British Medical Association, 2009).

Other alcohol control policies include taxation, prohibition, monopolies over production and/or sale, licensing, warning labels, restrictions on advertising and promotion and education. For instance, the recent introduction of warning labels on alcohol containers in New Zealand was designed to heighten awareness of the risks associated with alcohol consumption in pregnancy and was targeted to younger women and women of Maori and Pacific ethnicities. According to Parackal *et al.* (2010), while this might be a good first step, in order to effectuate behavioural change, complementary prevention approaches within a health promotion framework are needed. Alcohol (and drug) abuse is a complicated social problem that is unlikely to be resolved by education strategies alone.

Vital to any comprehensive health strategy for alcohol is the provision of adequate treatment facilities for alcohol dependence, but according to the WHO, very few countries have 'systematically evaluated various forms of treatment and the resources allocated for treatment are often very scarce, if existent. Globally, access to affordable and effective treatment is still largely inadequate' (2001: 13). No attempt is made here to summarize specific control policies, but it is important to reiterate that across our countries, with the possible exception of Singapore, public health measures towards alcohol remain equivocal and inadequately funded, thus undermining their effectiveness to combat the health problems raised by alcohol abuse.

So far this chapter has examined the structures and funding sources for public health and health promotion strategies and activities, particularly those surrounding obesity and tobacco and alcohol use. It is evident that many of these efforts lead us far from health care as medicine into the realm of health education and social welfare policy. The next two sections extend these linkages even further afield into housing and environmental policy areas. Still other dimensions of public health that we are unable to discuss here due to space limitations are occupational health, food safety, crime/violence, transportation safety and drug abuse. In combination, they all entail major health concerns neglected by the prevailing medical model.

Homelessness and inadequate housing

One health factor virtually ignored by the medical model, but which takes on importance in the more inclusive social model, is housing. A lack of adequate housing, especially when it involves homelessness, puts people, particularly children, at serious health risk. While homeless people suffer from the same acute and chronic illnesses as those in the general population, they do so at much higher rates. Among other deficiencies, homeless people often have little or no access to adequate bathing and hygienic facilities, survive on the streets or in unsafe and generally unsanitary shelters and suffer from inadequate diets and food preparation. As a result, upper respiratory tract infections, trauma and skin ailments are commonplace. High levels of alcohol abuse, drug abuse and mental illness among some homeless people complicate the picture.

Although the health impact of living on the streets is most severe, even inadequate housing can lead to poor health. Poor housing is linked to a wide array of physical and mental health problems as described in Box 7.20. Sub-standard housing is related to house fires and increased accidents. Furthermore, damp and cold living conditions are associated with respiratory ailments, while improperly ventilated housing is linked to heat-related health problems. In combination with overall poverty, unemployment, poor education, violence and crime, inadequate housing remains a significant health hazard for many citizens. These factors share

Box 7.20 Homelessness, poor housing and health in Britain

The poor health of homeless people is made worse by inadequate access to health services, as two reports on the health of 'rough sleepers' in the UK suggest. A report by the housing charity Crisis highlights the fact that they are often denied the right to register with a GP and instead must rely on overstretched casualty departments in hospitals after their health problem has become an emergency (Carvel, 2002b). Medical treatment can also be rendered useless when rough sleepers are discharged back on to the streets without any adequate support. This is echoed by a government report, which states that the health needs of homeless people in general are not met in a systematic and effective way (Ward, 2002). For example, only one-third of health improvement plans of Primary Care Trusts mention homeless people.

in common their isolation from the medical model. Although medical care is beneficial for many individuals affected by these health-threatening factors, 'medical care cannot compensate for economic deprivation, social disorganization, personal alienation, and low levels of education and social integration' (Mechanic, 1994: 3). In the end, solutions to these problems lie fully outside the medical community. Unfortunately, as argued by Kassler (1994: 166), health care reformers have focused so much on medical care that they have ignored those factors that ultimately make the biggest difference in people's health.

A report by the London School of Hygiene and Tropical Medicine (1999) lists the many health aspects on which housing has an impact, including excess winter morbidity because of inadequate home heating, respiratory problems because of damp and mould, and noise disturbance because of poor sound insulation. However, it is difficult to quantify the amount of ill health caused by poor housing because many health effects are qualitative in nature and concern poor quality of life and social isolation. Housing-related health problems are particularly acute in inner city areas, where the housing stock is comparatively old and often of poor quality.

Environmental health

The environment has always been intimately related to public health. Likewise, any major environmental change ultimately is a matter of health concern. 'There is an intrinsic relationship between the health of ecological systems, health of communities and the health of people' (Strand *et al.*, 2010: 442). However, while the health effects of environmental change have received considerable public attention, comprehensive policy efforts have been more subdued, in part because they are highly complex and often viewed as transnational problems. Although local and national environmental health hazards are endemic (see Quah and Boon, 2003), concern has recently been raised over new global threats.

Climate change

For instance, global climate change resulting from the accumulation of greenhouse gases is likely to have a significant impact on the health of the populations most affected (WHO, 2010; Kang, 2011; Huang *et al.*, 2011). After decades of debate, there is now general consensus that we are increasing the atmospheric concentration of energy-trapping gases, thus amplifying the natural 'greenhouse effect' that makes the Earth habitable. These greenhouse gases are comprised principally of carbon dioxide (mostly from fossil fuel combustion and forest burning) plus other heat-trapping gases such as methane (from irrigated agriculture, animal husbandry and oil extraction), nitrous oxide and various human-made halocarbons. In the last 100 years, the world has warmed by approximately 0.75°C. Over the last 25 years, the rate of global warming has accelerated, at over 0.18°C per decade. Sea levels are rising, glaciers are melting and precipitation patterns are changing. Extreme weather events are becoming more intense and frequent (WHO, 2010).

Although climate change may bring some localized benefits, such as fewer winter deaths in temperate climates and increased food production in certain areas, overall the effects of a changing climate are likely to have an overwhelmingly negative impact on the fundamental requirements for health, including clean air, safe drinking water, sufficient food and secure shelter (McMichael and Lindgren, 2011). Because of their complexity, measuring the health effects from climate change can only be very tentative. Nevertheless, a WHO assessment, taking into account only a subset of the possible health impacts, concluded that the modest warming that has occurred since the 1970s was already causing over 140,000 excess deaths annually by 2004 (WHO, 2010). Of this disease burden, 88 per cent fell upon children (Sheffield and Lanrigan, 2011).

Extreme high air temperatures contribute directly to deaths from cardiovascular and respiratory disease, particularly among elderly people. In the heat wave of summer 2003 in Europe, for example, more than 70,000 excess deaths were recorded (Robine *et al.*, 2008). High temperatures also raise the levels of ozone and other pollutants in the air that exacerbate cardiovascular and respiratory disease. Excess morbidity and mortality related to extremely hot weather and poor air quality are found in cities worldwide and can only get worse. The interactions of global climate change, urban heat islands and air pollution are predicted to place increasing health burdens on large cities. According to Ebi (2011), intense heat and air pollution increase mortality and morbidity in cities on six continents with urban air pollution alone causing about 1.2 million deaths every year. Pollen and other aeroallergen levels are also higher in extreme heat and can trigger asthma, which affects around 300 million people. Ongoing temperature increases are expected to increase this burden (WHO, 2010).

Climate change is also evidenced by the number of reported weather-related natural disasters, which have more than tripled since the 1960s. On average, these catastrophes result in over 60,000 deaths each year, predominantly in the poorest countries (WHO, 2010). Rising sea levels and increasingly extreme weather events also destroy homes, medical facilities and other essential services. More than half of the world's population lives within 60 km of the sea. Moreover, progressively variable rainfall patterns are likely to affect the supply of fresh water. A lack of safe water can compromise hygiene and increase the risk of diarrhoeal disease, which kills 2.2 million people every year (WHO, 2010). In extreme cases, water scarcity leads to drought and famine. Contrariwise, floods are also increasing in frequency and intensity that contaminate freshwater supplies, heighten the risk of water-borne diseases and create breeding grounds for disease-carrying insects such as mosquitoes.

Rising temperatures and variable precipitation are also likely to decrease the production of staple foods in many of the poorest regions – by up to 50 per cent in some African countries. This will increase the prevalence of malnutrition and under-nutrition, which currently cause 3.5 million deaths every year. Areas with weak health infrastructure, chiefly in the poorest developing countries, will be the least able to cope without assistance to prepare and respond. Moreover, many perilous diseases, including common vector-borne diseases such as malaria and dengue and yellow fever are highly sensitive to changing temperatures and precipitation (US Environmental Protection Agency, 2009). Transmitted by Anopheles mosquitoes, malaria kills almost 1 million people each year, mainly African children under five years old. The Aedes mosquito vector of dengue is also highly sensitive to climate conditions. Studies suggest that climate change could expose an additional 2 billion people to dengue transmission by the latter half of the century (WHO, 2010).

The Intergovernmental Panel on Climate Change (IPCC) Fourth Assessment Report found that 'warming of the climate system is unequivocal' and that 'most of the observed increase in globally averaged temperatures since the mid-20th century is very likely due to the observed increase in anthropogenic greenhouse gas concentrations' (IPCC, 2007). If even more conservative climate change predictions are accurate, the increase in the number of days with temperatures over 100°F (38°C) will produce a sharp rise in heat-related mortality from heat strokes, heart attacks and cerebral strokes, especially among the very young, the elderly and those with chronic respiratory diseases.

Climate change is also expected to trigger substantial increases in the scale of human population movement in coming decades. Forecasts of the number of people who are forced to relocate by mid-century in response to the effects of climate change vary from tens of millions to 250 million people (McMichael *et al.*, 2012). Climate-change–related migration is likely to amplify adverse health outcomes, both for displaced and host populations. Current scientific assessments project that climate change will, to varying extents among different regions and communities, exacerbate morbidity and mortality, reduce incomes and decrease access to important forms of natural capital.

Climate change, therefore, endangers human health, affecting all sectors of society, both domestically and globally. The environmental consequences of climate change, both already observed and those that are anticipated, such as sea-level rise, changes in precipitation resulting in flooding and drought, heat waves, more intense hurricanes and storms and degraded air quality, will affect human health both directly and indirectly (Portier *et al.*, 2010). Although indeterminate, the future health costs associated with predicted climate change are projected to be enormous. Knowlton *et al.* (2011) estimate that the health costs associated with six climate change-related events that struck the USA between 2000 and 2009 – ozone pollution, heat waves, hurricanes, infectious disease outbreaks, river flooding and wildfires – exceeded $14 billion, with 95 per cent due to the value of lives lost prematurely. Actual health care costs were an estimated $740 million with more than 760,000 encounters with the health care system.

Hess *et al.* (2012) contend that public health capacity must be increased to deal with climate-health threats. They argue that public health adaptation is imperative, but contend that there has been little discussion of how to increase adaptive capacity and resilience in public health systems. In the USA, the Environmental Protection Agency's mission to protect human health and the environment has focused on the potential for future climate change to cause air quality degradation via climate-induced changes in meteorology and atmospheric chemistry, posing challenges to the US air quality management system and the effectiveness of its pollution mitigation strategies (Post *et al.*, 2012).

Depletion of the ozone layer

In addition to climate change, the depletion of the ozone layer poses severe global health risks (Norval *et al.*, 2011). Higher levels of ultraviolet B radiation (UVB) reaching the surface of the earth can damage DNA and proteins and kill cells in all living organisms (see Box 7.21). The adverse effects of UV radiation are primarily on the eye and the skin. Overexposure to the sun is the major identified environmental risk factor in skin cancer (Ferguson, 2005). At highest risk are Australia and New Zealand, although the incidence of malignant melanomas, with mortality rates of 25 per cent, have increased faster than any other cancer – even in Scotland where the incidence of melanoma for men tripled between 1980 and 2000 (British United Provident Association, 2002). Worldwide, the WHO estimates there are 132,000 new cases of malignant melanoma (the most dangerous form of skin cancer) and 66,000 deaths from this and other skin cancers each year. One in three cancers worldwide is skin-related and in the USA that figure is one in two. Moreover, suppression of some aspects of immunity follows exposure to UV radiation and the consequences of this action for the immune control of infectious diseases, for vaccination and for tumours, are added concerns (Norval *et al.*, 2011).

Box 7.21 Depletion of the ozone layer

Stratospheric ozone absorbs much of the incoming solar ultraviolet radiation (UVR) especially the biologically more damaging shorter-wavelength. Various halogenated chemicals such as the chlorofluorocarbons (used in refrigeration, insulation and spray-can propellants) and methyl bromide, while inert at ambient Earth-surface temperatures, react with ozone in the extremely cold polar stratosphere. During the 1980s and 1990s the average year-round ozone concentration declined by around 4 per cent per decade at northern mid-latitudes and 6 to 7 per cent over the southern regions including Australia and New Zealand. Although estimating the resultant changes in actual ground-level ultraviolet radiation remains technically complex, exposures at northern mid-latitudes are likely to peak around 2020, with an estimated 10 per cent increase in effective ultraviolet radiation relative to 1980s levels. In the mid-1980s, governments recognized the emerging hazard from ozone depletion. The Montreal Protocol of 1987 was adopted, widely ratified, and the phasing out of major ozone-destroying gases began. The protocol was tightened in the 1990s (WHO, 2009a).

Australia has the highest rate of skin cancer in the world with exposure to ultraviolet radiation emitted by the sun being the primary cause. As a result, it is a significant public health issue and the country is a world leader in efforts to protect the ozone layer, the main line of defence against the ultraviolet radiation emitted by the sun. State cancer councils have developed sun safety and awareness campaigns, such as 'Slip! Slop! Slap!' and 'SunSmart', to educate the population about sun exposure and encourage early detection of skin cancers.

In addition to promoting cancer, burns, loss of elasticity, wrinkling and freckling of the skin, excess UV exposure can also harm the eyes and may compromise immune function. In terms of numbers, cataracts represent an even wider health threat. Some 20 million people worldwide are blinded by cataracts, with 20 per cent the result of UV exposure (WHO, 2008a). Because UVB exposure can be reduced by 90 per cent through a combination of the use of plastic lens glasses and a hat, this is one area where relatively straightforward strategies could easily be integrated in health promotion programmes such as that of Singapore to avert considerable health problems and costs. Ironically, however, there are major health benefits from exposure to sunshine and it is also implicated in protection against a wide range of diseases. According to Norval *et al.* (2011), it is difficult to provide easily understandable public health messages regarding 'safe' sun exposure, so that the positive effects of vitamin D production are balanced against the negative effects of excessive exposure.

Environmental health policy

Alongside the health threats of long-term environmental changes, more immediate and localized conditions can have considerable adverse health consequences for exposed populations. Despite efforts to reduce their impact, air and water pollution levels remain high in many locales and continue to put large numbers of persons at risk. Respiratory problems in urban areas caused or aggravated by air pollution are also likely to be exacerbated by global warming and population concentration (Epstein, 2000). Drinking water systems are not only threatened by industrial and waste disposal contamination, but also by the methods used for disinfecting them due to the toxic effects of the disinfectants and their by-products. The imminent breakdown of old and deteriorating water and sewage systems in some of the larger urban centres of many countries represents a growing health concern that requires urgent attention. Unfortunately, infrastructure funding in many countries has decreased as medical care consumes larger shares of state and local budgets.

All this is not to say that there have been no efforts to deal with environmental health problems. At the international level, a number of initiatives have followed the 1984 WHO 'Health for All' strategy (see page 59). Its definition of health as physical, mental and social well-being directed attention to the importance of the environment for promoting health. In 1989, the member states of the WHO's European region agreed on a 'European Charter on Environment and Health', which recognized the right to an environment conducive to health and the right to relevant information. In 1994, this was followed by an 'Environmental Action Plan for Europe' prepared by the WHO. The Plan calls for management instruments in the area of environmental protection where this is relevant to health. The participating member states committed themselves to implementing the Plan through 'National Action Plans on Environment and Health' (WHO, Regional Office for Europe, 2003c).

The WHO also established the European Environment and Health Committee to support the implementation of the Action Plan (WHO, Regional Office for Europe, 2003a). The member states of the WHO European Region reconfirmed their commitment to earlier policies as part of the Fourth Ministerial Conference on Environment and Health in 2004 (WHO, Regional Office for Europe, 2004). The work of the Committee is complemented by the WHO Programme on Global Change and Health, which is concerned with assessing and monitoring the health impact of global environmental changes (WHO, Regional Office for Europe, 2003b). In 2008, WHO member states passed a World Health Assembly resolution identifying five priority areas relating to health vulnerability, health protection, health impacts of mitigation and adaptation policies, decision-support and other tools and the costs of health protection from climate change (Hosking and Campbell-Lendrum, 2012).

In 2009, the World Health Assembly endorsed a new WHO work plan focused on climate change and health that includes: advocacy to raise awareness that climate change is a fundamental threat to human health; partnerships to coordinate with partner agencies within the UN system and ensure that health is properly represented in the climate change agenda; science and evidence to coordinate reviews of the scientific evidence on the links between climate change and health and develop a global research agenda; and health system strengthening to assist countries to assess their health vulnerabilities and build capacity to reduce health vulnerability to climate change (WHO, 2010).

Sweden considers environmental health an important issue and has had a pioneering role in environmental policies (Glenngård *et al.*, 2005). In Sweden, the municipalities are responsible for a wide range of areas of environmental health, including disease prevention, food quality, water management and chemical control. Municipalities are also experimenting with new forms of auditing and accounting as well as with new tariffs to improve environmental protection and food security. They were also at the forefront of implementing the UN's Local Agenda 21, a participatory process that targeted sustainable development, which includes health issues (Eckerberg *et al.*, 1998).

Public health: putting the medical model in perspective

There is considerable comparative data that demonstrate that the amount spent on medical care has little correlation with health improvement of populations or that medical care reduces health disparities (Lewis and Leeder, 2009; Unal *et al.*, 2005; Kabir *et al.*, 2007; McGinnis *et al.*, 2002). Medical care has a limited health effect, estimated to account at best for 10 to 15 per cent among the determinants of a nation's health (Isaacs and Schroeder, 2004). '[A]t the population level, more intensive use of supply-sensitive care – more frequent physician visits, hospitalizations, and stays in intensive care among the chronically ill – does not result in better health outcomes' (Center for the Evaluative Clinical Sciences, 2008). Although about half the decline of deaths from coronary heart disease are attributable to reductions in major risk factors and half to evidence-based medicine (Ford *et al.*, 2007), the proportion spent on medicine is about 30 times that of promotion. Moreover, health inequalities are associated heavily with the fundamental causes of health determinants such as the distribution of income and access to health promoting resources (Rainham, 2007). 'All the international evidence is that a health system oriented toward primary care achieves better health outcomes, lower rates of mortality and greater equity than a health system centred on hospitals' (Dragon, 2008).

If the goal of health care is to improve the health of populations, then the heavy dependence on the medical model must be reassessed. Over three decades ago, Ivan Illich (1976) vehemently criticized modern medicine as a nemesis and a cause, not a cure, of illness. Although Illich's critique of medicine was unduly severe, he raised many legitimate questions and forced placement of medicine in a social context. There is strong support, for instance, for his conclusion that major improvements in health derive from changes in the way in which people are able to live, thus suggesting the need to supplement the medical model with one based in subjective reality. Too much medicine is not good for health! Not only does it divert resources from more beneficial endeavours, but it also produces ill health and disrupts traditional social and cultural institutions and values that are central to good health in a broader sense. Moreover, medical misadventure contributes to a large number of deaths each year, over 100,000 in the USA alone (Kohn *et al.*, 1999; Starfield, 2000). Likewise, the prevalence of inappropriate drug use is alarming. From 1996 to 2005, an elderly individual had a 19 per cent chance of being prescribed an inappropriate medication (Costa-Font and Toyama, 2011).

Health, itself, must be put into perspective with a wide array of requisites of a good life including art, entertainment, music and work, as well as family and social interaction. To place health above everything else risks underestimating the contribution of myriad other factors that lead to the fulfilment of our goals and the enhancement of the human condition. According to Lamm (2003), we cannot live by health alone, but must also invest in education, infrastructure and other essential components. Satisfying health needs is vital, but human life has other worthy goals as well (Sade, 2007). Thus, it makes little sense to devote disproportionate amounts of societal resources to medicine at the expense of those things that make life worth living. 'No nation can continue to allow health care to drain away resources that would be more socially productive in education, the environment, security, and other policy areas' (Fuchs, 2007: 1544). It appears that while Western nations accept the notion that health is but one aspect of well-being at the personal level, as societies we expect the health care systems to resolve many problems that at their core are social, not medical, ones. The point here is not to undermine medical care, but rather to restore a proper balance between patient-centred and population-centred health care.

According to Schroeder (2007), the largest potential for further improvement in population health lies in reducing behavioural risk factors, especially smoking and obesity. We already have the tools at hand to make progress in tobacco control, and some of these are applicable to obesity. According to McGinnis *et al.* (2002), the determinants of health and their contribution to premature death are: behavioural patterns (40%); genetic predisposition (30%); social circumstances (15%); environmental exposures (5%); and, finally, health care (10%). Importantly, while lack of health care accounts for only 10 per cent of premature deaths, it receives by far the greatest share of resources and attention. Thus, if the public's health is to improve it is more likely to come from behavioural change than from technological innovation. The evidence is clear that when it comes to reducing early deaths, medical care has a relatively minor role. Moreover, because all the actionable determinants of health – personal behaviour, social factors, health care and the environment – disproportionately affect the poor, strategies to improve national health rankings must focus on the least well off.

The prevailing focus on medical care is flawed not only because it tends to emphasize only one dimension of health but also because it elevates health as the primary goal instead of as a means to broader life goals. Implicit in the conventional health care model is the assumption that improved health status is achieved primarily by higher expenditures on medical care, but, as noted above, beyond a minimal threshold there is little correlation between how much money is spent on doctors and hospitals and how healthy a society is. As illustrated in Table 7.5, countries that expend the highest amounts on health do not score higher on health outcomes and, in fact, often do considerably less well. Any relationship between medical care and health, even in its narrow physical

Table 7.5 ***Total health care expenditure, life expectancy at birth and infant mortality, 2010 (ranked by % GDP)***

	Total health care expenditure (as percentage of GDP)	*Life expectancy at birth (in years)*	*Infant mortality (in deaths per 1,000 live births)*
United States	17.6	78.7	6.1
Netherlands	12.0	80.8	3.8
Germany	11.6	80.5	3.4
New Zealand	10.1	81.0	5.2
Sweden	9.6	81.5	2.5
United Kingdom	9.6	80.6	4.2
Japan	9.5	83.0	2.3
Australia	9.1	81.8	4.1
Taiwan	6.4	79.2	4.2
Singapore	4.0	82.0	2.0

Sources: Data from OECD (2012b); Singapore (WHO, 2012c).

sense, is nominal compared to other determinants of health status such as heredity, personal behaviour and the physical and social environment. The impact of medical care is further limited because many health conditions are self-limiting, some are incurable and for many others there is little or no effective treatment. The cases where health care is effective and significantly affects health outcomes 'comprise only a small proportion of total medical care – too small to make a discernible impact on the statistics in populations' (Fuchs, 1994: 109).

Moreover, in those cases where health gains have been presumed to be the result of medical intervention, data indicate that medical technology has, in fact, not played the principal role. For instance, it has been estimated that at least two-thirds of the reduction in mortality rates during the 1970s and 98 per cent of the modest mortality rate improvement in the 1980s was tied to the reduction in death from cardiovascular disease (Drake, 1994: 133). Under the medical model, the reduction in deaths from cardiovascular disease is assumed to be the result of impressive innovations in treatment, especially coronary by-pass surgery and angioplasty. However, evidence suggests that most, if not all, of this drop is attributable to lifestyle changes reflected in the decline in smoking, increase in exercise and decrease in saturated fat consumption (Lewis and Leeder, 2009; Kabir *et al.*, 2007).

These findings regarding the inability to explain health status by health care alone have significant implications for any efforts to restructure the health care system. If a country really wants to achieve the goal of maximizing the health of its population, resources would better be directed towards alleviating poverty, reducing crime, changing lifestyles and so forth. A healthy person does not need medical care! According to Oliver (2011), a new paradigm, 'health in all policies', has generated a variety of models for the production of population health that: 1) recognize a broad range of social determinants of health and well-being; 2) highlight the impact of health inequalities on overall levels of population health; and 3) claim that responsibility for population health improvement rests not only with governmental health agencies and providers of health services but also with individuals and organizations across the spectrum of society.

An emphasis on lifestyle factors is accompanied by the recognition that systemic factors in the form of social relations, economic conditions, environmental hazards and a variety of public policies play as large a role, or an even larger role, in health outcomes than medicine (Fielding *et al.*, 2010; Lantz *et al.*, 2010). Health is improved or harmed by activities in many sectors of society including schools, businesses, housing, food systems, community design, law enforcement, transportation and the like. Simply increasing the funding for acute medical care, therefore, is not the answer to many contemporary 'health' issues.

As stated by Lewis and Leeder:

> No level of spending or rates of increase in spending definitively solve problems of access, quality, or equity. The natural experiment of the past decade has been to test whether it is possible to spend the way to excellence. The experiment failed because we mistook a structural and cultural problem for a financial shortfall. Buying more of the same proved ineffective, and it is now fiscally impossible to extend the experiment. The only option is to reinvent the delivery of care and invest more effectively in the production of health. For the foreseeable future, no country can continue to paper over the cracks in health care with hundred dollar bills. Abundance neither eliminated the fundamental problems in health care delivery nor reduced health disparities. Perhaps relative deprivation will create the urgency and courage to achieve both. (2009: 272)

In implementing the NHI in Taiwan, for example, many assumed, and the public expected, that the health of the population would be greatly improved and that health disparities would be reduced. However, recent studies indicate that it had only minor impact in these two areas. According to Wen *et al.* (2008), while it had high utilization and enjoyed strong support from the public, overall the NHI demonstrated minimal impact on the health of the population. Moreover, while disparities narrowed, this was very limited and major gaps remain. Similarly, Chen *et al.* (2007) conclude that while the NHI greatly increased the utilization both of inpatient and outpatient services, this increased consumption did not reduce mortality or lead to better self-perceived health status for the elderly. 'Relying on universal insurance alone to eliminate health disparity does not seem realistic. To further reduce health disparity, we believe universal health insurance programs should incorporate primary prevention, focusing on lifestyle risk reductions' (Wen *et al.*, 2008: 258).

On these grounds, many recent efforts to reform health care systems appear misguided because no amount of restructuring health care along the lines proposed by the various reformers will have a decisive impact on the health of their populations. Reforms for universal access, improved quality of care and cost containment might improve the medical care system, but they cannot be expected to improve public health substantially. As a result, 'there is little evidence . . . to suggest that providing universal coverage or changing the delivery system will have significant favourable effects on health, either in the aggregate or for particular socio-economic groups' (Fuchs, 1994: 109). This chapter unambiguously demonstrates that our countries vary significantly in the extent they are meeting the widespread challenges inherent in public health but that most still have an arduous path before them. It also demonstrates that public health is in fact a global issue that ultimately requires international cooperation transcending national boundaries. Chapter 8 brings these themes together.

Chapter 8

Understanding Health Policy Comparatively

In analysing health policy in a comparative context, the preceding chapters have covered a wide range of topics including the historical and cultural trajectories of health policy; systems of funding, providing and governing health care; policies of allocating health resources; health care in the home; and the diverse policies that constitute public health. As in any cross-country comparison, a tension emerges between similarities and difference, between common policy trends, such as the ubiquity of rationing, and policy divergence, such as welfare mix in the provision of hospital services. Similarly, in their study of 11 high income countries, Tenbensal *et al.* (2012: 29) found significant 'islands of difference' in an overall 'sea of similarity' among the health policy agendas of the selected countries.

This brings us back to cross-country comparison and the question of what analysing a range of countries can contribute to our understanding of health policy. Comparison is about juxtaposing health systems and health policies in different countries. This allows us to get a better idea about the range of variation that exists and also helps to avoid both false particularism ('everywhere is special') and false universalism ('everywhere is the same') (Saltman, 2012). Importantly, exploration often leads to deeper questions about why it is we find particular differences and similarities. As such, comparison can provide an important lever for explanation. Finally, comparison can also offer a basis for evaluation as a way of assessing the relative success and failure of specific health policies and offer a springboard for policy learning. This is a salient promise of comparison but the actual performance of comparative policy studies considerably lacks behind (Marmor *et al.*, 2005). The first rationale is central to the analysis presented in the preceding chapters and the next section critically discusses to what extent the concept of the health system does indeed help to explain health policies (see also Burau and Blank, 2006). The following section extends the discussion and assesses the potential for policy learning based on evaluating health policies across different countries. In short, in the light of *what* we found in our comparative analysis, this final chapter returns to the other two fundamental questions in comparative health policy, *how* and *why* we compare (Tuohy, 2012a and b).

Health systems and explaining health policies

The notion of different health systems, as ordered in a typology of health systems, has been central to the comparative turn in health policy analysis. The notion has been used to conceptualize the (institutional) context which shapes the politics and policies of health care (see, e.g., Freeman, 2000; Ham, 1997b; Raffel, 1997; Scott, 2001; Wall, 1996; for an overview see Marmor and Wendt, 2011a, 2012; Wendt *et al.*, 2009). Cross-country comparison generates an abundance of information, and ordering this information by using a typology of health systems is central to using comparison to build, review and revise explanations about health policy emergence and health policy making. Against this background, the following analysis critically discusses two things: the importance of institutional embeddedness beyond the health system and the use of the concept of the health system in relation to non-medical health policies. The key issue here is whether the concept of the health system helps us to discover how countries vary (or are similar) in the health policies they adopt and whether we can gain insights into why these differences (or similarities) exist.

Health systems and institutional embeddedness

Table 8.1 maps out our countries using the typology of health systems introduced in Chapter 1 as a basis, but it also defines in more detail different aspects of government involvement in the funding and provision of health care following on from the discussion in preceding chapters. The institutions of governing the funding of health care are concerned with the mechanisms by which individual patients have access to services (such as social citizenship and earned insurance entitlements) and the mechanisms that decide on the total volume of resources allocated to the financing of health care (such as governing through public management and setting regulatory frameworks). In contrast, the institutions of governing the provision of health care include the mechanisms for regulating hospitals (such as the amount of public regulation and the mix of differently owned hospitals) and the regulation of doctors (especially different forms of private interest government). This reflects the centrality of hospitals and doctors for the provision of health care.

Looking at the health systems in these countries across the different types and respective dimensions of governing health care, several findings stand out. Only five out of the ten countries included in the study fully fit one of the three types of health system (Britain, Sweden, Germany, Taiwan and the USA). In contrast, the remaining countries are more or less only close approximations of the individual ideal types. This

Table 8.1 *Health systems and their policies*

	Governance of funding • *Extent of public access to health care* • *Extent of public control of total health care costs*	*Governance of provision* • *Extent of public control of hospitals*[1] • *Extent of constraints on private interest government of doctors*[2]
National health service • Extensive public access, high public control of costs • High public control of hospitals, highly constrained private interest government of doctors	BRITAIN SWEDEN Australia (access/control) Japan (cost control) New Zealand (access) Netherlands (cost control) Singapore (cost control)	BRITAIN SWEDEN New Zealand
Social insurance systems • De facto public access, moderate public control of costs • Moderate public control of hospitals, some constraints on private interest government of doctors	GERMANY TAIWAN Japan (access) Netherlands (access) New Zealand (cost control)	GERMANY TAIWAN Australia Japan Netherlands Singapore
Private insurance system • Limited public access, low public control of costs • Little public control of hospitals, few constraints on private interest government of doctors	USA Singapore (access)	USA

[1] Share of hospitals in public ownership with degree of public regulation used as a proxy for extent of public control of hospitals.
[2] Share of publicly employed (hospital) doctors together with degree of professional self-regulation used as a proxy for extent of constraints on self-government of doctors.

highlights the fact that the institutional contexts of the governing of health care are more complex than suggested by the definition of the health system. Instead, institutional contexts are often highly specific in terms of how individual aspects combine themselves in individual countries. Such specificities also point to additional aspects of institutional context. Consequently, within a country the two sets of institutions associated with the governance of funding may actually fit different types of health systems thus making categorization problematic. The same problem might also apply to the comparison of the governance of funding and provision.

According to the typology, public control of the total resources allocated to health care can be expected to be highest in national health services with access to health care based on social citizenship and lowest in private insurance systems where access to health care is based on private insurance, with public control in social insurance health systems lying in between. This is true for four of our countries, but the picture is more complex in the remaining six countries, pointing to the importance of country-specific institutional contexts. In Australia, for example, federalism combined with the legacy of the private insurance systems weakens government authority over funding (Palmer and Short, 2000). In contrast, the unitary political system in Japan helps to concentrate authority in the hands of central government (Campbell and Ikegami, 2008). Despite significant decentralization of health services and insurance plans, for example, all billing and payment in Japan is centralized through the payment fund of National Health Insurance.

The Netherlands and Singapore are particularly interesting examples of how country-specific institutional contexts shape the public control of health care costs, thus making differences between countries particularly pertinent. In the Netherlands, the high public control of funding reflects the unusual combination of social insurance with strong universalist elements (for an overview, see Exter *et al.*, 2004; Maarse, 1997). Health funding combines a considerable diversity of sources, including private insurance for acute medical risks, and compulsory social insurance contributions to cover exceptional medical risks. This reflects the historical legacy of a society segmented into different groupings and the gradual weakening of this legacy in the Netherlands. The semi-federal political system also helps to concentrate authority in the hands of the central government, and, in contrast to Germany, corporatism is confined to the national level.

In Singapore, country-specific institutional contexts are such that public control is strong not only in relation to health care costs but also to other key aspects of health care (for an overview, see Barr, 2001; Ham, 2001). Strong government control of funding coexists with a strong focus on individual responsibility and limited familial risk pooling. Health care is funded in part by individual savings accounts that are compulsory. The government also caps contribution rates, while out-of-pocket payments are high. As such, Singapore defies the dictum that private funding is unlikely to make for public control. The strength of government control reflects not only the spatial concentration of political power typical of city-states, but also a strongly centralized approach to health policy. Government education programmes are aimed at lowering the demand for health care and also emphasize the importance of primary health care and prevention over hospital care. Not surprisingly, public health policies are strong, and the government heavily subsidizes health promotion and disease prevention programmes that emphasize the responsibility of the individual to look after his or her own health.

The importance of country specific institutional contexts also applies, though to a lesser extent, when comparing the governance of funding and provision. Singapore, for example, and as mentioned above, has a highly controlled health system but one based on individual savings accounts that give the impression of minimal government control over funding. Thus, it crosses the line between a social insurance and a private insurance health system. Furthermore, Singapore gives those persons with sufficient Medisave account balances considerable freedom of choice as to public and private doctors and hospitals as well as allowing them to purchase private insurance with their account should they so desire. While provision best fits a private insurance health system, a large proportion of health care is provided in publicly owned hospitals by government-set salaried doctors. Despite this, there are few controls on medical intervention in Singapore because in the end individuals have the choice of what services to use with their compulsory but private accounts.

The analysis suggests two things. First, the ideal type of the health system holds as an approximation of 'real' health systems. It is therefore a classical ideal type that is useful as a heuristic device that simplifies the complex real world of governing health care (following Weber, 1949). Thereby, the concept of the health system helps to move the analysis beyond the specificity of individual cases and towards more generalized observations, overcoming a salient tension inherent in comparative enquiry (Goodin and Smitsman, 2000). The health system as an ideal type, therefore, does not need to fit the real types completely in order to be useful.

Second, it is important to remember that it is primarily through the comparison and contrast with real types that explanations can be advanced (see Arts and Glissen, 2002). The central question, then, is how to explain the extent to which 'real' health systems do or do not fit the ideal types. The different degrees of 'misfits' among these countries and the types of health systems presented in the analysis raises many such 'why' questions. In turn, this underlines the fact that the concept of the health system indeed only provides a starting point for a comparative analysis and must be complemented by additional, more specific, institutional explanations. The importance of a detailed study of institutional contexts is well recognized in the comparative study of health policy (see, e.g., Döhler, 1991; Immergut, 1992; Wilsford, 1994).

Significantly, then, there is institutional embeddedness beyond the health system (more generally on this point Burau, 2012). As the analysis of our countries suggests, governing health care is embedded in institutional contexts that are broader than those institutions making up the health system, and institutional contexts that are often also highly specific to individual countries. Our analysis, for example, points to the importance of the specific characteristics of political systems (such as federalism in Australia), social structures (such as the legacy of societal pillars in the Netherlands) and social values (such as the high degree of individual self-reliance in Singapore). The governing of health care reflects specific configurations of these different aspects of institutional context, all of which are changeable over time. Therefore, more often than not, health policies follow trajectories that are highly complex and specific.

Similarly, in her comparative analysis of health reform Tuohy (2012b; similarly Schmid *et al.*, 2010) points to the emergence of distinct national hybrids in Britain and the Netherlands, reflecting politics of redesign driven by institutional entrepreneurs. In a similar vein, Saltman (2012) highlights the softening of boundaries of health systems, especially between public and private provision, between social insurance and tax funding and between individual and collective responsibility. In contrast, Freeman and Frisina (2012) in their review of the use of typologies of comparative health policy stress that classification, although highly problematic, remains integral to comparison. Instead, the authors call for a better understanding of how health systems actually work, using typologies as a first step (also see Denis and Forest, 2012).

Health systems and non-medical health policies

The analysis above suggests that the institutional context of governing health care itself is highly complex. This echoes Freeman's (2000: 7) observation that the organization of health care is actually not very systematic. The complex historical emergence of policies of health care often defies the order implied by the notion of a *system*. As a result, the health system perspective may be looking for order where there is little. Instead, the institutional context of governing health care is highly differentiated, to the extent that such contexts are often somewhat specific to individual countries. Importantly, there is also specificity in relation to sub-sectors of health care and policy. This is particularly apparent in relation to those sub-sectors that have traditionally been at the margins of the 'health system', but that are increasingly relevant to health policy. Focusing on home and community-based health care as an example, this section assesses the use of the notion of the health system for capturing the institutions central to non-medical health care and for explaining such 'new' health policies across countries.

Debates about ageing populations and their implications for health care costs and services have put home and community-based health care on the health policy agenda. At international level it is indicative, for example, that long-term care for elderly people was one of the components of a major OECD Health Project (OECD, 2005a). The OECD Health Project echoes developments across the countries included in our study in which there are many examples of major policy initiatives relating to home and community-based health care (see, e.g., Burau *et al.*, 2007; Jenson and Jacobzone, 2000). Such policies often aim at the expansion of existing services to support informal care givers by integrating home and community-based health care into the regular organization of health care. The expansion of social insurance in Germany and Japan are indicative examples. Starting in the late 1980s, the government in Japan introduced a publicly funded scheme, the so-called Gold Plan, to expand care services for older people. The scheme was extended in the late 1990s and in effect became a separate branch of social insurance, funded by a mixture of social insurance premiums and taxes. Considering the traditional strength of family responsibility for care of the elderly, this is a significant policy development (Furuse, 1996).

This emergence of non-medical based health care raises the question of how policies related to home and community-based health care fit into the concept of the health system. The concept focuses on institutions and policies related to medical care. In contrast, home and community-based health care is located on two sets of interfaces: between formal and informal care, and between health and social care. In relation to the first aspect, it is indicative that few older people receive home nursing care and even when they do it only accounts for a small share of their care. Instead, home care predominantly means unpaid (informal) care by women and often also includes social care, such as help with domestic tasks. This reflects not only the inadequacy of existing home nursing services, but also the fact that many of the health care needs of older people are often not principally medically related.

This puts a number of limitations on using the concept of the health system for capturing the institutions governing home and community-based health care and for explaining corresponding health policies. The institutions related to the governance of funding are relevant to the extent that home and community-based health care is part of the organization of medical health care. Traditionally, parts of home and community-based health care have by default been funded by the same scheme as medical health care. At the same time, parallel funding schemes relating to social care have existed. In Germany, for example, before the introduction of long-term care insurance, funding for home and community-based health care came from both health insurance and locally funded social assistance schemes. In many cases this organizational division continues and also applies to the newly established schemes. This also applies to Japan, whereas in Australia, New Zealand, the Netherlands and Sweden funding of home and community-based health care is integrated. Furthermore, there tends to be formal or de facto limits to the scope of collective consumption. Instead private consumption in the form of private payments for formal services and informal care paid by lost income are important complementary aspects of consumption. The last aspect even applies to countries like Sweden, where the level of publicly funded services is relatively high. A study in the mid-1980s, for example, found that informal care accounted for 64 per cent of the total care time (OECD, 1996: 166).

There are even more extensive limitations in relation to applying the definitions of the governance of provision. Hospitals as settings of care provision and doctors as providers of care are of little importance. Instead, care workers such as community nurses, care assistants and social workers together with informal carers, all working in home and community settings, are central for the provision of this type of health care. Taken together this suggests that shared values and beliefs (and corresponding practices) are important for understanding non-medical health policies. Freeman and Ruskin (1999) refer to this as 'cultural embeddedness' and thereby point to diversity beyond the macro level and, notably, a type of diversity that is shaped by organizational bases that are ethnic, gendered, local and personal, rather than national and public.

Where does this leave capturing institutional arrangements as they apply to home and community-based health care and explaining corresponding non-medical health policies across our countries? The concept of the health system is of some use, notably to the extent to which home and community-based health care is part the organization of medical health care. However, beyond that, using the concept of the health system has clear limits, as some institutions do not have the same importance, whereas others not included in the definition are central for understanding non-medical health policies. Instead, different aspects of institutional context need to be taken into consideration. This requires two things: first, redefining the institutions related to the governing of funding and provision so as to reflect the specific characteristics of home and community-based health care (and, where applicable, across the health and social care divide); and second, to include gender as a set of social and cultural institutions. In this respect Pfau-Effinger's (2004) concept of 'gender arrangements' is particularly useful. The concept consists of two components. Gender order describes existing structures of gender relations not least as reflected in gendered divisions of labour. Gender culture for its part refers to deeply embedded beliefs and ideas about the relations between the generations in the family and the obligations associated with such relations.

Against this background one way forward would be to combine the different, yet complementary, aspects of institutional context discussed above as part of an 'organizing framework'. In the context of their study of multilevel governance Bache and Flinders (2004: 94) define this as an analytical framework that provides a map of how things relate and that leads to a set of research questions. The value of such an approach is that it helps to explore complex issues and identifies interesting areas for further research.

Possibilities and limitations for cross-national learning

The discussion above concerning the extent to which the typology of health systems helps to explain health policy suggests three things. First, modelled on paradigmatic cases the concept of the health system holds as an ideal type. Second, as such the health system provides a useful springboard for the analysis of health policy, but one that needs to be complemented by more specific institutional explanations. Third, the concept of the health system is less applicable to increasingly important, non-medical areas of health policy. Instead, different aspects of institutional context come into play and they can be combined as part of a looser 'organizing framework'.

Nevertheless, cross-country comparison remains an attractive strategy for social enquiry, not least as it can also provide a basis for identifying the variety of policy options that exist in health policy. As such, comparison holds the implicit promise of learning from other countries and their policy successes and failures. Health policy learning occurs naturally as information about other countries has become more readily available as part of the process of globalization. Policy learning is also explicitly encouraged by international organizations such as the OECD and the WHO when they disseminate information about health systems and reforms in different countries. Policy learning, therefore, is becoming more explicitly transnational and global agendas for health reform increasingly are setting the scene for 'local' health policies. For example, this is what Burau and Kuhlmann (2012) found in their comparative analysis of primary health care policies in England, Germany and Russia. Similarly, in relation to tobacco control, Farquharson (2003) highlights the existence of global advocacy networks that either promote or oppose tobacco and their importance for shaping domestic policies.

To policy makers, cross-country comparison and the opportunity to identify which health policy/system works 'best' is attractive for several reasons. Looking at other countries offers a virtual 'test' of different policy options and as such promises 'evidence-based' policy making, policy innovation and, above all, policy success (Klein, 2009; Stone, 1999). This is particularly attractive in times of crisis, which are often rooted in a sense of converging policy problems and possible solutions, as it triggers a search for new policy ideas (Cortez, 2008a; Marmor *et al.*, 2005)

However, there are various models of policy learning as Freeman (2005, 2006) argues, two of which are particularly relevant in the present context. First, policy learning as transfer is based on a rationalist conception that policy input and policy output relate to each other as cause and effect. Policy learning emerges as an instrumental process that is based on evidence. In other words: policy makers learn in order to address specific problems and policies easily transfer from one country to the other. In contrast and second, policy learning as transplant is based on an institutionalist perspective and governments are seen to show different capacities for learning. The process of learning itself is related to experience and experiment. In other words, policy makers learn in an iterative way through trial and error, and the travel of policies from one country to the next is contingent upon there being a special institutional context.

The work of the OECD and its recent OECD Health Project powerfully represents a model of policy learning that is based on transfer. Indeed, this view is widespread among policy practitioners and analysts (Russell *et al.*, 2008). For example, in the foreword to the final report, the Direct General of the OECD stresses that the Project offers a means for member countries to learn from each other, drawing on 'the best expertise' that exists (OECD, 2005a: 3). Consequently, the report lists goals of health systems as generic to health policy and which, as such, are applicable across different countries. Similarly, the report presents policy initiatives in individual countries as equally possible policy options. In short, this is about evaluating health reforms to identify best practice for transfer, where the capacity of governments to learn is assumed. The analysis presented in the preceding chapters more or less explicitly challenges this model of policy learning that assumes that identifying what is 'best' and transferring what is 'best' from one country to another is straightforward. The complexity of health systems and policies in different countries emerging from our analysis suggests otherwise. Health policy making is not necessarily rationalist, driven by knowledge and evidence, but instead constitutes a struggle over ideas and values (Russell *et al.*, 2008). There are many definitions of what are 'best' health policies/systems, and transferring 'best practice' across countries is difficult because health policies are deeply embedded in country-specific contexts.

Health policy making is a complex process. Chapter 4 identifies quality, equity/access and cost containment/efficiency as the central goals of health policy. These three goals represent different and potentially competing ideas about what is the 'best' health policy/system. This makes learning from other countries a value-laden exercise, further complicated by the fact that different actors in health care have different ideas of what is 'best'. Thus, what is the 'best' health policy/system also depends on whom you ask. Importantly, the institutional set-up of different health systems means that actors enjoy different degrees of power. For example, providers are often particularly influential in private insurance systems, as the example of the USA demonstrates, whereas their power is more limited in national health services, as the example of the UK suggests. The same applies to patients, although in the USA the (until now) selective access to health insurance constrains the potential influence of patients.

As Figure 8.1 suggests, there are four sets of actors in health care: users, payers (including both third-party payers and the public), providers and the state. As mentioned, the different actors in health care often support different goals of health policy and as such have different ideas about what the 'best' health system or policy is. Payers are primarily concerned with cost containment and efficiency, whereas for providers the quality of health care is the key. In contrast, the goal orientation of the public is ambivalent; as patients the public put quality and access/equality first, whereas as payers the public has a predominant interest in cost containment/efficiency. Importantly, the different actors in health care may also have different ideas about the same goal. For users of health care, quality means a well-funded health system that allows for patient choice and fast access to medical technology. This definition of quality is shared by providers of health care, who also emphasize the importance of autonomy in the provision of health care services. In contrast, states are more likely to highlight the public health aspects of quality.

The discussion above suggests that health policies/systems are 'best' in relation to specific goals, and that the importance attached to the

		Actors in Health Care			
		Users	*Payers*	*Providers*	*The State*
Goals of Health Policy	*Quality*	X		X	X
	Equity/Access	X		X	
	Cost Containment/ Efficiency		X		X

Figure 8.1 *The goal orientation of actors in health care*

Quality	
Defined as ...	
Level of health care spending (percentage of GDP)	*High*: USA, Germany *Low*: Singapore, Taiwan, Britain, Japan
Speed of access to medical technology	*Fast*: USA, Germany, Taiwan *Slow*: Britain, Netherlands
Number of doctors (per 1,000 inhabitants)	*High:* Germany, Sweden *Low*: Taiwan, Singapore, Britain, Japan
Extent of patient choice	*High*: Singapore, Taiwan, USA *Medium*: Germany, Sweden *Low*: Australia, Britain, Netherlands, New Zealand
Commitment to public health	*High*: Singapore, Sweden *Low*: Germany, Taiwan, USA
Access/Equity	
Defined as ...	
Public funding of health care (percentage of total expenditure)	*High*: Sweden, Britain, Japan *Low*: Singapore, USA
Coverage of population	*High*: Britain (universality), Japan and Taiwan (social solidarity) *Low*: USA
Cost Containment/Efficiency	
Defined as ...	
Control of costs	*High (direct budget control)*: Britain, Japan, New Zealand, Sweden, Taiwan *Medium (contractual control)*: Germany, Netherlands *Low (decentralized, market-oriented systems)*: Australia, USA
Supply-side rationing	*High (national health services)*: Britain, New Zealand, Sweden *Low (market-based health systems)*: Singapore, Taiwan, USA

Figure 8.2 *Identifying 'best' health systems*

individual goals (and ideas about what is 'best') varies between different actors in health care. Figure 8.2 offers an overview of the 'best' health systems in relation to the goals of quality, equity/access and cost containment/efficiency for our countries. It also includes several definitions (or indicators) of each health policy goal. Considering the complexity of health care this overview uses selected indicators and examples and does not claim to be comprehensive.

Quality of health care is often measured in terms of the financial resources spent on health care. Based on the measure of the percentage of GDP spent on health care, the USA and the Netherlands are the 'best' health systems. Other measures of quality relate to the technical and human resources of health systems such as the speed of access to medical technology and the number of doctors, respectively. Subsidiary policy goals are patient choice and commitment to public health. The assumption is that the more money spent, the better the technical and human resources of health systems. Countries such as Germany and Britain support this assumption, although the relationship among different indicators of quality is far more complex than this. For example, while the health system in Singapore ranks very low in terms of the level of health care spending and the number of doctors, quality in terms of the extent of patient choice and commitment to public health is high. Similarly, Taiwan ranks low in both the number of doctors and the commitment to public health but high in patient choice and access to new technologies. Other cases highlight the tradeoffs between different indicators of quality. Germany, for example, does very well on all indicators except commitment to public health, suggesting that quality is primarily defined as high-tech medical care.

The share of health care expenditure coming from public sources is an important indicator of equity/access in health systems. Public funding in the form of taxes or social insurance contributions is underpinned by the principles of universality and social solidarity, respectively, and as such makes for universal or near universal (and in principle equitable) access to health care. On this count, Sweden, Britain and Japan are the three 'best' health systems, whereas Singapore and the USA are among the 'worst'. Here, low coverage means that a significant proportion of the population is excluded from what is otherwise a very 'high quality' health system.

Such tradeoffs also exist between the policy goals of cost containment/efficiency and quality. The extent of control of costs is an important indicator of cost containment/efficiency and here the 'best' health systems are characterized by extensive cost control. Direct budget control, such as in Britain, Japan, New Zealand, Sweden and Taiwan allows for greatest cost control, followed by contractual control as it exists in Germany and the Netherlands. Cost control is weakest in decentralized, market-oriented systems such as Australia and the USA. Health systems with extensive cost controls also make greater use of supply-side rationing. However, this comes at the price of quality in terms of the level of health care spending (such as in Japan), speed of access to medical technology (such as in Britain) and the extent of patient choice (such as in New Zealand). Not surprisingly, the 2000 World Health Report by the WHO ranked Britain 18th in terms of the responsiveness to patients (Laurance and Norton, 2000). The inverse is also true. In the USA and Germany, high quality in terms of level of health care spending and fast access to medical technology come at the price of low to medium control of costs.

Identifying the 'best' health system/policy is a highly complex process that depends on what is defined as 'best': that is, which policy goal is considered to be most important. In an ideal world, all three goals would be equally important. However, as health care resources are ultimately limited, the different policy goals in effect compete with each other. The emphasis put on individual goals and definitions of what is the 'best' health policy/system varies over time as well as between countries. This reflects historical trajectories and the health systems in individual countries together with the balance of power among the different actors in health care.

As such, and as suggested by the institutionally based, transplant approach to policy learning, the lessons policy makers want to learn from other countries also vary among individual health systems, not least because health systems have different policy agendas (Tenbensel *et al.*, 2012). Lesson learning is not necessarily a politically neutral process, but the value of policy lessons lies precisely in their power to bias policy choice (Marmor *et al.*, 2005; Stone, 1999). Lesson learning is politically motivated and selective and is often used to substantiate already made policy choices. Here, Britain is an indicative example. In response to the perceived funding crisis of the British NHS in the late 1980s, the government looked towards the USA and its models of managed care. The strong market orientation of the US health system resonated with the neo-liberal outlook of the Conservative government of the time. The focus on the organization of health services also helped to avoid the politically sensitive issue of making changes to the way in which the NHS was funded. Similarly, in their analysis of the introduction of DRGs across different countries, Gilardi *et al.* (2009) observe that introduction is most likely where existing policy is seen as ineffective and where experiences from other countries suggest the achievement of desired results. In their study of how quasi-market mechanisms become incorporated into national contexts, Hassenteufel *et al.* (2010) also underscore particularly the importance of actors, notably small groups of 'programmatic actors' like politicians, civil servants and medical doctors.

Moreover, there are only certain lessons policy makers in individual countries can learn, and this points to the limits of transferring 'best practice'. As Chapter 2 emphasizes, health policies are embedded in highly specific historical, cultural and political contexts, and any policy success is ultimately tied to a specific place and point in time. Irrespective of political will, not all policies work everywhere. Successful lesson learning is both about the substance of policies and about the circumstances in which policies succeed (Klein, 1997; Marmor *et al.*, 2009a). For instance, the New Zealand government's attempts to introduce partial charges for users for hospital care in the early 1990s were inspired by a series of reports by US-based health care consultants; but they failed. The policy engendered strong opposition not only from the public but also from the health care professions, which forced the government to withdraw the policy. A possible explanation is that the success of this policy was predicated on a health system that puts great emphasis on individual responsibility (as in the USA) rather than public responsibility (as in New Zealand). The relative match with institutional contexts is even less likely in relation to developing countries and as McPake (2002) demonstrates in relation to hospital reform and the introduction of co-payments, inadequate contextualization of policies can impose serious costs and be even worse than the absence of change.

The complexity and contingency of identifying 'best practice' and cross-country learning in health policy does not mean that it cannot or should not be done. Instead, cross-country learning requires sensitivity, notably in two respects. Cross-country learning requires sensitivity towards different and potentially competing ideas about what are the 'best' health policies/systems. There is no single, universally applicable definition of what is 'best', but rather there are as many definitions as there are goals of health policy. Some health systems are particularly successful in relation to cost containment/efficiency, whereas others score highly on quality as measured in terms of levels of spending and access to medical technology. Importantly, there are tradeoffs between different goals of health policy, and health systems are unlikely to be 'best' in respect of all policy goals. Which health policies are considered 'best' and worthy of lesson learning is ultimately a political decision.

Nevertheless, cross-country learning also requires sensitivity towards the specific contexts under which policies succeed (Klein, 2009). Indeed, this is one of the major conclusions from the experiences with an on-call facility for health care policy that the UK government created to facilitate learning from other countries (Nolte *et al.*, 2008). Okma (2008; also see Rovere and Barua, 2012) makes a similar observation in her commentary on the US interest in recent Dutch health reforms, while Or and colleagues (2010) argue that the heterogeneity in organizational design and governance within and across health systems makes it highly unlikely that a 'copy and paste' approach to health reform is effective. Rather, as Kirkpatrick and colleagues (2011) show in relation to the adoption of medical manager roles in European health systems, this involves extensive translation not least at the level of the organization. Such a process is shaped by a variety of aspects of institutional context, including the characteristics of hospital governance regimes and the position of the medical profession, as well as the timing/process of health management reform.

Contribution to the comparative study of health policy

In many respects the analysis presented in this book has covered familiar ground. Analyses of health systems, doctors and health reform are central topics in the comparative study of health policy. What, then, does the analysis presented in this book contribute to the debate? The contribution of the present analysis lies in the range of countries and policy issues covered. The breadth of the analysis results in a relatively comprehensive map in which specific health policies in individual countries can be located. As such, the analysis offers a basis for more in-depth analyses of a wide range of more specific cases that vary in terms both of countries and policy issues.

The map is based on an analysis that covers a diverse range of countries from the pioneers of publicly funded health systems (such as Germany and Sweden) to health systems that put individual responsibility first (such as Singapore and the USA) and hybrids (such as Australia and Taiwan); from health systems embedded in Western capitalist democracies to health systems embedded in Asian political systems; and from large health systems such as America's which covers 330 million people to small health systems such as New Zealand's which covers only 4.5 million people. The map is also based on an analysis that includes a diverse range of health policy issues including basic ones such as the funding and provision of health care, health policy issues that are high on the political agenda such as those relating to the allocation of health care resources, and health policy issues that are located on the margins of the health systems such as home care and public health. However, no matter how inclusive, such a loose framework has its own limitations. As Mabbett and Bolderson (1999) argue, the deconstruction of broad-brush categorizations and typologies makes all encompassing cross-country comparison and contrast more difficult.

Nevertheless, by offering a comprehensive map in which specific health policies in individual countries can be located, the analysis presented in this book contributes to the comparative study of health policy in another way. The map offers one way of moving away from the notion that health policies across countries are either different or similar and that they will either continue to be embedded in country-specific contexts or will be submerged by convergence. Over time, health policies across countries will be both different and similar in differing degrees and in different respects. Adopting a map also means embracing complexity, exploring differences in health policy within the same country, and analysing the interfaces with other, related policies. In short, using a map acknowledges the existence of similarities within differences and differences within similarities, and acknowledges that health policy includes more than just health systems. Although this more complex and dynamic view of health policy might lack the comfort that comes with the typology of health systems, the analysis in the earlier chapters demonstrates that it better reflects the real world of health care.

Glossary

Acute Care: Medical treatment rendered to people whose illnesses or medical problems are short term or don't require long-term continuing care. Acute care facilities are hospitals that mainly treat people with short-term health problems.

Ambulatory Care: All health services delivered outside hospitals (that is, in primary care settings).

Amenable Mortality: A premature death from causes that should not occur in the presence of timely and effective health care.

Capitation Fee: A payment system based on a fixed pre-payment, per patient, paid to a health care provider to deliver medical services to a particular group of patients. The payment is the same no matter how many services or what type of services each patient actually gets.

Case Management: Intended to improve health outcomes or control costs by tailoring services to a patient's needs.

Chronic Illnesses: Health problems that are long term and continuing. Nursing homes, mental hospitals and rehabilitation facilities are examples of chronic care facilities.

Clinical Guidelines: Carefully developed information on diagnosing and treating specific medical conditions. Guidelines are usually based on clinical literature and expert consensus, are designed to help physicians make decisions and to help funding organizations evaluate appropriateness and medical necessity of care.

Coordinated Care: Delivery of systematic, responsive and supportive care to people with complex needs, for example chronic illness. Coordinated care typically spans across different sectors of health care delivery and involves different health professions.

Co-payments: Flat fees or payments that a patient pays for each doctor visit or prescription or other health care service.

Core Services: A package of health care services deemed basic for all citizens.

Cost Containment: The method of constraining health care costs from increasing beyond a set level by controlling or reducing inefficiency and waste in the health care system.

Cost Sharing: The requirement that the patient pay a portion of the costs of covered services. Deductibles, co-insurance and co-payments are cost-sharing techniques.

Cost Shifting: When one group of patients does not pay the full cost for a service, health care providers pass on the costs for these services to other groups of patients.

Covered Services: Treatments or other services for which a health plan pays at least part of the charge.

Deductible: The amount of money, or value of certain services (such as one physician visit) a patient or family must pay before costs (or percentages of costs) are covered by the health plan or insurance company, usually per year.

Diagnosis-Related Groups (DRGs): A system for classifying hospital stays according to the diagnosis of the medical problem being treated for the purposes of payment.

Disease Management: Programmes for persons who have chronic illnesses such as asthma or diabetes that encourage them to live a healthy lifestyle and take medications as prescribed.

Effectiveness: A measure of the extent to which a specific intervention, procedure, regimen or service, when deployed in the field in routine circumstances, does what it is intended to do for a specified population.

Elective: A health care procedure that is not an emergency and that the patient and doctor plan in advance.

Electronic Health Record (EHR): Also electronic medical record (EMR). An evolving concept defined as a systematic collection of electronic health information about individual patients or populations. It is a record in digital format that is theoretically capable of being shared across many health care settings.

Fee-for-Service: The traditional payment method where the insurer (patient, insurance plan or government) pays providers per services rendered. The doctor charges a fee for each service provided.

Gate-Keeper: A primary care physician responsible for overseeing and coordinating all aspects of a patient's medical care. The gate-keeper usually has to pre-authorize other speciality care, diagnostic tests or hospital admission.

General Practitioners: Physicians without speciality training who provide a wide range of primary health care services to patients.

Global Budgets: Budgets set to contain health care costs. Common in national health systems that annually set the maximum amount of money that will be spent on health care.

Group Insurance: Health insurance offered through business, union trusts or other groups and associations. The most common system of health insurance in the USA is the one in which the cost of insurance is based on the age, sex, health status and occupation of the people in the group.

Halfway Technology: Focuses on alleviating problematic symptoms instead of the root causes of poor health.

Health Indicator: An indicator applicable to a health or health-related situation.

Health Inequalities: Differences in health among people and groups within and between countries that are the consequence of social injustice.

Health Inequities or Disparities: Systematic and potentially remediable differences in one or more aspects of health across population groups defined socially, economically, demographically or geographically.

Health Information Technology (HIT): The umbrella term to describe the comprehensive management of health information across computerized systems and its secure exchange between consumers, providers, government and quality entities and insurers.

Health Insurance: Financial protection against the health care costs caused by treating disease or accidental injury. A system of risk sharing through pooled resources.

Health Maintenance Organization (HMO): A health plan providing comprehensive medical services to its members for a fixed, prepaid premium. Members must use participating providers and are enrolled for a fixed period of time. HMOs can be either for-profit or not-for-profit. Most HMOs provide care through a network of doctors, hospitals and other medical professionals that their members must use in order to be covered for that care.

Health Outcomes: Measures of the effectiveness of particular kinds of medical treatment. This refers to research-based information that asks what difference a drug, procedure or other health care intervention really makes to a patient's health.

Health Sector: Part of the economy dealing with health-related issues in society.

Health System: The people, institutions and resources, arranged together in accordance with established policies, to improve the health of the population they serve, while responding to people's legitimate expectations and protecting them against the cost of ill-health through a variety of activities whose primary intent is to improve health. The set of elements and their relations in a complex whole, designed to serve the health needs of the population.

Home Health Care: Skilled nurses and trained aides who provide nursing services and related care to someone in his or her home.

Inpatient Care: Care for a person who has been admitted to a hospital or other health facility for a period of at least 24 hours.

Long-term Care: Health care, personal care and social services provided to people who have a chronic illness or disability and do not have full functional capacity. This care can take place in an institution or at home on a long-term basis.

Malpractice Insurance: Coverage for medical professionals which pays the costs of legal fees and/or any damages assessed by a court in a lawsuit brought against a professional who has been charged with negligence. Endemic in the USA.

Managed Care Organization: An umbrella term for HMOs and all health plans that provide health care in return for pre-set monthly payments and coordinate care through a defined network of primary care physicians and hospitals. Prepaid medical plans that attempt to control health care costs through a preventative health care approach.

Means Test: An assessment of a person's or family's income or assets so that it can be determined if they are eligible to receive public support.

Medical Home Model: An organizational and financing system that is meant to enhance primary care services through a financial mechanism (care management payments) and communications (information technology). It emphasizes continuity and coordination among specialists and first-contact practitioners without specifying who would coordinate the care.

Medical Tourism: Patient movement generally from highly developed nations to less developed ones to obtain medical treatment that is less expensive or unavailable in their home country. Medical tourism differs from the traditional model of international health travel where patients go from less developed countries to major medical centres in highly developed countries for medical treatment that is unavailable in their own communities.

Out-of-Pocket Payments: The amount of money that a person must pay directly for his or her health care, including: deductibles, co-payments, payments for services that are not covered, and/or in the US health insurance premiums that are not paid by his or her employer.

Outpatient Care: Health care services that do not require a patient to receive overnight care in a hospital (such as day surgery).

Preventive Health Care: An approach to medicine that attempts to promote and maintain the health of people by preventing disease or its consequences. It includes primary prevention to keep people from getting sick (such as immunizations), secondary prevention to detect early disease (such as Pap smears) and tertiary prevention to keep ill people or those at high risk of disease from getting sicker (such as helping someone with lung disease to quit smoking).

Primary Care: Preventive health care and routine medical care that is typically provided by a doctor trained in internal medicine, paediatrics or family practice, or by a nurse, nurse practitioner or physician's assistant.

Primary Care Provider: The health professional who provides basic health care services and may control patients' access to the rest of the health care system through referrals.

Private Insurance: Health insurance that is provided by commercial insurance companies and where insurance premiums are risk-based.

Quality Assessment/Assurance: A systematic process to improve the quality of health care by monitoring quality, finding out what is not working and fixing the problems of health care delivery.

Rationing: The denial of a treatment to a particular patient who would benefit from it.

Referral System: The process through which a primary care provider authorizes a patient to see a specialist to receive additional care.

Single Payer System: A health care system in which costs are paid by taxes or compulsory contributions to sickness funds or social insurance plans rather than by the employer and employee.

Social Determinants of Health: The broad and complex array of social, political, economic, environmental and cultural factors that strongly impact on health status and equity between and within countries.

Third Party Payer: An organization other than the patient or health care provider involved in the financing of personal health services.

Universal Coverage: This refers to health systems that guarantee health care to all people regardless of the way that the system is financed.

Waiting List Time: The amount of time a person must wait from the date he or she is deemed to need a procedure to the date they actually receive it.

Guide to Further Reading

1 Comparative health policy: an introduction

There are many useful works on comparative health systems and health policy for readers to explore for more information. The OECD (2011a) *Health at a Glance* presents the most current comparable data on key indicators of health and health systems across OECD countries. Matcha (2003) provides an analysis of health care systems in Canada, Germany, Sweden, Japan, the UK and the USA, including the history, financing and delivery of services. Masis and Smith (2010) detail health policies and systems from diverse countries such as Argentina, Bangladesh, Cambodia, Cameroon, Chile, Mexico, Nigeria, Peru, Sri Lanka and Taiwan. Similarly, Smith and Hanson (2012) examine health systems in low- and middle-income countries. Raffel (1997), DeVoe (2001), Okma and Crivelli (2009), Marmor and Wendt (2011b) and Hwang (2008) specifically look at health reform in an international context. Freeman (2000) offers a good overview of the politics of health in Europe, as does Moran (1999). Coulter and Ham (2000) specifically discuss the global challenge of rationing, and Ham and Robert (2003) place it in the international context. Gauld *et al.* (2006) and Wagstaff (2007) present excellent comparisons of Asian health systems, including Japan, Singapore, South Korea and Taiwan, while Blank and Merrick (2005) specifically examine end-of-life policies in 12 countries. Ranade (1998), Callahan and Wasunna (2006) and Harrison (2004) offer valuable comparative analyses of the role of markets. Scott (2001) compares private and public roles in health systems, while Thomson *et al.* (2009) focus on the international experience with private insurance and medical savings accounts across 20 countries. Lewis (2005) analyses health policy and politics in Australia, the Netherlands and the UK. Behan (2006) explores American health care policy failure by looking at the policies of Canada and Australia and provides a systematic comparison of these three countries while Lee *et al.* (2002) explore the global dimensions of health policy. For a look at how health care in developing countries differs from the countries analysed here, see Green (2007) and Mills *et al.* (2001). Green *et al.* (2009) offer a valuable overview of ethical issues raised by the globalization of health care.

2 The context of health care

There are many valuable resources on the context of health care for our countries. The Guide to Websites contains the most useful current data as well as contextual information. For Australia, the key books are Duckett (2004a), Dugdale (2008) and Palmer and Short (2000). A very useful contextual book on New Zealand health care is Davis and Dew (2000), while Blank (1994), Davis and Ashton (2001) and Gauld (2001) provide good overviews of the New Zealand health care system. There are numerous books on US society as it relates to health policy including an excellent historical perspective in Weissert and Weissert (2002). For a good analysis of the US legal context see Sage and Kersh (2006) and for one of the best of many books on recent reforms in the USA see Jacobs and Skocpol (2010). Also, valuable insights into the unique US value context are found in Musgrave (2006), Kleinke (2001) and Blank (1997). Still an excellent source on Japanese culture and health care is Ohnuki-Tiernev (1984). Other books on Japanese health policy and society include Campbell and Ikegami (2008), Powell and Anesaki (2011) and Feldman (2000) while Tatara and Okamoto (2009) provide a very comprehensive and current overview of Japan's health care system. Ham (2001) provides a useful article on values and health policy in Singapore and the work of Haseltine (2012) and Lim (2004) are most helpful in understanding the Singapore system. Some of the essays in Shih *et al.* (2009) are useful for understanding the transformation of Taiwan culture as a context for health policy. Klein (2001) provides a detailed analysis of the politics of the British NHS since it was established, while Ham (2009) offers excellent analysis of more recent health policy in the UK. Twaddle (1999) focuses on policies of health reform in Sweden. Marmot and Wilkinson (1999) offer a valuable review of the social determinants of health across countries and Kawachi *et al.* (1999) delve more deeply into the relationship between inequality and poor health.

3 Funding, provision and governance

Suggestions for further reading on the funding, provision and governance of health care must necessarily be highly selective. Scott (2001) examines public and private sector roles in health care funding, provision and regulation, drawing on the experiences of Australia, Canada, Germany, the Netherlands, New Zealand, the UK and the USA. Thomson *et al.* (2011) offer an excellent summary of health care systems of a variety of countries, including many of those in this book. The Marmor *et al.* (2009b) edited book includes chapters on health care regulation, financing and delivery across countries, while Okma *et al.* (2010)

analyse the health reform experiences of Chile, Israel, Singapore, Switzerland, Taiwan and the Netherlands and describe current provisions for funding, contracting and payment, ownership and governance of these health care systems. Verspohl (2012) specifically focuses on the introduction of market mechanisms in Germany, the Netherlands and Sweden, whereas Rothgang *et al.* (2010) examine the changing role of the state. Henderson and Peterson (2002) explore the diverse meanings and applications of the term 'consumer' in the health systems of Australia, the UK and Canada. The edited volumes by Altenstetter and Björkman (1997), Ham (1997a), Mossialos and Le Grand (1999) and Ranade (1998) together with the special issues of the *Journal of Health Politics, Policy and Law* (2005, volume 20, numbers 1–2) and *Health Economics, Policy and Law* (2012, volume 7, number 1) contain chapters on European countries, focusing on health policy from the perspective of reform, while Mladovsky *et al.* (2012) are specifically concerned with health policy responses to the financial crisis. As a complement, the reports by the European Observatory offer detailed overviews of health systems in Britain (Boyle, 2011), Germany (Busse and Riesberg, 2004), the Netherlands (Schäfer *et al.*, 2010) and Sweden (Anell *et al.*, 2012). For the Netherlands see Okma (2001) and for health reform in the UK see Harrison and McDonald (2008) and Hunter (2008). Davis and Ashton (2001) provide a detailed account of New Zealand health reforms while Ashton (2005) provides a useful summary of recent changes in funding. A good general work on Australia is Palmer and Short (2000), while Dugdale (2008) provides a comprehensive introduction to health policy in that country. Among the countless books on US health policy are Barr (2011), Porter and Teisberg (2006), Musgrave (2006) and Starr (2011). The publication on affordable health care published by the Singapore Ministry of Health (1995) is invaluable in explaining its unique system. For good summaries of the Japanese health care system, see Campbell and Ikegami (2008), Imai and Fushimi (2012) and especially the Japan Ministry of Health, Labour and Welfare (2004). For those with a special interest in Asia, Kwon (2011) examines the major elements of health care financing of 26 South Pacific and Asian countries.

4 Setting priorities and allocating resources

Twaddle (2002) looks at market-oriented health care reforms in numerous countries and analyses the recent concern with the efficiency of medical care while Jacobs *et al.* (2006) examine the pursuit of efficiency across health systems and the techniques available to measure it. General books on rationing medicine include Wütscher *et al.* (2010), Syrett

(2008) and Ubel (2001), while Sauerland (2009) specifically focuses on issues of quality assurance in Germany. Locock (2000) deals with rationing in Britain and Lamm and Blank (2007) in the USA. Coulter and Ham (2000) and Ham and Robert (2003) provide very useful comparative analyses of rationing and argue it is a global issue, whereas Williams *et al.* (2011) and Thomson and Dixon (2006) specifically focuses on priority setting and choice in health care respectively. Sabik and Lie (2008) offer a good overview of priority setting in eight countries, whereas the volumes by Garrido *et al.* (2008a) and Schlander (2010) specifically look at health technology assessment. Ranade's (1998) and Harrison's (2004) comparative analyses of health care markets are a good introduction to this topic. Ikegami and Campbell (1999) provide an important analysis of cost containment in Japan, and Campbell and Ikegami (2008) extend this analysis to priority setting. More technical books on health allocation techniques include Drummond *et al.* (2005) and McKie *et al.* (1998). McIntosh *et al.* (2010) offer a good introduction to cost–benefit analysis in health care and Morris *et al.* (2012) to economic analyses.

5 The medical profession

Johnson (1995) and Light (1995) provide useful introductions to the conceptual issues surrounding doctors and health policy, as do Moran and Wood (1993) and Moran (1999) in their comparative analyses of Britain, Germany and the USA. The edited collection by Bovens *et al.* (2001) contains chapters on recent medical reform in our European countries, whereas the special issue edited by Burau (2009) focuses on reforms of the governance of medical performance. Harrison (2001) and Harrison *et al.* (2002) have written widely about doctors in Britain, whereas Garpenby (1997, 1999, 2001) has focused on Sweden. Allsop and Saks (2003) offer a critical perspective on regulation of the medical profession in the UK. Yoshikawa *et al.* (1996) provide good coverage of the medical profession in Japan. A good introduction to the medical profession in the USA is provided by Badasch (1993), while Birenbaum (2002) looks at the impact of managed care on US doctors. Judson and Harrison (2012) analyse the legal and ethical issues that all health care professionals face.

6 Beyond the hospital: health care in the home

Among the few comparative works that focus specifically on home care are Burau *et al.* (2007) and Doyle and Timonen (2007). In addition,

Alber and Kohler (2006), Anttonen *et al.* (2003a) and Tester (1998) offer more general introductions to key issues and concepts for comparing home care. Glendinning (1998), Hutten and Kerkstra (1996) and Tester (1996) include useful overviews of our European countries, whereas Duff (2001) and OECD (2005b, 2011b) adopt a broader international perspective. Ranci and Pavolini (2013) analyse current reforms and Lundsgaard (2004) focuses on payments of informal carers. More specific country perspectives include works by Campbell and Morgan (2005) on Germany and the USA, Theobald (2012) and Rothgang (2010) on Germany, Schut and Berg (2010) on the Netherlands, Ashton (2000) and Davey and Keeling (2004) on New Zealand, Comas-Herrera *et al.* (2010) and Glendinning (2013) on Britain and Meagher and Szebehely (2013) and Rauch (2006) on Sweden. Campbell and Ikegami (2003), Izuhara (2003), Fukuda *et al.* (2008) and Noguchi and Shimizutani (2005) provide a useful range of perspectives on home care policy in Japan, while Reisman (2009) analyses the challenges of the ageing Singapore population. Watson and Mears' (1999) book on women and care of the elderly is a good overview of the social issues surrounding home care in Australia. The encyclopaedia of home care for the elderly by Romaine-Davis *et al.* (1995) is a valuable sourcebook while Kitchener *et al.* (2007) and Centers for Medicare and Medicaid Services (2008, 2009a) review home and community-based services in the USA. Marrelli (2011) is a useful handbook of home health standards and documentation guidelines.

7 Public health

Since public health comprises such a broad range of areas, many of which fall outside the scope of health care, the resources here are expansive. Among the most helpful recent general works on public health per se are Schneider (2012), Merson *et al.* (2011), Henderson *et al.* (2001) and Wallace (2007). For public health nursing, see Stanhope and Lancaster (2011). Dawson and Verweij (2007) offer constructive insights on the ethical aspects of prevention and public health, while Levy and Sidel (2009) look at social justice and public health. Bennett *et al.* (2010) look at the problems of communicating risk to the public. One of the best general books on health promotion is DiClemente *et al.* (2002). For a comprehensive guide to the frameworks, theories and methods used to evaluate health promotion programmes see Valente (2002). For a good analysis of occupational health and safety see Tompa *et al.* (2008). More specific country perspectives on public health include books on Europe by Greer and Kurzer (2012), the USA by Milio (2000) and Turnock (2011), Australia by Leeder (1999) and Hancock (1999), Britain by

Baggott (2010) and Japan by Okamoto (2001). Reynolds (2011) looks at health and environmental law in Australia and New Zealand. Recent books on environmental and global health include Ball (2006), Skolnick (2011), Moeller (2011) and the huge edited collections of Merson *et al.* (2011) and Koop *et al.* (2002). For global health care governance, see Keefe and Zacher (2011), Davies (2010), Harman (2012a) and Crisp (2010). Moreover, Ferri *et al.* (2012) examine mortality among older people as a neglected topic in global health with a focus on Latin America, India and China. Taylor (2009) analyses the relationship between economic growth and equitable health within globalization, while Talbot and Verrinder (2010) address public health challenges emerging from the social and environmental consequences of globalization. Finally, Levy and Sidel (2007) document the public health consequences of war. Holtz (2012) offers a comprehensive set of articles on a variety of global health topics and perspectives, and Birn and Pillay (2009) synthesize historical, cultural, environmental, economic and political considerations to provide a comprehensive global overview of the many factors that determine the health of individuals and populations.

Guide to Websites

In the light of the growing importance of the Internet for transferring health policy information, below is a selection of health-related websites for our countries and for key international health organizations. Where possible, we have included English language sites; otherwise an English option is often available. This list of websites is also available online at www.palgrave.com/politics/blank, where it will be updated periodically.

Australia

Bureau of Statistics: www.abs.gov.au
Commonwealth Government: www.australia.gov.au
Department of Health and Ageing: www.health.gov.au
Department of Health, Australian Capital Territory: www.health.act.gov.au
Health Communication Network: www.hcn.net.au
Health Insurance Commission: www.hic.gov.au
Institute of Health and Welfare: www.aihw.gov.au
Public Health Association of Australia: www.phaa.net.au

Germany

Expert Panel for the Evaluation of Developments in the Health System (*Sachverständigenrat zur Begutachtung der Entwicklung im Gesundheitswesen*): www.svr-gesundheit.de/Startseite/Startseite.htm
Federal Association of Insurance Funds (*Spitzenverband Bund der Krankenkassen*): www.gkv-spitzenverband.de/Home.gkvnet
Federal Association of Insurance Fund Doctors (*Kassenärztliche Bundesvereinigung*): www.kbv.de
Federal Association of Welfare Organizations (*Bundesarbeits-gemeinschaft der Freien Wohlfahrtspflege*): www.bagfw.de
Federal Centre for Health Education (*Bundeszentrale für Gesundheitliche Aufklärung*): www.bzga.de/?uid=e02ec89ebda9ff1178fb4d37c1a668c0&id=home
Federal Chamber of Doctors (*Bundesärztekammer*): www.bundesaerztekammer.de/page.asp?his=4.3569

Federal Joint Committee (*Gemeinsamer Bundesausschuss*): www.g-ba.de/institution/sys/english/
Federal Ministry for Health (*Bundesministerium für Gesundheit*): www.bmgesundheit.de
Federal Ministry of Labour and Social Affairs (*Bundesministerium für Arbeit und Soziales*): www.bmas.bund.de
German Hospital Association (*Deutsche Krankenhaus Gesellschaft*): www.dkgev.de
Institute for Quality and Efficiency in Health Care (*Institut für Qualität und Wirtschaftlichkeit im Gesundheitswesen*): www.iqwig.de/index.2.en.html

Japan

Ministry of Health, Labour and Welfare: www.mhlw.go.jp/english

The Netherlands

Association of Dutch Municipalities (*Vereniging van Nederlandse Gemeenten*): www.vng.nl/smartsite.dws?ch=,DEF&id=41361
Association of Health Insurance Providers (*Zorgverzekeraars Nederland*): www.zn.nl
Association of Municipal Health Services (*Vereniging vor GGD'en*): www.ggd.nl/ggdnl/statpagina/show_pagina.asp?dmod=statpagina&paginanr=101&style=1&headerparam=1017
Central Agency for Health Care Tariffs (*College Tarieven Gezondheidszorg*): http://www.ctgzorg.nl/
Health Insurance Board *(College voor zorgverzekeringen)*: www.cvz.nl
Ministry for Health, Welfare and Sport (*Ministerie van Volksgezondheid, Welzijn en Sport*): www.minvws.nl/en/
Statistics Netherlands (*Centraal Bureau voor de Statistiek*): www.cbs.nl/en-GB/menu/home/default.htm?Languageswitch=on
Royal Dutch Medical Association (*Koninklijke Nederlansche Maatschappij tot bevordering der Geneeskunst*): http://knmg.artsennet.nl/

New Zealand

Maori Health Policy: www.nzgg.org.nz/maori_health.cfm
Ministry of Health: www.moh.govt.nz
New Zealand Health Information Service: www.nzhis.govt.nz

New Zealand Health Network: www.nzhealth.net.nz
New Zealand Health Technology Assessment: nzhta.chmeds.ac.nz

Singapore

Health Sciences Authority: www.hsa.gov.sg
Ministry of Health: www.moh.gov.sg
National Centre for Policy Analysis: www.ncpa.org

Sweden

Medical Responsibility Board (*Hälso- och sjukvårdens ansvarsnåmnd*): www.hsan.se/eng/start.asp
Ministry for Health and Social Affairs (*Socialdepartementet*): www.sweden.gov.se/sb/d/2061
National Board of Health and Welfare (*Socialstyrelsen*): www.socialstyrelsen.se/
National Institute for Public Health (*Statens Folkhälsoinstitutet*): www.fhi.se
Swedish Association of Local Authorities and Regions (*Sveriges Kommuner och Landsting*): http://www.skl.se/startpage_en.asp?C=6390
Swedish Medical Association (*Sveriges läkarförbund*): www.slf.se/templates/Page.aspx?id=2033

Taiwan

Bureau of National Health Insurance: http://www.nhi.gov.tw/english/index.asp
Department of Health: http://www.doh.gov.tw/EN2006/index_EN.aspx
National Health Research Institutes: http://english.nhri.org.tw/

UK

British Medical Association: www.bma.org.uk
Care Quality Commission: www.cqc.org.uk
Department of Health: www.doh.gov.uk
General Medical Council: www.gmc-uk.org
The King's Fund: www.kingsfund.org.uk
National Institute for Health and Clinical Excellence: www.nice.org.uk

NHS Confederation: www.nhsconfed.org
Office of Public Sector Information: www.opsi.gov.uk

USA

Agency for Healthcare Research and Quality: www.ahcpr.gov
American Hospital Association: www.aha.org
Center for Disease Control and Prevention: www.cdc.gov
Center for Medicare and Medicaid Services: www.medicare.gov
Department of Health and Human Services: www.hhs.gov
Department of Veterans Affairs: www.va.gov
Health Resources and Services Administration: www.hrsa.gov
Institute of Medicine: www.iom.edu
National Center for Health Statistics: www.cdc.gov/nchs
National Institutes of Health: www.nih.gov
National Library of Medicine/National Institutes of Health: www.nlm.nih.gov

International organizations

European Observatory on Health Care Systems and Policies: www.euro.who.int/observatory
Organisation for Economic Co-operation and Development: www.oecd.org
World Health Organization: www.who.org
World Health Organization, Regional Office for Europe: www.who.dk

Bibliography

Aaron, H.J. (2003) 'Should Public Policy Seek to Control the Growth of Health Care Spending?', *Health Affairs*, 8 January.

Abrams, J. (2002) 'Divided Congress Puts off Many Issues Until after the Election', *Associated Press*, 17 October.

Adams, P.J., J. Raeburn and K.A. de Silva (2009) 'Question of Balance: Prioritizing Public Health Responses to Harm from Gambling', *Addiction* 104: 688–91.

Alber, J. (1995) 'A Framework for the Comparative Study of Social Services', *Journal of European Social Policy* 5 (2): 131–49.

Alber, J. and U. Kohler (2006) *Health and Care in an Enlarged Europe*, Luxembourg, Official Publications of the European Communities, European Foundation for the Improvement Working Conditions, www.fr.eurofound.eu.int/publications/files/ EF03107EN.pdf, 10 July.

Alber, J. and M. Schöllkopf (1999) *Seniorenpolitik. Die soziale Lage älterer Menschen in Deutschland und Europa*. Berlin: Verlag Fakultas.

Allen, P. and P.R. Hommel (2006) 'What are "Third Way" Governments Learning? Health Care Consumers and Quality in England and Germany', *Health Policy* 76 (2): 202–12.

Allen, J. (2012) 'New York OKs nation's first ban on supersized sugary drinks', Reuters, 13 September.

Allsop, J. and M. Saks (2003) *Regulating the Health Profession*. London: Sage.

Altenstetter, C. and J.W. Björkman (eds) (1997) *Health Policy Reform, National Variations and Globalization*. London: Macmillan.

Altenstetter, C. and R. Busse (2005) 'Health Care Reform in Germany: Patchwork Change within Established Governance Structures', *Journal of Health Politics, Policy and Law* 30: 121–42.

Altman, S.H., C.P. Tompkins, E. Eilat and M.P.V. Glavin (2003) 'Escalating Health Care Spending: Is It Desirable or Inevitable?', *Health Affairs*, 8 January.

Amelung, V., S. Glied and A. Topan (2003) 'Health Care and the Labor Market: Learning from the German Experience', *Journal of Health Politics, Policy and Law* 28 (4): 693–714.

American College of Physicians (2008) 'Achieving a High-Performance Health Care System with Universal Access: What the United States Can Learn from Other Countries', *Annals of Internal Medicine* 148: 55–75.

American Hospital Association (2009) 'Fast Facts on US Hospitals', www.aha.org.

American Society for Bariatric Surgery (2006) 'Rationale for the Surgical Treatment of Morbid Obesity', http://asbs.org/html/rationalerationale.html.

Anderson, G.F., B.K. Frogner, R.A. Johns and U.E. Reinhardt (2006) 'Health Care Spending and Use of Information Technology in OECD Countries', *Health Affairs* 25 (3): 819–31.

Andeweg, R.B. and G.A. Irwin (2005) *Governance and Politics of the Netherlands*, 4th edn. Basingstoke: Palgrave Macmillan.

Andrews, M. (2010) 'Health Insurance Premiums and Other Costs Will Rise for Many Workers in 2011', *The Washington Post*, 11 October.

Anell, A. (2008) 'The Health System in Sweden', *Eurohealth* 14 (1): 10–11.

Anell, A. (2010) 'Choice and Privatisation in Swedish Primary Care', *Health Economics, Policy and Law* 6 (4): 549–69.

Anell, A. and P. Svarvar (1998) 'Health Care Reforms and Cost Containment in Sweden', in E. Mossialos and J. Le Grand (eds) *Health Care and Cost Containment in the European Union*. Alderhot: Ashgate.

Anell, A., A.H. Glengård and S. Merkur (2012) 'Sweden: Health System Review', *Health Systems in Transition* 14 (5): 1–144.

Angell, M. (1993) 'Privilege and Health – What is the Connection?', *New England Journal of Medicine* 329 (2): 126–7.

Anttonen, A., J. Baldock and J. Sipila (eds) (2003a) *The Young, the Old and the State. Social Care Systems in Five Industrial Nations*. Cheltenham: Edward Elgar.

Antonnen, A., J. Sipilä and J. Baldock (2003b) 'Patterns of Social Care in Five Industrial Societies: Explaining Diversity', in A. Antonnen, J. Baldock and J. Sipilä (eds) *The Young, the Old and the State. Social Care Systems in Five Industrial Nations*. Cheltenham: Edward Elgar.

Appleby, J. (1992) *Financing Health Care in the 1990s*. Buckingham: Open University Press.

Arts, W. and J. Glissen (2002) 'Three Worlds of Welfare Capitalism or More? A State-of-the-Art Report', *Journal of European Social Policy* 12: 137–48.

Asher, M., M. Ramesh and A. Maresso (2008) 'Medical Savings Accounts: Can They Improve Health System Performance in Europe?', *EuroObserver* 10 (4): 9–11.

Ashton, T. (2000) 'New Zealand: Long-Term Care in a Decade of Change', *Health Affairs* 19 (3): 72–81.

Ashton, T. (2005) 'Recent Developments in the Funding and Organisation of the New Zealand Health System', *Australia and New Zealand Health Policy* 2 (9), http://www.anzhealthpolicy.com/content/2/1/9.

Aslan, A. (2009) 'Convergence of Per Capita Health Care Expenditures in OECD Countries', *International Research Journal of Finance and Economics* 24: 48–53.

Association of American Medical Colleges (2008) 'Residences Revolve around Rural Care', *AAMC Reporter*, July.

Associated Press (2006) 'Singapore Takes Strict Steps against Obesity', www.msnbc.msn.com/id/6124732 (12 October).

Astolfi, R., L. Lorenzoni and J. Oderkirk (2012) 'Informing Policy Makers about Future Health Spending: A Comparative Analysis of Forecasting Methods in OECD Countries', *Health Policy* 107: 1–10.

Attia, N. and V. Bérenger (2009) 'European Integration and Social Convergence: A Qualitative Appraisal', *Panoeconomicus* 364 (4): 3–19.

Australian Department of Health and Ageing (2002) *A Summary of the National Program Guidelines for the Home and Community Care Program 2002*. Canberra: Commonwealth of Australia.

Australian Department of Health and Ageing (2003) 'Home and Community Care', www.health.gov.au/acc/hacc/index.htm.

Australian Department of Health and Ageing (2006a) 'Home and Community Care Programme', www.health.gov.au/acc/hacc/index.htm.

Australian Department of Health and Ageing (2006b) 'Evaluation of the Home and Community Care Program: National Standards Three Year Appraisal', http://www.health.gov.au/internet/wcms/publishing.nsf/Content/ageinghacc-haccevaluation-standards.htm.

Australian National Health and Hospital Reform Commission (2009) *A Healthier Future for All Australians*. http://www.health.gov.au/internet/nhhrc/publishing.nsf/Content/nhhrc-report.

Bache, I. and M. Flinders (2004) 'Multi-level Governance and British Politics', in I. Bache and M. Flinders (eds) *Multi-level Governance*. Oxford: Oxford University Press.

Badasch, S.A. (1993) *Introduction to Health Occupations*. New York: Regents/Prentice Hall.

Baggott, R. (2010) *Public Health: Policy and Politics*, 2nd edn. Basingstoke: Palgrave Macmillan.

Baggott, R. (2004) *Health and Health Care in Britain*, 3rd edn. Basingstoke: Palgrave Macmillan.

Baird, P. (1993) *Proceed with Care: Final Report of the Royal Commission on New Reproductive Technologies*. Ottawa: Minister of Government Services Canada.

Baker, L., H. Birnbaum, J. Geppert, D. Mishol and E. Moyneur (2003) 'The Relationship between Technology Availability and Health Care Spending', *Health Affairs* 5, November.

Baldock, J. (2003) 'Social Care in the United Kingdom: A Pattern of Discretionary Social Administration', in A. Anttonnen, J. Baldock and J. Sipilä (eds) *The Young, the Old and the State. Social Care Systems in Five Industrial Nations*. Cheltenham: Edward Elgar, pp. 109–41.

Ball, D. (2006) *Environmental Health Policy*. Buckingham: Open University Press.

Bandelow, N.C. (2007) 'Health Policy: Obstacles to Policy Convergence in Britain and Germany', *German Politics* 16 (1): 150–63.

Banks, J., M. Marmot, Z. Oldfield and J.P. Smith (2006) 'Disease and Disadvantage in the United States and in England', *Journal of the American Medical Association* 295: 2037–45.

Banta, D. (2002) 'The Development of Health Technology Assessment', *Health Policy* 63 (2): 121–32.

Bäringhausen, T. and R. Sauerborn (2003) 'One Hundred and Eighteen Years of the German Health Insurance System: Are there any Lessons for Middle- and Low-Income Countries?', *Social Science and Medicine* 54: 1559–87.

Barr, M.D. (2001) 'Medical Savings Accounts in Singapore: A Critical Inquiry', *Journal of Health Politics, Policy and Law* 26 (4): 709–26.

Barr, D.A. (2011) *Introduction to U.S. Health Policy: The Organization, Financing, and Delivery of Health Care in America*, 3rd edn. Baltimore: Johns Hopkins University Press.

Bartholomée, Y. and H. Maarse (2006) 'Health Insurance Reform in the Netherlands', *Eurohealth* 12 (2): 7–9.

Barwick, H. (1992) *The Impact of Economic and Social Factors on Health*. Wellington: Public Health Association of New Zealand.

BBC News (2002) 'Being Single Worse than Smoking', www.news.bbc.co.uk/1/hi/health/2195609.stm.

BBC News (2005) 'Obese Patients Denied Operations', http://news.bbc.co.uk/go/pr/fro/1/hi/england/suffolk/4462310.stm.

Begley, S. (2012) 'Fat and Getting Fatter: U.S. Obesity Rates to Soar by 2030', http://www.reuters.com/article/2012/09/18/health-obesity-us-dUSL1E8KHGGJ20120918.

Behan, P. (2006) *Solving the Health Care Problem: How Other Countries Have Succeeded and Why the United States Has Failed*. Albany: State University of New York Press.

Bejerot, E. and H. Hasselbladh (2011) 'Professional Autonomy and Pastoral Power: The Transformation of Quality Registers in Swedish Health Care', *Public Administration* 89 (4): 1604–21.

Belsky, L., R. Lie, A. Mattoo, E.J. Emanuel and G. Sreenivasan (2004) 'The General Agreements on Trade in Services: Implications for Health Policymakers', *Health Affairs* 23 (3): 137–45.

Bennett, P., K. Calman, S. Curtis and D. Smith (2010) *Risk Communication and Public Health*. New York: Oxford University Press.

Bennett, C.J. (1991) 'What is Policy Convergence and What Causes It?', *British Journal of Political Science* 21 (2): 215–33.

Bennett, B. and T. Carney (2010) 'Law, Ethics and Pandemic Preparedness: The Importance of Cross-Jurisdictional and Cross-Cultural Perspectives', *Australian and New Zealand Journal of Public Health* 34 (2): 106–17.

Bensoussan, A. and S.P. Myers (1996) *Towards a Safer Choice: The Practice of Traditional Chinese Medicine in Australia*. Sydney: University of Western Sydney Press.

Berg, M., K. Horstman, S. Plass and M. van Heusden (2000) 'Guidelines, Professionals and the Production of Objectivity: Standardisation and the Professionalism of Insurance Medicine', *Sociology of Health and Illness* 22 (6): 765–91.

Bergh, A. and T. Nilsson (2010) 'Good for Living? On the Relationship between Globalization and Life Expectancy', *World Development* 38 (9): 1191–203.

Berk, M.L. and A.C. Monheit (2001) 'The Concentration of Health Care Expenditures Revisited', *Health Affairs* 20 (2): 9–18.

Bertelsmann Foundation (2003a) 'Diagnosis-Based Hospital Reimbursement', Japan Survey No. 1. Gütersloh: Bertelsmann Foundation, www.reformmonitor.org.

Bertelsmann Foundation (2003b) 'PHI Incentive Scheme', Australia Survey No. 1. Gütersloh: Bertelsmann Foundation, www.reformmonitor.org.

Bertelsmann Foundation (2004a) 'Medicare Safety Net', Australia Survey No. 4. Gütersloh: Bertelsmann Foundation, www.reformmonitor.org.

Bertelsmann Foundation (2004b) 'Graphic Health Warning on Cigarette Packs', Singapore Survey No. 4. Gütersloh: Bertelsmann Foundation, www.reformmonitor.org.

Bertelsmann Foundation (2004c) 'Australian Primary Care Collaborative Program', Australia Survey No. 4. Gütersloh: Bertelsmann Foundation, www.reformmonitor.org.

Bertelsmann Foundation (2005a) 'Global Budget', Singapore Survey No. 5. Gütersloh: Bertelsmann Foundation, www.reformmonitor.org.

Bertelsmann Foundation (2005b) 'Merger of Municipalities', Japan Survey No. 5. Gütersloh: Bertelsmann Foundation, www.reformmonitor.org.

Bertelsmann Foundation (2006) 'Liberalization of Medisave Use', Singapore Survey No. 7. Gütersloh: Bertelsmann Foundation, www.reformmonitor.org.

Bevan, G. and W. P. M. M. van den Ven (2010) 'Choice of Providers and Mutual Healthcare Purchasers. Can the English National Health Service Learn from the Dutch Reforms?', *Health Economics, Policy and Law* 5 (3): 343–63.

Birenbaum, A. (2002) *Wounded Profession: American Medicine Enters the Age of Managed Care*. Westport, CT: Praeger Press.

Birn, A.-E. and Y. Pillay (2009) *Textbook of International Health: Global Health in a Dynamic World*. New York: Oxford University Press.

Bitton, A. and J.G. Kahn (2003) 'Government Share of Health Care Expenditures', *Journal of the American Medical Association* 289 (9):1165.

Björkman, J.W. and K.G.H. Okma (1997) 'Restructuring Health Care Systems in the Netherlands: The Institutional Heritage of Dutch Health Policy Reforms', in C. Altenstetter and J.W. Björkman (eds) *Health Policy Reform, National Variations and Globalization*. London: Macmillan.

Blank, R.H. (1994) *New Zealand Health Policy: A Comparative Study*. Auckland: Oxford University Press.

Blank, R.H. (1997) *The Price of Life: The Future of American Health Care*. New York: Columbia University Press.

Blank, R.H. and V. Burau (2006) 'Setting Health Priorities across Nations: More Convergence than Divergence?', *Journal of Public Health Policy* 27 (3): 265–81.

Blank, R.H. and J.C. Merrick (eds) (2005) *End-of-Life Decision Making: A Cross-National Study*. Cambridge, MA: MIT Press.

Blendon, R.J., M. Kim and J.M. Benson (2001) 'The Public versus the World Health Organization on Health System Performance', *Health Affairs* 20 (3): 10–20.

Blendon, R.J., R. Leitman, R. Morrison and K. Donelan (1990) 'Satisfaction with Health Systems in Ten Nations', *Health Affairs* 9 (2): 188–9.

Blomgren, M. (2007) 'The Drive for Transparency: Organizational Field Transformations in Swedish Healthcare', *Public Administration* 85 (1): 67–82.

Blondel, Jean (1990) *Comparative Government: An Introduction*. Hemel Hempstead: Philip Allan.

Bodenheimer, T. (2005) 'High and Rising Health Care Costs. Part 2: Technologic Innovation', *Annals of Internal Medicine* 142 (11): 932–7.

Bodenheimer, T. and A. Fernandez (2005) 'High and Rising Health Care Costs. Part 4: Can Costs Be Controlled While Preserving Quality?', *Annals of Internal Medicine* 143 (1): 26–31.

Boom, H. v.d. (2008) *Home Nursing in Europe: Patterns of Professionalisation and Institutionalisation of Home Care and Family Care to Elderly People in Denmark, France, the Netherlands and Germany*. Amsterdam: Aksant.

Boonen, L.H.M. and F.T. Schut (2011) 'Preferred Providers and the Credible Commitment Problem in Health Insurance: First Experiences with the

Implementation of Managed Competition in the Dutch Health Care System', *Health Economics, Policy and Law* 6: 219–35.

Borgor, C., S. Smith, C. Truffer, S. Keehan, A. Sisko, J. Poisal and M.K. Clemens (2006) 'Health Spending Projections Through 2015: Changes on the Horizon', *Health Affairs* 25 (2): w61–w73.

Borland, R., L. Li, P. Driezen, N. Wilson, D. Hammond, M.E. Thompson, G.T. Fong, U. Mons, M.C. Willemsen, A. McNeill,, J.F. Thrasher and K.M. Cummings (2011) 'Cessation Assistance Reported by Smokers in 15 Countries Participating in the International Tobacco Control (ITC) Policy Evaluation Surveys', *Addiction* 107 (1): 197–205.add05

Bovens, M., P. t'Hart and B.G. Peters (eds) (2001) *Success and Failure in Public Governance. A Comparative Analysis*. Cheltenham: Edward Elgar.

Boxall, A.-M. and S.D. Short (2006) 'Political Economy and Population Health: Is Australia Exceptional?', *Australia and New Zealand Health Policy* 3 (6), doi:10.1186/1743-8462-3-6.

Boyle, S. (2011) United Kingdom (England). Health System Review, Health Systems in Transition, 13/1, Copenhagen: European Observatory on Health Systems and Policies.

Brabers, A.E.M., M. Reitsma-van Rooijen and J.D. de Jong (2012) 'The Dutch Health Insurance System: Mostly Competition on Price rather than Quality of Care', *European Observatory on Health Systems and Policies* 18 (1): 30–4.

Brenner, M.H. (2001) 'Unemployment, Employment Policy and the Public Health', paper presented at European Commission Expert Meeting on Unemployment and Health in Europe, Berlin, 6–7 July.

British Medical Association (2009) *The Human Cost of Alcohol Misuse: Doctors Speak Out*. Edinburgh: British Medical Association Scotland.

British United Provident Association (2002) 'Skin Cancer on the Rise', www.bupa.co.uk/health information/html/health news/250602skin.htm.

Brodhurst, S. and C. Glendinning (2001) 'The United Kingdom', in T. Blackmann, S. Brodhurst and J. Convery (eds) *Social Care and Social Exclusion: A Comparative Study of Older People's Care in Europe*. Basingstoke: Palgrave Macmillan.

Brownell, K.D., T. Farley, W.C. Willett, B.M. Popkin, F.J. Chaloupka, J.W. Thompson and D.S. Ludwig (2009) 'The Public Health and Economic Benefits of Taxing Sugar-Sweetened Beverages', *New England Journal of Medicine* 361: 1599–605.

Bulman, E. (2006) 'WHO: TB Poses Greatest Threat to Europe', Associated Press, 9 October.

Burau, V. (2001) 'Medical Reform in Germany: The 1993 Health Care Legislation as an Impromptu Success', in M. Bovens, P. t'Hart and B.G. Peters (eds) *Success and Failure in Public Governance: A Comparative Analysis*. Cheltenham: Edward Elgar.

Burau, V. and R.H. Blank (2006) 'Comparing Health Policy – An Assessment of Typologies of Health Systems', *Journal of Comparative Policy Analysis* 8 (1): 63–76.

Burau, V., L. Henriksson and S. Wrede (2004) 'Comparing Professional Groups in Health Care: Towards a Context Sensitive Analysis', *Knowledge, Work and Society* 2 (2): 49–68.

Burau, V. and T. Kröger (2004) 'Towards Local Comparisons of Community Care Governance: Exploring the Relationship between Policy and Politics', *Social Policy & Administration* 38 (7): 793–810.

Burau, V., H. Theobald and R.H. Blank (2007) *Governing Home Care: A Cross-National Comparison*. Cheltenham: Edward Elgar.

Burau, V. (2007a) 'Comparative Health Research', in M. Saks and J. Allsop (eds) *Researching Health*. London: Sage.

Burau, V. (2007b) 'The Complexity of Governance Change: Reforming the Governance of Medical Performance in Germany', *Health Economics, Policy and Law* 2 (4): 391–407.

Burau, V. (ed.) (2009) 'Governing Medical Performance: A Comparative Analysis of Pathways of Change', *Health Economics, Policy and Law* 4 (3): 265–382.

Burau, V., D. Wilsford and G. France (2009) 'Reforming Medical Governance in Europe. What is it about Institutions?', *Health Economic, Policy & Law* 4 (3): 265–82.

Burau, V. and L. Fenton (2009) 'How Health Care States Matter: Introducing Clinical Standards in Britain and Germany', *Journal of Health Organization and Management* 23 (3): 289–303.

Burau, V. (2012) 'Transforming Health Policy and Services: Challenges for Comparative Research', *Current Sociology* 60 (4): 569–78.

Burau, V. and E. Kuhlmann (2012) *Transnational Health Policy: Comparing Policy Transformations of the Global Primary Healthcare Agenda in England, Germany and Russia*, unpublished manuscript.

Bureau of National Health Insurance (BNHI) (2008) *National Health Insurance Statistics*, http://www.nhi.gov.tw/english/index.asp.

Bureau of National Health Insurance (BNHI) (2012) 'Statistics', http://www.nhi.gov.tw/English/webdata/webdata.aspx?menu=11&menu_id=296&WD_ID=296&webdata_id=4229

Burstrom, B. (2004) 'User Charges in Sweden', *Euro Observer* 6 (3): 5–6.

Busse, R. (1999) 'Priority-setting and Rationing in German Health Care', *Health Policy* 50: 71–90.

Busse, R. (2008) 'The Health System in Germany', *Eurohealth* 14 (1): 5–6.

Busse, R. and A. Riesberg (2004) *Health Systems in Transition: Germany*. Copenhagen: WHO Regional Office for Europe on behalf of the European Observatory on Health Care Systems.

Busse, R. and C. Howorth (1999) 'Cost Containment in Germany: Twenty Years' Experience', in E. Mossialos and J. Le Grand (eds) *Health Care and Cost Containment in the European Union*. Aldershot: Ashgate.

Butler, P. (2002) 'How Nice Works', *The Guardian*, 22 March.

Callahan, D. (1990) *What Kind of Life? The Limits of Medical Progress*. New York: Simon & Schuster.

Callahan, D. and A.A. Wasunna (2006) *Medicine and the Market: Equity v. Choice*. Baltimore: The Johns Hopkins University Press.

Campbell, J.C. and N. Ikegami (2003) 'Japan's Radical Reform of Long-Term Care', *Social Policy and Administration* 37 (1): 21–34.

Campbell, J.C. and N. Ikegami (2008) *The Art of Balance in Health Policy: Maintaining Japan's Low-Cost, Egalitarian System*. Cambridge: Cambridge University Press.

Campbell, A.L. and K.J. Morgan (2005) 'Federalism and the Politics of Old-Age Care in Germany and the United States', *Comparative Political Studies* 38 (8): 1–28.

Campillo-Artero, C. (2011) 'When Health Technologies Do Not Reach Their Effectiveness Potential: A Health Service Research Perspective', *Health Policy* 104 (1): 92–8.

Carrera, P.M., K.K. Siemens and J. Bridges (2008) 'Health Care Financing in Germany: The Case for Rethinking the Evolutionary Approach to Reforms', *Journal of Health Politics, Policy and Law* 33 (5): 979–1005.

Carvel, J. (2002a) 'Britons Say Non to C'est la Vie Philosophy', *The Guardian*, 16 October.

Carvel, J. (2002b) 'Homeless Suffer for Want of a GP', *The Guardian*, 9 December.

Casciani, D. (2002) 'Asylum Seeker Health Crisis in London', *BBC News*, 12 November, http://news.bbc.co.uk/1/hi/2453263.stm.

Castles, F.G. (1999) *Comparative Public Policy. Patterns of Post-war Transformation*. Cheltenham: Edward Elgar.

Cawley, J. (2007) 'The Cost-Effectiveness of Programs to Prevent or Reduce Obesity: The State of the Literature and a Future Research Agenda', *Archives of Pediatrics and Adolescent Medicine* 161: 611–14.

Center for the Evaluative Clinical Sciences (2008) *The Care of Patients with Severe Chronic Illness: An Online Report on the Medicare Program. The Dartmouth Atlas of Health Care*, http://www.dartmouthatlas.com, accessed 5 August 2008.

Centers for Disease Control and Prevention (CDC) (2007) *The State of Aging and Health in America*. Atlanta, GA: Centers for Disease Control and Prevention.

Centers for Medicare and Medicaid Services (2008) 'Home Health PPS', www.cms.hhs.gov/HomeHealthPPS/.

Centers for Medicare and Medicaid Services (2009a) 'Program of All-Inclusive Care for the Elderly (PACE)', www.cms.hhs.gov.

Centers for Medicare and Medicaid Services (2009b) 'Regulations and Guidance', www.cms.hhs.gov.

Centers for Medicare and Medicaid Services (2010) http://cciio.cms.gov /programs/marketreforms/prevention/index.html.

Chang, L. and J.-H. Hung (2008) 'The Effects of the Global Budget System on Cost Containment and the Quality of Care: Experience in Taiwan', *Health Services Management Research* 21: 106–16.

Chang, T., J. Liang and S. Ransom (2005) 'How Taiwan Does It: Seeing More Patients for Less', *Physician Executive* 31 (4): 38–42.

Charlie Rose–Peter Orszag Interview-November 3 (2009), http://www.charlierose.com/download/transcript/10697 (accessed 12 January 2012).

Chaudhry, B., J. Wang, S. Wu, M. Maglione, W. Mojica, E. Roth, S.C. Morton and P.G. Shekelle (2006) 'Systematic Review: Impact of Health Information Technology on Quality, Efficiency, and Costs of Medical Care', *Annals of Internal Medicine* 144 (10): 742–52.

Checkland, K. (2004) 'National Service Frameworks and UK General Practitioners: Street-Level Bureaucrats at Work?', *Sociology of Health and Illness* 26 (7): 951–75.

Chen, L.K., W. Yip, M.-C. Chang, H.-S. Lin, S.-D. Lee, Y.-L. Chiu and Y.-H. Lin (2007) 'The Effects of Taiwan's National Health Insurance on Access and Health Status of the Elderly', *Health Economics* 16 (3): 223–42.

Chen, Y.T., C.M. Huang, P.P. Huang and W.C. Chu (2008) 'Design a Wireless Radio Frequency Identification Based Intelligent Drug Preparation System', *Technology and Applications in Biomedicine* 30–1: 549–51.

Cheng, T.M. (2003) 'Taiwan's New National Health Insurance Program: Genesis and Experience So Far', *Health Affairs* 22: 61–76.

Cheng, S-H. and W-L. Chang (2007) 'Hospital Response to the Global Budget Program Implemented by Taiwan's National Health Insurance', iHEA 2007 6th World Congress: Explorations in Health Economics Paper. http://ssrn.com/abstract=992643.

Cheng, S.-H., Y.-J. Wei and H-J. Chang (2006) 'Quality Competition among Hospitals: The Effects of Perceived Quality and Perceived Expensiveness on Health Care Consumers', *American Journal of Medical Quality* 21 (1): 68–76.

Chernichovsky, D. (1995) 'Health System Reforms in Industrialized Democracies: An Emerging Paradigm', *The Milbank Quarterly* 73 (3): 339–56.

Chi, C., J.L. Lee and R. Schoon (2012) 'Assessing Health Information Technology in a National Health Care System: An Example from Taiwan', *Advances in Health Care Management* 12: 75–109.

Chiu, Y.-C., K.C. Smith and L. Morlock (2007) 'Gifts, Bribes and Solicitations: Print Media and the Social Construction of Informal Payments to Doctors in Taiwan', *Social Science & Medicine* 64 (3): 521–30.

Churchill, L.R. (2005) 'Age-rationing in Health Care: Flawed Policy, Personal Virtue', *Health Care Analysis* 13 (2): 137–46.

Ciarini, A. (2008) 'Family, Market and Voluntary Action in the Regulation of the "Care System": A Comparison between Italy and Sweden', *World Political Science Review* 4 (1), Doi: 10.2202/1935-6226.1043.

Clasen, J. (ed.) (1999) *Comparative Social Policy*. Oxford: Blackwell.

Clinical Advisory Board (2001) *Elevating the Standard of Critical Care*. Washington, DC: The Advisory Board Company.

Collier, D. and J.E. Mahon, Jr. (1993) 'Conceptual "Stretching" Revisited: Adapting Categories in Comparative Analysis', *American Political Science Review* 87: 845–55.

Collier, D. and S. Levitsky (1997) 'Democracy with Adjectives: Conceptual Innovation in Comparative Research', *World Politics* 49: 430–51.

Comas-Herrera, A., R. Wittenberg and L. Pickard (2010) 'The Long Road to Universalism? Recent Developments in the Financing of Long-term Care in England', *Social Policy & Administration* 44 (4): 375–91.

Commonwealth Fund Commission on a High Performance Health System (2009) *The Path to a High Performance U.S. Health System: A 2020 Vision and the Policies to Pave the Way*. New York: The Commonwealth Fund.

Conceição, C. and M. McCarthy (2011) 'Public Health Research Systems in the European Union', *Health Research Policy and Systems* 9: 38–53.

Conference of the Parties to the WHO FCTC (2008) *Guidelines for Implementation of Article 11 of the WHO Framework Convention on*

Tobacco Control on Packaging and Labelling of Tobacco Products, Decision FCTC/COP3 (10) (November 2008).

Coolen, J. and S. Weekers (1998) Long-Term Care in the Netherlands: Public Funding and Private Provision within a Universalistic Welfare State', in C. Glendinning (ed.) *Rights and Realities. Comparing New Developments in Long-term Care for Older People.* Bristol: Policy Press.

Cooper, Z., F.P. Rivara, J. Wang and E.J. MacKenzie (2012) 'Racial Disparities in Intensity of Care at the End-of-Life: Are Trauma Patients the Same as the Rest?', *Journal of Health Care for the Poor and Underserved* 23 (2): 857–74.

Cortez, N. (2008a) 'International Health Care Convergence: The Benefits and Burdens of Market-Driven Standardization', *Wisconsin International Law Journal* 26 (3): 646–704.

Cortez, N. (2008b) 'Patients without Borders: The Emerging Global Market for Patients and the Evolution of Modern Health Care', *Indiana Law Journal* 83: 71–132.

Costa-Font, J. and M.G. Toyama (2011) 'Does Cost Sharing Really Reduce Inappropriate Prescriptions among the Elderly?' *Health Policy* 101 (2): 195–208.

Costa-Font, J. and C. Hernández-Quevedo (2012) 'Measuring Inequalities in Health: What do We Know? What do We Need to Know?', *Health Policy* 106: 195–206.

Coulter, A. and C. Ham (eds) (2000) *The Global Challenge of Health Care Rationing.* Buckingham: Open University Press.

Creagh, H. (2008) 'Strategy to Stem the Rise of Obesity Criticised as "Feeble Fantasy"', *British Medical Journal* 336: 240–1.

Crisp, A. (2010) *Turning the World Upside Down: The Search for Global Health in the 21st Century.* London: CRC Press.

Cubit, K.A. and C. Meyer (2011) 'Aging in Australia', *Gerontologist* 51 (5): 583–9.

Cuellar, A.E. and J.M. Wiener (2000) 'Can Social Insurance for Long-term Care Work? The Experience of Germany', *Health Affairs* 19 (3): 8–25.

Culyer, A.J., J.E. Brazier and O. O'Donnell (1988) *Organising Health Service Provision: Drawing on Experience.* London: Institute of Health Services Management.

Daatland, S.O. (1996) 'Adapting the "Scandinavian Model" of Care for Elderly People', in OECD (ed.) *Caring for Frail Elderly People: Policies in Evolution.* Social Policy Studies no. 19. Paris: OECD.

Dalton, R.J. (2008) 'Politics in Germany', in G.A. Almond, G.B. Powell, R.J. Dalton and K. Strøm (eds) *Comparative Politics Today*, 9th edn. New York: Pearson Longman.

Davey, J.A. and S. Keeling (2004) 'Combining Work and Eldercare: A Neglected Work-Life Balance Issue', *Labour, Employment and Work in New Zealand.* Wellington: Victoria University Institute for Research on Ageing.

Davies, G.P., W. Hu, J. McDonald, J. Furier, E. Harris and M. Harris (2006) 'Developments in Australian General Practice 2000–2002: What Did These Contribute to a Well Functioning and Comprehensive Primary Health Care System?', *Australia and New Zealand Health Policy* 3 (1), http://www.anzhealthpolicy.com/content/3/1/1.

Davies, S.E. (2010) *Global Politics of Health*. Cambridge. UK: Polity Press.

Davis, P. and T. Ashton (eds) (2001) *Health and Public Policy in New Zealand*. Auckland: Oxford University Press.

Davis, P. and K. Dew (eds) (2000) *Health and Society in Aotearoa New Zealand*. Auckland: Oxford University Press.

Davis, K., M.M. Doty, K. Shea and K. Stremikis (2009) 'Health Information Technology and Physician Perceptions of Quality of Care and Satisfaction', *Health Policy* 90 (2–3): 239–46.

Davis, C. and J.C. Carter (2009) 'Compulsive Overeating as an Addiction Disorder: A Review of Theory and Evidence', *Appetite* 53: 1–8.

Day, S.E., K. Alford, D. Dunt, S. Peacock, L. Gurrin and D. Voaklander (2005) 'Strengthening Medicare', *Australia and New Zealand Health Policy* 2 (18), http://www.anzhealthpolicy.com/content/2/1/18.

Dawson, A. and M. Verweij (eds) (2007) *Ethics, Prevention, and Public Health*. New York: Oxford University Press.

De Ferranti, D. (1985) *Paying for Health Services in Developing Countries: An Overview*. Washington, DC: World Bank Staff Working Paper 721.

de Silva-Sanigorski, A., L. Prosser, L. Carpenter, S. Honisett, L. Gibbs, M. Moodie, L. Sheppard, B. Swinburn and E. Waters (2010) 'Evaluation of the Childhood Obesity Prevention Program Kids – "Go for your life"', *BMC Public Health* 10: 288, doi:10.1186/1471-2458-10-288.

Deleon, P. and P. Resnick-Terry (1999) 'Comparative Policy Analysis: Déjà vu all over Again?', *Comparative Policy Analysis* 1: 9–22.

Denis, J.-L. and P.-G. Forest (2012) 'Real Reform Begins Within: An Organizational Approach to Health Care Reform', *Journal of Health Politics, Policy and Law* 37 (4): 633–45.

Dent, M. (2003) *Remodelling Hospitals and Health Professions in Europe. Medicine, Nursing and the State*. Basingstoke: Palgrave Macmillan.

Department of Health and Ageing (2008) *Report on the Operation of the Aged Care Act 1997 – 1 July 2007 to 30 June 2008*. Canberra: Commonwealth of Australia.

Department of Health (2008) *Departmental Report. The Health and Personal Social Services Programmes*. London: Her Majesty's Stationery Office.

Department of Health (2009) *Review Body on Doctors' and Dentists' Remuneration*. Thirty-eighth report 2009 (Cm 7579). London: Her Majesty's Stationery Office.

Department of Health (2012a) *Clinically-led Commissioning – The Health and Social Care Act 2012*. Factsheet B1. London: Department of Health, www.dh.gov/healthandsocialcarevill (18 December 2012).

Department of Health (2012b) *Greater Accountability Locally and Nationally – The Health and Social Care Act 2012. Factsheet B5*. London: Department of Health, www.dh.gov.uk/healthandsocialcarebill (18 December 2012).

Department of Health (2012c) *Overview of Health and Care Structures – The Health and Social Care Act 2012. Factsheet A3*. London: Department of Health, www.dh.gov.uk/healthandsocialcarebill (18 December 2012).

Department of Health (2012d) *Provider Regulation to Support Innovative and Efficient Services – The Health and Social Care Act*. Factsheet B2. London: Department of Health, www.dh.gov/healthandsocialcarevill (18 December 2012).

Department of Health (2012e) *The Health and Social Care Act 2012*. Factsheet A1. London: Department of Health, www.dh.gov/healthandsocialcarevill (18 December 2012).

DeVoe, J.E. (2001) *The Politics of Health Care Reform: A Comparative Study of National Health Insurance in Britain and Australia*. Kensington, NSW: School of Health Services Management.

DiClemente, R.J., R.A. Crosby and M.C. Kegler (2002) *Emerging Theories in Health Promotion Practice and Research: Strategies for Improving Public Health*. San Francisco: Jossey-Bass.

Derrett, S., T.H. Bevin, P. Herbison and C. Paul (2009) 'Access to Elective Surgery in New Zealand: Considering Equity and the Private and Public Mix', *International Journal of Health Planning and Management* 24: 147–60.

Dixon, J. (2012) 'Reform and the National Health Service', *The Political Quarterly* 83 (2): 143–52.

Dobbin, F., B.A. Simmons and G. Garrett (2007) 'The Global Diffusion of Public Policies: Social Construction, Coercion, Competition, or Learning', *Annual Review of Sociology* 33: 449–72.

Docteur, E., H. Suppanz and J. Woo (2003) 'The US Health System: An Assessment and Prospective Directions for Reform', *Economics Department Working Papers* No. 350, www.oecd.org/eco.

Döhler, M. (1991) 'Policy Networks, Opportunity Structures and Neo-conservative Reform Strategies in Health Policy', in B. Marin and R. Mayntz (eds) *Policy Networks: Empirical Evidence and Theoretical Considerations*. Boulder, CO: Westview Press.

Donato, R. and L. Segal (2010) 'The Economics of Primary Healthcare Reform in Australia – Towards Single Fundholding through Development of Primary Care Organisations', *Australia and New Zealand Journal of Public Health* 34 (6): 613–19.

Doorslaer, E.V., P. Clarke, E. Savage and J. Hall (2008) 'Horizontal Inequities in Australia's Mixed Public/Private Health Care System', *Health Policy* 86: 97–108.

Dovey, S., M. Tilyard, W. Cunningham and M. Williamson (2011) 'Public and Private Funding of General Practice Services for Children and Adolescents in New Zealand', *Health Policy* 103 (1): 24–30.

Doyle, M. and V. Timonen (2007) *Home Care for Ageing Populations: A Comparative Analysis of Domiciliary Care in Denmark, the United States and Germany*. Cheltenham: Edward Elgar.

Dragon, N. (2008) 'Health Reform: Finding the Way', *Australian Nursing Journal* 15 (7): 20–3.

Drake, D.F. (1994) *Reforming the Health Care Market*. Washington, DC: Georgetown University Press.

Drummond, M.F., M.J. Sculpher, G.W. Torrance and B.J. O'Brien (2005) *Methods for the Economic Evaluation of Health Care Programmes*. New York: Oxford University Press.

Duckett, S.J. (2004a) *The Australian Health Care System,* 2nd edn. Melbourne: Oxford University Press.

Duckett, S.J. (2004b) 'The Australian Health Care Agreements, 2003–2008',

Australia and New Zealand Health Policy 1 (5), http://www.anzhealthpolicy.com/content/1/1/5.

Duff, J. (2001) 'Financing to Foster Community Health Care: A Comparative Analysis of Singapore, Europe, North America, and Australia', *Current Sociology* 49 (3): 135–54.

Dugdale, P. (2008) *Doing Health Policy in Australia*. Sydney: Allen and Unwin.

Dunne, R. (2002) 'Analysis: GPs and Asylum Seekers', BBC News, 7 November, http://news.bbc.co.uk/1/hi/health/2414887.stm.

Dwyer, J.M. (2004) 'Australian Health System Restructuring: What Problem Is Being Solved?', *Australia and New Zealand Health Policy,* 19 November: 1–6.

Ebi, K. (2011) 'Climate Change and Health Risks: Assessing and Responding to Them through "Adaptive Management"', *Health Affairs* 30 (5): 924–30.

Eckerberg, K., B. Fordberg and P. Wickenberg (1998) 'Sweden: Setting the Pace with Pioneers, Municipalities and Schools', in W.M. Lafferty and K. Eckerberg (eds) *From the Earth Summit to Local Agenda 21*. London: Earthscan.

Ehrlich, C., E. Kendall, H. Muenchberger and K. Armstrong (2009) 'Coordinated Care: What Does That Really Mean?', *Health and Social Care in the Community* 44 (2): 147–52.

Eichler, M. and B. Pfau-Effinger (2009) 'The "Consumist Principle" in the Care of Elderly People: Free Choice and Actual Choice in the German Welfare State', *Social Policy & Administration* 43 (6): 617–33.

Elston, M.A. (1991) 'The Politics of Professional Power: Medicine in a Changing Health Service', in J. Gabe, M. Calnan and M. Bury (eds) *The Sociology of the Health Service*. London: Routledge.

Epstein, P.R. (2000) 'Is Global Warming Harmful to Health?', *Scientific American,* 20 August.

Esping-Andersen, G. (1990) *The Three Worlds of Welfare Capitalism*. Oxford: Polity Press.

Ettelt, S., M. Fazekas, N. Mays and E. Nolte (2012) 'Assessing Health Care Planning: A Framework-led Comparison of Germany and New Zealand', *Health Policy* 106: 50–9.

European Observatory on Health Care Systems (1999) *Health Care Systems in Transition: United Kingdom*. Copenhagen: European Observatory on Health Care Systems.

Eurostat (1999) '"Profound Consequences" as EU Grows Older', *News Release* no. 75/99, 29 July.

Evans, J.G. (1997) 'Rationing Health Care by Age: The Case Against', *British Journal of Medicine* 314: 822–6.

Evers, A. and I. Svetlik (eds) (1993) *Balancing Pluralism. New Welfare Mixes in Care for the Elderly*. Aldershot: Avebury.

Executive Office of the President (2010) *Report to the President: Realizing the Full Potential of Information Technology to Improve Healthcare for Americans: The Path Forward*. Washington, DC: President's Council of Advisors on Science and Technology.

Exter, A. den, H. Hermans, M. Dosljak and R. Busse (2004) *Health Care*

Systems in Transition: Netherlands. Copenhagen: WHO Regional Office for Europe on Behalf of the European Observatory on Health Care Systems.

Farquharson, K. (2003) 'Influencing Policy Transnationally: Pro- and Anti-tobacco Global Advocacy Networks', *Australian Journal of Public Administration* 62 (4): 80–92.

FarmOnline (2009) '$120,000 Lure for Doctors to go Bush'. Canberra: National News Bureau.

Fattore, G. (1999) 'Cost Containment and Health Care Reforms in the British NHS', in E. Mossialos and J. Le Grand (eds) *Health Care and Cost Containment in the European Union*. Aldershot: Ashgate.

Feldman, E.A. (2000) *The Ritual of Rights in Japan: Law, Society, and Health Policy*. Cambridge: Cambridge University Press.

Fenton, L. and B. Salter (2009) 'Competition and Compromise in Negotiating the New Governance of Medical Performance: The Clinical Governance and Revalidation Policies in the UK', *Health Economics, Policy and Law* 4 (3): 283–304.

Ferguson, J. (2005) 'WHO Says Skin Cancer Incidence Is Rising', *Journal Watch*, http://dermatology.jwatch.org/cgi/content/full/2005/426/1#primary content.

Ferri, C.P., D. Acosta, M. Guerra, Y. Huang, J.J. Llibre-Rodriguez, A. Salas, A.L. Sosa, J.D. Williams, C. Gaona, Z. Liu, L. Noriega-Fernandez and M.J. Prince (2012) 'Socioeconomic Factors and All Cause and Cause-Specific Mortality among Older People in Latin America, India, and China: A Population-Based Cohort Study', *PLoS Med* (2):e1001179.doi:10.1371/journal.pmed.1001179.

Field, M.G. (1999) 'Comparative Health Systems and the Convergence Hypothesis: The Dialectics of Universalism and Particularism', in F.D. Powell and A.F. Wessen (eds) *Health Care Systems in Transition: An International Perspective*. Thousand Oaks, CA: Sage.

Fielding, J.E., S. Teutsch and L. Breslow (2010) 'A Framework for Public Health in the United States', *Public Health Reviews* 32 (1): 174–89.

Fielding, J.E., S. Teutsch and H. Koh (2012) 'Health Reform and Healthy People Initiative', *American Journal of Public Health* 102 (1): 30–3.

Finkelstein, E.A., J.G. Trogdon, J.W. Cohen and W. Dietz (2009) 'Annual Medical Spending Attributable to Obesity: Payer- and Service-Specific Estimates', *Health Affairs* 28 (5): w822–w831.

Fleck, L.M. (2002) 'Rationing: Don't Give Up: It's Not Only Necessary, but Possible, if the Public Can Be Educated', *The Hastings Center Report* 32 (2): 35–8.

Ford, E.S., U.A. Ajani, J.B. Croft, J. Critchley, D.R. Labarthe, T.E. Kottle, W.H. Giles and S. Capewell. (2007) 'Explaining the Decrease in U.S. Deaths from Coronary Disease, 1980–2000', *New England Journal of Medicine* 356: 2388–98.

Foster, D. (2001) 'Frequent Flyer Racks up Big Bill', *Detroit News*, 10 October.

Foundation for AIDS Research (2012), http://www.amfar.org/About_HIV_and_AIDS/Facts_and_Stats/Statistics__Worldwide/

Franck, M.J. (1996) *Against the Imperial Judiciary. The Supreme Court vs. the Sovereignty of the People*. Lawrence: University of Kansas Press.

Fredriksson, M. and U. Winblad (2008) 'Consequences of a Decentralized Healthcare Governance Model: Measuring Regional Authority Support for Patient Choice in Sweden', *Social Science and Medicine* 67 (2): 271–9.

Fredriksson, M., P. Blomqvist and U. Winblad (2012) 'Conflict and Compliance in Swedish Health Care Governance: Soft Law in the "Shadow of Hierarchy"', *Scandinavian Political Studies* 35 (1): 48–70.

Freeman, B., S. Chapman and M. Rimmer (2008) 'The Case for Plain Packaging of Tobacco Products', *Addiction* 103: 580–90.

Freeman, R. (1998) 'Competition in Context: The Politics of Health Care Reform in Europe', *International Journal of Quality in Health Care* 10 (5): 395–401.

Freeman, R. (2000) *The Politics of Health in Europe*. Manchester: Manchester University Press.

Freeman, R. (2005) 'Learning in Health Policy', Text of a Presentation to the Social Policy Forum, Bogazici University, Istanbul, 17–18 June, 2005, unpublished manuscript, University of Edinburgh, http://www.pol.ed.ac.uk/freeman.

Freeman, R. (2006) 'Of Transfers, Transplants and Translations: How Health Policy Makers Learn from Abroad', Presentation at the Dansk Forum for Sundhedstjenesteforskning (Danish Forum for Health Services Research), University of Aarhus, Denmark, 28 November.

Freeman, R. and J. Clasen (1994) 'The German Social State: An Introduction', in J. Clasen and R. Freeman (eds) *Social Policy in Germany*. Hemel Hempstead: Harvester Wheatsheaf.

Freeman, R. and M. Ruskin (1999) 'Introduction: Welfare, Culture and Europe', in P. Chamberlayne *et al.* (eds) *Welfare and Culture in Europe: Towards a New Paradigm in Social Policy*. London: Jessica Kingsley.

Freeman, R. and L. Frisina (2012) 'Health Care Systems and the Problem of Classification', *Journal of Comparative Policy Analysis: Research and Practice* 12 (1–2): 163–78.

Freidson, E. (1994) *Professionalism Reborn: Theory, Prophecy and Policy*. Cambridge: Polity.

Fry, C.L. (2010) 'Critical Questions We Should Ask in a Changing Australian Preventative Health Landscape: Competing Interests, Intervention Limits and Permissible Health Identities', *Health Promotion Journal of Australia* 21 (3): 170–5.

Fuchs, V.R. (1994) 'The Clinton Plan: A Researcher Examines Reform', *Health Affairs* 13 (2): 102–14.

Fuchs, V.R. (2004) 'Reflections on the Socio-economic Correlates of Health', *Journal of Health Economics* 23 (4): 653–61.

Fuchs, V.R. (2005) 'Health Care Expenditures Reexamined', *Annals of Internal Medicine* 143 (1): 76–8.

Fuchs, V.R. (2007) 'What are the Prospects for Enduring Comprehensive Health Reform?', *Health Affairs* 26 (6): 1542–4.

Fujisawa, R. and F. Colombo (2009) 'The Long-term Care Workforce: Overview and Strategies to Adapt Supply to Growing Demand', *Health Working Papers* no. 44. Paris: OECD.

Fujisawa, R. and G. Lafortune (2008) *The Remuneration of General*

Practitioners and Specialists in 14 OECD Countries. What are the Factors Influencing Variations across Countries?, OECD Health Working Papers no. 41. Paris: OECD.

Fukuda, Y., K. Nakamura and T. Takano (2004) 'Wide Range of Socioeconomic Factors Associated with Mortality Among Cities in Japan', *Health Promotion International* 19 (2): 177–87.

Fukuda, Y., H. Nakao, Y. Yahata and H. Imai (2008) 'In-depth Descriptive Analysis of Trends in Prevalence of Long-term Care in Japan', *Geriatrics and Gerontology International* 2008 (8): 166–71.

Furuse, T. (1996) 'Changing the Balance of Care: Japan', in OECD (ed.) *Caring for Frail Elderly People*. Paris: OECD.

Gallego, G., R. Casey, R. Norman and S. Goodall (2011), 'Introduction and Uptake of New Medical Technologies in the Australian Health Care System: A Qualitative Study,' *Health Policy* 102 (2): 152–8.

Garpenby, P. (1997) 'Implementing Quality Programmes in Three Swedish County Councils: The Views of Politicians, Managers and Doctors', *Health Policy* 39 (2): 195–206.

Garpenby, P. (1999) 'Resource Dependency, Doctors and the State: Quality Control in Sweden', *Social Science and Medicine* 49: 405–24.

Garpenby, P. (2001) 'Making Health Policy in Sweden: The Rise and Fall of the 1994 Family Doctor Scheme', in M. Bovens, P. t'Hart and B.G. Peters (eds) *Success and Failure in Public Governance. A Comparative Analysis*. Cheltenham: Edward Elgar.

Garrido, M.V., F.B. Kristensen, C.P. Nielsen and R. Busse (eds) (2008a) *Health Technology Assessment and Health-policy Making in Europe. Current Status, Challenges and Potential*. Copenhagen: European Observatory on Health Systems and Policy.

Gauld, R. (2001) *Revolving Doors: New Zealand's Health Reforms*. Wellington: Institute of Policy Studies and Health Services Research Centre.

Gauld, R., N. Ikegami, M.D. Barr, T.-L. Chiang, D. Gould and S. Kwon (2006) 'Advanced Asia's Health Systems in Comparison', *Health Policy* 79: 325–36.

Gauld, R. (2008) 'The Unintended Consequences of New Zealand's Primary Health Care Reforms', *Journal of Health Politics, Policy and Law* 33: 93–115.

Gauld, R. (2010) 'Big Country, Small Country: How the United States Debated Health Reform while New Zealand Just Got On with It', *International Journal of Clinical Practice* 64: 1334–6.

Gauld, R., R.H. Blank, J. Burgers, A.B. Cohen, M. Dobrow, N. Ikegami, S. Kwan, K. Luxford, C. Millett and C. Wendt (2012) 'The World Health Report 2008: Primary Health Care: How Wide is the Gap between its Agenda and Implementation in 12 High-income Health Systems?', *Healthcare Policy* 7 (3): 38–58.

Gerdtham, U-G., B. Jönsson, M. MacFarlan and H. Oxley (1998) 'The Determinants of Health Care Expenditure in OECD Countries: A Pooled Data Analysis', *Developments in Health Economics and Public Policy* 6: 113–34.

Gerlinger, T. (2010) 'Health Care Reform in Germany', *German Policy Studies* 6 (1): 107–42.

Germain, D., M.A. Wakefield and S.J. Durkin (2010) 'Adolescents' Perceptions of Cigarette Brand Image: Does Plain Packaging Make a Difference?', *Journal of Adolescent Health* 46 (4): 385–92.

Get America Fit (2012) 'Obesity in America', http://www.getamericafit.org/statistics-obesity-in-america.html.

Gesundheitsreform (2007) 'Die Gesundheitsreform 2007 – Fundament der neuen Gesundheitsverischerung',http://www.bmg.bund.de/cln_110/nn_1210508/SharedDocs/Standardartikel/DE/AZ/G/Glossar-Gesundheitsreform/Die-Gesundheitsreform-2007-Fundament-der-neuen-Gesundheitsversicherung.html.

Giamo, S. (2002) *Markets and Medicine: The Politics of Health Care Reform in Britain, Germany and the United States*. Ann Arbor, MI: The University of Michigan Press.

Giamo, S. and P. Manow (1999) 'Adapting the Welfare State: The Case of Health Care Reform in Britain, Germany and the United States', *Comparative Political Studies*, 31 (8): 967–1000.

Gibson, D. and R. Means (2000) 'Policy Convergence: Restructuring Long-term Care in Australia and the UK', *Policy and Politics* 29 (1): 43–58.

Gilardi, F., K. Füglister and S. Luyet (2009) 'Learning from Others: Diffusion of Hospital Financing Reforms in OECD Countries', *Comparative Political Studies* 42 (4): 549–73.

Glendinning, C. (1998) 'Health and Social Care Services for Frail Older People in the UK: Changing Responsibilities and New Developments', in C. Glenndinning (ed.) *Rights and Realities. Comparing New Developments in Long-term Care for Older People*. Bristol: Policy Press.

Glendinning, C. (2008) 'Increasing Choice and Control for Older and Disabled People: A Critical Review of New Developments in England', *Social Policy & Administration* 42 (5): 451–69.

Glendinning, C. (2013) 'Long Term Care Reform in England: A Long and Unifinished Story', in C. Ranci and E. Pavolini (eds) *Reforms in Long-Term Care Policies in Europe*. New York: Springer Science+Business Media.

Glennerster, H. and R.C. Lieberman (2011) 'Hidden Convergence: Toward a Historical Comparison of U.S. and U.K. Health Policy', *Journal of Health Politics, Policy and Law* 36 (1): 5–31.

Glenngård, A.H., F. Hjalte, M. Svensson, A. Anell and V. Bankauskaite (2005) *Health Systems in Transition: Sweden*. Copenhagen: WHO Regional Office for Europe on behalf of the European Observatory on Health Care Systems.

Glied, S. (2008) 'Medical Savings Accounts: Can They Improve Health System Performance in Europe?', *EuroObserver* 10 (4): 5–6.

Globerman, S. and A. Vining (1998) 'A Policy Perspective on "Mixed" Health Care Financial Systems of Business and Economics', *Journal of Risk Insurance* 65: 57–80.

Glover, J.D., D.M.S. Hetzel and S.K. Tennant (2004) 'The Socioeconomic Gradient and Chronic Illness and Associated Risk Factors in Australia', *Australia and New Zealand Health Policy* 1 (8).

Goetzel, R.Z., D. Shechter, R.J. Ozminkowski, P.F. Marmet, M.J. Tabrizi and E.C. Roemer (2007) 'Can Health Promotion Programs Save Medicare Money?', *Clinical Interventions in Aging* 2 (1): 117–22.

Goodin, R.E. and A. Smitsman (2000) 'Placing Welfare States: The Netherlands as a Crucial Test', *Journal of Comparative Public Policy* 2: 39–64.

Gostin, L.O., P.D. Jacobson, K.L. Record and L.E. Hardcastle (2011) 'Restoring Health to Health Reform: Integrating Medicine and Public Health to Advance the Population's Well-Being', *University of Pennsylvania Law Review* 159: 1777–824.

Gough, R. (1994) 'Från Hembiträden till Social Hemtjänst', in A. Baude and C. Rundström (eds) *Kvinnans plats i det tidiga välfardssamhället*. Stockholm: Carlsson, pp. 39–56.

Government Offices of Sweden (2007) *How Sweden is Governed*. Stockholm: Government Offices of Sweden.

Green, A. (2007) *An Introduction to Health Planning for Developing Health Systems*. New York: Oxford University Press.

Green, R.M., A. Donovan and S.A. Jauss (eds) (2009) *Global Bioethics: Issues of Conscience for the Twenty-First Century*. New York: Oxford University Press.

Green, R. (2011) 'The Ethics of Sin Taxes', *Public Health Nursing* 28: 68–77, doi: 10.1111/j.1525-1446.2010.00907.x.

Greenlee, G. (2003) 'Singapore is Right to Get Tough', www.ctnow.com/news/opinion/oped.

Greer, S.L. and M. Mätzke (2012) 'Bacteria without Borders: Communicable Disease Politics in Europe', *Journal of Health Politics, Policy and Law*, doi: 10.1215/03616878-1813763.

Greer, S.L. (2012) 'The European Centre for Disease Prevention and Control: Hub or Hollow Core?', *Journal of Health Politics, Policy and Law*, doi: 10.1215/03616878-1813817.

Greer, S. and P. Kurzer (2012) *European Union Public Health Policy: Regional and Global Trends*. London: Routledge.

Greiner, W. and J.-M.G. v.d. Schulenburg (1997) 'Germany', in M.W. Raffel (ed.) *Health Care and Reform in Industrialized Countries*. University Park, PA: Pennsylvania State University Press.

Greß, S., S. Gildemeister and J. Wasem (2004) 'The Social Transformation of American Medicine: A Comparative View from Germany', *Journal of Health Politics, Policy and Law* 29 (4–5): 659–99.

Greß, S., P. Groenewegen, J. Kerssens, B. Braun and J. Wasem (2002) 'Free Choice of Sickness Funds in Regulated Competition: Evidence from Germany and the Netherlands', *Health Policy* 60: 235–54.

Grignon, M. (2012) 'A Democratic Responsiveness Approach to Real Reform: An Exploration of Health Care Systems' Resilience', *Journal of Health Politics, Policy and Law* 37 (4): 665–76.

Grossman, B.R., M. Kitchener, J.T. Mullan and C. Harrington (2007) 'Paid Personal Assistance Services: An Exploratory Study of Working-Age Consumer's Perspectives', *Journal of Aging and Social Policy* 19 (3): 27–45.

Gruber, J. (2011) 'The Impacts of the Affordable Care Act: How Reasonable Are the Projections?', *National Tax Journal* 64 (3): 893–908.

Hacker, J.S. (2011) 'Why Reform Happened', *Journal of Health Politics, Policy and Law* 36 (3): 437–41.

Haddon, K. (2006) 'Britain is Fattest Country in Europe', *Agence France Presse*, 10 October.

Hague, R. and M. Harrop (2004) *Comparative Government and Politics. An Introduction*, 6th edn. Basingstoke: Palgrave Macmillan.
Håkansson, S. and S. Nordling (1997) 'Sweden', in M.W. Raffel (ed.) *Health Care and Reform in Industrialized Countries*. University Park, PA: Pennsylvania State University Press.
Ham, C. (ed.) (1997a) *Health Care Reform: Learning from International Experience*. Buckingham: Open University Press.
Ham, C. (1997b) 'Priority Setting in Health Care: Learning from International Experience', *Health Policy* 42 (1): 49–66.
Ham, C. (1999) *Health Policy in Britain*, 4th edn. London: Macmillan.
Ham, C. (2001) 'Values and Health Policy: The Case of Singapore', *Journal of Health Politics, Policy and Law* 26 (4): 739–45.
Ham, C. (2009) *Health Policy in Britain*, 6th edn. Basingstoke: Palgrave Macmillan.
Ham, C. and G. Robert (eds) (2003) *Reasonable Rationing: International Experience of Priority Setting in Health Care*. Buckingham: Open University Press.
Ham, C. (2010) 'The Ten Characteristics of the High-performing Chronic Care System', *Health Economics, Policy and Law* 5 (1): 71–90.
Hammond, D., D. Arnott, M. Dockrell, A. Lee and A.C. McNeill (2009) 'Cigarette Pack Design and Perceptions of Risk among UK Adult and Youth: Evidence in Support of Plain Packaging', *European Journal of Public Health* 19 (6): 631–7.
Hancock, L. (ed.) (1999) *Health Policy in the Market State*. St Leonard's, NSW: Allen & Unwin.
Hanibuchi, T., T. Nakaya and C. Murata (2010) 'Socio-economic Status and Self-rated Health in East Asia: A Comparison of China, Japan, South Korea and Taiwan', *European Journal of Public Health* 22 (1): 47–52.
Hantrais, L. and S. Mangen (eds) (1996) *Cross-national Research Methods in the Social Sciences*. London: Pinter.
Harman, S. (2012a) *Global Health Governance* (Global Institutions). London: Routledge.
Harman, S. (2012b) *The World Bank and HIV/AIDS: Setting a Global Agenda*. London: Routledge.
Harris, M.F., N.A. Zwar, C.F. Walker and S.M. Knight (2011) 'Strategic Approaches to the Development of Australia's Future Primary Care Workforce', *Medical Journal of Australia* 194 (11): s88–s91.
Harrison, M.I. (2004) *Implementing Change in Health Systems. Market Reforms in the United Kingdom, Sweden and the Netherlands*. London: Sage.
Harrison, M.I. and J. Calltrop (2000) 'The Reorientation of Market-Oriented Reforms in Swedish Health Care', *Health Policy* 50: 219–40.
Harrison, S. (1998) 'The Politics of Evidence-based Medicine in the United Kingdom', *Policy and Politics* 26 (1): 15–31.
Harrison, S. (2001) 'Reforming the Medical Profession in the United Kingdom, 1989–97: Structural Interests in Health Care', in M. Bovens, P. t'Hart and B.G. Peters (eds) *Success and Failure in Public Governance. A Comparative Analysis*. Cheltenham: Edward Elgar.

Harrison, S. (2002) 'New Labour, Modernisation and the Medical Labour Process', *Journal of Social Policy* 31 (3): 465–85.

Harrison, S., M. Moran and B. Wood (2002) 'Policy Emergence and Policy Convergence: The Case of "Scientific-bureaucratic Medicine" in the United States and United Kingdom', *British Journal of Politics and International Relations* 4 (1): 1–24.

Harrison, S. and R. McDonald (2007) 'Fixing Legitimacy? The Case of NICE and the National Health Service', in A. Hann (ed.) *Health Policy and Politics*. Aldershot: Ashgate.

Harrison, S. and R. McDonald (2008) *The Politics of Healthcare in Britain*. London: Sage.

Haseltine, W.A. (2012) *Affordable Excellence: The Singapore Health System*. Singapore: National University of Singapore Press.

Hassenteufel, P., M. Smyrl, W. Genieys and F.J. Moreno-Fuentes (2010) 'Programmatic Actors and the Transformation of European Health Care States', *Journal of Health Politics, Policy and Law* 35 (4): 517–38.

Haverland, M. and P. Marier (2008) 'Introduction: Adapting Public Policies for an Ageing Society', *Journal of Comparative Policy Analysis* 10 (1): 1–6.

Havighurst, C.C. (2000) 'Freedom of Contract: The Unexplored Path to Health Care Reform', in R.D. Feldman (ed.) *American Health Care*. New Brunswick: Transaction, pp. 145–67.

Haynes, P., M. Hill and L. Banks (2010) 'Older People's Family Contacts and Long-term Care Expenditure in OECD Countries: A Comparative Approach Using Qualitative Comparative Analysis', *Social Policy and Administration* 44 (1): 67–84.spSocial

Henderson, J.N., J. Coreil and C. Bryant (2001) *Social and Behavioural Foundations of Public Health*. London: Sage.

Henderson, S. and A. Peterson (2002) *Consuming Health: The Commodification of Health Care*. London: Routledge.

Herk, R.v., N.S. Klazinga, R.M.J. Schepers and A.F. Casparie (2001) 'Medical Audit: Threat or Opportunity. A Comparative Study of Medical Audit among Medical Specialists in General Hospitals in the Netherlands and England, 1970–1999', *Social Science and Medicine* 53 (12): 1721–32.

Hernández-Quevedo, C., A.M. Jones and N. Rice (2008) 'Persistence in Health Limitations: A European Comparative Analysis', *Journal of Health Economics* 27 (6): 1472–88.

Herper, M. (2004) 'Cancer's Cost Crisis', *Forbes,* 8 June.

Herwartz, H. and B. Theilen (2010) 'The Determinants of Health-Care Expenditure: New Results from Semiparametric Estimation', *Health Economics* 19: 964–78.

Hess, J.J., J.Z. McDowell and G. Luber (2012) 'Integrating Climate Change Adaptation into Public Health Practice: Using Adaptive Management to Increase Adaptive Capacity and Build Resilience', *Environmental Health Perspectives* 120: 171–9.

Heywood, A. (2002) *Politics*. Basingstoke: Palgrave.

Hieda, T. (2012) 'Comparative Political Economy of Long-Term Care for Elderly People: Political Logic of Universalistic Social Care Policy Development', *Social Policy and Administration* 46 (3): 258–79.

Hill, M. (2009) *The Public Policy Process*, 5th edn. New York: Longman.
Hilless, M. and J. Healy (2001) *Health Care Systems in Transition: Australia*. Copenhagen: The European Observatory on Health Care Systems.
Hillestad, R., J. Bigelow, A. Bower, F. Girosi, R. Meili, R. Scoville and R. Taylor (2005) 'Can Electronic Medical Record Systems Transform Healthcare? An Assessment of Potential Health Benefits, Savings, and Costs', *Health Affairs* 24 (5): 1103–17.
Hitiris, T. and J. Nixon. (2001) 'Convergence of Health Care Expenditure in the EU Countries', *Applied Economic Letters* 8: 223–8.
Hobson, K. (2011) 'Big Employers Estimate Health-care Costs Will Rise 8.9% in 2011', available at:www.ncpa.org/sub/dpd/index.php?Article_ID=19726 (accessed 8 August 2011).
Hochschild, A.R. (1995) 'The Culture of Politics: Traditional, Post-Modern, Cold-Modern and Warm-Modern Ideals of Care', *Social Politics* 2 (3): 333–46.
Hoffman, A.K. (2010) 'Oil and Water: Mixing Individual Mandates, Fragmented Markets, and Health Reform', *American Journal of Law and Medicine* 36 (1): 7–77.
Holtz, C. (2012) *Global Health Care*, 2nd edn. Burlington, MA: Jones and Bartlett Publishers.
Holzinger, K. and C. Knill (2005) 'Causes and Conditions of Cross-national Policy Convergence', *Journal of European Public Policy* 12 (5): 775–96.
Hosking, J. and D. Campbell-Lendrum (2012) 'How Well Does Climate Change and Human Health Research Match the Demands of Policymakers? A Scoping Review', *Environmental Health Perspectives*, http://dx.doi.org/10.1289/ehp.1104093.
Howell, B. (2005) 'Restructuring Primary Health Care Markets in New Zealand: From Welfare Benefits to Insurance Markets', *Australia and New Zealand Health Policy* 2 (2), http://www.anzhealthpolicy.com/content/2/1/20.
Howlett, M. and M. Ramesh (2009) *Studying Public Policy: Policy Cycles and Policy Subsystems*, 3rd edn. Oxford: Oxford University Press.
Howse, G. (2004) 'Managing Emerging Infectious Diseases: Is a Federal System an Impediment to Effective Laws?', *Australia and New Zealand Health Policy* 1 (7), http://www.anzhealthpolicy.com/content/1/1/7.
Hsiao, C.-T. and H.-H. Huang (2012) 'A Causal Model for the Development of Long-term Facilities: A Case in Taiwan', *Qual Quant* 46: 471–81.
Huang, C., P. Vaneckova, X. Wang, G. FitzGerald, Y. Guo and S. Tong (2011) 'Constraints and Barriers to Public Health Adaptation to Climate Change: A Review of the Literature', *American Journal of Preventive Medicine* 40 (2): 183–90.
Huang, J.-H. and C.-M. Tung (2008) 'The Effects of Outpatient Co-Payment Policy on Healthcare Usage by the Elderly in Taiwan', *Archives of Gerontology and Geriatrics* 43: 101–16.
Huggins, C.E. (2002) 'Poor Face Multitude of Environmental Health Threats', *Reuters*, 17 October.
Hummelgaard, H., M. Baadsgaard and J.B. Nielsen (1998) *Unemployment and Marginalisation in Danish Municipalities*. Copenhagen: Institute of Local Government Studies.

Hunter, D.J. (2008) *The Health Debate*. Bristol: Policy Press.

Hurst, J. and J.-P. Poullier (1993) 'Paths to Health Reform', OECD *Observer* 179: 4–7.

Hutten, J.B.F. and A. Kerkstra (eds) (1996) *Home Care in Europe: Country-Specific Guide to its Organization and Financing*. Aldershot: Ashgate.

Hwang, G.-J. (2008) 'Going Separate Ways? The Reform of Health Insurance Funds in Germany, Japan and South Korea', *Policy Studies* 29 (4): 421–35.

Ikegami, N. (1992) 'Japan: Maintaining Equity through Regulated Fees', *Journal of Health Politics, Policy and Law* 17 (4): 689–713.

Ikegami, N. and J.C. Campbell (1999) 'Health Care Reform in Japan: The Virtues of Muddling Through', *Health Affairs* 18 (3): 56–75.

Ikegami, N. (2007) 'Rationale, Design and Sustainability of Long-Term Care Insurance in Japan – In Retrospect', *Social Policy & Society* 6 (3): 423–34.

Iliffe, S. and J. Munro (2000) 'New Labour and Britain's National Health Service: An Overview of Current Reforms', *International Journal of Health Services* 30 (2): 309–34.

Illich, I. (1976) *Limits to Medicine: Medical Nemesis: The Expropriation of Health*. Harmondsworth: Penguin Books.

Imai, H. and K. Fushimi (2012) 'Factors Associated with the Use of Institutional Long-term Care in Japan', *Geriatrics and Gerontology International* 12: 72–9.ggi_9

Immergut, E.M. (1992) *Health Politics: Interests and Institutions in Western Europe*. Cambridge: Cambridge University Press.

Inagaki, K. (2006) 'Japan Battles Rising Obesity: Frets Disease May Cut World-Class Longevity', www.ABCNews.go.com.

Institute of Alcohol Studies (2002) 'Alcohol Consumption and Harm in the UK and EU', www.ias.org.uk/factsheets/default.htm.

Institute of Medicine (2002) *The Future of the Public's Health in the 21st Century*. Washington, DC: Institute of Medicine.

Institute of Medicine (2008) *Knowing What Works in Health Care: A Roadmap for the Nation*. Washington, DC: National Academy Press.

Intergovernmental Panel on Climate Change (2007) *Climate Change 2007: Impacts, Adaptation, and Vulnerability*. Cambridge: Cambridge University Press.

Isaacs, S.L. and S.A. Schroeder (2004) 'Class – the Ignored Determinant of the Nation's Health', *New England Journal of Medicine* 351: 1137–42.

Izuhara, M. (2003) 'Social Inequality under a New Social Contract: Long-Term Care in Japan', *Social Policy & Administration* 37 (4): 395–410.

Jacobs, A. (1998) 'Seeing Differences: Market Health Reform in Europe', *Journal of Health Politics, Policy and Law* 23 (1): 1–33.

Jacobs, R., P.C. Smith and A. Street (2006) *Measuring Efficiency in Health Care: Analytic Techniques and Health Policy*. Cambridge: Cambridge University Press.

Jacobs, L.R. and T. Skocpol (2010) *Health Care Reform and American Politics: What Everyone Needs to Know*. New York: Oxford University Press.

Jacobs, L.R. (2011) 'America's Critical Juncture: The Affordable Care Act and Its Reverberations', *Journal of Health Politics, Policy and Law* 36 (3): 625–31.

Jacobson, P.D., L.M. Napiewocki and L.A. Voigt (2011) 'Regulating the U.S. Health Care System: Failure in Motion', *Journal of Health Politics, Policy and Law* 36 (3): 583–9.

Jacobson, P.D. (2012) 'The Role of Networks in the European Union Public Health Experience', *Journal of Health Politics, Policy and Law*, doi: 10.1215/03616878-1813836.

Jacobzone, S. (1999) *Ageing and Care for Frail Elderly Persons: An Overview of International Perspectives*. Labour Market and Social Policy Occasional Papers no. 38. Paris: OECD.

Jacobzone, S., E. Cambois, E. Chaplain and J.M. Robine (1999) *The Health of Older Persons in* OECD *Countries: Is it Improving Fast Enough to Compensate for Population Ageing?* Labour Market and Social Policy Occasional Paper no. 37. Paris: OECD.

Jamieson, A. (1996) 'Issues in Home Care Services', in OECD (ed.) *Caring for Frail Elderly People. Policies in Evolution*. Social Policy Studies no. 19. Paris: OECD.

Japan Ministry of Health, Labour and Welfare (2004) *Direction of Health and Welfare Policies for the Elderly over the Next 5 Years*. Tokyo: Ministry of Health, Labour and Welfare.

Jatrana, S. and P. Crampton (2009) 'Affiliation with a Primary Care Provider in New Zealand: Who Is and Who Isn't', *Health Policy* 91: 286–96.

Jegers, M., K. Kesteloot, D. De Graeve and W. Gilles (2002) 'A Typology for Provider Payment Systems in Health Care', *Health Policy* 60: 255–73.

Jenkin, G.L., L. Signal and G. Thomson (2011) 'Framing Obesity: The Framing Contest between Industry and Public Health at the New Zealand Inquiry into Obesity', *Obesity Review* 12: 1022–30.

Jenson, J. and S. Jacobzone (2000) *Care Allowances for the Frail Elderly and Their Impact on Women Care-givers*. Labour Market and Social Policy Occasional Papers no. 41. Paris: OECD.

Jha, A.K., D. Doolan, D. Grandt, T. Scott and D.W. Bates (2008) 'The Use of Health Information Technology in Seven Nations', *International Journal of Medical Informatics* 77 (12): 848–54.

Johansson, S. (2000) 'Women's Paradise Lost? Social Services and Care in the Quasi-Markets in Sweden', in B. Hobson (ed.) *Gender and Citizenship in Transition*. Basingstoke: Palgrave Macmillan.

Johnson, M. and L. Cullen (2000) 'Solidarity Put to the Test. Health and Social Care in the UK', *International Journal of Social Welfare* 9 (4): 228–37.

Johnson, T. (1995) 'Governmentality and the Institutionalization of Expertise', in T. Johnson, G. Larkin and M. Saks (eds) *Health Professions and the State in Europe*. London: Routledge.

Joung, I.M., H. van der Mheen, K. Stranks, F.W. van Poppel and J.P. Mackenbach (1994) 'Differences in Self-Reported Morbidity by Marital Status and Living Arrangement', *International Journal of Epidemiology* 23: 91–7.

Jost, T.S. (2011) 'The Real Constitutional Problem with the Affordable Care Act', *Journal of Health Politics, Policy and Law* 36 (3): 501–6.

Judson, K. and C. Harrison (2012) *Law & Ethics for the Health Professions*. New York: McGraw Hill.

Kabir, Z., K. Bennett, E. Shelley, B. Unal, J.A. Critchley and S. Capewell (2007) 'Life-Years-Gained from Population Risk Factor Changes and Modern Cardiology Treatments in Ireland', *European Journal of Public Health* 17: 193–8.

Kam, Y.W. (2012) 'The Contributions of the Health Decommodification Typologies to the Study of the East Asian Welfare Regime', *Social Policy and Administration* 46 (1): 108–28.spol_

Kassler, J. (1994) *Bitter Medicine: Greed and Chaos in American Health Care*. New York: Birch Lane Press.

Kawachi, I., B.P. Kennedy and R.G. Wilkinson (eds) (1999) *The Society and Population Health Reader: Income Inequality and Health*. New York: New Press.

Kay, A. (2001) 'Beyond Policy Community. The Case of the GP Fundholding Scheme', *Public Administration* 79 (3): 561–77.

Keefe, T.J. and M.W. Zacher (2011) *The Politics of Global Health Governance: United by Contagion*. Basingstoke, UK: Palgrave Macmillan.

Kelly, E. and J. Hurst (2006) *Health Care Quality Indicators Project: Initial Indicators Report*. Paris: OECD.

Kenner, D. (2001) 'The Role of Traditional Herbal Medicine in Modern Japan', *Acupuncture Today,* August.

Kerkstra, A. (1996) 'Netherlands', in J.B.F. Hutten and A. Kerkstra (eds) *Home Care in Europe: Country-Specific Guide to its Organization and Financing*. Aldershot: Ashgate.

Kersh, R. and J. Morone (2002) 'The Politics of Obesity: Seven Steps to Government Action', *Health Affairs* 21 (November/December): 142–53.

Kiil, A. (2012) 'What Characterises the Privately Insured in Universal Health Care Systems? A Review of the Empirical Evidence', *Health Policy* 106: 60–72.

Kim, I.-H., C. Muntaner, F.V. Shahidie, A. Vivesd, C. Vanroelen and J. Benach (2012) 'Welfare States, Flexible Employment, and Health: A Critical Review,' *Health Policy* 104: 99–127.

Kirkpatrick, I., B. Bullinger, M. Dent and F. Lega (2011) 'The Translation of Medical Manager Roles in European Health Systems: A Framework for Comparison'. Paper presented at the 27th EGOS Colloquium, Gothenberg, Sweden.

Kitchener, M., T. Ng and C. Harrington (2007) 'Medicaid State Plan Personal Care Services: Trends in Programs and Policies', *Journal of Aging and Social Policy* 19 (3): 9–26.

Klazinga, N. (2005) 'Re-engineering Trust: The Adoption and Adaptation of Four Models of External Quality Assurance of Health Care Services in Western European Health Care Systems', in J. Watson and P. Ovseiko (eds) *Health Care Systems. Major Themes in Health and Social Welfare. Volume I Reforming Health Care Systems*. London: Routledge.

Klazinga, N. (2008) 'The Health System in the Netherlands', *Eurohealth* 14 (1): 8–10.

Klein, R. (1997) 'Learning from Others: Shall the Last Be the First?', *Journal of Health Politics, Policy and Law* 22 (5): 1267–78.

Klein, R. (2001) *The New Politics of the NHS*, 4th edn. Harlow: Prentice Hall.

Klein, R. (2005) 'A Middle Way for Rationing Healthcare Resources', *British Medical Journal* 330: 1340–1.

Klein, R. (2006) 'The Troubled Transformation of Britain's National Health Service', *The New England Journal of Medicine* 355 (4): 409–15.

Klein, R. (2009) 'Learning from Others and Learning from Mistakes', in T.R. Marmor, R. Freeman and K.G.H. Okma (eds) *Comparative Studies and the Politics of Modern Medical Care*. New Haven, London: Yale University Press.

Klein, R. (2010) 'The Eternal Triangle: Sixty Years of the Centre-Periphery Relationship in the National Health Service', *Social Policy & Administration* 44 (3): 285–304.

Klein, R. and A. Williams (2000) 'Setting Priorities: What is Holding Us Back – Inadequate Information or Inadequate Institutions?', in A. Coulter and C. Ham (eds) *The Global Challenge of Health Care Rationing*. Buckingham: Open University Press, pp. 15–26.

Kleinke, J.D. (2001) *Oxymorons: The Myth of a U.S. Health Care System*. San Francisco: Jossey-Bass.

Kludt, R. (2012) 'Poll: "Obamacare" Gains Support, Public Opinion Now Split', http://livewire.talkingpointsmemo.com/entry/poll-obamacare-gains-support-public-opinion-now-split.

Knijn, T. (1998) 'Social Care in the Netherlands', in J. Lewis (ed.) *Gender, Social Care and Welfare State Restructuring in Europe*. Aldershot: Ashgate.

Knijn, T. (2000) 'Marketization and the Struggling Logics of (Home) Care in the Netherlands', in M.H. Meyer (ed.) *Care Work: Gender, Labor and the Welfare State*. New York: Routledge.

Knijn, T. (2001) 'Care Work: Innovations in the Netherlands', in M. Daly (ed.) *Care Work: The Quest of Security*. Geneva: International Labour Office.

Knijn, T. and S. Verhagen (2007) 'Contested Professionalism. Payments for Care and the Quality of Home Care', *Administration and Society* 39 (4): 451–75.

Knowlton, K., M. Rotkin-Ellman, L. Geballe, W. Max and G.M. Solomon (2011) 'Six Climate Change-Related Events in the United States Accounted for About $14 Billion in Lost Lives and Health Costs', *Health Affairs* 30 (11): 2167–76.

Kobayashi, Y. and M.R. Reich (1993) 'Health Care Financing for the Elderly in Japan', *Social Science and Medicine* 37 (3): 343–53.

Kodate, N. (2012) 'Events, Politics and Patterns of Policy-Making: Impact of Major Incidents on Health Sector Regulatory Reforms in the UK and Japan', *Social Policy and Administration* 46 (3): 280–301.4

Kohn, L., J. Corrigan and M. Donaldson (eds) (1999) *To Err is Human: Building a Safer Health System*. Washington, DC: National Academy Press.

Konrad, R. (2006) 'E. coli Fears Prompt Recall of Lettuce', *Associated Press,* October 7.

Koop, C.E., C. Pearson and M.R. Schwartz (eds) (2002) *Critical Issues in Global Health*. San Francisco: Jossey-Bass.

Kremer, M. (2005) 'Consumers in Charge of Care: The Dutch Personal Care Budget (PGB) and Its Impact on The Market, Professionals and the Family', unpublished manuscript.

Kreng, V.B. and C.-T. Yang (2011) 'The Equality of Resource Allocation in Health Care under the National Health Insurance System in Taiwan', *Health Policy* 100: 203–10.

Kröger, T. (2001) *Comparative Research on Social Care. The State of the Art*. Brussels: European Commission.

Kröger, T. (2005) 'Interplay between Formal and Informal Care for Older People: The State of the Nordic Research', in M. Szebehely (ed.) *Äldreomsorgsforskning i Norden. En kunstkapsöversikt*. Copenhagen: Nordic Council of Ministers.

Kuhlmann, E. (2006) *Modernising Health Care. Reinventing Professions, the State and the Public*. Bristol: Policy Press.

Kulkarni, S.C., A. Levin-Rector, M. Ezzati and C.J.L. Murray (2011) 'Falling Behind: Life Expectancy in U.S. Counties from 2000 to 2007 in an International Context', *Population Health Metrics* 9: 16, doi:10.1186/1478-7954-9-16.

Kwon, S. (2011) 'Health Care Financing in Asia: Key Issues and Challenges', *Asia-Pacific Journal of Public Health* 23 (5): 651–61.

Lamm, R.D. (2003) *The Brave New World of Health Care*. Golden, CO: Fulcrum Press.

Lamm, R.D. and R.H. Blank (2007) *Condition Critical: A New Moral Vision for U.S. Health Care*. Golden, CO: Fulcrum Press.

Lancet, The (ed.) (2006) 'Rationing is Essential in Tax-Funded Health Systems', *The Lancet* 368 (9545): 1394.

Landwehr, C. and K. Böhm (2011) 'Delegation and Institutional Design in Health-Care Rationing', *Governance: An International Journal of Policy, Administration, and Institutions* 24 (4): 665–88.

Lang, T. and G. Rayner (2005) 'Obesity: A Growing Issue for European Policy?', *Journal of European Social Policy* 15 (4): 301–32.

Lantz, P.M., R.L. Lichtenstein and H.A. Pollack (2007) 'Health Policy Approaches to Population Health: The Limits of Medicalization', *Health Affairs* 26: 1253–7.

Lantz, P.M., E. Golberstein, J.S. House and J. Morenoff (2010) 'Socioeconomic and Behavioral Risk Factors for Mortality in a National 19-Year Prospective Study of U.S. Adults', *Social Science and Medicine* 70: 1558–66.

Lasser, K.E., D.U. Himmelstein and S. Woolhandler (2006) 'Access to Care, Health Status and Health Disparities in the United States and Canada: Results of a Cross-National Population-Based Survey', *American Journal of Public Health* 96: 1300–7.

Laurance, J. and C. Norton (2000) '"Unresponsive" NHS Ranked 18th in the World', *The Independent*, 21 June.

Lee, K., K. Buse and S. Fustukian (eds) (2002) *Health Policy in a Globalising World*. Cambridge: Cambridge University Press.

Lee, S.-Y., C.-B. Chun, Y.-G. Lee, Y.-G. and N.K. Seo (2008) 'The National Health Insurance System as One Type of New Typology: The Case of South Korea and Taiwan', *Health Policy* 85 (1): 105–13.

Leeder, S.R. (1999) *Healthy Medicine: Challenges Facing Australia's Health Services*. St Leonard's, NSW: Allen & Unwin.

Leiber, S., S. Greß and M.-S. Manouguian (2010) 'Health Care System Change and the Cross-Border Transfer of Ideas: Influence of the Dutch Model on the 2007 German Health Reform', *Journal of Health Politics, Policy and Law* 35 (4): 539–66.

Leichter, H.M. (1991) *Free to be Foolish: Politics and Health Promotion in the United States and Great Britain*. Princeton, NJ: Princeton University Press.

Leiter, A.M. and E. Theurl (2009) 'The Convergence of Health Care Financing Structures: Empirical Evidence from OECD-countries', *The European Journal of Health Economics* 13 (1): 7–18.

Leutwyler, K. (1995) 'The Price of Prevention', *Scientific American*, April: 124–29.

Levy, B.S. and V.W. Sidel (2007) *War and Public Health*. New York: Oxford University Press.

Levy, B.S. and V.W. Sidel (2009) *Social Injustice and Public Health*. New York: Oxford University Press.

Lewis, J. (2001) 'Older People and the Health–Social Care Boundary in the UK: Half a Century of Hidden Policy Conflict', *Social Policy and Administration* 35 (4): 343–59.

Lewis, J. (2005) *Health Policy and Politics: Networks, Ideas and Power*. Melbourne: IP Communications.

Lewis, S.J. and S.R. Leeder (2009) 'Why Health Reform?', *Medical Journal of Australia* 191 (5): 270–2.

Lian, O.S. (2003) 'Convergence or Divergence? Reforming Primary Care in Norway and Britain', *The Milbank Quarterly* 81 (2): 305–30.

Lieverdink, H. and J.H. van der Made (1997) 'The Reform of Health Insurance Systems in the Netherlands and Germany: Dutch Gold and German Silver', in C. Altenstetter and J.W. Björkman (eds) *Health Policy Reform, National Variations and Globalization*. London: Macmillan.

Light, D. (1995) 'Countervailing Powers: A Framework for Professions in Transition', in T. Johnson, G. Larkin and M. Saks (eds) *Health Professions and the State in Europe*. London: Routledge.

Light, D.W. (2011) 'Historical and Comparative Reflections on the U.S. National Health Insurance Reforms', *Social Science and Medicine* 72 (2): 129–32.

Lijphart, A. (1999) *Patterns of Democracy*. New Haven, CT: Yale University Press.

Lim, M.-K. (2004) 'Shifting the Burden of Health Care Finance: A Case Study of Public–Private Partnership in Singapore', *Health Policy* 69: 83–92.

Lim, W.T.L. (2006) 'Development of Medical Informatics in Singapore: Keeping Pace with Healthcare Challenges', a paper presented at the Asia Pacific Association for Medical Informatics meeting, October 27–29, 2006, Taipei, Taiwan. Retrieved from http://www.apami.org/apami2006/papers/wlim%28sg%29.pdf.

Lim, J. and V.D. Joshi (2008) 'Public Perceptions of Healthcare in Singapore', *Annals Academy of Medicine* 37 (2): 91–5.

Lin, V. and P. Robinson (2005) 'Australian Public Health Policy in 2003–2004', *Australia and New Zealand Health Policy* 2 (7), http://www.anzhealthpolicy.com/content/2/1/7.

Lin, Y.Y. (2006) 'Update on Medishield Reform: Early Results', MOH Information Paper: 2006/013. Singapore: Ministry of Health.

Lin, Y.-J., W.-H. Tian and C.-C. Chen (2011) 'Urbanization and the Utilization of Outpatient Services under National Health Insurance in Taiwan', *Health Policy* 103 (2–3): 236–43.

Lin, B.Y.-J., C.C.C. Lin and Y.K. Lin (2010) 'Patient Satisfaction Evaluations in Different Clinic Care Models: Care Stratification under a National Demonstration Project', *Health and Place* 16 (1): 85–92.

Locock, L. (2000) 'The Changing Nature of Rationing in the UK National Health Service', *Public Administration* 78 (1): 91–109.

Lombarts, M.J.M.H. and N.S. Klazinga (2001) 'A Policy Analysis of the Introduction and Dissemination of External Peer Review (Visitatie) as a Means of Professional Self-regulation amongst Medical Specialists in the Netherlands in the Period 1985–2000', *Health Policy* 58 (3): 191–213.

London School of Hygiene and Tropical Medicine (1999) *Rapid Reviews of Public Health for London. Housing and the Built Environment*. London: London School of Hygiene and Tropical Medicine.

Long, A.-J. and P. Chang (2012) 'The Effect of Using the Health Smart Card vs. CPOE Reminder System on the Prescribing Practices of Non-obstetric Physicians during Outpatient Visits for Pregnant Women in Taiwan', *International Journal of Medical Informatics* 81: 605–11.

Loo, M.v.h., J.P. Kahan and K.G.H. Okma (1999) 'Developments in Health Care Cost Containment in the Netherlands', in E. Mossialos and J. Le Grand (eds) *Health Care and Cost Containment in the European Union*. Aldershot: Ashgate.

Low, J.A., W.C. Ng, K.B. Yap and K.M. Chan (2000) 'End-of-life Issues: Preferences and Choices of a Group of Elderly Chinese Subjects', *Annals of the Academy of Medicine* 29 (1): 50–6.

Lowi, T.A. (1972) 'Four Systems of Policy, Politics and Choice', *Public Administration Review* 32: 298–310.

Lu, J.-FR. and W.C. Hsiao (2003) 'Does Universal Health Insurance Make Health Care Unaffordable? Lessons from Taiwan', *Health Affairs* 22: 77–88.

Lundsgaard, J. (2004) 'Consumer Direction and Choice in Long-Term Care for Older Persons, Including Payments for Informal Care: How Can It Help Improve Care Outcomes, Employment and Fiscal Sustainability?', *Health Working Papers*, No. 20. Paris: OECD.

Luzio, G. di (2004) 'The Irresistible Decline of the Medical Profession? An Empirical Investigation of Its Autonomy and Economic Situation in the Changing German Welfare State', *German Politics* 13 (3): 419–48.

Lyon, D. and M. Gluckmann (2008) 'Comparative Configurations of Care Work across Europe', *Sociology* 42 (1): 101–18.

Maarse, H. and A. Paulus (2003) 'Has Solidarity Survived? A Comparative Analysis of the Effect of Social Health Insurance Reforms in Four European Countries', *Journal of Health Politics, Policy and Law* 28 (4): 585–614.

Maarse, J.A.M. (1997) 'Netherlands', in M.W. Raffel (ed.) *Health Care and Reform in Industrialized Countries*. University Park, PA: Pennsylvania State University Press.

Maarse, H. and R. Ter Meulen (2006) 'Consumer Choice in Dutch Health Insurance after Reform', *Health Care Annals* 14: 37–49.

Mabbett, D. and H. Bolderson (1999) 'Theories and Methods in Comparative Social Policy', in J. Clasen (ed.) *Comparative Social Policy*. Oxford: Blackwell.

MacDaid, D. (2001) 'European Health Technology Assessment Quo Vadis?', *Eurohealth* 7 (1): 27–8.

Macer, D. (1999) 'Bioethics in and from Asia', *Journal of Medical Ethics* 25: 293–5.

MacIntyre, C.R. (2011) 'Public Health and Health Reform in Australia', *Medical Journal of Australia* 194 (1): 38–40.

Mackenbach, J.P., I. Stirbu, A.-J.R. Roskam, M.M. Schaap, G. Menvielle, M. Leinsalu and A.E. Kunst (2008) 'Socioeconomic Inequalities in Health in 22 European Countries', *The New England Journal of Medicine* 358: 2468–81.

Mackey, T.K. and B.A. Liang (2012) 'Lessons from SARS and H1N1/A: Employing a WHO–WTO Forum to Promote Optimal Economic-Public Health Pandemic Response', *Journal of Public Health Policy* 33: 119–30.

Maclennan, A.H., D.H. Wilson and A.W. Taylor (1996) 'Prevalence and Cost of Alternative Medicine in Australia', *Lancet* 347: 569–73.

Maher, J.M., S. Fraser and J. Wright (2010) 'Framing the Mother: Childhood Obesity, Maternal Responsibility and Care', *Journal of Gender Studies* 19 (3): 233–47.

Mariner, W.K. (2010) 'Health Reform: What's Insurance Got to Do With It – Recognizing Health Insurance as a Separate Species of Insurance', *American Journal of Law and Medicine* 36: 436–51.

Marmor, T.R., R. Feeman and K. Okma (2005) 'Comparing Perspectives and Policy Learning in the World of Health Care', *Journal of Comparative Policy Analysis* 7 (4): 331–48.

Marmor, T.R. and J. Oberlander (2011) 'The Patchwork: Health Reform, American Style', *Social Science and Medicine* 72: 125-28.

Marmor, T.R. and C. Wendt (2011a) 'Introduction', in T. Marmor and C. Wendt (eds) *Reforming Healthcare Systems. Volume 1. Ideas, Interests and Institutions*. Chelthenham, UK: Edward Elgar Publishing Ltd.

Marmor, T.R. and C. Wendt (eds) (2011b) *Reforming Heathcare Systems*. Chelthenham, UK: Edward Elgar Publishing Ltd.

Marmor, T.R. and C. Wendt (2012) 'Conceptual Frameworks for Comparing Healthcare Politics and Policy', *Health Policy* 107: 11–20.

Marmor, T.R., R. Freeman and K.G.H. Okma (2009a) *Comparative Studies and the Politics of Modern Medical Care*. New Haven, CT: Yale University Press.

Marmor, T.R., R. Freeman and K.G.H. Okma (2009b) 'Comparative Policy Analysis and Health Care: An Introduction', in T.R. Marmor, R. Freeman and K.G.H. Okma (eds) *Comparative Studies and the Politics of Modern Medical Care*. New Haven, London: Yale University Press.

Marmot, M. and R.G. Wilkinson (eds) (1999) *Social Determinants of Health*. Oxford: Oxford University Press.

Marnoch, G. (2003) 'Scottish Devolution: Identity and Impact and the Case of Community Care for the Elderly', *Public Administration* 81 (2): 253–73.

Marrelli, T.M. (2011) *Handbook of Home Health Standards, Revised Reprint*. Maryland Heights, MO: Mosby.

Marshall, T. (2003) 'The Silent Revolution: Recent Developments in the Organisation of General Medical Practice in New Zealand', *Business Review* 5 (1): 1–8.

Martin, J. and G. Salmond (2001) 'Policy Making: The "Messy Reality"', in P. Davis and T. Ashton (eds) *Health and Public Policy in New Zealand*. Auckland: Oxford University Press.

Martin, R. and A. Conseil (2012) 'Public Health Policy and Law for Pandemic Influenza: A Case for European Harmonization?', *Journal of Health Politics, Policy and Law*, doi: 10.1215/03616878-1813854.

Masis, D.P. and P.C. Smith (eds) (2010) *Health Care Systems in Developing and Transition Countries: The Role of Research Evidence (Global Development Network)*. London: Edward Elgar.

Matcha, D.A. (2003) *Health Care Systems of the Developed World: How the United States' System Remains an Outlier*. Westport, CT: Praeger Publishers.

Matsushige, T., T. Tsuisui and M. Otaga (2012) '"Mutual Aid" beyond Formal Institutions: Integrated Home Care in Japan', *Current Sociology* 60 (4): 538–50.

Matsushita, Y., N. Yoshiike, F. Kaneda, K. Yoshita and H. Takimoto (2004) 'Trends in Childhood Obesity in Japan over the Last 25 Years from the National Nutrition Survey', *Obesity Research* 12: 205–14.

Maynard, A. and K. Bloor (2001) 'Our Certain Fate: Rationing in Health Care', Office of Health Economics Briefings Page, www.ohe.org/our.htm.

McClellan, M. and D. Kessler (1999) 'A Global Analysis of Technological Change in Health Care: The Case of Heart Attacks', *Health Affairs* 18 (3): 250–5.

McConahy, K. (2002) 'Food Portions Are Positively Related To Energy Intake and Body Weight in Early Childhood', *Journal of Pediatrics* 140 (March): 340–7.

McGinnis, J.M., P. Williams-Russo and J.R. Knickman (2002) 'The Case for More Active Policy Attention to Health Promotion', *Health Affairs* 21 (2): 78–93.

McIntosh, E., P. Clarke, E.J. Frew and J.J. Louviere (2010) *Applied Methods of Cost-benefit Analysis in Health Care*. New York: Oxford University Press.

McKie, J., J. Richardson, P. Singer and H. Kuhse (1998) *The Allocation of Health Care Resources: An Ethical Evaluation of the 'QALY' Approach*. Aldershot: Dartmouth.

McMichael, C., J. Barnett and A.J. McMichael (2012) 'An Ill Wind? Climate Change, Migration, and Health', *Environmental Health Perspectives* 120: 646–54. http://dx.doi.org/10.1289/ehp.1104375.

McMichael, A.J. and E. Lindgren (2011) 'Climate Change: Present and Future Risks to Health, and Necessary Responses', *Journal of Internal Medicine*, doi: 10.1111/j.1365-2796.2011.02415.x.

McPake, B. (2002) 'The Globalisation of Health Sector Reform Policies: Is "Lesson Drawing" Part of the Process?', in K. Lee, K. Buse and S. Fustukian (eds) *Health Policy in a Globalising World*. Cambridge: Cambridge University Press.

McRae, I., L. Yen, J. Gillespie and K. Douglas (2010) 'Patient Affiliation with GPs in Australia: Who Is and Who Is Not and Does it Matter?', *Health Policy* 103:16–23.

Meagher, G. and M. Szebehely (2013) 'Long-Term Care in Sweden: Trends, Actors and Consequences', in C. Ranci and E. Pavolini (eds) *Reforms in Long-Term Care Policies in Europe*. New York: Springer Science+Business Media.

Means, R., S. Richards and R. Smith (2003) *Community Care: Policy and Practice*, 3rd edn. Basingstoke: Palgrave.

Mechanic, D. (1994) *Inescapable Decisions: The Imperatives of Health Care*. New Brunswick, NJ: Transaction.

Mechanic, D. and D.D. McAlpine (2010) 'Sociology of Health Care Reform: Building on Research and Analysis to Improve Health Care', *Journal of Health and Social Behavior* 51 (s): s147–s159.

Mehta, K.K. and C. Briscoe (2004) 'National Policy Approaches to Social Care for Elderly People in the United Kingdom and Singapore 1945–2002', *Journal of Aging and Social Policy* 16 (1): 89–111.

Mendelson, D.N., R.G. Abramson and R.J. Rubin (1995) 'State Involvement in Medical Technology Assessment', *Health Affairs* 14 (2): 83–98.

Merson, M.H., R.E. Black and A.J. Mills (2011) *Global Health*, 3rd edn. New York: Jones and Bartlett Publishers.

Mernagh, P., K. Coleman, J. Cumming, T. Green, J. Harris, D. Paech and A. Weston (2011) 'Cost-Effectiveness Analysis of Public Health Interventions to Prevent Obesity in New Zealand', *Value in Health* 14 (7): A382.

Meyer, J.A. (1996) *Der Weg zur Pflegeversicherung. Position, Akteure, Politikprozesse*. Frankfurt am Main: Mabuse Verlag.

Milio, N. (2000) *Public Health in the Market: Facing Managed Care, Lean Government, and Health Disparities*. Ann Arbor, MI: University of Michigan Press.

Miller, A.S. and A. Hagihara (1997) 'Organ Transplanting in Japan: The Debate Begins', *Public Health* 111: 367–72.

Miller, E.A., M. Booth and V. Mor (2008) 'Meeting the Demographic Challenges Ahead: Toward Culture Change in an Ageing New Zealand', *Australia and New Zealand Health Policy* 5 (5): 5–16.

Miller, E.A., V. Mor and M. Clark (2010) 'Reforming Long-Term Care in the United States: Findings from a National Survey of Specialists', *Gerontologist* 50 (2): 238–52.

Mills, A., S. Bennett, S. Russell and N. Attanayake (eds) (2001) *The Challenge of Health Sector Reform: What Governments Must Do?* Basingstoke: Palgrave.

Mills T.C. (2009) 'Forecasting Obesity Trends in England', *Journal of the Royal Statistical Society* 172 (1): 107–17.

Mills, S.Y. (2001) 'The House of Lords Report on Complementary Medicine: A Summary', *Complementary Therapies in Medicine* 9 (1): 34–9.

Ministry of Health and Social Affairs (2001) 'Towards Public Health on Equal Terms', Fact Sheet no. 3. Stockholm: Ministry of Health and Social Affairs.

Mitchell, A.D. (2010) 'Australia's Move to the Plain Packaging of Cigarettes and Its WTO Compatibility', *Asian Journal of WTO and International Health, Law and Policy* 5: 405–25.

Mladovsky, P., D. Srsivastava, J. Cylus, M. Karanikolos, T. Evetovits, S. Thomson and M. McKee (2012) *Health Policy Responses to the Financial Crisis in Europe*. Copenhagen: World Health Organization.

Moeller, D.W. (2011) *Environmental Health*, 4th edn. Cambridge: Harvard University Press.

Mokdad, A.H., J.S. Marks, D.F. Stroup and J.L. Gerberding (2004) 'Actual Causes of Death in the United States, 2000', *Journal of the American Medical Association* 291:1238–45.

Monheit, A.C. (2003) 'Persistence in Health Expenditures in the Short Run: Prevalence and Consequences', *Medical Care* 41 (7):11153–64.

Mooney, G. (2009) 'Is It Not Time for Health Economists to Rethink Equity and Access?', *Health Economics, Policy and Law* 4: 209–21.

Moran, M. (1999) *Governing the Health Care State: A Comparative Study of the United Kingdom, the United States and Germany*. Manchester: Manchester University Press.

Moran, M. (2000) 'Understanding the Welfare State: The Case of Health Care', *British Journal of Politics and International Relations* 2 (2): 135–60.

Moran, M. and B. Wood (1993) *States, Regulation and the Medical Profession*. Cheltenham: Edward Elgar.

Morris, S., N. Devlin, D. Parkin and A. Spencer (2012) *Economic Analysis in Healthcare*. New York: Wiley.

Mosebach, K. (2006) 'Institutional Change or Political Stalemate? Health Care Financing Reform in Germany', *Eurohealth* 12 (4): 11–14.

Mossialos, E. and J. Le Grand (eds) (1999) *Health Care and Cost Containment in the European Union*. Aldershot: Ashgate.

Moszczynski, W. (2008) 'Why Britain needs Polish Migrants', *Telegraph*, 3 April.

Mueller, K.J. (1993) *Health Care Policy in the United States*. Lincoln, NE: University of Nebraska Press.

Muennig, P.A. and S.A. Glied (2010) 'What Changes in Survival Rates Tell Us about U.S. Health Care', *Health Affairs* 29 (11): 2105–13.

Mullen, P. (1998) 'Rational Rationing?', *Health Services Management Research* 11: 113–23.

Muramatsu, N. and H. Akiyama (2012) 'Japan: Super-Aging Society Preparing for the Future', *The Gerontologist* 51 (4): 425–32.

Musgrave, F.W. (2006) *The Economics of U.S. Health Care Policy: The Role of Market Forces*. New York: M.E. Sharpe.

Musgrave, P., R. Zeramdini and G. Carrin (2002) 'Basic Patterns in National Health Expenditure', *Bulletin of the World Health Organization* 80 (2): 1–17.

Nadash, P. and Y.-C. Shih (2012) 'Introducing Social Insurance for Long-term Care in Taiwan: Key Issues', *International Journal of Social Welfare*, DOI: 10.1111/j.1468-2397.2011.00862.x.

Nakahara, T. (1997) 'The Health System of Japan', in M.W. Raffel (ed.) *Health Care and Reform in Industrialized Countries*. University Park, PA: Pennsylvania State University Press.

Nathan, S.A., E. Develin, N. Grove and A.B. Zwi (2005) 'An Australian Childhood Obesity Summit: The Role of Data and Evidence in "Public" Policy Making', *Australia and New Zealand Health Policy* 2 (17), http://www.anzhealthpolicy.com/content/2/1/17.

National Board of Health and Welfare (2000) *Social Services in Sweden in 1999. Needs – Interventions – Development*. Stockholm: National Board of Health and Welfare.

National Center for Health Care Statistics (2012) *Chartbook on Trends in the Health of Americans*. Washington, DC: Government Printing Office.

National Commission for Quality Long-Term Care (2007) *From Isolation to*

Integration: Recommendations to Improve Quality in Long-Term Care. Washington, DC: National Commission for Quality Long-Term Care.

National Contract for Public Health (2001) *National Contract for Public Health. Declaration of Intent to Cooperate. 2001–2003*. Leiden, 22 February, www.minvws.nl/documents/ Health/natcontract.pdf.

National Health Service (2008) 'Statistics on NHS Stop Smoking Services in England, April to September 2007 (Q2-Quarterly Report)', www.ic.nhs.uk/pubs.sss07q2.

National Rural Health Association (2009) 'Recruiting Rural Doctors', *Policy Brief*, May, http://www.ruralcenter.org/recruitment.

Navarro, V. (1999) 'Health and Equity in the World in the Era of "Globalization"', *International Journal of Health Services* 29 (2): 215–26.

Navarro, V. and L. Shi (2001) 'The Political Context of Social Inequalities and Health', *International Journal of Health Services* 31 (1): 1–21.

Navarro, V., C. Borrell, J. Benach, C. Muntaner, A. Quiroga, M. Rodriquez-Sanz, N. Verges, J. Guma and M.I. Pasarin (2003) 'The Importance of the Political and the Social in Explaining Mortality Differentials among the Countries of the OECD, 1950–1998', *International Journal of Health Services* 33 (3): 419–94.

New Zealand Core Services Committee (1992) *The Core Debate: How We Define the Core*. Wellington: National Advisory Committee on Core Health and Disability Support Services.

New Zealand Medical Association (2013) *NZMA Strategic Plan 2011–2016*. http://www.nzma.org.nz/sites/all/files/nzmastrategicplan.pdf.

New Zealand Ministry of Health (2003) *Achieving Health for All People: A Framework for Public Health Action*. Wellington: Ministry of Health.

New Zealand Ministry of Health (2008) *Annual Report, 2008*. Wellington: Ministry of Health.

New Zealand Ministry of Health (2009) Primary Health Organisations (PHOs) http://www.moh.govt.nz/moh.nsf/indexmh/phcs-pho.

Noguchi, H. and S. Shimizutani (2005) 'Supplier-Induced Demand in Japan's At-Home Care Industry', *ESRI Discussion Paper Series* 148: 1–131.

Nolte, E., S. Ettelt, S. Thomson and N. Mays (2008) 'Learning from Other Countries: An On-call Facility for Health Care Policy', *Journal of Health Services Research Policy*, 13 (2): 58–64.

Nolte, E. and C.M. McKee (2011) 'Measuring the Health of Nations: Updating an Earlier Analysis', *Health Affairs* 27: 58–71.

Norval, M., R.M. Lucas, A.P. Cullen, F.R. de Gruijl, J. Longstreth, Y. Takizawa and J.C. van der Leun (2011) 'The Human Health Effects of Ozone Depletion and Interactions with Climate Change', *Photochemical and Photobiological Sciences* 10: 199–225.

Nyman, J.A. (2008) 'American Health Policy: Cracks in the Foundation', *Journal of Health Politics, Policy and Law* 32 (5): 759–83.

OECD (1987) *Financing and Delivering Health Care: A Comparative Analysis of* OECD *Countries*. Paris: OECD.

OECD (1992) *The Reform of Health Care Systems: A Comparative Analysis of Seven* OECD *Countries*. Paris: OECD.

OECD (1996) *Caring for Frail Elderly People. Policies in Evolution*. Social Policy Studies no. 19. Paris: OECD.

OECD (2005a) *OECD Health Project*, http://www.oecd.org/document/28/0,2340,en_2649_37407_2536540_1_1_1_37407,00.html.

OECD (2005b) *The OECD Health Project: Long-term Care for Older People*. Paris: OECD.

OECD (2005c) *Health at a Glance*. Paris: OECD.

OECD (2006) *OECD Health Data 2006. A Comparative Analysis of 30 Countries*. Paris: OECD, Version: 26 June.

OECD (2008) *OECD Health Data 2008*. Paris: OECD.

OECD (2009a) 'Health at a Glance 2009: OECD Indicators', http://dx.doi.org/10.1787/717877483033

OECD (2009b) 'OECD Health Data 2009 – Comparing Health Statistics across OECD Countries', http://search.oecd.org/officialdocuments/displaydocumentpdf/?cote=PAC/COM/NEWS%282009%2917&docLanguage=En.

OECD (2011a) *Health at a Glance 2011: OECD Indicators*, OECD Publishing. http://dx.doi.org/10.1787/health_glance-2011-en.

OECD (2011b) *Health Reform: Meeting the Challenge of Ageing and Multiple Mobilities*, OECD Publishing. http://dx.doi.org/10.1787/9789264122314-en.

OECD (2011c) *Help Wanted? Providing and Paying for Long-Term Care*. Paris: OECD.

OECD (2012a) *Health: Key Tables from OECD*, No. 2. Paris: OECD. doi: 10.1787/hlthxp-cap-table-2012-2-en

OECD (2012b) *OECD Health Statistics* (database). Paris: OECD doi: 10.1787/data-00349-en. (Accessed on 26 March 2013)

OECD (2013) 'Smoking', in OECD Factbook 2013: *Economic, Environmental and Social Statistics*, OECD Publishing. http://dx.doi.org/10.1787/factbook-2013-98-en.

Ohnuki-Tiernev, E. (1984) *Illness and Culture in Contemporary Japan: An Anthropological View*. Cambridge: Cambridge University Press.

Okamoto, K. (2001) *Public Health of Japan 2001*. Osaka: National Institute of Public Health.

Okma, K.G.H. (2001) *Health Care, Health Policies and Health Care Reforms in the Netherlands*. International Publication Series Health, Welfare and Sport no. 7. The Hague: Ministry of Health, Welfare and Sport.

Okma, K.G. (2008) 'Commentary. Learning and Mislearning across Boarders: What Can we (not) Learn from the 2006 Health Care Reform in the The Netherlands? Commentary on Rosenau and Lako', *Journal of Health Politics, Policy and Law* 33 (6): 1057–71.

Okma, K.G.H. and L. Crivelli (2009) *Six Countries, Six Reform Models: The Healthcare Reform Experience of Israel, The Netherlands, New Zealand, Singapore, Switzerland and Taiwan: Healthcare Reforms 'Under the Radar Screen'*. Singapore: World Scientific Publishing Company.

Okma, K.G.H. and A.A. de Roo (2009) 'The Netherlands: From Polder Model to Modern Management', in T.R. Marmor, R. Freeman and K.G.H. Okma (eds) *Comparative Studies and the Politics of Modern Medical Care*. New Haven, London: Yale University Press.

Okma, K.G.H., T.-M. Cheng, D. Chinitz, L. Crivelli, M.-K. Lim, H. Maarse and M.E. Labra (2010) 'Six Countries, Six Health Reform Models? Health Care

Reform in Chile, Israel, Singapore, Switzerland, Taiwan and The Netherlands', *Journal of Comparative Policy Analysis: Research and Practice* 12 (1–2): 75–113.

Olivares-Tirado, P., N. Tamiya, M. Kashiwagi and K. Kashiwagi (2011) 'Predictors of the Highest Long-term Care Expenditures in Japan', *BMC Health Services Research* 11: 103–16.

Oliver, A. (2008) 'Personal Financial Incentives to Improve Health', *Health Policy Monitor*, no.12, http://www.hpm.org/en/Surveys/LSE/12/Personal_financial_incentives_to_improve_health.html?p_c:254=254&content_id=251&p_c:257=257&a=sn&y=13&p_c:66=66&p_i=97&language=en&x=55.

Oliver, A. (2009) 'Tackling Alcohol Problems', *Health Policy Monitor*, no. 13, http://www.hpm.org/en/Surveys/LSE/13/Tackling_alcohol_problems.html?p_c:254=254&content_id=251&p_c:257=257&a=sn&y=13&p_c:66=66&p_i=97&language=en&x=55.

Oliver, T.R. (2011) 'Health Care Reform as a Halfway Technology', *Journal of Health Politics, Policy and Law* 36 (3): 603–9.

O'Malley, S.P. (2006) 'The Australian Experiment: The Use of Evidence Based Medicine for the Reimbursement of Surgical and Diagnostic Procedures (1998–2004)', *Australia and New Zealand Health Policy* 3 (3), http://www.anzhealthpolicy.com/content/3/1/3.

Or, Z., C. Cases, M. Lisac, K. Vrangbaek, U. Winblad and G. Bevan (2010) 'Are Health Problems Systemic? Health Reforms under Beveridge and Bismarck Systems', *Health Economics Policy and Law* (5): 269–93.

Outshoorn, J. (2008) 'The Provision of Home Care as a Policy Problem', *Journal of Comparative Policy Analysis* 10 (1): 7–27.

Øvretveit, J. (1998) *Comparative and Cross-cultural Health Research*. Abingdon, UK: Radcliffe Medical Press.

Oxley, H. (2009) 'Policies of Healthy Ageing: An Overview', *Health Working Papers,* No. 42. Paris: OECD.

Ozegowski, S. and L. Sundmacher (2012) 'Ensuring Access to Health Care – Germany Reforms Supply Structures to Tackle Inequalities', *Health Policy* 106: 105–9.

Palmer, G.R. and S.D. Short (2000) *Health Care and Public Policy: An Australian Analysis*, 3rd edn. Melbourne: Macmillan.

Panopoulou, E. and T. Pantelidis (2011) 'Convergence in Per Capita Health Expenditures and Health Outcomes in the OECD Countries', *Applied Economics*, DOI : 10.1080/00036846.2011.583222.

Parackal, S.M., M.K. Parackal and J.A. Harraway (2010) 'Warning Labels on Alcohol Containers as a Source of Information on Alcohol Consumption in Pregnancy among New Zealand Women', *International Journal of Drug Policy* 21 (4): 302–5.

Paris, V., M. Devaux and L. Wei (2010) 'Health Systems Institutional Characteristics: A Survey of Twenty-Nine OECD Countries', *OECD Health Working Paper No. 50*. Paris: Organisation for Economic Co-operation and Development.

Paton, C. (1997) 'The Politics and Economics of Health Care Reform: Britain in a Comparative Context', in C. Altenstetter and J.W. Björkman (eds) *Health Policy Reform, National Variations and Globalization*. London: Macmillan.

Paton, C. (2007) 'Visible Hand or Invisible Fist? The New Market and Choice in the English NHS', *Health Economics, Policy and Law* 2 (4): 317–25.

Peckham, S. and M. Exworthy (2003) *Primary Care in the UK*. Basingstoke: Palgrave.

Peckham, S., M. Exworthy, M. Powell and I. Greener (2008) 'Decentralizing Health Services in the UK: A New Conceptual Framework', *Public Administration* 86 (2): 559–80.

Pelone, F., M.L. Specchia, M.A. Veneziano, S. Capizzi, S. Bucci, A. Mancuso, W. Ricciardi and A.G.de Belvis (2012) 'Economic Impact of Childhood Obesity on Health Systems: A Systematic Review', *Obesity Reviews* 13 (5): 431–40.

Perleth, M., R. Busse and F.W. Schwartz (1999) 'Regulation of Health-related Technologies in Germany', *Health Policy* 46 (2): 105–26.

Perry, N. (2012) 'A Smoke-free Country? New Zealand Taxes Aim for It', http://news.yahoo.com/smoke-free-country-zealand-taxes-aim-063909666—finance.html.

Peters, B.G. (1998) *Comparative Politics: Theory and Methods*. Basingstoke: Macmillan.

Peterson, C.L. (2006) *Alternatives for Modeling Results from the RAND Health Insurance Experiment*. Washington, DC: Congressional Research Service.

Pfau-Effinger, B. (2004) *Development of Culture, Welfare State and Women's Employment in Europe*. Aldershot: Ashgate.

Pitts, S.R., E.R Carrier, E.C. Rich and A.L. Kellermann (2010) 'Where Americans Get Acute Care: Increasingly, It's Not At Their Doctor's Office', *Health Affairs* 29 (9): 1620–9.

Pocock, N.S. and K.H. Phua (2011) 'Medical Tourism and Policy Implications for Health Systems: A Conceptual Framework from a Comparative Study of Thailand, Singapore and Malaysia', *Globalization and Health* 7: 12–24.

Pollack, H.A. (2011) 'Prevention and Public Health', *Journal of Health Politics, Policy and Law* 36 (3): 515–20; doi:10.1215/03616878-1271189.

Porter, M.E. and E.O. Teisberg (2006) *Redefining Health Care: Value-Based Competition on Results*. Cambridge, MA: Harvard Business School Press.

Portier, C.J., T.K.Thigpen, S.R. Carter, C.H. Dilworth, A.E. Grambsch, J. Gohlke, J. Hess, S.N. Howard, G. Luber, J.T. Lutz, D.M. Wolcock and M.R. Meador (2010) *A Human Health Perspective On Climate Change: A Report Outlining the Research Needs on the Human Health Effects of Climate Change*. Research Triangle Park, NC: Environmental Health Perspectives/National Institute of Environmental Health Sciences.

Post E.S., A. Grambsch, C. Weaver, P. Morefield, J. Huang, L.-Y. Leung, C.G. Nolte, P. Adams, X.-Z. Liang, J.-H. Zhu, and H. Mahoney (2012) 'Variation in Estimated Ozone-Related Health Impacts of Climate Change due to Modeling Choices and Assumption', *Environmental Health Perspectives*, http://dx.doi.org/10.1289/ehp.1104271.

Powell, M. and M. Anesaki (2011) *Health Care in Japan*. New York: Routledge.

Pratt, B. and B. Loff (2012) 'Health Research Systems: Promoting Health Equity or Economic Competitiveness?', *Bulletin of the World Health Organisation* 90: 55–62.

Quah, E. and T.L. Boon (2003) 'The Economic Cost of Particulate Air Pollution on Health in Singapore', *Journal of Asian Economics* 14 (1): 73–90.

Quah, S.R. (2003) 'Traditional Healing Systems and the Ethos of Science', *Social Science and Medicine* 57 (10): 1997–2012.

Quesnel-Vallée, A., E. Renahy, T. Jenkins and H. Cerigo (2012) 'Assessing Barriers to Health Insurance and Threats to Equity in Comparative Perspective: The Health Insurance Access Database', *BMC Health Services Research* 12: 107, http://www.biomedcentral.com/1472-6963/12/107.

Radin, B.A. (2010) 'When is a Health Department not a Health Department? The Case of the US Department of Health and Human Services', *Social Policy and Administration* 44 (2): 142–54.

Raffel, M.W. (ed.) (1997) *Health Care and Reform in Industrialized Countries*. University Park, PA: University of Pennsylvania Press.

Rainham, D. (2007) 'Do Differences in Health Make a Difference? A Review for Health Policymakers', *Health Policy* 84 (2–3): 123–32.

Ranade, W. (ed.) (1998) *Markets and Health Care: A Comparative Analysis*. London: Longman.

Ranci, C. and E. Pavolini (eds) (2013) 'Reforms in Long-Term Care Policies in Europe', New York: Springer Science+Business Media.

Raphael, D. and T. Bryant (2006) 'The State's Role in Promoting Population Health: Public Health Concerns in Canada, USA, UK, and Sweden', *Health Policy* 78: 39–55.

Rasanathan, K., E.V. Montesinos, D. Matheson, C. Etienne and T. Evans (2011) 'Primary Health Care and the Social Determinants of Health: Essential and Complementary Approaches for Reducing Inequities in Health', *Journal of Epidemiology and Community Health* 65: 656–60.

Rauch, D. (2006) 'Institutional Fragmentation, Institutional Engineering and the Development of Elderlycare and Childcare in Sweden', *Scandinavian Political Studies* 29 (4): 285–307.

Rechel, B., M. Suhrcke, S. Tsolova, J.E. Suk, M. Desai, M. McKee, D. Stucklerc, I. Abubakar, P. Hunter, M. Senek and J.C. Semenza (2011) 'Economic Crisis and Communicable Disease Control in Europe: A Scoping Study among National Experts', *Health Policy* 103: 168–75.

Reese, P.P., A.L. Caplan, R.D. Bloom, P.L. Abt and J.H. Karlawish (2010) 'How Should We Use Age to Ration Health Care? Lessons from the Case of Kidney Transplantation', *Journal of the American Geriatric Society* 58: 1980–6.

Reisman, D.A. (2006) 'Medisave and Medishield in Singapore: Getting the Balance Right', *Savings and Development* 2: 189–215.

Reisman, D.A. (2009) *Social Policy in an Ageing Society*. Cheltenham, UK: Edward Elgar.

Reiss, C. (2003) 'Malpractice Debate Now A Blame Game', *Sarasota Herald Tribune* 13 January, p. 1A.

Republic of China Yearbook (2008) Taipei: Government Information Office.

Reuters (2005) 'Expert Sees Obesity Hitting U.S. Life Expectancy', http://news.yahoo.com/news?tmpl=story&cid=5718cu./nm/20050202/html.

Reuters (2006) 'Hospitals Prepare for Growing Ranks of Obese', 6 June.

Reynolds, C. (2011) *Public and Environmental Health Law*. Annandale, NSW: Federation Press.

Rico, A., R.B. Saltman and W.G.W. Boerma (2003) 'Organizational Restructuring in European Health Systems: The Role of Primary Care', *Social Policy and Administration* 37 (6): 592–608.

Riksdagen (2009) 'The History of the Rigsdag', http://www.riksdagen.se/templates/R_Page____798.aspx.

Riska, E. and K. Wegar (1995) 'The Medical Profession in the Nordic Countries. Medical Uncertainty and Gender-based Work', in T. Johnson, G. Larkin and M. Saks (eds) *Health Professions and the State in Europe*. London: Routledge.

Rix, M., A. Owen and K. Eagar (2005) '(Re)form with Substance? Restructuring and Governance in the Australian Health System 2004/05', *Australia and New Zealand Health Policy* 2 (19), http://www.anzhealthpolicy.com/content/2/1/19.

Robine, J.M., S. Cheung, S. LeRoy, H. Van Oyen, C. Griffiths and J.M. Michel (2008) 'Death Toll Exceeded 70,000 in Europe during the Summer of 2003', *Les Comptes Rendus/Série Biologies* 331: 171–8.

Robone, S., N. Rice and P.C. Smith (2011) 'Health Systems' Responsiveness and Its Characteristics: A Cross-Country Comparative Analysis', *Health System Research* 46 (6, pt.2): 2079–100.

Romaine-Davis, A., J. Boondas and A. Lenihan (eds) (1995) *Encyclopedia of Home Care for the Elderly*. Westport, CT: Greenwood Press.

Ros, C.C., P.P. Groenwegen and D.M.J. Delnoij (2000) 'All Rights Reserved, or Can We Just Copy? Cost Sharing Arrangements and Characteristics of Health Care Systems', *Health Policy* 52 (1): 1–13.

Rose, R. (2008) 'Politics in Britain', in G.A. Almond, G. Bingham Powell, R.J. Dalton and K. Strøm (eds) *Comparative Politics Today*, 9th edn. New York: Pearson Longman.

Rosenau, P. Vaillancourt and C.J. Lako (2008) 'An Experiment with Regulated Competition and Individual Mandates for Universal Health Care: The New Dutch Health Insurance System', *Journal of Health Politics, Policy and Law* 33 (6): 1032–55.

Rosenbrock, R. and T. Gerlinger (2004) *Gesundheitspolitik. Eine systematische Einführung*. Bern: Verlag Hans Huber.

Ross, E. (2003) 'WHO Links SARS to Three Small Mammals', *Associated Press News Story*, 23 May.

Rostron, B. (2011) 'Smoking-attributable Mortality in the United States', *Epidemiology* 22 (3): 350–5.

Rothgang, H. (2010) 'Social Insurance for Long-term Care: An Evaluation of the German Model', *Social Policy & Administration* 44 (4): 436–60.

Rothgang, H., M. Cacace, L. Frisina, S. Grimmeisen, A. Schmid and C. Wendt (2010) *The State and Healthcare. Comparing OECD Countries*. Basingstoke: Palgrave Macmillan.

Rovere, M. and B. Barua (2012) 'Opportunity for Health Reform: Lessons from the Netherlands', *Fraser Forum*, October. http://www.fraserinstitute.org/uploadedFiles/fraser-ca/Content/research-news/research/articles/opportunity-for-health-reform-lessons-from-the-netherlands.pdf.

Rummery, K. and M. Fine (2012) 'Care: a Critical Review of Theory, Policy and Practice', *Social Policy & Administration* 46 (3): 321–43.

Russell, J., T. Greenhalgh, E. Bryne and J. McDonnell (2008) 'Recognizing Rhetoric in Health Care Policy Analysis', *Journal of Health Services Research Policy* 13 (1): 40–6.

Ryburn, B., Y. Wells and P. Foreman (2009) 'Enabling Independence: Restorative Approaches to Home Care Provision for Frail Older Adults', *Health and Social Care in the Community* 17 (3): 225–34.

Sabik, L.M. and R.K. Lie (2008) 'Priority Setting in Health Care: Lessons from the Experiences of Eight Countries', *International Journal for Equity in Health* 7 (4): 1–13.

Sade, R.M. (2007) 'Ethical Foundations of Health Care System Reform', *Annals of Thoracic Surgery* 84: 1429–31.

Sage, W.M. and R. Kersh (eds) (2006) *Medical Malpractice and the U.S. Health Care System*. Cambridge, MA: Cambridge University Press.

Saks, M. (2002) *Orthodox and Alternative Medicine: Politics, Professionalization, and Health Care*. London: Sage.

Saltman, R.B. (1997) 'Convergence Versus Social Embeddedness. Debating the Future Direction of Health Systems', *European Journal of Public Health* 7 (4): 449–53.

Saltman, R.B. (1998) 'Health Reform in Sweden: The Road Beyond Cost Containment', in W. Ranade (ed.) *Markets and Health Care: A Comparative Analysis*. London: Longman.

Saltman, R.B. (2002) 'Regulating Incentives: The Past and Present Role of the State in Health Care Systems', *Social Science and Medicine* 54 (11): 1677–84.

Saltman, R.B. (2012) 'The Role of Comparative Health Studies for Policy Learning', *Journal of Health Politics, Policy and Law* 7 (1): 11–13.

Saltman, R.B. and V. Bankauskaite (2006) 'Conceptualizing Decentralization in European Health Systems: A Functional Perspective', *Journal of Health Economics, Policy and Law* 1: 127–47.

Saltman, R.B. and S.-E. Bergman (2005) 'Renovating the Commons: Swedish Health Care Reforms in Perspective', *Journal of Health Politics, Policy and Law* 30 (1): 253–76.

Saltman, R.B., A. Rico and W. Boerma (eds) (2006a) *Primary Care in the Driver's Seat? Organizational Reform in European Primary Care*. Maidenhead: Open University Press.

Saltman, R.B., H.F.W. Dubois and M. Chawla (2006b) 'The Impact of Aging on Long-term Care in Europe and Some Potential Policy Responses', *International Journal of Health Services* 36 (4): 719–46.

Sassi, F., M. Devaux, M. Cecchini and E. Rusticelli (2009) *The Obesity Epidemic: Analysis of Past and Projected Future Trends in Selected OECD Countries*. Paris: OECD, Health Working Papers No. 45.

Sauerland, D. (2009) 'The Legal Framework for Health Care Quality Assurance in Germany', *Health Economics, Policy and Law* 4 (1): 79–98.

Schäfer, W., M. Kroneman, W. Boerma, M.v.d. Berg, G. Westert, W. Devillé and E.v. Ginneken (2010) 'The Netherlands. Health System Review', *Health Systems in Transition* 12 (1): 1–198.

Schlander, M. (2010) *Health Technology Assessments by the National Institute for Health and Clinical Excellence: A Qualitative Study*. Berlin: Springer.

Schmid, A. and R. Götze (2009) 'Cross-national Policy Learning in Health System Reform: The Case of Diagnosis Related Groups', *International Social Security Review* 62 (4): 21–39.

Schmid, A., M. Cacace, R. Götze and H. Rothgang (2010) 'Explaining Health

Care System Change: Problem Pressure and the Emergence of "Hybrid" Health Care Systems', *Journal of Health Politics, Policy and Law* 35 (4): 455–86.

Schneider, M.J. (2012) *Introduction to Public Health w/Healthy People 2020*. New York: Jones and Bartlett Publishers.

Schoen, C., R. Osborn, M.M. Doty, M. Bishop, J. Peugh and N. Murukulta (2007) 'Toward Higher-Performance Health Systems: Adults' Health Care Experiences in Seven Countries', *Health Affairs* 26 (6): w717–34.

Schoenbaum, S.C., C. Schoen, J.L. Nicholson and J.C. Cantor (2011) 'Mortality Amenable to Health Care in the United States: The Roles of Demographics and Health Systems Performance', *Journal of Public Health Policy* 32: 407–29.

Schroeder, S.A. (2007) 'We Can Do Better: Improving the Health of the American People', *New England Journal of Medicine* 357: 1221–8.

Schut, F.T. and B.v.d. Berg (2010) 'Sustainability of Comprehensive Universal Long-term Care Insurance in the Netherlands', *Social Policy & Administration* 44 (4): 411–35.

Schwartz, F.F. and R. Busse (1997) 'Germany', in C. Ham (ed.) *Health Care Reform: Learning from International Experience*. Buckingham: Open University Press.

Schwartz, M.D. (2011) 'Health Care Reform and the Primary Care Workforce Bottleneck', *Journal of General Internal Medicine* 27 (4): 469–72.

Scott, C.D. (2001) *Public and Private Roles in Health Care: Experiences from Seven Countries*. Buckingham: Open University Press.

Scott, W.G., H.M. Scott and T.S. Auld (2005) 'Consumer Access to Health Information on the Internet: Health Policy Implications', *Australia and New Zealand Health Policy* 2 (13), http://www.anzhealthpolicy.com/content/2/1/13.

Seedhouse, D. (1991) *Liberating Medicine*. Chichester: Wiley.

Semansky, R., C. Willging, D.J. Ley and B. Rylko-Bauer (2012) 'Lost in the Rush to National Reform: Recommendations to Improve Impact on Behavioral Health Providers in Rural Areas', *Journal of Health Care for the Poor and Underserved* 23 (2): 842–56.

Sexton, S. (2001) 'Trading Health Care Away? GATS, Public Services and Privatisation', www.thecornerhouse.org.uk/pdf/briefing/23gats.pdf.

Sheffield, P.E. and P.J. Landrigan (2011) 'Global Climate Change and Children's Health: Threats and Strategies for Prevention', *Environmental Health Perspectives* 119 (3): 291–8.

Sheldon, G.F. (2011) 'The Evolving Surgeon Shortage in the Health Reform Era', *Journal of Gastrointestinal Surgery* 15: 1104–11.

Shih, F.-L., S. Thompson and P. Tremlett (eds) (2009) *Rewriting Culture in Taiwan*. New York: Routledge.

Shortt, J. (2004) 'Obesity: A Public Health Dilemma', *AORN Journal* 80 (6): 1069–76, 78.

Singapore Ministry of Health (1995) 'Traditional Chinese Medicine', *Report of the Committee on Traditional Chinese Medicine*, October.

Singapore Ministry of Health (2008) Singapore: Singapore Ministry of Health, http://www.moh.gov.sg/corp/index.do.

Singapore Ministry of Health (2009) 'Healthcare Services: Intermediate and Long-Term Care', www.gov.sg/moh/mohinfo/mohinfo-a.html.

Skinner, J.S., D.O. Staiger and E.S. Fisher (2006) 'Is Technological Change in Medicine Always Worth It? The Case of Myocardial Infarction', *Health Affairs* 25: w34–w47.

Skolnick, R. (2011) *Global Health 101*. Burlington, MA: Jones and Bartlett.

Sloane, T. (2005) 'The Long-Term Problem', *Modern Healthcare* 35 (30): 18.

Smith, J. and N. Mays (2007) 'Primary Care Organizations in New Zealand and England: Tipping the Balance of the Health System in Favour of Primary Care?', *International Journal of Health Planning and Management* 23: 3–19.

Smith, R.D. and K. Hanson (eds) (2012) *Health Systems in Low- and Middle-Income Countries: An Economic and Policy Perspective*. New York: Oxford University Press.

Smith, P.C., A. Anell, R. Busse, L. Crivelli, J. Healy, A.K. Lindahl, G. Westert and T. Kene (2012) 'Leadership and Governance in Seven Developed Health Systems', *Health Policy* 106: 37–49.

'Smoking in Taiwan' (2012) http://en.wikipedia.org/wiki/Smoking_in_Taiwan.

Sodaro, M.J. (2004) *Comparative Politics. A Global Introduction*. Boston: McGraw-Hill.

Someya, Y. and Y. Wells (2008) 'Current Issues on Ageing in Japan: A Comparison with Australia', *Australasian Journal on Ageing* 27 (1): 8–13.

Stanhope, M. and J. Lancaster (2011) *Public Health Nursing: Population-Centered Care in the Community*, 8th edn. Maryland Heights, MO: Mosby.

Stanton, G.T. (2003) 'How Marriage Improves Health', www.divorcereform.org/ mel/abetterhealth.html.

Stanton, M.W. and M.K. Rutherford (2005) 'The High Concentration of U.S. Health Care Expenditures', Research in Action Issue 19. AHRQ Pub. No. 06–0060. Rockville, MD: Agency for Healthcare Research and Quality.

Starfield, B. (2000) 'Is US Health Really the Best in the World?', *Journal of the American Medical Association* 284 (4): 483–85.

Starfield, B., J. Gervas and D. Mangin (2012) 'Clinical Care and Health Disparities', *Annual Review of Public Health* 33: 89–106.

Starr, P. (2011) *Remedy and Reaction: The Peculiar American Struggle over Health Care Reform*. New Haven, CT: Yale University Press.

Steinberg, E.P. and B.R. Luce (2005) 'Evidence Based: Caveat Emptor!', *Health Affairs* 24 (1): 80–93.

Stenger, R.J. and J.E. DeVoe (2010) 'Policy Challenges in Building the Medical Home: Do We Have a Shared Blueprint?', *Journal of the American Board of Family Medicine* 23: 384–92.

Strand, L.B., S. Tong, R. Aird and D. McRae (2010) 'Vulnerability of Eco-environmental Health to Climate Change: The Views of Government Stakeholders and Other Specialists in Queensland, Australia', *BMC Public Health* 10: 441–50.

Stone, D. (1999) 'Learning Lessons and Transferring Policy across Time, Space and Disciplines', *Politics* 19 (1): 51–9.

Straits Times, The (2000) 'Singapore's Health System is Best in Asia', 21 January.

Stukel, T.A., F.L. Lucas and D.E. Wennberg (2005) 'Long-term Outcomes of

Regional Variations in Intensity of Invasive vs. Medical Management of Medicare Patients with Acute Myocardial Infarction', *Journal of the American Medical Association* 293: 1329–37.

Sullivan, L.W. (1990) 'Healthy People 2000', *New England Journal of Medicine* 323: 1065–7.

Swedish Institute (2007) *The Swedish System of Government*. Stockholm: Swedish Institute.

Swerissen, H. (2004) 'Australian Primary Care Policy in 2004: Two Tiers or One for Medicare?' *Australia and New Zealand Health Policy* 1 (2), http://www.anzhealthpolicy.com/content/1/1/2.

Syrett, K. (2003) 'A Technocratic Fix to the "Legitimacy Problem"? The Blair Government and Health Care Rationing in the United Kingdom', *Journal of Health Politics, Policy and Law* 28 (4): 715–46.

Syrett, K. (2008) *Law, Legitimacy and the Rationing of Health Care*. Cambridge: Cambridge University Press.

Szebehely, M. (2005) 'Anhörigas betalda och obetalda äldreomsorgsinsatser', in Statens Offentliga Utredningor (SOU) (2005:66), *Forskingsrapporter till Jämställdhetspolitiska utredningen*. Stockholm: Social Department.

Taiwan Medical Association (2004) 'Statistics of Practicing Doctors and Medical Associations in the Taiwan Area, Republic of China'. Taipei: Taiwan Medical Association.

Takano, T. and K. Nakamura (2004) 'Participatory Research to Enhance Vision Sharing for Healthy Town Initiatives in Japan', *Health Promotion International* 19 (3): 299–307.

Talbot, L. and G. Verrinder (2010) *Promoting Health: The Primary Health Care Approach*. Chatswood, NSW: Churchill Livingstone Australia.

Tamiya, N., H. Noguchi, A. Nishi, M.R. Reich, N. Ikegami, H. Hashimoto, K. Shibuya, I. Kawachi and J.C. Campbell (2011) 'Population Ageing and Wellbeing: Lessons from Japan's Long-term Care Insurance Policy', *The Lancet* 378 (9797): 1183–92, DOI: 10.1016/S0140-6736(11)61176-8.

Tan, A.S.L. (2011) 'An Approach to Building the Case for Nutrition Policies to Limit Trans-fat Intake – A Singapore Case Study', *Health Policy* 100: 264–72.

Tanner, L. (2006) 'U.S. Newborn Survival Rate Ranks Low', *Associated Press*, 5 May.

Tatara, K. and E. Okamoto (2009) 'Japan: Health System Review', *Health Systems in Transition* 11 (5): 1–164.

Tay, J., F.N. Yeuk, J. Cutter and L. James (2010) 'Influenza A (H1N1-2009) Pandemic in Singapore: Public Health Control Measures Implemented and Lessons Learnt', *Annals of the Academy of Medicine Singapore* 39: 313–24.

Taylor, S. (2009) 'Wealth, Health and Equity: Convergence to Divergence in Late 20th Century Globalization', *British Medical Bulletin* 91: 29–48.

Taylor, V.H., C.M. Curtis and C. Davis (2010) 'The Obesity Epidemic: The Role of Addiction', *CMAJ* 182 (4): 327–8.

Taylor-Gooby, P. and L. Mitton (2008) 'Much Noise, Little Progress: The UK Experience of Privatization', in D. Béland and B. Grand (eds) *Public and Private Social Policy. Health and Pension Policies in a New Era*. Basingstoke: Palgrave Macmillan.

Teo, P., A. Chan and P. Straughan (2003) 'Providing Health Care for Older Persons in Singapore', *Health Policy* 64 (3): 399–413.

Tenbensel, T., J. Cumming, T. Ashton and P. Barnett (2008) 'Where There's a Will, Is There a Way? Is New Zealand's Publicly Funded Health Sector Able to Steer Towards Population Health?', *Social Science and Medicine* 67: 1143–52.

Tenbensel T., S. Eagle and T. Ashton (2012) 'Comparing Health Policy Agendas across Eleven High Income Countries: Islands of Difference in a Sea of Similarity', *Health Policy* 106 (1): 29–36.

Tester, S. (1996) *Community Care for Older People. A Comparative Perspective*. London: Macmillan.

Tester, S. (1998) 'Comparative Approaches to Long-Term Care for Adults', in J. Clasen (ed.) *Comparative Social Policy: Theories and Methods*. Oxford: Blackwell, pp. 136–58.

Thacker, S.B., D.F. Stroup, V. Carande-Kulis, J.S. Marks, K. Roy and J.L. Gerberding (2006) 'Measuring the Public's Health', *Public Health Reports* 121: 14–22.

Theobald, H. (2003) 'Welfare System, Professionalisation and the Question of Inequality', *International Journal of Sociology and Social Policy* 23 (4/5): 159–85.

Theobald, H. (2004) 'Care Services for the Elderly in Germany. Infrastructure, Access and Utilisation from the Perspective of Different User Groups', Discussion paper (SP I 2004-302), Working Group on Public Health Policy. Berlin: Social Science Research Centre (WZB) Berlin.

Theobald, H. (2012) 'Combining Welfare Mix and New Public Management: The Case of Long-term Care Insurance in Germany', *International Journal of Social Welfare* 1–10.

Theobald, H. and S. Hampel (2013) 'Radical Institutional Change and Incremental Transformation: Long-Term Care Insurance in Germany', in C. Ranci and E. Pavolini (eds) *Reforms in Long-Term Care Policies in Europe*. New York: Springer Science+Business Media.

Thomas, R.L. (2011) 'Convergence: It's What's Next in Healthcare IT', *Healthcare Financial Management* 65 (1): 130–2.

Thomas, S.L., S. Lewis, J. Hyde, D. Castle and P. Komesaroff (2010) 'The Solution Needs to be Complex: Obese Adults' Attitudes about the Effectiveness of Individual and Population Based Interventions for Obesity', *BMC Public Health* 10: 420, http://www.biomedcentral.com/1471-2458/10/420.

Thomson, S. and E. Mossialos (2008) 'Medical Savings Accounts: Can They Improve Health System Performance in Europe?', *EuroObserver* 10 (4): 1–4.

Thomson, S., E. Mossialos and R.G. Evans (2009) *Private Health Insurance and Medical Savings Accounts: Lessons from International Experience*. Cambridge: Cambridge University Press.

Thomson, S. and A. Dixon (2006) 'Choices in Health Care: The European Experience', *Journal of Health Services Research Policy* 11 (3): 167–71.

Thomson, S., R. Osburn, D. Squires and S.J. Reed (eds) (2011) *International Profiles of Health Care Systems 2011*. New York: The Commonwealth Fund.

Thorpe, K.E., C.S. Florence, D.H. Howard and P. Joski (2004a) 'The Impact of Obesity on Rising Medical Spending', *Health Affairs*, 20 October.

Thorpe, K.E., C.S. Florence and P. Joski (2004b) 'Which Medical Conditions Account for the Rise in Health Care Spending?', *Health Affairs*, 25 August.

Thorpe, K.E., L.L. Ogden and K. Galactionova (2010) 'Chronic Conditions Account for Rise in Medicare Spending from 1987 to 2006', *Health Affairs* 29 (4): 718–24.

Timmermans, A. (2001) 'Arenas as Institutional Sites for Policymaking: Patterns and Effects in Comparative Perspective', *Journal of Comparative Policy Analysis* 3: 311–37.

Tjadens, F. and M. Duijnstee (2000) 'The Netherlands', in F. Tjadens and M. Pijl (eds) *The Support Of Family Carers and Their Organisations in Seven Western-European Countries: State of Affairs in 1998*. Utrecht: Netherlands Institute for Care and Welfare.

Tompa, E., A.J. Culyer and R. Dolinschi (2008) *Economic Evaluation of Interventions for Occupational Health and Safety*. New York: Oxford University Press.

Trappenburg, M. and M. De Groot (2001) 'Controlling Medical Specialists in the Netherlands: Delegating the Dirty Work', in M. Bovens, P. t'Hart and B.G. Peters (eds) *Success and Failure in Public Governance. A Comparative Analysis*. Cheltenham: Edward Elgar.

Thrasher, J.F., M.C. Rousuc, D. Hammond, A. Navarro and J.R. Corrigane (2011) 'Estimating the Impact of Pictorial Health Warnings and "Plain" Cigarette Packaging: Evidence from Experimental Auctions among Adult Smokers in the United States', *Health Policy* 102: 41–8.

Trydegård, G.-B. (2000) *Tradition, Change and Variation: Past and Present Trends in Public Old-Age Care*. Dissertation. Stockholm: Department of Social Work, University of Stockholm.

Trydegård, G.-B. (2003) 'Swedish Elderly Care in Transition: Unchanged National Policy but Substantial Changes in Practice', paper presented at the 2003 ESPAnet Conference, 13–15 November, Copenhagen.

Trydegård, G.-B. and M. Thorslund (2001) 'Inequality in the Welfare State? Local Variation in Care of the Elderly – the Case of Sweden', *International Journal of Social Welfare* 10 (3): 174–84.

Tsai, J.C.-H., W.-Y. Chen and Y.-W. Liang (2011) 'Nonemergent Emergency Department Visits under the National Health Insurance in Taiwan', *Health Policy* 100: 189–95.

Tsutsui, T. and N. Muramatsu (2007) 'Japan's Universal Long-Term Care System Reform of 2005: Containing Costs and Realizing a Vision', *Journal of the American Geriatric Society* 55: 1458–63.

Tully, S. (2010) 'Documents Reveal AT&T, Verizon, Others Thought about Dropping Employer Sponsored Benefits', *Fortune*, 6 May.

Tuohy, C.H. (2012a) 'Reform and the Politics of Hybridization in Mature Health Care States', *Journal of Health Politics, Policy and Law* 37 (4): 611–32.

Tuohy, C.H. (2012b) 'Shall We Dance? The Intricate Project of Comparison in the Study of Health Policy', *Health Economics, Policy and Law* 7 (1): 21–3.

Turnock, B.J. (2011) *Public Health: What It Is and How It Works*, 5th edn. New York: Jones and Bartlett Publishers.

Twaddle, A.C. (1999) *Health Care Reform in Sweden, 1980–1994*. London: Auburn House.

Twaddle, A.C. (ed.) (2002) *Health Care Reform around the World*. Westport, CT: Auburn House.

Twigg, J. (1989) 'Models of Carers: How Do Social Care Agencies Conceptualise Their Relationship with Informal Carers?', *Journal of Social Policy* 18 (1): 53–66.

Ubel, P.A. (2001) *Pricing Life: Why it's Time for Health Care Rationing*. Cambridge, MA: MIT Press.

Ueda, H., F. Armada, M. Kashiwabara and I. Yoshimi (2011) 'Street Smoking Bans in Japan: A Hope for Smoke-free Cities?', *Health Policy* 102: 49–55.

Unal, B., J.A. Critchley, D. Fidan and S. Capewell (2005) 'Life-years Gained from Modern Cardiological Treatments and Population Risk Factor Changes in England and Wales, 1981–2000', *American Journal of Public Health* 95: 103–8.

UNAIDS (2010) *Report on the Global AIDS Epidemic*. http://www.unaids.org/GlobalReport/Global_report.htm.

UNAIDS (2012) Press Release, 20 November, http://www.unaids.org/en/resources/presscentre/pressreleaseandstatementarchive/2012/november/20121120prresults/.

United States Department of Health and Human Services (2001) *The Surgeon General's Call to Action to Prevent and Decrease Overweight and Obesity*. Washington: US Government Printing Office.

United States Department of Health and Human Services (2004) 'HHS Announces Revised Medicare Obesity Coverage Policy' (accessed 10 October 2006).

United States Department of Health and Human Services (2005) *National Guideline for Overweight and Obesity in Children and Adolescents: Assessment, Prevention, and Management*. Washington, DC: US Government Printing Office.

United States Environmental Protection Agency (2009) 'Climate Change – Health and Environmental Effects', www.epa.gov/climatechange/effects/health.html (accessed 15 May 2009).

Valente, T.W. (2002) *Evaluating Health Promotion Programs*. New York: Oxford University Press.

Van Wave, T.W., F.D. Scutchfield and P.A. Honore (2010) 'Recent Advances in Public Health Systems Research in the United States', *Annual Review of Public Health* 31: 283–95.

Verspohl, I. (2012) *Health Care Reforms in Europe. Convergence towards a Market Model?* Baden-Baden: Nomos Verlagsgesellschaft.

Victorian Department of Human Services (1996) *Towards a Safer Choice: The Practice of Traditional Chinese Medicine*. Melbourne: Department of Human Services.

Victorian Ministerial Advisory Committee on Traditional Chinese Medicine (1998) *Traditional Chinese Medicine: Report on Options for Regulation of Practitioners*. Melbourne: Department of Human Services.

Visser-Jansen, G. and C.P.M. Knipscheer (2004) *Eurofamcare: National Background Report for the Netherlands*. Amsterdam: Free University.

Volkow, N.D. and C.P. O'Brien (2007) 'Issues for DSM-V: Should Obesity be Included as a Brain Disorder?', *American Journal of Psychiatry* 164: 708–10.

Von Lengerke, T. and C. Krauth (2011) 'Economic Costs of Adult Obesity: A Review of Recent European Studies with a Focus on Subgroup-specific Costs', Maturitas 69 (3): 220–9.

Vrangbaek, K., R. Robertson, U. Winblad, H.v.d. Bovenkamp and A. Dixon (2012) 'Choice Policies in Northern European Health Systems', *Health Economics, Policy and Law* 7: 47–71.

Wagenaar, A.C. and M. Wolfson (1995) 'Deterring Sales and Provision of Alcohol to Minors: A Study of Enforcement in 295 Counties in Four States', *Public Health Reports* 995 (110): 419–27.

Wagner, A.K., A. Johnson Graves, S.K. Reiss, R. LeCates, F. Zhang, D. Ross-Degnan (2011) 'Access to Care and Medicines, Burden of Health Care Expenditures, and Risk Protection: Results from the World Health Survey', *Health Policy* 100: 151–8.

Wagstaff, A. (2007) 'Health Systems in East Asia: What Can Developing Countries Learn from Japan and the Asian Tigers?' *Health Economics* 16: 441–56.

Wall, A. (ed.) (1996) *Health Systems in Liberal Democracies*. London: Routledge.

Wallace, R.B. (2007) *Public Health and Preventive Medicine*, 15th edn. Columbus, OH: McGraw-Hill.

Walton, M., J. Waiti, L. Signal and G. Thomson (2010) 'Identifying Barriers to Promoting Healthy Nutrition in New Zealand Primary Schools', *Health Education Journal* 69 (1): 84–94.

Wang, K.Y-T. (2011) 'Child Care and Elder Care Arrangements in Taiwan', *Journal of Comparative Social Welfare* 27 (2): 165–74.

Wang, Y.C., K. McPherson, T. Marsh, S.L. Gortmaker and M. Brown (2011) 'Health and Economic Burden of the Projected Obesity Trends in the USA and the UK', *The Lancet* 378 (9793): 815–25.

Ward, L. (2002) 'Health Service Failing Homeless', *The Guardian*, 17 December.

Watson, E.A. and J. Mears (1999) *Women, Work and Care of the Elderly*. Aldershot: Ashgate.

Weale, A. (1998) 'Rationing Health Care', *British Medical Journal* 316: 410–26.

Weber, M. (1949) *The Methodology of the Social Sciences*. New York: Free Press.

Webster, C. (1998) *The National Health Service. A Political History*. Oxford: Oxford University Press.

Weinstein, M.C. (2001) 'Should Physicians be Gatekeepers of Medical Resources?', *Journal of Medical Ethics* 27: 268–74.

Weissert, C.S. and W.G. Weissert (2002) *Governing Health: The Politics of Health Policy*. Baltimore: The Johns Hopkins University Press.

Wells, D.A., J.S. Ross and A.S. Detsky (2007) 'What is Different about the Market for Health Care?', *Journal of the American Medical Association* 298 (23): 2785–87.

Wen, C.-P., S.-P. Tsai and W.-S. Chung (2008) 'A 10-Year Experience of Universal Health Insurance in Taiwan: Assessing the Health Impact and Disparity Reduction', *Annals of Internal Medicine* 148 (4): 258–67.

Wendt, C., H. Rothgang and U. Helmert (2005) *The Self-Regulatory German Health Care System between Growing Competition and State Hierarchy*. TranState Working Papers no 32. Bremen: University of Bremen.

Wendt, C., L. Firsina and H. Rothgang (2009) 'Healthcare System Types: A Conceptual Framework for Comparison', *Social Policy and Administration* 43 (1): 70–90.

Wenger, E.L. (2001) 'Restructuring Care for the Elderly in Germany', *Current Sociology* 49 (3): 175–88.

Werkö, L., J. Chamova and J. Adolfson (2001) 'Health Technology Assessment. The Swedish Experience', *Eurohealth* 7 (1): 29–31.

Wessen, A.F. (1999) 'The Comparative Study of Health Care Reform', in F.D. Powell and A.F. Wessen (eds) *Health Care Systems in Transition: An International Perspective*. Thousand Oaks, CA: Sage.

Wharam, J.F. and N. Daniels (2007) 'Toward Evidence-Based Policy Making and Standardized Assessment of Health Policy Reform', *Journal of the American Medical Association* 298 (6): 676–79.

White, C. (2011) *The Personal Touch – The Dutch Experience of Personal Health Budgets*. London: Health Foundation.

Whitehead, M. (1998) 'Diffusion of Ideas on Social Inequalities in Health: A European Perspective', *The Milbank Quarterly* 76 (3): 469–92.

WHO (1946) 'Preamble to the Constitution of the World Health Organization as adopted by the International Health Conference', New York, 19–22 June, 1946; signed on 22 July 1946 by the representatives of 61 States, and entered into force on 7 April 1948.

WHO (1996) 'Traditional Medicine', Fact Sheet no. 134, September. Geneva: WHO.

WHO (2001) *Global Status Report on Alcohol*. Geneva: WHO, June.

WHO (2002) *Alcohol Control Policies*. Geneva: WHO, www.WHO.int/substanceabuse/PDFfiles/global_alcohol_status_report/8Alcoholcontrol policies.pdf.

WHO (2003) *Moving towards a Tobacco-free Europe: The European Report on Tobacco Control Policy, 1997–2002*. European Ministerial Conference for a Tobacco-free Europe. Copenhagen: WHO.

WHO (2008a) 'Climate Change and Human Health', www.who.int/globalchange/climate/summary/en/print.html (accessed 16 May 2009).

WHO (2009a) *Global Database on Body Mass Index*. Geneva: WHO.

WHO (2008b) *WHO Report on the Global Tobacco Epidemic, 2008: The MPOWER Package*. Geneva: WHO.

WHO (2009b) *WHO Report on the Global Tobacco Epidemic, 2009: Implementing Smoke-free Environments*. Geneva: WHO.

WHO (2010) 'Climate Change and Health', Fact Sheet No. 266.
http://www.who.int/mediacentre/factsheets/fs266/en/.

WHO (2012a) 'Obesity and Overweight', Fact Sheet No. 311. http://www.who.int/mediacentre/factsheets/fs311/en/index.html.

WHO (2012b) 'HIV/AIDS, Data and Statistics', http://www.who.int/hiv/data/en/.

WHO (2012c) 'Singapore', http://www.who.int/countries/sgp/en/.

WHO Regional Office for Europe (2003a) *European Environment and Health Committee*, www.euro.who.int/eprise/main/who/progs/eehc/home.

WHO Regional Office for Europe (2003b) 'Global Change and Health', www.euro.who.int/eprise/main/who/progs/gch/home.

WHO Regional Office for Europe (2003c) 'National Environmental Action Plans', www.euro.who.int/envhealthpolicy/ Plans/20020807_1.

WHO Regional Office for Europe (2004) Declaration. Fourth Ministerial Conference on Environment and Health, 23–25 June 2004. Budapest, (EUR/o4/5046267/06). Copenhagen: WHO, Regional Office for Europe.

WHO Regional Office for Europe (2006) *European Charter on Counteracting Obesity*. Copenhagen: WHO Regional Office for Europe.

Wilensky, Gail R. (2005) 'The Challenges of Medicaid', *Healthcare Financial Management* 59 (6): 34–5.

Wilkinson, R.G. (1992) 'National Mortality Rates: The Impact of Inequality?', *American Journal of Public Health* 82: 1082–4.

Wilkinson, R.G. (1997) *Unhealthy Societies: The Afflictions of Inequality*. London: Routledge.

Wilkinson, R.G. and K.E. Pickett (2006) 'Income Inequality and Population Health: A Review and Explanation of the Evidence', *Social Science and Medicine* 62 (7): 1768–84.

Williams, A. (1997) 'Rationing Health Care by Age: The Case For', *British Medical Journal* 314: 820–2.

Williams, B.O. (2000) 'Ageism Helps to Ration Medical Treatment', *Health Bulletin* 58 (3): 198–202.

Williams, I., S. Robinson and H. Dickinson (2011) *Rationing In Health Care: The Theory and Practice of Priority Setting*. Bristol, UK: Policy Press.

Wilsford, D. (1994) 'Path Dependency, or Why History Makes it Difficult, but Not Impossible to Reform Health Systems in a Big Way', *Journal of Public Policy* 14 (3): 285–306.

Winkleby, M.A., D.E. Jatulis, E. Frank and S.P. Fortmann (1992) 'Socioeconomic Status and Health: How Education, Income, and Occupation Contribute to Risk Factors for Cardiovascular Disease', *American Journal of Public Health* 82 (6): 816–21.

Wipfli, H. and G. Huang (2011) 'Power of the Process: Evaluating the Impact of the Framework Convention on Tobacco Control Negotiations', *Health Policy* 100: 107–15.

Withrow, D. and D.A. Alter (2011) 'The Economic Burden of Obesity Worldwide: A Systematic Review of the Direct Costs of Obesity', *Obesity Reviews* 12 (2): 131–41.

Witz, A. and E. Annandale (2006) 'The Challenge of Nursing', in D. Kelleher, J. Gabe and G. Williams (eds) *Challenging Medicine*, 2nd edn. London: Routledge.

Wong, M. (2003) 'WHO Removes Hong Kong from SARS List', *The Associated Press*, 23 June.

Woodman, R. (2001) 'UK Hospitals Face 3.9 Billion Negligence Bill', *Reuters News*, 4 May, http://dailynews.yahoo.com/h/nm/20010504/hl/hospitals_1.htm.

Woods, K.J. (2004) 'Political Devolution and the Health Services in Great Britain', *International Journal of Health Services* 34 (2): 323–39.

World Fact Book (2012) https://www.cia.gov/library/publications/the-world-factbook/

Worldwide Market for the Clinical Management of Obesity, 2007–2015 (2007) Report #825. MedMarket Diligence.

Wroe, D. (2003) 'Australia: Home Care Programs for Elderly "In Crisis"', *The Age*, 13 June.

Wütscher F., F. Breyer, H. Kliemt and F. Thiele (eds) (2010) *Rationing in Medicine: Ethical, Legal and Practical Aspects*. Berlin: Springer.

Yamashita, J. (2011) 'Exploring the Impact of the Japanese Long-Term Care Insurance Act on the Gendered Stratification of the Care Labour Market through an Analysis of the Domiciliary are Provided by Welfare Non-Profit Organisations', *Social Policy and Society* 10: 433–43

Yang, C.-M. (2010) 'The Road to Observer Status in the World Health Assembly: Lessons from Taiwan's Long Journey', *Asian Journal of WTO & International Health Law and Policy* 5 (2): 3311–54.

Yoshikawa, A., J. Bhattacharya and W.B. Vogt (eds) (1996) *Health of Japan: Patients, Doctors, and Hospitals under a Universal Health Insurance System*. Tokyo: University of Tokyo Press.

Youde, J. (2012) *Global Health Governance*. Cambridge UK: Polity Press.

Zuckerman, S., T.A. Waidmann and E. Lawton (2011) 'Undocumented Immigrants, Left Out Of Reform, Likely To Continue To Grow as Share of the Uninsured', *Health Affairs* 30 (11): 1997–2004.

Zwillich, T. (2001) 'Medical Technologies May Drive Up Health Costs', *Reuters News Service*, 6 March.

Index